Early French Cookery

Early French Cookery

Sources, History, Original Recipes and Modern Adaptations

D. Eleanor Scully

Terence Scully

with illuminations by

J. David Scully

Ann Arbor

THE UNIVERSITY OF MICHIGAN PRESS

First paperback edition 2002

Copyright © by the University of Michigan 1995

All rights reserved

Published in the United States of America by

The University of Michigan Press

Manufactured in the United States of America

♾ Printed on acid-free paper

2005   2004   2003   2002   4   3   2

A CIP catalog record for this book is available from the British Library.

Library of Congress Cataloging-in-Publication Data

Scully, D. Eleanor, 1932-
    Early French cookery : sources, history, original recipes and
    modern adaptions / D. Eleanor Scully, Terence Scully ; with
    illuminations by J. David Scully.
        xii + 377 p.   cm.
    English, with some recipes in English and French.
    Includes index.
    ISBN 0-472-10648-1
    1. Cookery, French–History.   2. Food habits–France–History.
    3. Civilization, Medieval.   I. Scully, Terence, 1935-   .
    II. Title.
TX719.S3895   1995
641.5944'0902—dc20   95-17396
                                                      CIP

ISBN 0-472-08877-7 (pbk. : alk. paper)

        We are grateful to our many friends, colleagues and students who
for many years have shared our interest in things medieval. A special thank you
to Eileen and David Scully, both of whom not only collaborated in the banquets
but above all tolerated a kitchen forever filled with the fragrances of medieval
food and hundreds of loaves of trencher bread. David's artistic talents have
added another dimension to this book.
        It has been a very pleasant experience to work with Ellen Bauerle,
her assistants and colleagues at the University of Michigan Press. Their
competence and enthusiasm are very much appreciated.
                                                      The Authors

Contents

Introduction

The Recipes

Menu Suggestions and Meals

Appendix

Introduction

1. **Early French Cookery**
   - a. **Culinary traditions of early France**
   - b. **The late Middle Ages**
2. **The Manuscript Sources**
   - a. **The *Viandier of Taillevent***
   - b. **The *Menagier de Paris***
   - c. **Chiquart's *Du fait de cuisine***
3. **Foods and Cookery**
   - a. **Foodstuffs unknown in medieval France**
   - b. **Foods peculiar to medieval France**
   - c. **Cookery**
   - d. **Food supply and preservation**
4. **Beverages**
   - a. **Wines**
   - b. **Beers**
   - c. **Ciders**
5. **Kitchens**
   - a. **Physical features**
   - b. **Utensils**
6. **The Hall and Banquets**
7. **The Late-Medieval Cook**
8. **Advice to the Newly Medieval Cook**
   - a. **Authenticity**
   - b. **Adaptations**

Introduction

1. Early French Cookery

In most people's minds the label "medieval," and even "late Middle Ages," usually conjures up the misty, romantic image of an indefinitely long period blemished above all by what we snobbishly condemn as cultural decadence and a lack of social refinement. Many people presume that the Middle Ages was a period that was miserably wanting in those values and practices that, with some conceit, we moderns often term the proprieties of true civilization. Yet in many respects societies today benefit richly from refinements that were wrought many generations ago. In particular an undeniable fact is that we moderns did not discover the pleasures and graces of the table—simply by virtue of the fact that we are more modern than older societies and must therefore somehow always be "better off" than them.

In the areas of cookery and food at least, the late Middle Ages can show us that modern progress has not always been inevitable.

a. Culinary traditions of early France

In a great many respects the Roman province of Gaul benefitted from the civilization that the conquerors brought with them from the first century B.C. on. Not only were efficient administrative procedures put in place across the large territory, and the basis for a coherent written law code gradually imposed on the newly subdued tribes, but Roman soldiers, merchants, professionals, colonists and administrators naturally tried in the new lands to retain some of the refinements to which they had been accustomed in the Eternal City. Of these refinements the customary pleasures of the table undoubtedly represented for displaced Romans the essence of what it was to be a Roman. Roman food habits continued to live in Gaul, at least to the extent that the usual foodstuffs were available or could be obtained, during the five centuries that the Empire lasted.

i. Apicius

In the area of Roman cookery one name stands out, almost by itself, as representative of customs and practice during the most glorious age of the Empire. M. Gavius Apicius (c.25 B.C.–c.35 A.D.) was a notoriously profligate debauchee and gourmet, whose self-inflicted death was, according to Seneca and others[1] occasioned by his realization that his wealth had been so

---

[1] Lucius Annæus Seneca, *Ad Helviam matrem de consolatione* (or, *Ad Abinam*), 10, 8–9; Isidore of Seville, *Origanum*, 20, 1, 1. In the *Mythographi tres* edited by Angelo Mai, we likewise read: *Apicius quidam voracissimus fuit, qui de condituris multa scripsit. Postquam ergo omne patrimonium dilapidavit, cum egere cœpisset, non ferens pudorem, veneno periit (Mythographus secundus,* N° 225: *Classicorum Auctorum e Vaticanis Codicibus Editorum,* 10 vols., Rome (Typis Vaticanis), 1828–38; Vol. 3, p. 160.

squandered as to have declined to a level at which he was unable to maintain the style of life to which he had become accustomed. Pagan stoics and Christians alike held up this death as a moral lesson on the inevitable end for a life of excesses, in large part gastronomic. While there were in fact several Romans called Apicius, it is tempting to see this particular individual as the author of the *De re coquinaria*, particularly given that Tertullian at the beginning of the third century wrote that the name of this Apicius had become synonymous with the word "cook"[2] and that this Apicius was known to have written about food and the culinary inventions he was famous for having created. At any rate there is no doubt that by the end of the fourth century the *De re coquinaria*, to which the name of Apicius was firmly attached, did exist and was respected as a definitive source of information on the best in food and cookery in Imperial Rome.[3]

Few books on the culinary art have enjoyed a more widespread or more lasting reputation than the *De re coquinaria*. While it is true that numerous learned Latin writers produced treatises on dietetics or monographs on specific foodstuffs, such as fish or vegetables or baking, and several other writers detailed cookery recipes more or less incidentally in their works, there is no collection of recipes that is as extensive and relatively well-rounded as the *De re coquinaria*. This appears to be a composite work which was compiled at least three centuries after Apicius's death and which incorporates material from several sources. Containing some 450 recipes for dishes and sauces—these 138 latter recipes perhaps constituting the bulk of Apicius's real contribution to the collection—this cookbook afforded its readers in the fifth century a fine survey of the best culinary practice at the heart of the civilized Western world.

When the Roman Empire was finally overrun and collapsed in the century following the compilation of the *De re coquinaria*, the name of Apicius lived on, and so did the renown of the cookery book that was associated with his name. Despite the general disruption of refined society and the destruction of libraries, Apicius's book continued to be reproduced faithfully by scribes throughout the Middle Ages, so that medieval copies were available when the first edition was printed, anonymously, at Venice in 1498. However, even given the lasting celebrity of the *De re coquinaria* during these one thousand years, to what extent the cookery of Imperial Rome continued to exert any substantial influence in the aristocratic and bourgeois kitchens of fourteenth- and fifteenth-century France remains moot.

ii. Anthimus

A little less problematic is the relationship to actual culinary practice represented by a second

---

[2] *Apology*, 3, 6.

[3] The text of the *De re coquinaria* may be read in any of several modern editions: Jacques André, *Apicius, l'Art culinaire*, Paris (Les Belles Lettres), 1974 (originally 1965); Mary Ella Milham, *De Re Coquinaria*, Leipzig (Teubner), 1969; and, with English translations, in the following three publications: Joseph Dommers Vehling, *Apicius, Cookery and Dining in Imperial Rome*, New York (Dover), 1977 (originally Chicago (Walter M. Hill), 1936); Barbara Flower and Elizabeth Rosenbaum, *The Roman Cookery Book*, London (Harrap), 1958; and John Edwards, *Roman Cookery Revised. Elegant & Easy Recipes from History's First Gourmet*, Point Roberts, WA and Vancouver, B.C. (Hartley & Marks), 1986.

early work, the "Letter of Anthimus to Theodoric".[4] This letter, written about 520 A.D., expressly embodies medical and culinary advice about foods offered by a Greek physician to an Ostragoth ruler. It is, in fact, a practical dietetic, often resembling an informal cookery manual as its paragraphs evaluate a succession of foodstuffs.

> LXVIII. Of Chickpeas. Chickpeas, if they are well cooked, so that they are entirely liquid, seasoned with salt and oil, are good, and agreeable to the kidneys. But if they are not well done, I urge not even well people to eat them, because they cause serious bloating, bad indigestion and disorder of the stomach.

> III. Of Beef. Beef, ... steamed and cooked in a casserole should be eaten in a gravy. First it should be put to soak in one water, and then it should cook in a reasonable quantity of fresh water, without adding any water (as it cooks). When the meat is cooked, put in another vessel about a half-mouthful of vinegar, and add thereto the heads of leeks and a little pennyroyal, parsley root or fennel, and let them cook for an hour; then add honey to half the quantity of the vinegar, or make it sweeter according to taste. Then let it cook on a slow fire, shaking the pot frequently with the hands, and the sauce will season the meat well. Then grind the following: pepper, fifty grains; *costum* and spikenard, a half *solidus* each; cloves, one *tremissis*; all these grind well in an earthen mortar, adding a little wine to them; when well ground, put them into a vessel and stir well, so that before it is taken from the fire it may warm up a little and put its strength into the gravy. Moreover, where there is honey or must or *caroenum*, put in one of these as is said above. And do not let it cook in a copper kettle, but in an earthen vessel: this makes the flavor better.

> XLII. Of Plaice. Plaice or sole are the same thing; they are good and agreeable boiled in salt and oil, and agree very well even with sick people.

> XLVIII. Of Oysters. Oysters must be permitted when wanted, but seldom, because they are cold and phlegmatic. ... But if oysters smell, and anyone eat of them, he has need of no other poison.

The Letter of Anthimus demonstrates two features in early medieval food and cooking: firstly, the elite of the Frankish tribes that broke across the frontiers of the Roman Empire looked to *Roman* usage for the standards they would adopt in their own social practice; and secondly, the best advice that could be offered about food and food preparation at this time was presented by a physician and founded upon the best medical concepts. The text of this letter seems to have achieved a certain modest celebrity; the copies of it that continued to be made in the tenth, eleventh and twelfth centuries demonstrate a persistent and lively interest in good culinary practice.

---

[4] Shirley Howard Weber, *Anthimus, De Observatio Ciborum. Text, Commentary and Glossary, with a Study of the Latinity*, Leiden (E.J. Brill), 1924. The full *incipit* of the work reads "Here beginneth the letter of Anthimus, a notable personage, count and legatarius, to the most renowned Theodoric, King of the Franks, on the regulation of diet."

The Franks themselves, for whom the physician Anthimus's advice was written, ultimately established themselves in the land to which they gave their name, France. In matters of food the French, right through to the end of the Middle Ages, continued to respect the doctrines of medical science.

b. The late Middle Ages

i. The time period

Just when was this period from which the recipes contained in this book come down to us? For Europe, the centuries that stretch between the calamitous years at the end of the 400s—those years of violence and destruction marking the Fall of the Roman Empire—up until the end of the 1400s make up the millennium that we glibly call the Middle Ages. No historical period has ever had to labor under a less accurate or less descriptive name. By this name alone the ignorance of nineteenth-century scholars did an enormous injustice to one thousand years of several European civilizations. Even today it remains difficult for us to free ourselves of criminally unfair simplifications whenever we refer to "the Middle Ages." These one thousand years were very far from being the amorphous glob of ignorant barbarity—the "Gothic night," as Renaissance writers termed this period which they strove to denigrate in order to glorify themselves all the more.

In particular the twelfth to the fifteenth centuries are now recognized as harboring a span of generations that contributed much of lasting worth to modern European culture. It may be because the populations of Europe were beginning to enjoy longer periods of relative peace; it may be because in very general terms the different societies were becoming richer, and consequently more interested in creating a more pleasant life for themselves; it may simply be that we moderns are in a better position to understand the nature of human existence during this particular four-hundred-year span than, say, between 500 and 900 A.D. The late Middle Ages were by no means an epoch of unbroken tranquility and progress, any more than the twentieth century has been.

It is perhaps useful to realize that these four hundred years at the end of the medieval period were made up of roughly the same number of generations of human living that separate us today from the Renaissance itself. And the late Middle Ages had its share of troubles in the form of disease (the recurrent plagues) and warfare (between ambitious, bellicose feudal vassals and between nations). Yet despite the great length of the period and its frequent troubles, we *are* beginning to appreciate some of the many remarkable things Europeans were managing to do in the late Middle Ages. These were things that they found pleasurable and useful, and from which in many cases we, too, can continue to derive pleasure and worth.

ii. French-speaking territory

By virtue of its geographical position, the size of its growing territory and population, and its more or less cohesive system of administration, France came very gradually during the late Middle Ages to be respected by the states surrounding it, both as a power in political matters and as an arbiter of taste in social matters. Occasionally its kings turned out to be capable and effective even though their reign might be brief. The armies of its monarchs, dukes and counts were occasionally successful in winning an expansion of its boundaries—even if an Eleanor of Aquitaine in 1154 could jeopardize the territorial integrity of the country by marrying Henry of Anjou, the future King Henry II of England. On the whole the kingdom known as France was becoming a country which could fight to assert itself, and over which other kingdoms, especially England, thought it worthwhile to fight.

But France proper was not quite the France we see on the map today. The domains of the crown were at times only a slender slice of modern France. It was only by struggle and accident that the various parts were added, and sometimes almost lost. In the northeast, Brittany remained as fiercely independent as Wales remained from the English crown; in the southwest, Navarre was haughtily the appanage of its own king, and the Counts of Toulouse for a while continued to rule much of the land south of the Massif Central; in the southeast, Provence belonged variously to either Anjou or Savoy—and the Church was to lay exclusive claim to the area around Avignon; in the east, the Counts and Dukes of Savoy were usually successful in affirming their possession of lands from the Alps down to the Rhone River; while northward from Savoy at the end of the Middle Ages stretched the lands of that mightiest of all European potentates, the Duke of Burgundy. When the quarrel over vassalage between the Kings of France and England finally came to a boil in the fourteenth century, and the English territorial claims to the Aquitaine and to Normandy looked as if they could be enforced, the majestic French crown had shrunk away to a pitiful condition. By the beginning of the fifteenth century the King of France could mockingly be styled the *roi de Bourges*, in reference to the tiny town in the middle of France to which his glorious authority had for all practical purposes been reduced.

But, no matter who was from time to time sovereign in any region at any given moment, all of the area within the modern boundaries of France could by the end of the Middle Ages be said to be French-speaking—at least in the sense that the many dialects of the whole area were certainly related. (Here we still have to allow the exception of the Duchy of Brittany, whose people, generally of Celtic stock, spoke, and in some places today still speak, a form of Gaelic.) Culturally there was always some degree of exchange of social customs between the Kingdom of France and its effectively independent duchies and counties. Particularly when the King was strong and his court life helped ensure his glory, the cultural borrowing from France, quite naturally practiced in French-speaking England, Flanders, Burgundy, Savoy and Navarre, was readily evident. Despite their continual efforts to resist French political hegemony or full absorption by France, these satellite states were not really foreign to travelling aristocrats or wealthy bourgeois. Furthermore royal intermarriage (such as that of the Charles V's granddaughter, Catherine of Bar, with the King of Aragon) and conquest (as of the Angevin dynasty in Naples) took French taste abroad into somewhat more "foreign" lands.

iii. The society

Despite our modern prejudices and presumptions, in many respects Western Europe in the fourteenth and fifteenth centuries was in fact a remarkably civilized place. In the face of the common double tribulations of warfare and disease, social organization in France in particular allowed two small classes of individuals, landed aristocrats and relatively wealthy bourgeois, to develop the arts of comfort and pleasure to quite a high degree.

Of these arts of comfort and pleasure the most important were undoubtedly those that derive from the two fundamental necessities of human beings, shelter and food. As much as those affluent classes in society could afford to, they chose refinements in building and in eating that conferred real advances on the art of living. To the extent that culture must be defined collectively as varieties of behavior after fundamental human needs have been taken care of, a great deal of the culinary practices of these classes in the late Middle Ages may indeed properly be called cultural.

The cuisine of late-medieval France is one of the glories of that period. It contributed to the history of human culture an enormous amount that deserves to be remembered by us moderns. Some of us who perhaps like to be thought of as gastronomes point back to that renowned triumvirate of French culinary egos, Escoffier, Brillat-Savarin and Dumas, as the founders of an ideal of excellence in cookery, to say nothing of gastronomy. However, in glorifying a culinary "tradition" that dates only to the middle of the last century, we would be sadly short-sighted.

For the real origin of the high standards to which all western cooks aspire nowadays—and for which modern gourmets should indeed be grateful—we have to look a little further back in history. In the kitchens of fourteenth- and fifteenth-century Paris and Dijon (Burgundy) and Chambéry (Savoy) and Riom (Auvergne) we would find chefs whose ingenuity, whose sensitive taste and whose devotion to their profession were responsible for the true basis of the esteem in which French cuisine is held today.

2. The Manuscript Sources

In France the concern about eating well dates from the time many generations ago when the French began to become French. As we mentioned above, one of the earliest reports coming out of Romanized Gaul was the letter written in the sixth century about food customs among the best and most civilized classes in that province. "If anyone," wrote Anthimus, "pleases to eat any food whatsoever, let him at least eat food that is well prepared, and of other things sparingly, so that what he has eaten first may profit him, and that he may digest it well." Anthimus goes on to assess the value of all of the foodstuffs in common use among the Franks, the future French, in his time, and to describe a selection of exemplary dishes that could be prepared for Theodoric, king of the Frankish nation.[5]

Between then and now many of the French have written about food. From the Middle Ages on, they have described, prescribed, criticized and analysed at exhaustive length what should be prepared for the dining table and consumed by the most discerning members of society. And among these writers-about-food there have been many of a practical bent who, being concerned about the well-being of posterity, have bequeathed enough documentation to allow future generations to reproduce their culinary triumphs of imagination and taste. The recipe book was far from being a rare bird among late-medieval manuscripts.

From the end of the thirteenth century we possess precious documentary evidence of just what French chefs were busy doing in contemporary kitchens. This evidence is preserved mostly in a group of five recipe books, two of them in Latin and three in French. We shouldn't think that this flourishing of the cookbook *genre* in France indicates some sort of spontaneous stirring of canny ingenuity among a handful of chefs. High standards in cookery—to say nothing of the highly valued recipes themselves—undoubtedly developed over many generations of apprenticeship, over an endless succession of many huge cauldrons. If nothing else, the sudden appearance of this small array of cookbooks shows that the French themselves now realized that good cookery was indeed a legitimate and worthy branch of knowledge. Records of the professional cooks' activities could take their place alongside valuable learned documents in aristocratic libraries.

What the chefs, and their masters and patrons and scribes, quite consciously tried to do toward the end of the thirteenth century was to set about recording the best of current culinary practice—in much the same way as other writers of this period were trying to record all that was known about physical nature, philosophy or medicine. It was the age of the compendium, a forerunner of the modern encyclopedia. The French recognized that cooking deserved its place among the other great sciences. And so we are really very fortunate to have good, reliable sources of information about the nature of food and cookery at this relatively early time in France.

---

[5] *De observatione ciborum*, ed. cit., p. 9.

That two of the first recipe collections were in Latin[6] should not surprise us. The use of this eternal, universal language was reserved for any subject matter that was held in the highest respect by both the authors and an international audience. Of the three other works, those written in the language of the French chefs themselves, two are relatively short, each containing only some forty recipes for meat, fowl and fish. Of these one was probably written in England, where the aristocracy was still conscious of its French roots.[7] This latter collection is called *Coment l'en deit fere viande et claree*. Despite its name, the space given over here to the preparation of the spiced beverage *claree* is minimal—one recipe out of twenty-nine; the bulk of the collection describes prepared dishes of food, or *viande*.

The other short work is certainly continental in origin and has been given the name of the *Enseignements*, or "Instructions" on food preparation because of the first words of its text.[8]

Almost all of the dishes outlined briefly in the *Enseignements* are described in a little more detail in the other French recipe book of this early period, a manuscript roll whose first lines, probably containing the title of the work, have unfortunately been torn away. We have no way of knowing just where this manuscript roll was copied out, or whether its author was trying merely to transmit its recipes more or less faithfully from some earlier source—such as the *Enseignements*. Its appearance, though, rather worn and grease-splotched in a few particular places, lets us guess that the odd chef had unrolled it in his kitchen to check on the ingredients of a particular *brouet* or *civé*!

In its later versions, copied and recopied over more than a century, this last, anonymous work eventually became known as the *Viandier of Taillevent*. In its earliest, title-less form it incorporated some 133 recipes; future versions of the *Viandier* would inflate this number to 220. Whatever its identity before it became baptized with Taillevent's name, this basic collection undoubtedly exercised a profound influence directly and indirectly upon the majority of subsequent recipe manuals in medieval and Renaissance France and England, and perhaps beyond.

With the mention of the great work attributed to Taillevent, we come to the first of *our* great sources for medieval cookery. The *Viandier* is itself the first of a trio of really important cookery books in France. The others of this trio are the anonymous *Menagier de Paris* and the *Du fait de cuisine* (that is, *On Cookery*) of Chiquart. These three collections of recipes and of cooking advice provide us with a remarkably clear view of French culinary customs and methods in the later Middle Ages. Together, they afford a good understanding both of what was the regular daily fare in a comfortable Parisian household of the day as well as of the gastronomic delights available

---

[6] These two Latin works are the *Tractatus de modo preparandi et condiendi omnia cibaria* and the *Liber de coquina*. They were edited together by Marianne Mulon in "Deux traités inédits d'art culinaire médiéval," *Bulletin Philologique et Historique*, Paris (Comité des Travaux Historiques et Scientifiques), 1968 [published in 1971], pp. 369-435.

[7] Constance B. Hieatt and Robin F. Jones, "Two Anglo-Norman Culinary Collections Editied from British Library Manuscripts Additional 32085 and Royal 12.C.xii," *Speculum*, 61 (1986), pp. 859–882.

[8] The most recent and best of a series of editions of this work is by Grégoire Lozinski and appears as an appendix to his edition of the *Bataille de Caresme et de Charnage*, Paris (Champion), 1933, pp. 181–190.

from the hands of the French-speaking world's most respected master chefs. They describe dishes created in order to flatter the refined palates of French bourgeois, aristocrats and royalty.

The recipes we offer here to the readers of *our* copy of these old recipe collections are a selection of the best of what has been preserved by these three early masterworks of French culinary genius.

a. The *Viandier of Taillevent*

The *Viandier of Taillevent* in its numerous manuscript copies acquired a solid reputation for usefulness and dependability that far outlasted the life of its compiler.[9] Even down into the sixteenth century, cooks and householders were still buying printed editions of the *Viandier* in what was still a more or less original version. For Rabelais, the worldly *farceur* of the French Renaissance, "The Taillevent," as the book had become known universally, still remained the ultimate guide in matters of cuisine.

While it is questionable whether the historic personage nicknamed Taillevent was in actual fact the author of the *Viandier* in its original form, he certainly did revise the collection of recipes that he adopted from his thirteenth-century source. He amplified and clarified some, he added others, and finally he endowed the book with his own *nom-de-cuisine*, Taillevent—"Wind-Slicer."

This nickname appears to have been a professional pseudonym that the chef Guillaume Tirel had earned in the royal kitchens of France during a remarkably long career. He was so respected by his employer, King Charles V, that he was actually ennobled. His eminently appropriate coat of arms can still be seen on his tombstone: portrayed across his shield is his personal heraldic motif, a diagonal string of three stew-pots! On the same tombstone he himself is depicted dressed in knightly armor, a dog at his feet, and flanked in most domestic fashion by effigies of his two wives![10] Unfortunately we can still only speculate just what heroic deeds with his chef's knife had won for Guillaume Tirel, the first known professional French chef, such a durable epithet as "Wind-Slicer."

Taillevent's professional career was surely one of the most illustrious ever to have been enjoyed by a cook at that time, or probably at any time since. He began it in a way that was thoroughly normal for the period, as a humble apprentice, a kitchen-boy, a lowly scullion. Then

---

[9] See *The Viandier of Taillevent. An Edition of all Extant Manuscripts*, edited, with a translation of the text, by Terence Scully, Ottawa (University of Ottawa Press), 1988. From the first half of the sixteenth century alone, twelve distinct printed editions have been identified. This exceptional number of printings for the time amply demonstrates the great celebrity of this cookbook. See the edition of *Le Viandier de Guillaume Tirel dit Taillevent* by Jérôme Pichon and Georges Vicaire, Paris, 1892; reprinted, Geneva (Slatkine), 1967; pp. lii–lxvi.

[10] The tomb can be seen in the priory of Our Lady of Hennemont, near Saint Germain en Laye in the western suburbs of modern-day Paris. In that place are buried Guillaume Tirel, in the chapel that he had founded for the purpose, together with his wives, Jeanne Bonard, who died in 1363, and Isabeau Le Chandelier, who must have died just before 1404. As for Guillaume Tirel himself, who in the engraving of his tombstone is qualified as both cook and sergeant at arms of the the King, he was probably born about 1315 and died in 1395.

he rose through a succession of stages and ranks in the household that was exclusively devoted to the service of the Queen of France. And finally he entered into the august service of the King himself, Charles V.

Taillevent arrived at the pinacle of his career in 1370 when he became the King's chief cook. In that particularly eminent position, in which he was responsible for all of the dishes that were set before the king, he was in a very real sense the arbiter of the taste of Europe, censor and innovator of preparations worthy of royal consumption. While he would naturally be guided by royal whims and pleasures, he must surely also have been free to experiment, to demonstrate his own particular talents. And what the King of France ate in Paris was undoubtedly of great interest at noble tables and in noble kitchens throughout the rest of Europe.

In an age of increasing wealth and increasingly lavish lifestyles, Guillaume Tirel acquired such honor and acclaim in the various dining halls of the royal court that his name came almost to define the essence of excellence in cookery during some three centuries. The work that was universally known in bourgeois, aristocratic and royal circles as the *Viandier of Taillevent* was recognized as the ultimate repository of the best in culinary practice.

Taillevent's collection of recipes of dishes for a princely table opens in typically sober, laconic fashion:

> Here begins the *Viandier* of Taillevent, master chef of our Lord the King of France, by means of which can be prepared all manner of foods worthy to be served before kings, dukes, counts, lords, prelates, bourgeois, and others.

The *Viandier* is a recipe book produced by an individual who enjoyed the exalted status of chief cook of the sovereign of the mightiest kingdom of Europe. As such it is the work of a supreme professional, destined to serve as a guide and resource for all other professional cooks of his age.

b. The *Menagier de Paris*

A striking instance of the new breadth of intellectual curiosity stirring France in the fourteenth century is afforded by the second great culinary treatise we depend on for our knowledge of the art of food preparation in medieval France. Toward the end of the 1300s, an elderly but affluent bourgeois living in Paris decided to take a wife. There were two remarkable circumstances of this decision. In the first place, the new bride was a mere girl of fifteen years, who could offer only (what *he* condescendingly termed) a "petit et ignorant service" to her much more mature husband.

In the second place, this particular elderly individual possessed a truly encyclopedic interest in the arts, crafts, theology and commerce of his day. Moreover, he seems to have been determined, in what we can only imagine to be a charitable frame of mind, generously to pass on as much of this knowledge as he possibly can to his innocent and unsuspecting bride. He will do this, he claims, in order to nurture her housekeeping abilities for the satisfaction that these developed skills will give her personally—in being able to serve him better in the course of this present, and likely brief, marriage—as well as for the benefits that such a domestic education will allow her to bring to her future husband when the writer is dead and gone!

This remarkable book is known as the *Menagier de Paris*, "The Goodman of Paris" as one translator called it.[11] In the mind of its writer the work must have been intended to constitute a sort of bridegroom's marriage gift. Our frugal bourgeois bridegroom himself would probably also have called it a canny investment of labor. It must have taken a great deal of labor to assemble all the anecdotes, apologues, admonitions, advice and just plain instruction he offers his bride. We may perhaps be forgiven for guessing that any gratitude expressed by the young wife may not have been wholly sincere. The book is close to 300 pages in length, and provides detailed information on everything from hawking and horse husbandry to personal piety and pruning. The bourgeois's diatribe against gluttony (among the six other Deadly Sins, which, of course he has to treat *in extenso*) is nicely offset—fortunately, as we feel for the poor girl—by the very last section of his book in which he has assembled as rich a series of food recipes as exists in one place in the medieval period. These he magnanimously puts at the disposition of his inexperienced bride—or at least within the reach of those members of the bourgeois's household, the cook and steward, who will be having to work directly under her orders.

Many of the recipes in the *Menagier de Paris* are undoubtedly inspired by dishes described in the *Viandier of Taillevent*: it is clear that the bourgeois owned or had managed to borrow a copy of this earlier work because entire passages are textually identical in the two. Even so, a good number of the dishes that the bourgeois recommends to his wife are quite unrelated to those in the *Viandier*, and they seem to point either to a tradition of cuisine independently alive in his Parisian milieu, or to the author's inventiveness, or to the strength of his own personal taste—this latter being quite positively marked in every section of his treatise. He certainly lets his wife know what he thinks about things!

In any case what we have in the extensive set of recipes that the bourgeois has compiled is a very broad representation of the dishes that could be served, respectably and avoiding any possible sense of shame, on an average upper-middle-class table in one of the most important cities of Europe of the day.[12]

More than in the *Viandier*, the recipes in the *Menagier de Paris* are designed to be understood and followed by the amateur cook. The bourgeois himself was, after all—despite his encyclopaedic knowledge of things having to do with domestic science in its broadest sense—still only a dilettante

---

[11] The *Menagier de Paris* is available in two satisfactory editions: that of Jérôme Pichon, published for the Société des Bibliophiles Français, Paris, 1847 and reprinted by Slatkine in Geneva in 1970; and that of Georgine E. Brereton and Janet M. Ferrier, Oxford (Clarendon Press), 1981. A modern English translation of a large part of the work was published by Eileen Power, London (Routledge), 1928, under the title *The Goodman of Paris*. A slightly more literal translation of the French title might be *The Householder of Paris*. In our book we offer references to both editions of the original text: to the page numbers of Volume II of Pichon, and to the section numbers (§) in Distinction 2, Article 5 (pp. 191 ff.) in that of Brereton and Ferrier.

[12] There exists some reason for thinking that the Ménagier himself may have been an affluent lawyer, associated with the Court of Parliament in Paris, or with those who were members of it. The preachy tone he slips into so easily makes us inclined to think even that he may have been a royal judge. Internal references make it clear likewise that he was acquainted with persons intimate with the Duke of Berry; a copy of the *Menagier* is known to have been in the Duke's library.

in matters of cookery. His book as a whole, while it never popularizes or simplifies its complex subject matters, is still aimed at an "ignorant" fifteen-year-old girl who has assumed a social role and obligations for the moment much beyond her.

At the beginning of his compilation the bourgeois places a Prologue in which he speaks to his new bride in these terms:

> My dear, because, in the week following our marriage, you (being fifteen years of age) begged me to forgive you your youth and the slight and imperfect service you could render until such time as you had seen and learned more fully—to which apprenticeship you promised that you would bend your whole effort and care, for my sake and for love of me, as you said wisely, and by a wiser counsel than your own—beseeching me humbly in our bed, as I recall, for the love of God that I not chastise you harshly before outsiders or before our own servants but that I should correct you each night, or from day to day, in our chamber, and that I should review your improprieties or foolishness of the day or days just past, and that I should give you proper instruction, should I wish to do so. Then you would have all you needed to improve yourself according to my teaching and instruction, and you would do all in your power to fulfil my wishes, as you said. And I hold it well and commend you, and am grateful to you for having spoken to me about this, and I have since remembered it frequently. . . .
>
> As for the service that you say you would gladly render me greater than at present, that you wish you might learn and have me instruct you in, you may be assured, my dear, that I am content to receive such service as the good wives of our neighborhood render their husbands, who are alike to us and of our station, the same service as your kinswomen render their husbands, who are of the same station as us. Take counsel from them, then follow their advice more or less as you will. For I am not so arrogant, seeing your good sense and your good will, that I should consider whatever service of any sort you may render me not to be fully sufficient, provided there be on your part neither deceit, nor despising, nor disdain.
>
> Yet for this I must thank you, for while I realize that you are of a higher lineage than I, yet this will not protect you. For, by God, the women-folk of your family are so good that they, by themselves without any need for my intervention, would sternly rebuke you should they learn by anyone of any misdemeanor of yours. But I have no anxieties over you: I have full confidence in your good intentions.

If the poor girl *herself* had any anxieties about what was expected of her in the new capacity she was assuming, the treatise her husband had compiled was at least designed to relieve her of some of them. The First Distinction of the *Menagier de Paris* deals with personal morality, examples or models for the new wife to follow since they are conventionally drawn from the lives of "good" women in history and legend. The Second Distinction is more properly a treatise on domestic science, and includes, as its fifth chapter, a very extensive lesson on how to "order, set out, arrange and cause to be made all sorts of soups, stews, sauces, and all other dishes; the same, for the sick."

Whatever his life may have been *before* this marriage, it seems quite likely that the old bourgeois continued to eat very well indeed at home!

c. Chiquart's *Du fait de cuisine / On Cookery*

The third great cookery book of the French Middle Ages belongs to a milieu that is somewhat different from each of the other two. In 1420 the Duke of Savoy, Amadeus VIII,[13] prevailed upon his chief cook, a certain Master Chiquart Amiczo, to put down in writing—for the benefit of posterity and for the greater glory of the Duchy of Savoy—all that he knew about cooking and about the preparation of a noble banquet. Before rising to his lofty position as head of the Duke's kitchens, Chiquart, like Taillevent a half-century before, had many years of scullery drudgery and apprenticeship behind him. They were undoubtedly years during which he had acquired a thorough understanding and mastery not only of food preparation but of planning and arranging enormous gala feasts of several days' duration.

In finally acceding to his lord's urging that he compile a book on the art and craft of cookery, Chiquart set about it by dictating to one of the Duke's secretaries a sort of *summa* of his professional experience. The result, on 236 folio pages, can properly be termed Europe's first true cookbook. More than a mere collection of recipes (which in large part it is, having 81 of them), the *Du Fait de Cuisine*—"On the Matter of Cookery"—is a series of detailed explanations of how a broad variety of dishes should actually be put together into a formal meal.[14]

---

[13] At the beginning of his reign, Amadeus was the Eighth *Count* of Savoy. When, with much pomp and pride, his domain was elevated into a Duchy by the Emperor Sigismund in 1416, he automatically became Amadeus, First Duke of Savoy. Despite his renumbering in a new series, he is usually still referred to nowdays as Amadeus VIII.

[14] Edited by Terence Scully, *Vallesia*, 40 (Sion, Switzerland), 1985, pp. 101–231. This work is available in an English translation also by the same editor, *Chiquart's 'On Cookery'. A Fifteenth-Century Savoyard Culinary Treatise*, New York, Berne & Frankfurt (Peter Lang), 1986.

Chiquart himself must have been an enormously capable and intelligent man. He had mastered all of the culinary techniques of his day; he had to account financially for all the foodstuffs that passed through his kitchen; he must direct the diverse daily activities of the numerous kitchen personnel efficiently. As chief cook of the Duke he had, among his many routine responsibilities, to oversee all of the arrangements for any banquets that his master might decide to offer. A potential difficulty associated with this latter duty was, of course, that these banquets might be arranged not only in the familiar setting of the ducal castle at Chambéry, but also in lesser castles throughout the Duchy, castles where kitchen facilities and normal supplies of foodstuffs were totally inadequate for anything more grand than feeding the day-to-day garrison and the castle's small administration.

In his book Chiquart tells us of the staggering logistics involved in preparing for such a feast, even of only two days' duration. In order to allow for something like 57 dishes to be served, the cook must ensure the availability of 100 head of cattle—to be slaughtered on the spot—along with 130 sheep, 120 pigs, 200 piglets, 200 lambs, 100 calves, 2,000 hens and 12,000 eggs (!)—to say nothing of incredible quantities of wild game and fish, spices, herbs, fruit, sugar, wines, candles, firewood, filter-cloth and so forth.

All of these foodstuffs, one must remember, are to be prepared, cooked, served and consumed in a 36-hour period! For a banquet, it fell to the cook's responsibility also to assemble the wide variety of cooking utensils, from those that were extraordinarily huge in capacity all the way down to modestly standard items—every single object that was required for this grandiose undertaking. Furthermore, during the repeated use of these utensils, containers, cutlery and dishware over the course of the four huge meals, the chief cook had to ensure that they remained constantly and properly scoured clean. He himself had to see to engaging a small army of assistant cooks and their helpers, numerous scullions, butchers, sauce-makers, pastry chefs and bread bakers. Chiquart advises his reader, presumably a neophyte in the profession, that the first plans for such a banquet—a relatively short one, since it will last *only* two days—have to be made at least four months in advance!

Besides being an intelligent man, Chiquart was also rather a vain man. This tends to be so of highly successful chefs at any time. However, as the highly respected chief cook of the Duke of Savoy, Chiquart probably had every right to be—vain, that is, about his professional competence. His master had married the daughter of the Duke of Burgundy, the wealthiest and most powerful individual in all of contemporary Europe. Amadeus himself had just been elevated from Count to Duke by the Emperor of Rome. And later, in 1439, he was to be elected to the even more exalted throne of the Pope, under the name of Felix V. Through his court at Chambéry, on the "French" side of a busy route over the Alps that Amadeus controlled, passed much of the nobility and aristocracy of Europe. It was Chiquart's repeated task to feed these grandees decently, just as their station and his master's honor demanded. The *Du Fait de Cuisine / On Cookery* tells how this should be done.

Chiquart prefaces his *On Cookery* with a dedication to his master. This is properly couched in the humblest, most servile language, and depends for its effect upon conventionally hyperbolic modesty:

To you, exalted, renowned and mighty Prince and Lord, Amadeus, First Duke of Savoy, be all honor and reverence, together with ready will, proffered with humble and devoted commendation, to obey all your commands. In the past, most respected Lord, on many occasions you have requested and ordered me, Chiquart—even though the least of your humble subjects yet nevertheless your devoted servant in great affection and desire— that, the memory of man being unsure and faulty, and there being no record of things were it not for the art of writing—*"Quoniam memoria hominis est labilis, et sepe memorie injuriatur oblivio nisi scripture suffragio innaretur, idcirco ad infrascripta per scripture memoriam decernanda"*[15] —and you being occasionally desirous of and inclined to making feasts and solemn banquets, I should set in writing some knowledge of cooking and of cookery, particularly, so you state and affirm, as I am learned in this science and art, for your consideration and pleasure; yet, as you know, I have several times refused and even demured, for in knowledge as well as in life I sit in the lowest places— *"in ymis locis"*—and have never, whether through ignorance or negligence, turned my understanding to such knowledge or learning; nor have I any books or writings bearing on this subject; and I have told you that I have no capability or understanding in such things. But you, my most respected Lord, responding constantly and firmly, have told me that, no matter what excuses I might allege before you, I am not to be excused; and that, if only I were to set the hand of my will to this task, God would grant me the resolution and the strength; and that whatsoever tends to the use, profit and pleasure of many, particulary of yourself among all others, great merit, commendation and honor would accrue to me. And so, my most respected Lord, finally won and overcome by these and many other arguments of yours, yet fearful and trembling, but with the help of God and your goodwill and pleasure, bending to your desire and command, I very humbly tender my assent. And, animated and encouraged by these things, not without great pain and great labor, I have undertaken to accomplish this work, by my own abilities, in the manner that follows.

Firstly, God granting there be an honorable feast attended by kings, queens, dukes, duchesses, counts, countesses, princes, princesses, marquis, marquises, barons, baron- esses, and prelates of various conditions, and nobles too in great number, one needs, for the supply of the kitchen and to prepare the banquet honorably to the honor of the Lord giving it, the following things: . . .

And so Chiquart launches into his long list of necessary ingredients, utensils and kitchen personnel that it would be necessary to provide in order even to begin to work on a model banquet. Following this sort of preamble, Chiquart comes to the "meat" of his treatise: a series of recipes whose order would be that of the dishes served in a banquet at any respectably noble court of his day. These recipes constitute what properly we may call menus, and they are among

---

[15] "For the memory of man is unsteady, and oblivion would often harm the recollection of things, were it not for the intervention of writing; and so what follows is given over to the memory of script."

the first such clearly defined menus that we possess. They comprise, in the order in which the various dishes are to be prepared and presented to the diners: the first serving (six regular dishes and an extraordinary preparation known as an *entremets*, or diversion) for the dinner of the first day of the banquet; the second serving (again, six dishes and yet another *entremets*) for this same dinner of the first day; then the supper (five dishes) of the first day; after this follow in exactly the same sequence the dishes for the servings, first and second, and meals, dinner and supper, of the second day of the banquet. In all, Chiquart mentions some thirty-nine servings whose preparation the chef will have to oversee during those hectic two days.

Having successfully disposed of all these prescribed courses and arrived—for anyone other than Chiquart himself this would likely be in utter exhaustion—at the end of his imaginary banquet, Chiquart quite coolly acknowledges a consideration that was of enormous importance for the medieval cook. What if, he points out, the banquet were to happen to be held on fasting days, that is to say on those days of the week (usually Wednesday, Friday and Saturday, and in some jurisdictions Monday as well), or on any day in Lent, on which according to canonic ordinance no meat or animal products, such as milk, eggs, cheese, fat and grease, could be eaten. So Chiquart begins all over again. He retraces all of the menus of his two-day feast and all of the recipes he has just explained in such minute detail, and substitutes, for every single one of the servings, just as rich and elaborate a variety of meatless or fish preparations as he had outlined for meat days. The need to know how to cook the original "lean cuisine" effectively doubled any medieval chef's working repertoire!

A third section of Chiquart's treatise is made up of some twenty additional recipes: these are provided, our canny master cook explains to his neophyte, as suggestions just in case your lord should take a fancy to prolong his banquet beyond the time foreseen for it. Whatever the circumstances, the accomplished chef must never be short of ideas for additional dishes that offer just as much by way of variety and delightful savor as those of his basic menus.

And the final section of the *Du Fait de Cuisine / On Cookery* takes into account the possibility that some of the guests at his master's court might be sick, or at least be of a sickly constitution. The seigneurial cook should always be able to concoct any of a dozen dishes whose medicinal virtues would be approved by the patient's physician. Not only did the early cook have to be totally trusted not to endanger his master's life, or that of his master's guests, with the food he handled, but regularly he had also to work closely with the court doctors in order to be able to prepare dishes that were therapeutic in effect. In this last section of his book Chiquart shows that he fully understood the contemporary scientific theories of food values.

Chiquart was very conscious of the honor that his master, Duke Amadeus, was bestowing upon him in commanding that he compile this treatise on cookery. When he dictated it, both he and the Duke intended the volume to serve as a guide to the state of culinary art in their "modern" day and age. The Duke's chief cook could indeed take quite justifiable pride in the clear, detailed and always practical manner in which he acquitted himself of his master's charge. Even after more than five and a half centuries, the *Du Fait de Cuisine / On Cookery* remains perhaps the most useful and enlightening means we possess of recreating the best in late medieval European cooking.

One further small collection of French recipes should be mentioned. This the so-called *Recueil de Riom*—an assortment of forty-eight more-or-less standard recipes which are also found in one or the other of the three principal manuscript collections.[16] The main body of this manuscript is dated 1466. Its 232 folios contain a wide variety of medical, moral, literary, philosophical, theological, historical and botanical material, all copied from other sources, including four folios of culinary recipes. It appears to have been a personal compilation of useful information, a sort of household encyclopedia after the fashion of the *Menagier de Paris*, but designed for (if not actually executed by) a minor noble or rich bourgeois in the Auvergnese town of Riom.

---

[16] This work is edited by Carole Lambert, *Le recueil de Riom et la Maniere de henter soutillement. Un livre de cuisine et un récepteur sur les greffes du XVe siècle* (*Le Moyen Français*, 20), Montréal (CERES), 1987.

3. Medieval Foods and Cookery

a. Foodstuffs unknown in medieval France

People at one time or another have tried to eat virtually everything that has come to hand—or foot, or net or arrow. By means of cooking, after reduction by chopping and grinding, and in combinations with other substances, virtually everything *is* indeed edible in some quantity. And, as the very old adage goes, there is no accounting for taste. Much of what determines food habits is to be found quite simply in a listing of what is available, and is considered edible, in any locality. Hunger will eventually determine what is considered edible for every individual or society.

In Medieval Europe not all of the foodstuffs that we know about (even if we are not accustomed to using them as such) were available. Certain foods that we consider even to be fundamental staples nowadays are nonexistent in the written recipes of early Europe. While some of these foodstuffs might be thought of as manufactured convenience ingredients, such as jelly powders, and some, such as potatoes, have assumed what amounts to an almost indispensable role in a modern meal, it should never be thought that the medieval cook, or diner, ever missed such ingredients. They never conceived of themselves as "doing without" *any* variety of foodstuff except for the economic or commercial reasons of current available supply.

However, the modern cook should be aware which foodstuffs did *not* normally pass through a medieval kitchen, and were unknown on medieval dining tables, simply because they were still "foreign" to the Europe of the fourteenth and fifteenth centuries. Occasionally a late-medieval writer will show that he has only a vague awareness of a particular food: in his analysis of foodstuffs, what the author of the *Tacuinum sanitatis* writes about bananas offers a case in point:

> Bananas. It is no surprise that Ellbochasim [the supposed original author of the *proto-Tacuinum*, an Arab] mentions this plant and its fruit, but as far as we are concerned we know of it only from texts or tales from merchants from Cyprus or pilgrims from the Holy Land. Sicilians, on the other hand, know them well. The leaves are fan-shaped and have a hard rib and a thin blade, which dries up in the summer. The banana has a yellow skin when ripe and white pulp. It seems at first to be very insipid-tasting, but then they say that one can never eat enough of them due to their delicious flavor, which gradually emerges very pleasantly. They weigh heavily on the stomach, and their only virtue is that they are sexually arousing.[17]

Even more revealing than this fanciful *exposé* of the qualities of the banana is the illuminator's

---

[17] Judith Spencer, trans., *The Four Seasons of the House of Cerruti*, New York and Bicester, England (Facts on File), 1984, p. 82. This edition is the most convenient source for reading the Vienna manuscript of the *Tacuinum sanitatis*, and we have used it in the following pages. Generally speaking, the *tacuina* afford an interesting introduction to the medical and scientific lore of the Middle Ages.

attempt to reproduce with credible realism a "plant" that he has never seen and of which he has only read the description in the author's text.

A banana bush

The person who is anxious to be as authentic as possible in reconstructing a medieval meal will avoid the anachronism of serving tea or coffee, will keep potatoes (whether boiled, fried *or* baked) rigorously off the menu, will use tomatoes very sparingly—like the rare exotic fruits they were in fifteenth-century France. Chocolate is likewise out altogether, as are green string-beans, green peas (white peas are the variety to use), red and green peppers, maize or Indian corn (which we call simply "corn"), and that wonderful New-World bird, the turkey. And of course we have no bananas.

There may be a temptation to fall back upon these commonplace fixtures of the modern diet, particularly in the cases of coffee and potatoes which have become so integral a part of North-American meals. It is particularly because they have become so commonplace that we do tend to look upon them almost as a necessity to any meal. In the days before potatoes, string-beans and turkeys were ever heard of, though, meal-planners managed quite nicely, thank you. Rice (colored or not) and frumenty (a wheat porridge) fulfilled much the same function in a meal as potatoes today. White peas and round or flat beans were as much a staple serving as sliced carrots and string-beans seem to be in restaurants nowadays. And as for our ritualistic offer of coffee at the end of a meal, who could possibly prefer this bitter, burnt-tasting potion to a soothing cup of rich grape juice or mulled hypocras?

As for turkey, the early cook exercised an ample choice between wildfowl (ducks, pheasants, partridges, and so forth) and domestic birds (chickens, doves and geese). The goose was, after all, the festive fowl on the gourmet's table, as it often appears today. It seems advisable *not* to fall back on the elegant standbys of swans and peacocks—even if you have some way of getting one or the other: they need extensive treatment to render them palatable.

For the medieval cook, as we say, it was never a matter of having to "do without" these unknown foods. We ourselves have as much, and perhaps more, to discover about their foods and how they used them as their successors had still to discover about foodstuffs during the twenty generations that have followed their age.

b. Foods peculiar to medieval France

Certain of the foodstuffs that entered the medieval kitchen on a normal basis are not those that the modern cook expects to be using as a matter of course somewhere in every meal. The relative importance of these foodstuffs in the cookery of the time can be considered a peculiar feature of that cookery. To a very large extent they determined its nature.

i. Spices

That medieval food was highly spiced, even overspiced, is a modern myth founded upon ignorance. It is true that spices were used, and used ubiquitously, in "noble" cookery of the period. However the questions that remain concerning the place of spices in this food have to do with quantity, quality and purpose. And they are fundamental questions.

It might be best to begin with "purpose." The people of twenty generations ago knew perfectly well the difference between fresh food and rotten food. They knew of several very effective ways to preserve foods over long periods, and they had enough common sense not to try to prepare or to eat rotten food by dousing it in strong spices! Injurious bacteria could make their continued presence known just as effectively in a medieval digestive system as in a modern one. And certainly anyone who could afford to stock his larder with expensive exotic spices sufficiently potent to function as a mask for a putrifying joint of mutton could afford to replace that mutton with something a little more wholesome.

Greek, and later Arabic, humoral theory taught medieval physicians that all things were constituted of a delicate balance of four qualities, warmth and cold, moisture and dryness. Human beings, in a healthy state, possessed a nature that was warm and moist, to a moderate degree. Anything a human ate that was not moderately warm and moist was apt to upset his temperament and engender in him such bad humors as choler (warm and dry), melancholia (cold and dry), phlegm (cold and moist) or an excessively sanguine disposition (too warm and too moist). To resist this bad influence that might come from foods that were not precisely suited to the human temperament, such inappropriate complexions had to be corrected in the foods. In the first instance the correction could be effected by cooking (with dry or moist heats of variable intensity); in the second instance the cook could resort to the use of appropriate condiments.

Condiments—particularly herbs and spices—had their own peculiar qualities, in the same way as all other foodstuffs, each one differing somewhat from the next. Among his principal responsibilities, the cook had to determine, as rationally as possible, firstly how ill-suited a foodstuff—such as beef or pork—might be to the human temperament of those whose food he was preparing; then, drawing upon his knowledge of the respective virtues of his condiments, he had to compose an efficacious mixture herbs and spices which would act with neutralizing or mitigating force on the undesirable elements in the complexion of the foodstuff he was preparing. The mixture of condiments could be used either in the cooking pot or in the pie shell, or could be served as a sauce accompanying the foodstuff when it was presented to the table.

Despite modern prejudices about the medieval cook's ungoverned and unconscionable use of spices, this person really *did* know what he was doing. In the case of Chiquart at the court of Savoy, even as the Duke's chief cook he still had to apply to the Duke's apothecary, with a formal request, to be dispensed those spices that he would be requiring for his cooking; he did this in exactly the same way as any physician would have to lodge a request for drugs. Spices (including sugar) were considered to be simply that, varieties of drugs, to be employed only with a full, conscious understanding of their respective strengths and virtues. Besides this procedural control to be followed in obtaining spices, in larger households the cook usually had one or two of the staff physicians leaning over his shoulder to make absolutely certain their master's health would not be harmed by what was being done in the kitchen!

As to the quantity and quality of these spices, there are three observations we might make. Firstly, exotic spices—and most spices were not produced locally—were expensive; even wealthy households kept very strict accounting of the quantities of spices that were bought and used. Secondly, being exotic and having to be imported from distant sources,[18] spices normally spent a very long time in transit, and without the benefit of efficient sealed packaging. When finally they arrived in a kitchen in northern France—perhaps a year and a half or more after being plucked or dug or scraped in the Indies or in West Africa—they were apt to have lost much of their original potency. In all likelihood the spices the medieval cook had at his disposal did not have nearly the strength that we are used to expecting today. Thirdly, it would probably be sensible not to think that "medieval people" were vastly different from ourselves: their sense of taste in foods was not that either of barbarians or of prehistoric cave dwellers. Twenty generations ago, people's tastes were most likely very similar to ours. Some people were enthusiastic about foods that were tangy with herbs and spices; others preferred dishes whose seasoning merely tickled the palate. The

---

[18] Most of the spices dealt with in the *Libre de conexenses de spicies, e de drogues e de avissaments de pessos, canes e massures de diverses terres*, a Barcelona merchant's manual from 1455, come from the Levant. One of the primary concerns of this treatise is the quality of the products the merchant will be travelling far abroad to buy, and especially how he should be able to distinguish good, fresh spices from the bad or from those that were past their prime. As well he had to know how to deal with the whole question of fraud on the part of producers. The work is edited by Miguel Gual Camarena in "Un manual catalan de mercadería," *Anuario de Estudios Medievales*, 1 (Barcelona, 1964), pp. 431–50.

highly competent author of an Italian recipe compilation keeps noting repeatedly in the outlines of his dishes that the potent taste of an onion does not agree with everyone and that, unless the cook's master insists on them, it might be best to leave onions out.[19] There is, in sum, no evidence in these recipes that a modern individual of "refined" and delicate gastronomic taste, dining in the fourteenth or fifteenth century, would have found the dishes anything but deliciously flavorful.

The modern cook should have little difficulty in obtaining most of the condiments in common culinary use in the Middle Ages, certainly those that are called for in the recipes of this book. One exception might be the spice popularly called grains of paradise. This seed, similar in appearance to a greyish peppercorn, is still commercially produced in West Africa[20] and makes its way into specialty stores in North America and Europe, particularly those stocking Arabic foods. Though it is sometimes called melegueta pepper, it is not biologically related to pepper; and though some early food historians understood the name to represent cardamom, it is not. If you need to identify grains of paradise by its botanical name, ask for *Amomum melegueta*. Its gingery flavor is responsible for much that is deliciously unique in medieval flavors; only as a very last resort—*in extremis*, as it were—should you omit it from any recipe that lists it.

ii. Colorants

For the modern cook the color of a dish is very often just the net result of the combined colors of all of the ingredients of that dish, ingredients that are chosen primarily for their flavor. This was not so in the fourteenth and fifteenth centuries. A very important consideration in the mind of any medieval cook who set to work on a dish was its color. Frequently the color alone, incorporated into its name, distinguished one dish from another: White Dish, Pink Dish, Black Porée, White Porée, Yellow Pottage, Georgé (Orange) Brewet, Russet Brewet, Bright-Green Brewet, Ruddy Rice, Blue Jelly, Green Sauce, Sandy-Colored Sauce. Many recipes from the period conclude with an injunction that the cook must take care to give the dish such-and-such a hue; he must pay heed, says Chiquart, that such-and-such a colorant is measured into a preparation in a judicious amount "in order to give it the color it should have." Clearly the cook had to be very sensitive about the appearance of his creations and the stimulating effect that color exercised upon the diners' appetites.

As colorants, many resources were available and regularly used in medieval kitchens. The cook had recourse to a remarkably wide variety of roots, plants, fungi, woods and minerals—all of them yielding a usable dye. Most were even more or less edible! Among the ingredients lists of recipes we find, for instance, alkanet, sandalwood, lapis lazuli (finely ground, of course) and one particularly useful orchil lichen (in Old French, *tornesoc*). This last source of color possessed the valuable characteristic of being able to infuse a blue into the food mixture if this mixture were alkaline in its chemical properties, or a red if it were acidic: it was in fact and quite remarkably

---

[19] *The Neapolitan Cookbook*: New York, Pierpont Morgan Library, Bühler 19.

[20] A distiller of a popular modern brand of English gin advertises that grains of paradise enter into his vats, along with cubebs, coriander, cassia and almonds—a regular medieval potion, it would seem.

an early version of the modern litmus. These colorants, together with more "natural" ones such as egg yolks or burnt toast, afforded the cook access to an extensive spectrum of tints and hues. Occasionally a dish is party-colored: for one version of the *Viandier*'s White Dish (*sic*), for example, the cook must prepare the same basic ingredients in pink, red, blue and green, and then present these portions together on a single plate. "White Dish" indeed! At least the author takes care to instruct us how to ensure that the various colors not run together!

To judge by the frequency with which they appear in the names of dishes in these early recipe collections, the two favorite colors on the late-medieval table in France are yellow and green. Generally the yellow is obtained by the use of saffron or, whenever a binding agent is required as well as a yellow colorant, by a generous use of egg yolks. For the color green the virtually universal source is parsley, ground, moistened and strained, occasionally with the admixture of sage. It might be observed that neither saffron or parsley is ever called upon in the cookery of this time in order to provide flavor but solely for the chromatic virtue in each. The phrases "add saffron for color," or "grind sufficient parsley to make the mixture green," recur regularly in all of the cookery books of the period. To such an extent is there a predilection for the colors yellow and green that they are commonly combined to produce a hue known generically as *vergay*, "gay green" or "bright green." This yellow-green can perhaps fairly be taken as representative and typical of the colors the early cook felt were necessary in the dishes he prepared in his kitchen.

Some decoration seems in effect to have been just a particular variation of this love of color. Such, for instance, was likely the case of thinly beaten metals which were commonly glued, with an adhesive of egg-whites, to the top surface of a pie. For one preparation, that of an *entremets* of a cock mounted astride a pig, both of them roasted, the *Viandier* stipulates that gold-leaf or silver-leaf is to be stuck on the cock's breast according to the relative grandeur of the nobility to whom the *entremets* is to be presented; however, where the dish is to be served to persons of lesser social significance only pewter-leaf, whether colored white, red or green, says the author, is to be used.

At the same time as the decoration lent artistic grace and nobility to the dish, it served as well to distinguish the diners along the lines of social rank: there was always some advantage to be had in flattering the most exalted persons present at a table.

iii. Sweeteners

As was the case with spices, sugar was classified as a substance whose keeping was appropriately entrusted to the household pharmacist. The sugar cane was cultivated only in the Near East, and hard cones of refined sugar entered Europe in the trade of Mediterranean merchants. As a variety of exotic spice, its earliest function was strictly pharmaceutical: sugar syrups were frequently mixed with other "drugs" and, then as now, helped the medicine go down.

Sugar was particularly valued by the physicians of the time because its humoral qualities were identified as being moderately warm and moderately moist—exactly those qualities of the human temperament. (We may be tempted to debate whether the scholarly perception of this ideal temperament in sugar preceded or, cynically, followed the pleasure that sugar gave to the tongue of a sick person.) Were it not for its costliness, sugar could almost become a sort of panacea, to be prescribed and taken as an elixir in therapeutic treatment or as part of restorative potion. And if sugar was beneficial to the sick and sickly, then what about those who wanted to safeguard their good health? . . . .

The assessment that the *Tacuinum sanitatis* accords to sugar reads like an encomium:

> Sugar. Ask the grocer for refined sugar which is hard, white as salt and brittle. It has a cleansing effect on the body and benefits the chest, kidneys and bladder. It causes thirst and stimulates the bilious humors [yellow bile, choler, is particularly warm and dry], which can be remedied by eating unripe pomegranates. It is good for the blood and therefore suitable for every temperament, age, season and place. Artificially white, it is very effective for tightness in the chest and when the tongue is unusually dry.

It would be very hard to resist doing your body so much good!

There is a very noticeable increase in the use of sugar in recipes from the fourteenth to the fifteenth centuries. In the earliest, thirteenth-century versions of the *Viandier* sugar appears as an ingredient only in dishes which are being prepared for the sick. In the *On Cookery* (dating from 1420) and in the fifteenth-century revisions of the *Viandier* sugar is being dumped into the mixing bowl for just about every dish almost as if it were salt. Most recipes tended to conclude (then as now) with the instruction: "Salt to taste."[21] We might suspect that the recipe authors of the fifteenth century may also have been inclined to write, "Sugar to taste." The taste of the times, at least among the wealthy, was definitely sweet.

But honey had been relied upon for a very long time as a sweetener in early European cookery. Anthimus, the Greek physician whom we saw advising the Gothic monarch Theodoric in matters of food, attests to its use (in a bitter-sweet combination with vinegar) for a beef dish back in the sixth century. What is apparent at the end of the Middle Ages is that a decreasing number of dishes call for honey. It is found above all in German cookery, and to a less important degree in that of England. In French and Italian cookery of this late period honey is almost unknown as an ingredient in prepared dishes. Although bee-keeping remained a common, if lowly, industry we may reasonably guess that there was considerably more money to be made from the wax which the comb yielded than from its honey when the hive was destroyed at the end of each season.

Where honey does remain in fairly constant demand, however, is in the confection of fruits and nuts. An instance of this is the lengthy, complex elaboration of a *Composte* described by the *Menagier de Paris* (p. 243/§312). Beginning on St. John's Day (June 24, according to the *Menagier*) and continuing over the several months of harvest-time, into this fruit and nut preserve are dumped: honey, walnuts, cloves, ginger, turnips, carrots, pears, gourds (squash or zucchini), peaches, parsley root, fennel root, mustard seed, aniseed, coriander, fennel seed, caraway seed (these last all ground into powder), horse-radish, cloves, cinnamon, pepper, ginger, nutmeg, grains of paradise (these spices powdered also), saffron and cedarwood (for color), more honey, wine and vinegar, seedless grapes and must. Other recipes in the *Menagier* similarly call for honey in

---

[21] For some peculiar reason German recipes of the period often end with a negative formulation of this instruction: " . . . And do not oversalt!"

making fruit conserves, for instance the *Condoignac*, a quince jam (p. 247/§313), and *Confiture de noiz*, a honey-nut confection (p. 247/§315); we have included these two preparations among our recipes in Chapter 10, Recipes 7 and 9.

The making of a variety of confections by means of honey was common enough in Antiquity and across Europe during the Middle Ages, but seems to have become particularly studied in fifteenth- and sixteenth-century Spain. The practice remains, of course, not altogether unknown in more modern times.

iv. Fats and grease

In about 1415 the Brothers Limbourg illustrated a Book of Hours for John, Duke of Berry, a volume that has become famous under the name of the *Très riches heures*. For the month of November the miniature painters have executed a rural scene in an oak grove where swineherds have driven a dozen or more pigs to feed on ripe acorns on the ground. What is remarkable about this picture is not so much what is in it—these domestic boar, with their pointed snouts, sharp teeth and lean, bristly brown bodies, look still very closely related to their wild cousins—but rather the fact that the chore of fattening a herd of swine on acorns was, in the mind of the artists, what best represented this whole autumn month in the calendar of the year's activities.

Pigs and pork were extremely important in the medieval economy and diet. Not only was the meat of the pig a staple among roast joints prepared for the table, but bacon seems to have been added into a large number of pottages along with the principal meat, whatever it might be, of that pottage. In a similar fashion bacon is cut into the filling of meat pies. Chiquart indicates that fat pork is used in these ways for the flavor it adds to a dish. The cooks of the time undoubtedly recognized as well that the addition of fat to a mixture adds useful moisture wherever this is necessary.

The grease of the pig was also a highly valued commodity in medieval kitchens. Lard, crude or rendered, was used constantly as the frying (and deep-frying) medium at some stage in all sorts of dishes, from the frying of puréed peas to that of batter-coated cheese-sticks and turnovers. It was only on lean-days that dietary restrictions forbade the use of pork fat for any purpose; on those days olive oil or, rarely, various sorts of nut oil were resorted to as substitutes for pork grease and fat.

One final observation here has to do with bone marrow. In more modern times marrow tends to be ignored by most cooks, perhaps because it is not commonly available in butcher shops. In the Middle Ages bone marrow was as much used as any other animal offal, tongue, kidneys, mesentery. Chiquart cautions his cook to make sure that butchers carefully set aside the marrowbones when they cut up a carcass and that they later dig out all of the marrow. Deep-fried in a batter covering, for instance, bone marrow was considered a delicacy worthy of designation as an *entremets*.

v. Grape products

From the thirteenth century in France the juice of the grape was not only, in a fermented state, the principal table beverage but, in both fermented and unfermented state also, the principal liquid ingredient in cookery. Wine, vinegar, verjuice and must (this last being normal, unfermented grape juice) were stocked in large quantities in the cellars of affluent households; to one or more individuals was usually assigned the sole responsibility of maintaining these stocks in good condition. So important was the supply of wines, and so valuable was the investment for a bourgeois or noble, that both the *Viandier of Taillevent* and the *Menagier de Paris* contain a chapter devoted solely to "recipes" for curing "sick" wines. These were wines that were turning, were becoming viscous or cloudy, had been subject to lactic or acetic spoilage, had absorbed the tannin from improperly prepared wooden casks, and so forth.

As cooking ingredients, grape products were valued for their flavors. The alcohol content of medieval wines may not have been as high as we are accustomed to—which does not matter particularly when the broth to which they are added is boiled—but the tastes of red, rosé and white wines were undoubtedly just as rich as today. The one flavor that we might not be familiar with is that of verjuice. Verjuice is a variety of grape that is fully formed by midsummer but whose taste is acidic and bitter. Because this taste was so highly esteemed in the late Middle Ages,[22] and because both the juice and the mash of verjuice grapes are used so extensively in the recipes of this period, it is vital for us, if we cannot obtain these ingredients, to be able to substitute something that is very similar. What seems in most instances to be a satisfactory alternative to verjuice is plain grape juice invigorated with a dash of lemon juice for tartness.

c. Cookery

There is nothing that the medieval cook did to his ingredients that we cannot do today, and usually a little more easily.

i. Chopping and grinding

The explanation may have been the state of people's teeth, it may have been the absence of forks, it may have been a consequence of humoral theories—or, more or less, for all of these reasons. At any rate three of the medieval cook's constant chores were to chop, grind and sieve. A large sharp knife, a mortar and pestle, and bolting cloth were essential items in his or her kitchen and were in never-ending use.

Just how many adults retained a full set of teeth by their thirtieth year is a moot question. There are extremely few references to toothbrushes in medieval fiction or in testamentary inventories. There are, however, many literary references to toothaches (a commonplace metaphor for the pangs

---

[22] A frequent combination in favorite dishes was of verjuice or vinegar with something sweet; this produced a sweet-and-sour effect. On the making of verjuice itself we have the evidence of one of the medieval health handbooks, the *Tacuina sanitatis*: "[Verjuice] is made from sour grapes which have been harvested before the sun enters Leo. They are condensed by being left in tubs for several days together with the marc, covered with a heavy cloth, until the marc rises and the dregs are deposited on the bottom, clarifying the verjuice. . . . It is kept for a year and may be used either as a condiment or as a medicament. . . . " *The Four Seasons of the House of Cerruti*, ed. cit., p. 62.

of love: *everybody* knew what suffering toothache brought!); and medical treatises often contain chapters on the making of poultices to ease the discomfort of caries of the cuspids, as well as the more practical techniques of extracting mouldering molars. It remains a matter of speculation to what extent a growing use of sugar in the fourteenth and fifteenth centuries undermined dental hygiene. One may wonder, again, on what basis the popular image of the Neanderthal gnawing at a huge joint of roast meat is generalized universally for the medieval table. And one may wonder whether the ravages of sugar on teeth may have had anything to do with the widespread and growing practice of reducing many of these roast joints to dainty dice-sized cubes.

Then, too, there is the matter of the fork. Cooks had always had forks—long spears that were useful for handling meat in or out of a cauldron. They were simply a double or triple sort of skewer, itself a kitchen utensil of venerable history. But the dining table did not generally see a smaller version of the kitchen fork until well on in the fifteenth century. At first, French diners thought the table fork was an affectation, an ultra-refinement in dining manners that should remain in Italy; spoons, pointed knives and fingers had long served adequately even at the royal table. But in order for the spoon, the knife and the fingers to do the job cleanly, with a modicum of decorum, foods had to be served either *a*) in bite-sized morsels, or *b*) in a liquid, mash or paste. Most prepared dishes were just that, either *a*) or *b*), dishes for the eating of which either the pointed knife or the spoon were respectively adequate. The whole development at this time of meat- and fish-pies (chopped meat or fish cooked and contained between pastry crusts: the late-medieval sandwich *par excellence*) can be attributed at least in part to an ongoing desire to find clean finger-foods.

The mortar and pestle were apothecaries' instruments but, because the cook as well had to reduce many of his foodstuffs to a finer state than a cleaver or a grater could produce, it was natural that these grinding tools became the ubiquitous fixtures of every kitchen. Humoral theory helped promote such grinding. The finer the particle of any foodstuff the more completely it mixed with particles of other foodstuffs, and so the more effective was any moderating influence that each foodstuff worked upon the nature of the other. Spices in particular had to be ground, of course. Most herbs were chopped and ground. Green vegetables were chopped, ground and pureed. Beans and peas were chopped, ground, pureed and reduced to paste. Liver, bread and toast were ground before they could be used as thickeners. That fundamental staple, almond milk, began its multifarious life in the mortar. Onions and garlic must commonly have passed by the mortar because Chiquart warns his cook to be absolutely certain to scour away their residue before using a mortar to grind any food for a sick person. Meat-, fowl- and fish-paste all came out of the mortar.

It sounds like a lot of mush was created in the medieval kitchen. There probably was. But there were as many preparations in which pieces of each serving could be picked up with the fingers or a pointed knife rather than the spoon. Still, though, a good deal of mush. But at least it was tasty mush.

ii. Binding agents

Because the cooking pot was used for a broad range of preparations, the cook made use of an equally broad range of thickeners. Wheat flour, then as now, was most useful as a thickener, but strangely enough not just as flour. It is in the form of bread—sliced, ground, moistened and sieved—that flour is most commonly called upon in our recipes to bind liquid ingredients more or less together. Depending upon the color that was desired for the finished dish, the bread could be toasted lightly or darkly, or even burnt. Starch (*amidon*), too, could be used: a recipe tells us that starch is made from soaking wheat, then grinding it, soaking it again, straining it, and finally drying it into a powder.[23] Egg yolks, ground liver and ground almonds were similarly relied upon to thicken broths and, less commonly, sauces.

To the modern palate the early dependence upon bread as a binder gives sauces a granular texture which is unusual. To some extent the old sieve or bolting cloth—for a banquet Chiquart requires his cook to have about 200 yards (!) of this cloth on hand for filtering purposes—made such sauces a little smoother, but the modern cook, even with the help of a high-speed blender, should not expect or aim to produce a *velouté* every time.

iii. Cooking

Modern physicists tell us that cooking changes the chemical characteristics of a substance. Medieval physicists—or physicians—told their contemporaries that cooking added either warmth and moisture or warmth and dryness to the foodstuff that was cooked: the cook chose his cooking method according to the inherent nature of the foodstuff and any need he had to correct this nature.

Roasting, the application of direct heat at close proximity, was appropriate for a cold, moist meat such as pork, because an open fire would warm and dry. A grill was convenient for flat meats, a spit for larger cuts. The distance of both grill and spit from the flame could be regulated fairly well, although the intensity of the flame itself was a different matter. Boiling, on the other hand, offered a relatively constant heat, and boiling better suited beef because its cold dry nature needed to be both warmed and moistened. If the ignorant cook were to subject beef to a roasting, so further drying its already dry nature, this could be quite dangerous to the unfortunate person who was to eat it later, and could even put him or her at risk of an attack of melancholia or a bilious upset. That medieval French cooks took this warning seriously and rarely roasted their beef[24] is evident in the large stocks of beef bouillon that our recipes imply was always on hand for ready use in other preparations. The serious modern-medieval cook should take note and either

---

[23] The process had been described long before by Pliny the Elder (A.D. 23–79) in his *Natural History*. Randle Cotgrave defined *amydon* in much the same way, as "Fine wheat flower steeped in water; then strained, & let stand untill it settle at the bottome; then drained of the water, & dried at the Sunne; used for bread, or in brothes it is very nourrishing." *A Dictionarie of the French and English Tongues*, London, 1611; repr. Columbia (University of South Carolina), 1950.

[24] Chiquart's course of roast meats calls for the serving of roast kid, piglet, loin of veal, loin of pork and shoulders of mutton—but *no roast beef*: all of these meats considered appropriate for roasting were held to be of a moist nature. It is in the serving of "large joints" of boiled meats that we find beef and salted meats.

(preferably) prepare quantities of beef and poultry stock, or else lay in a good supply of bouillon cubes, both beef and chicken!

The effects of the process of frying, whether sauteeing or deep-frying, fell theoretically between those of boiling and roasting. Frying added heat moderately, but it also added moisture moderately—in the form of oil or grease—to the foodstuff. Because neither heat nor moisture was added to the foodstuff in any excessive amount, frying was declared appropriate for foods possessing a relatively moderate temperament, such as chicken.

The theorists tend not to have too much to say about baking, but did at least indicate that this cooking method did not present any serious dangers. After all, they might reason, people had eaten bread safely for a long time. Baking was particularly valued as a means to retain the natural moisture in a food without adding any to it, and so this cooking procedure was suitable for meats that were themselves only moderately moist. Thus lamb, mutton and wildfowl were theoretically good candidates for the oven. What we find is that actual practice put a wide variety of foodstuffs between layers of pastry, making pies in a wide variety of shapes, heights and diameters, and that these foodstuffs seem to have been baked with little apparent concern for theoretical doctrine.

After all, what do you do with veal, held by many to be the "best" of all meats? Its humoral qualities were the most moderate, but they tended in an ideal way already toward the slightly warm and slightly moist. The *Viandier* boils veal with bacon and serves it with herbs, verjuice, saffron and ginger; but then, in another recipe, the same book makes a veal stew by roasting the veal, *then* frying it with onions, and *then* boiling it with beef bouillon, vinegar and spices. Yet another recipe in the same collection parboils the veal, then roasts it, then puts it with a smattering of spices into a pie. Such a quasi-ideal meat as veal could lend itself to a variety of preparations, provided that added condiments corrected any "superfluities" of warmth, dryness or moisture that the method of cooking might impart.

However, in a few recipes it is occasionally difficult to demonstrate patently that humoral theory was indeed the factor that determined either the cooking method(s) or the saucing that were chosen. When all is said and done, we may be excused for thinking that in some cases theory may simply have followed practice: maybe some "inspired" preparations just tasted too good to let logic interfere with them.

Two problems were inherent in the techniques of medieval cookery: heats and times. The difficulties of regulating the heat to which a pot, a pan or a pie was exposed while the contents cooked can be imagined easily enough—even by anyone who is not familiar with the tribulations of cooking over a campfire. To a large extent the cook of this time could rely upon a set of quite clever mechanisms (described below) that had been invented over time and had been further refined by many generations of his professional predecessors who had faced and largely solved exactly the same difficulties. For the most part these mechanisms allowed a cooking vessel to be hung or held at a variable distance from an open flame. The cook had only to know how direct or intense a heat the fire was producing and his food needed; he could then adjust the distance the food was from the heat.

Quite often a recipe will direct that a pot should be placed far from the fire in order to simmer. It is clear that cooks understood that certain ingredients (such as eggs) should be added to a mixture only when it has been removed from the fire and stopped boiling.

But the source of the heat complicated the problem as well. Firewood varied in nature and consequently in the sort of flame it produced. Some recipes demanded a constant heat, but it was not simple for the cook to ensure this. A cook could, and did, occasionally specify glowing embers in order to make sure that a pot received a low but especially even heat over a relatively long time. By the late-fourteenth and the fifteenth century a partial solution to the problem of heats was being adopted regularly, and that was in the substitution of coal for wood. Chiquart insists that his kitchen have access to vary large stocks of coal. While much more expensive than firewood, coal offered the late-medieval cook the double virtue of yielding a more even heat while it was burning, and a longer-lasting heat while its "coals" were merely glowing.

The definition of heats posed a supplemental difficulty for the writer of recipes. Lacking our scientifically exact description of heat, the cook who had learned by experience and *feel* just how much heat was appropriate for such and such a dish, faced some perplexity when he came to putting this knowledge into words on paper (or vellum). He might write "Swing the pot over a hot fire," for instance, but what exactly is hot? How hot? Really hot-hot, or just moderately hot—you know, "hot"? Even the great Taillevent never solved this problem of defining the heats that he knew he wanted: he could in actual fact specify only two, a "big" fire ("avoid," he writes "a *grant feu* that would burn the food") and a "little" fire ("have," he writes in another place, "a *petit feu* such that the pan be hot"). The author of the *Recueil de Riom* writes of a "fine little fire" (*beau petit feu*). Chiquart will sometimes make use of descriptive qualifications in order to give an idea of the heat he has in mind: "on a fine bright fire" (*sur beau feu cler*); "on a pretty little fire" (*sur joli pitit feu*); and in one recipe he calls for a "sprightly fire" (*sur gracieux feu*). It would have been ever so much easier for the medieval cook to have been able to write, "Expose the pot to 375° Fahrenheit of heat." Such a definition of temperatures might have had more practical sense for us when we are reading their recipes.

As well as describing the heat of his fire, the cook sometimes found it necessary to try to tell his reader just how hot the food or mixture should be. Since the boiling point of a liquid is more or less universal, recipes frequently refer to the moment when a pot just comes to a boil, or begins a rolling boil. Modern cooks would feel quite comfortable with this definition of temperature. They might not, however, feel too happy when the late-medieval recipe instructs them to let the boiled mixture cool to the point where they can bear to put their hand into it! For the medieval cook heat is largely a relative matter.

The other major difficulty, cooking times, was a matter of relativity, too. In the fourteenth and fifteenth centuries mechanical clocks were still extremely rare, and even such a simple time-measuring device as a sand-glass or a marked candle would likely be thought quite unnecessary in a kitchen.[25] What was the profession of cooking, after all, but, in part, that of knowing *when* a food was properly cooked? But if a cook were trying to transmit his knowledge about the proper

---

[25] By the second half of the fifteenth century, Italian kitchens seem to have had access normally to devices for measuring time absolutely, because some recipe collections instruct that such-and-such a mixture cook for, say, a third of an hour.

time a dish should be cooked, what could he say or write? How could he tell another cook *how long* to cook the stew or the sauce? In our age, when even wristwatches are so ubiquitous, the seriousness of this problem might not be all that apparent. But for the medieval cook it was a real one.

For the reader of medieval food recipes, the solutions that cooks found were interesting ones. Again, they were relative solutions, relative, that is, to certain normal activities that everyone engaged in or could imagine engaging in. The most commonly used means by which a medieval recipe reader was asked to measure cooking times was by referring to the time it took to recite the "Our Father": a sauce should, for instance, be boiled and stirred for three *Paternoster*'s. Alternatively a reader might be instructed[26] that a pot be boiled "the length of time it takes to say a *miserelle*—that is, Psalm 51, *Miserere mei, Deus*, probably under two minutes. Another possible procedure could measure time by referring to a normal pace of walking over a certain distance: the time it takes to walk half a mile; for as long as it takes to walk around an acre field.[27] While perhaps not as precise a measure of time as some modern cooks might prefer, such relative directions must have been considered adequate by those for whom the recipes were written and the collections compiled.

One final observation might be made about cooking problems in the medieval kitchen, and that has to do with smoke. Whether in an open pit or in a huge, hooded fireplace, a wood-fire could produce smoke that might taint the dish cooking over it. Cooks were, of course, well aware of this risk, and written recipes often direct expressly that delicate dishes be cooked far from any possible contamination from a fire's smoke. A conscientious cook ought always to take the necessary precautions that the fastidious palate of his master or patron not be offended by the after-flavor of the cook-fire smoke.

d. Food supply and preservation

The late-medieval household, both noble and bourgeois, rarely had occasion to be seriously anxious about supplies of fresh foods. Towns abounded with shops specializing in all sorts of foodstuffs, from bakeries and wafer-makers to fishmongers (whose supplies came from local inland fish-farms) and stalls offering animal viscera.

If these shops, which were apparently well supplied in the best of times, were not convenient enough, a host of itinerant peddlers who roamed the streets of towns and the by-ways of populous rural areas could usually be counted upon throughout the year to supply most of the needs of the kitchen. These peddlers cried their goods, with the result that the medieval street must surely have been the theatre of a tumult of different sounds. The cook or housewife likely had little difficulty in identifying the peculiar cries that announced the sellers of fresh herrings, small fry, garlic sauce, honey, peas, beans, garlic, onions, scallions, water cress, garden cress, chervil, chard, lettuce, turnips, melons, cheese from Champagne, cheese from Brie, butter, oatmeal, wheat meal, flour,

---

[26] As the *Menagier de Paris* writes at p. 243/§312.

[27] *Buch von guter Spise*, ed. Hans Hajek, Berlin (Erich Schmidt), 1958; Recipe 14.

milk, peaches, several varieties of pears, cherries, horse-plums, several standard varieties of apple, sorb-apples, service-berries, sloe-berries, mushrooms, walnuts, walnut oil, hazel-nuts, chestnuts, wine, vinegar, verjuice grapes, vine sprouts, hawthorn sprouts, mustard vinegar, sourdough, bread, pasties, cakes, biscuits, several varieties of wafer, rissoles, flans, tarts, simnel cakes, bean cakes, pepper, anise, figs and raisins.[28] The list is astonishingly long and varied.

What this list shows very clearly is that the late-medieval table in an affluent household did not have to lack interest or variety. What it also demonstrates equally clearly is that the medieval diet was not, as a reading of only its recipes might suggest, a diet of heavy meats and stews and pies. The recipes were devised to help prepare dishes in which foodstuffs had to be treated or mixed in some unusual way; but medieval cuisine is not at all restricted to what we read in these recipes. The cuisine that could avail itself of the variety of seasonal fresh foodstuffs—to say nothing of the prepared foods, the medieval equivalent of our delicatessen items—that were hawked regularly by street peddlers was a rich, appetizing and potentially healthy one.

In the days before freezers, or even refrigerators, a household could make use of a variety of means to ensure that some foodstuffs that had been produced or acquired remained available for eating throughout the year. The principal means to which people had recourse were fourfold: drying, salting, candying and jelling.

It may have been because physical theory identified the cause of corruption to be fundamentally a matter of superfluous moisture that it was felt to be entirely reasonable to resort to drying and salting in order to preserve foodstuffs. Or maybe the theory was formulated, *a posteriori*, after the practice in order to explain its efficacy.

Whatever the rationale for this sort of preserving, it was a thoroughly common practice. A good number of recipes simply assume that the cook is apt to be starting with dried (or smoked) fish, or with salted meat. Our fish and meat is less likely nowadays to be dried or salted, but we should understand just why so many medieval recipes open with directions that the fish or meat to be prepared should first be subject to a soaking or parboiling. Clearly for the sake of authenticity the enthusiastic modern reader can go out and purchase a filet of dried cod or a slab of salt pork, in order to begin the dish with that just as the medieval recipe does. In the recipes that follow here, though, we have assumed that all of the major ingredients are fresh.

Both honey and sugar were used in medieval confections initially for the purpose of preserving certain foodstuffs. When refined sugar became more generally available on the European market during the fourteenth century its virtue was still largely understood as medicinal. Its warm and moist nature ensured that it was accorded a preeminent place as a safe, readily digestible and highly beneficial condiment. These qualities made it analogous also to many spices, and conferred upon sugar the same potential as was recognized in spices for correcting undesirable qualities in other foodstuffs. In particular this potential was exploited in the use of sugar or honey for preserving fruits and vegetables. The *Menagier de Paris* offers several recipes for candying walnuts, carrots,

---

[28] See the poem of Guillaume de la Villeneuve, *Les Crieries de Paris* ed. by Etienne Barbazan in his *Fabliaux et contes des XIe, XIIe, XIIIe et XVe siècles*, 2 vols., Paris, 1808; repr. Geneva (Slatkine), 1976; Vol. I, pp. 276–86.

pears, peaches, quince, gourds, parsley and fennel roots, or for making confitures or compotes of them.

The word *dragée* was of course a medieval coinage, but originally it usually designated a piece of spiced candy (which we spell *dragee* here) distributed and eaten as a digestive after a meal. It is easy to see how the word *dragee* came to be applied to a nut preserved in a coating of sugar.

The final means of conserving foods was by using the natural gelatin in certain fish and meats. All three of the major medieval French collections contain recipes outlining the procedures to be followed in making jellied meat or fish dishes. The medieval cook had no way of extracting gelatin from its source and of refining it for use elsewhere, say, with fruits. But he was very familiar with the techniques of boiling the gelatin off fish skins or out of sheep's hooves. To the vat of chopped fish or meat he would add a complex array of warming and drying spices, perhaps adding in a little sugar too, for good measure. Then the broth would be strained and the mixture allowed to set in a cool place.

This jelling procedure was held to be an economical way to avoid wasting leftovers. Besides, cool jelly dishes were much appreciated on summer dining tables, and were even recommended by the physicians' health handbooks as being beneficial during this season.

4. Beverages

It should be enough for the purposes of this book merely to enumerate the beverages which the French butler could serve to the table of his medieval master during a meal. For the modern cook they are the regular, everyday accompaniment to food *instead of* water, tea, coffee, milk, cocoa or, maybe, carbonated drinks. One other medieval drink is not listed here and that is mead. While common enough in early English and German gastronomy, mead never enjoyed much acceptance among the French—except perhaps those early Franks who remained near the Rhineland.

In every case these beverages are alcoholic, at least to some degree. Their alcohol content ensured a quality that "plain" water rarely could in the Middle Ages: from whatever source, generally the alcoholic beverage was bacteriologically safer to drink. The modern cook should have no difficulty in choosing an entirely appropriate beverage to accompany a medieval meal.

a. Wines

The medieval French family drank wine. For everyone, from the tenderest youthful age right through to the most elderly member of the household, wine, albeit perhaps watered, was considered to be the normal table beverage in most parts of France. Depending upon the relative affluence of the household the selection of wines stored in the household's wine cellar and available for serving at a meal might be surprisingly broad. Not only regional wines could be kept on hand but "foreign" wines from other provinces of France and exotic wines from other countries and from across the sea (the Mediterranean sea) from such places as Corsica, Cyprus, Greece and Syria were imported by merchants and distributed in large barrels to the wealthier houses. In ordinary households the staple beverages were clearly the local wines.

There are good grounds for thinking that medieval wines were not normally as strong in alcoholic content as the 10–13 percent alcohol/volume that we think of as usual today. The modern host or hostess who is conscientiously determined to be authentic even in the matter of wine will have to decide whether *a*) to cut commercially available wine by the same amount of water—and so to have a somewhat *un*-medieval watery wine; or *b*) to try to find or to make a good, rich-tasting wine with about 5 percent of alcohol.

b. Beers

The normal drinking of beer and cider was limited in late-medieval France to those regions in which, for one reason or another, the grape vine did not become entirely acclimatized. Historically this amounted to the more northerly provinces, and especially in the northeast of the kingdom to the grain-growing areas where the brewing of beer was cheaper than vinification and had, furthermore, become culturally traditional. The aristocracy and the wealthier members of the bourgeois class in these provinces could well afford to import any wines for which they may have cultivated a predilection, but documentary evidence testifies that in Flanders and Vermandois beer remained the preferred drink.

A thirteenth-century health handbook, written in French in 1256 for the Countess of Provence, affords us what may be a prejudiced view of the merits of beer—particularly as the author of this work, Aldobrandino of Siena, was an Italian.

> Beer (*ciervoise*). Beer is a variety of drink made from oats, from wheat and from barley; but that which is made from oats and from wheat is better because it does not produce gas. But from whatever it may be made, whether from oats or barley or wheat, it harms the head and the stomach, gives bad breath, hurts the teeth and fills the brain with bad fumes; consequently whoever drinks beer with wine becomes quickly intoxicated; but it does have the virtue of promoting urine, and it makes soft, white flesh. And beer that is made from rye or from rye bread containing mint and wild celery, this beer is to be preferred.[29]

c. Ciders

Several beverages were made from the juice that had been expressed from locally grown fruits in the Middle Ages, juice that was usually allowed to ferment for a short time in order to make an effervescent, mildly alcoholic drink. In particular, the French consumed *poiree* from pears, *moree* from blackberries, a quince cider and, especially, an apple cider.

Across the north of France, and particularly in Normandy—as is still the case today—apple cider was the normal drink of preference. The preparation of these fruit ciders was to all intents and purposes identical with the preparation of grape wines; only regional agriculture and regional habits determined local taste. Aldobrandino, the Italian physician whom we consulted above, offers a commentary on cider that tends to be more a scientific analysis than a gastronomic appreciation.

> Cider (*vin de pume*). Wine that is made from ripe apples is temperately warm and moist, but it is hardly healthy to drink because it blows up and swells the stomach and stops up the passages of the liver and of the lungs; but it does have the virtue of putting on fat and yields good nourishment, and it is especially useful for those who have a rough, dry chest and who cannot cough easily. If this wine is made from bitter apples, it is of the same nature as vinegar, and is suitable for those who have bitter bile in the stomach and who have a heated liver. Everyone may drink this wine when the weather is very warm.[30]

---

[29] *Le régime du corps de maître Aldebrandin de Sienne*, ed. Louis Landouzy and Roger Pépin, Paris (Champion), 1911, pp. 118–19.

[30] *Le régime du corps, ed. cit.*, p. 119.

5. Kitchens

a. Physical features

There are no "ideal" kitchens in the Middle Ages except to the extent that each new kitchen incorporated features that someone had perceived as marking an advance over those in use elsewhere. In this sense one might hypothesize that there was some sort of gradual progress in kitchen design during the Middle Ages. From the archeological evidence that we have in those medieval French kitchens that are still extant, the picture we can form of the cook's professional setting is both simple and fairly straightforward.

In large princely castles, the kitchen could be located apart from the main structure of the castle hall itself. In part this separation lessened the danger of accidental conflagration in the rest of the castle; in part it diminished the migration of any unpleasant cooking odors that were apt to originate in the kitchen. Numerous manuscript illuminations show a procession of dish-bearers entering the dining hall from the open air, and a few show them entering from the protection of a covered walkway.

At the Royal Abbey of Fontevrault the layout of an efficient kitchen must surely have occupied the thoughts either of the founder (Robert d'Abrissel) or of the abbess, nuns or monks who in the twelfth century designed the Abbey's kitchen. This dressed-stone structure, originally separate from the other conventual buildings, is octagonal in plan and 88 feet in height. Five great fireplaces are situated in semi-circular recesses around the perimeter; they and a number of firepits are vented through twenty tall circular chimneys; the central roof, sitting on a square which is formed by pairs of chimneys, is an octagonal pyramid on whose peak is set a fresh-air in-take to supply both a free draft to the fireplaces and clean, cool air to the workers. This kitchen is architecturally, on the outside, a symmetrically graceful structure, most remarkable for such a utilitarian domestic purpose, but above all it is on the inside a highly functional building designed to make cooking as efficient and pleasant as possible. The kitchen brothers who were assigned to labor there enjoyed the advantage of an environment of which most professional cooks of the time could only dream, perhaps with envy.

What were the criteria for a useful kitchen in the fifteenth century? Very fortunately Chiquart's *On Cookery* spells out in detail the concerns which a cook should satisfy about a kitchen, its equipment and a good supply of foodstuffs, if ever he is called upon to prepare a banquet in some locale away from his regular place of work.

Besides his principal place of residence where he normally held court, the cook's master usually owned a number of other manors or castles. It was entirely likely that in the normal course of a year he would travel and spend some days in these secondary residences, so that the cook, in accompanying his master wherever he went, was required to make use of facilities that he might be inclined otherwise to consider less than adequate. In any one of these secondary residences, as political or seasonal circumstances might dictate, the master might even direct his cook and his household steward to prepare a formal banquet. In such a case, as well as the enormity of the task of planning the menu and overseeing the preparation of a vast array of dishes, the cook faced the additional difficulty of having to work in a kitchen with whose layout he was not comfortably familiar. He had to make absolutely certain in advance that he could produce, just as creditably as in his home kitchen, the elegant meal or series of meals for which he would be responsible.

As a structure a kitchen provided the cook with space, light, heat and what we would call a reasonably tolerable if not entirely convenient environment. It must have room enough for a suitable number of work tables, chopping blocks and mortars, all of the different bulky equipment that has its place in the large late-medieval kitchen, along with all the personnel who work at them and must move around there freely. During daylight hours its windows must admit sufficient light to work by. Its doorways must allow access and egress of sacks and carcasses, and the men carrying them; these doors must communicate directly with storage rooms or with "offices," such as the bakery and fruitery, where other kitchen functions are being performed. It must have several fireplaces, of a good range of suitable sizes, all of which draw well and cleanly, and all of which are usefully equipped with andirons and the mechanisms to hang pots and hold pans. It must have adequate sinks for washing, with a good supply of running water (piped in, ideally) and drains. Perhaps above all, a *sine qua non* for the medieval cook and his staff, there must be a means to provide large quantities of fresh air: for when, at the height of the preparation of a score of dishes for a mid-summer banquet, a number of large fires around the kitchen are blazing and smoking, oil is boiling in deep pans, and all of the staff are working strenuously at chopping, pounding and stirring, a current of fresh air can be a true blessing.

b. Utensils

The facilities in a secondary castle were quite likely not in themseves sufficient to provide for the exceptional challenge of a banquet. So Chiquart tells us what we must consider to be the bare minimum as far as cooking utensils are concerned. To handle the preparations for a banquet with any sort of competence, the cook would have to assemble—beg, borrow or, on the authority of his master, otherwise procure—a large variety of kitchen equipment: cauldrons of all sizes, pans (20 of them), pots (50 regular and 60 large, two-handled models), kettles (one dozen large), hampers, baskets (to move raw and semi-cooked foodstuffs around within the kitchen), grills, graters, rasps, wooden stirring-spoons (some one hundred of those), holed spoons (25 large and small), knives (several dozen, both large, of a two-handed variety, and small), pot-hooks, oven shovels, roasting spits and supports (20 of several varieties), and iron[31] skewers (120 of them, 13 ft/4 m long, a further three dozen of the same length but not as thick, along with a further [!] four dozen that are even more slender). Huge quantities of dishware are needed for both kitchen use and for serving, in gold, silver, pewter and wood: 4,000 plates is an absolute minimum, he assures us, but even so what is used for the first course will have to be washed and readied for re-use for the third

[31] In defence of his specification that the cook hold out for stout *iron* skewers, Chiquart explains that, given the risk of losing the meat into the fire, along with all of the labor that has gone into its preparation, it really is false economy to make use of the cheaper wooden skewers!

course. The cook must procure bolting cloth (130 yards/120 meters), white cloth (750 yds/690 m, for sanitary kitchen use), fine linen (75 yds/70 m, for strainers), and additional white sheeting. He must foresee the need for torches, candles and tapers to light all the areas of the cooking kitchen, the bakery, butchery and fish kitchen.

The work of a large medieval kitchen was subdivided into several specialized areas, or "offices," as in any large kitchen today. In the company of the Household Steward, Chiquart tells us, the Chief Cook must inspect the proposed locale of the banquet in order to make certain that there will be enough space for all the multifarious labor the preparation of a banquet called for: room for tables for chopping and mixing, room for grinding in the mortars, well ventilated room to set out open hearth fireplaces, room to make ovens and for the bakery, for pastry-making, for meat and fish preparation.

Fuel was also the cook's concern: the cooking fires of even a simple banquet would consume one thousand cartloads of good dry firewood and a large *barnfull* of coal. (It is difficult for us today to have an accurate impression of the huge quantity of firewood that would have to be transported to the kitchen in *one thousand* cartloads, let alone imagine the amount of shovelling of coal that would be involved first to fill and then empty a barn. Just think of the filthy, sweating runner—a young lad, undoubtedly—with his coal-scuttle, scarcely set down during two whole days!) And, furthermore, the cook must never run the slightest risk of running out of this fuel; he must always know where, at a pinch, he can send immediately for more.

And workers: the Chief Cook would undoubtedly have to recruit helpers—competent ones ideally—even if he were given permission to transport some of his regular staff to an outlying castle. Cooking in the Middle Ages was labor intensive. How many butchers would be needed to cut up and dress 100 oxen, 130 sheep, 180 pigs, 200 piglets, 400 goat kids, 100 calves and 2,000 chickens? (And how much space would these butchers need in order to wield their cleavers?) How many scullions would be needed to scrub 4,000 plates? (And how much water would *they* need?) How many assistant cooks would be needed for a banquet without the risk of spoiling its broth?

Above all, then, space, equipment, fuel and workers—without even beginning to calculate the horrendous figures of foodstuffs. The logistics for even a relatively simple banquet must have been daunting. For a large one, over two lean days, in a small, outlying castle, a duke could depend on no one of less competence than a Chiquart.

6. The Hall and Banquets

In 1550 King Henry II of France offered a grand reception to the ambassadors of his English royal counterpart, Edward VI. The French Marshal of the day, a certain François de Sceppeaux, Lord of Vielleville, noted in his memoirs that "Nobody can doubt, since this took place in the abode of a King of France, that it was incomparable and unrivalled; for no other kings in Christendom, or in the world, can approach our triumphant success in the matter of feasting. Nor are their cooks so accomplished in preparing and dressing their viands. No greater proof of this is needed," the Marshal goes on to claim, "than the fact that all the foreign princes seek their cooks and pastry makers in France."[32]

Modern readers may well be sceptical of such rodomontade, particularly when it was uttered by a Frenchman whose very status depended upon the good graces of the sovereign master he served. However, despite any inclination we may have to be perhaps a little cynical about such conceit, there is a good deal of evidence that the Marshal's bragging did indeed have a solid basis in fact during the sixteenth century. Banquetting, together with all of the ceremonial associated with formal dining, had long been areas in which French monarchs prided themselves for their elegance, refinement and taste, to say nothing of their splendid magnificence. And foreign nobility willingly acknowedged French preeminence in this area. Most of the early French cookery manuals, themselves produced in royal or noble households, include directions to the chef on how to prepare dishes appropriate for an extraordinary meal, a feast or banquet. At such meals the food served and the entertainment provided ought to make a lasting impression upon the guests.

The origins of the medieval banquet undoubtedly reach back to times before Classical Antiquity, even to pre-historic times when the earliest men and women celebrated some exceptional occasion by the serving, with formal ceremony, of some unusual food. We may be certain, though, that it was at French courts that the formal medieval banquet developed to the point where it became a recognized model of the genre, emulated throughout Europe. And it was in French kitchens, of the fourteenth and fifteenth centuries, that cooks worked on recipes and prepared banquets which were talked about and imitated to a large extent in all of the contemporary courts of the western world.

It is particularly revealing that the Bayeux Tapestry places the scene of a mini-banquet at a point in the narrative where William of Normandy has landed safely in England in 1066 and is about to engage King Harold. As a dramatic formal pause before one of the greatest conquests of all time, that by a Norman duke of the English kingdom, the banquet brings together the Norman principals, the Duke and his two (half-)brothers, Bishop Odo and Robert of Mortain. The banquet serves here specifically (as it tends to do generally) to affirm, and in a sense to sanctify, the solidarity of the Norman cause: in the scene the Bishop is praying the grace and perhaps asking

---

[32] Colin Clair, *Kitchen and Table*, London, New York, Toronto (Abelard-Schuman), 1964, p. 60.

a blessing upon the whole Norman undertaking.

What was a medieval French banquet, then, and what were these remarkable dishes which became so celebrated among aristocratic and even bourgeois gourmets of the period? The banquet was one of the most useful, effective means a lord possessed of honoring a guest. In essence this consisted of lavishing hospitality upon him. To impress his banquet guest, the lord, or an exceptionally wealthy bourgeois, might depend upon sheer quantity of food, or upon the variety of dishes which were borne to the table over an extended period of time. Or he might direct his Chief Cook to prepare some remarkable plate in which art and skill, imagination and craftsmanship would be combined to delight all those who had been invited to share in the lord's prodigality at his board. In the full sense of the word a lord depended upon his cook to provide the *honors* of his house on these occasions. French cooks show throughout this period that they fulfilled their masters' expectations honorably with dishes of ever-increasing variety and delectability.

At the same time as it provided exceptional gastronomic pleasure, the medieval banquet drew a lot of its effect from the set of formal rules of procedure which governed it. Just as proper, rigorously observed procedure was assumed to be of paramount importance in the law courts in the late Middle Ages, so the sequence of acts and the actual words spoken as a part of any formal event were fixed and sacrosanct. The tournament, the hunt, the rites of ennoblement and of homage, and the banquet—all of these occasions had certain formulæ, in action, gesture and word, that had to be realized. Because the banquet was in many respects an affirmation of the exclusivity of the donor's social class, and a reflection of its glory, the "style" in which the banquet was offered, its procedure, was formulated into a fairly firm set of rules.

A banquet began of course with a decision on the part of the noble lord or rich bourgeois. According to Chiquart, a period of between two months and six weeks was the necessary lead-time for those preparations that lasted longest.[33] Of course cooks in any establishment have always had much the same concerns when a formal meal has to be prepared. In the Middle Ages, however, the state banquet posed two additional problems. One of these had to do with provisions; the other concerned the date of the banquet and the unfixed nature of its duration.

Firstly there was the matter of a supply of foodstuffs. For Chiquart the list is extensive: domestic meats, game meats, fish (in remarkable quantities and varieties, both fresh-water fish and sea-fish), eggs (12,000!), spices (certain of these were absolutely *de rigueur* on the cook's procurement list: ginger, cinnamon, cloves, grains of paradise, long pepper, spikenard, black and white pepper, mace, saffron, galingale and nutmeg, according to the *Viandier of Taillevent*, Recipe

---

[33] All of these precise details on the arrangements for a banquet are again provided in the opening pages of the *On Cookery*. Chiquart's banquet is for two days, with both dinner and supper on each day. It is to take place away from the lord's principal residence and, because in the book it is merely a hypothetical exercise, Chiquart suggests a parallel set of menus in case the dates decided for the banquet should happen to fall on lean days. Chiquart is never specific about the number of guests attending his banquet, but we may guess about five hundred, of mixed ranks but all from decidedly the upper end of the social hierarchy: "Kings," he begins his hypothetical guest-list, and then continues quite explicitly with "queens, dukes, duchesses, counts, countesses, princes, princesses, marquesses, marchionesses, barons, baronesses, and prelates of various classes, and nobles."

170), nuts, fruits, cheeses, flour (3,600 lbs/1636 kg of wheat-flour), colorants (including 18 lbs/8 kg of gold-leaf) and a large number of spiced candies, vinegar (832 gallons/3,740 liters), verjuice (1,040 gal/4,680 l), oil (520 gal/2,340 l), and wines for the use of the kitchen *alone*!

The Chief Cook had to be assured of adequate supplies of game and wild fowl. The gathering of these provisions was the responsibility of the game purveyors—these functionaries being sometimes "free-lance" operatives and sometimes members of the noble household. Ultimately they would require that forty horses be requisitioned for their use in order to transport all of the necessary game: deer, hare, rabbits, partridge, pheasants, doves (and any other small wildfowl they could come by), cranes, herons, and so forth. The game purveyors were enjoined to deliver their acquisitions to the site of the banquet in time to allow them to hang for three days in order to become tender. Within this same minimum period of lead-time the Chief Cook had also to work his way down an enormous check-list of supplies for the four meals of a two-day banquet. These supplies were both edible and non-edible and had to be determined with a view to ensuring that every single thing needed for the food, for the making of it and for the serving of it, should be on hand at the crucial moment.

The second problem unique to the medieval cook who found himself responsible for a banquet was itself twofold: that he must allow for the possibility that the banquet might happen to fall on a lean day or over several lean days; and that he had to plan his menus and determine the quantities of his foodstuffs always with the thought in mind that his lord might, on a mere whim, decide to prolong the banquet for an additional meal,[34] or two, or three, ... ! Such a prolongation of the festivities might realize the medieval cook's worst nightmare, but it would certainly separate the apprentices from the master cooks! When Chiquart dictates his *On Cookery*, he goes so far as to duplicate his extensive banquet menu for meat days with a second and parallel banquet menu for fish days. Then, cannily, he appends a section of additional dishes upon which the cook can fall back in the case of an unforeseen extension of the banquet. Just as much as his modern counterpart, the medieval cook had to be flexible and to possess a repertoire and abilities that were much broader than he might think he would ever need to draw upon.

Following the lord's decision to hold a banquet, it was above all the cook who made it happen. The food was prepared, dish by dish, it was laid out on platters or in bowls on the kitchen "dressers" and then presented to the guests in the banquet hall.

The hall was set with tables in an open U or square horseshoe. Such tables were normally rather narrow and not permanent fixtures, consisting merely of trestles upon which boards were laid—hence we must "set" the table (up), and the word "board" has become synonymous with food and eating. Those invited to partake at the lord's board assembled as soon as they received a summons to come and wash their hands. Then they sat in the hierarchical order indicated to them by the lord's Herald (or by the person who functioned as such), as that order descended in distance from the lord's high board. They sat on benches, set up likewise expressly for meals, on only the outer side of the table; often only the lord, who presided over the meal, enjoyed a

---

[34] For a banquet thrown by the Duke of Savoy a single meal, a dinner, normally contained something in the order of 26 different preparations!

cushioned bench with a back—or even a chair, so that he became the "chairman of the board."

Tables were laid with a white cloth; a wealthy household might lay a second, narrower cloth, a runner, that fell on the laps of the diners and was to be used as a modern napkin. A spoon was provided each guest, but a sharp, pointed knife was a more personal item commonly carried by everyone, man or woman, and used for eating. The knife was in a sense the vital eating utensil, important for cutting food but useful also for spearing chunks that might be served in the common bowls or on the common platters. The knife amply fulfilled all of the functions that moderns reserve for their forks. Large forks were well known in the kitchen, but in France and England were not conceived as appropriate as an eating utensil until the sixteenth century when the dainty Italian practice of spearing morsels of food with a dining fork, a miniature of the kitchen instrument, became generally imitated.[35]

Also marking each place-setting with the spoon was the diner's personal plate, usually a trencher of tough bread. The *Menagier de Paris* describes the bread trencher that was available commercially in Paris at the end of the fourteenth century. As part of the provisions for a formal meal he advises his young wife to instruct one of their servants to go off to the bakery and purchase

> trencher bread, three dozen, six inches across, four finger widths high, baked four days before; it should be brown; or else get Corbeil bread at the Halles.[36]

The bread that was known by the name of the town of Corbeil where it was made was a particularly dense bread of coarsely ground brown flour. Rather than slicing one's own trenchers from this especially coarse bread that was sold at the Paris market, however, the medieval householder who was preparing a formal dinner could buy trenchers "ready made" for the purpose, square and baked smoothly with a hard flat surface on both sides. The *Menagier*'s purchases are with a view to

---

[35] One hundred years after the "end" of the Middle Ages a peregrinating, and presumably cosmopolitan, Englishman is still marvelling at the Italian use of dining forks.

I observed a custom in all those Italian cities and towns through which I passed, that is not used in any other country that I saw in my travels, neither do I think that any other nation of Christendom doth use it, but only Italy. The Italians . . . do always at their meals use a little fork when they cut their meat. For while, with their knife, which they hold in one hand, they cut the meat out of the dish, they fasten their fork, which they hold in their other hand, upon the same dish, so that whatsoever he be that, sitting in the company of any others at meal, should unadvisedly touch with his fingers the dish of meat from which all at the table do cut, he will give occasion of offence unto the company, as having transgressed the laws of good manners, in so much that, for his error, he shall be at the least brow-beaten, if not reprehended in words. This form of feeding I understand is generally used in all places of Italy, their forks being for the most part made of iron or steel, and some of silver, but those are used only by Gentlemen. The reason of this their curiosity is, because the Italian cannot by any means endure to have his dish touched with fingers, seeing all men's fingers are not alike clean. . . .

Thomas Coryate, *Coryats Crudities*, 1611.

[36] *Pain de tranchouers, .iii. douzaines de demy pié d'ample et .iiii. dois de large de haut, cuit de .iiii. jours devant; et sera brun; ou qu'il soit pris es Halles pain de Corbueil.* Ed. Brereton and Ferrier, p. 184/ed. Pichon, II, p. 109.

a wedding banquet being planned for for a Tuesday (hence a meat day) in May; at dinner there would be twenty bowls (therefore approximately 40 persons), and at supper ten bowls (20 persons). For these sixty-odd place-settings the *Menagier* suggests 36 trencher "loaves," each about three inches/seven centimeters thick. We may deduce that such commercial trencher slabs as these were normally split in half, the broad outer crusts being placed upwards. Aging the hard-crusted trencher loaf by four days further ensured that it would be even more resistent to penetration by dripping sauces and gravies.

A cup, goblet or tumbler served every two guests, and in the same way as each new dish was served, a serving platter or bowl was set before every two guests. With one exception the medieval banquet table was otherwise bare: of all the condiments, the oldest, salt, was alone available on the table. Traditionally it sat in one principal source, a more or less elegant and preciously crafted vessel, often of silver, that conventionally had the form of a boat and that sat near the lord; if you were not honored by a seat at the lord's elevated table, you sat "below the salt." Because of the rich elegance of the salt boat, and because it was a personal possession of the lord and master, in a way it signified his presence at table. While this artifact formed in effect a sort of symbolic focal point for the whole dining board, salt was available to the other guests whose places might be far removed from the boat. In the *Menagier*'s time it was customary to set out salt in cubes of hard bread of which one side was either depressed or hollowed out. Again, the *Menagier* provides revealing evidence; the passage is interesting enough to reproduce fully.

> You need [by way of personnel for your formal meal] two bread-assistants (*porte-chappes*), one of whom will slice bread to make trenchers and bread salt cellars; and they will bear the salt, bread and trenchers to the tables; for the hall they will obtain two or three large baskets (*couloueres*) into which to throw the solid left-overs such as bread sops, sliced or broken bread, trenchers, meat and so forth, and two buckets into which to throw and collect broth, sauces and other liquid substances.[37]

As the *Menagier*'s passage indicates, each diner received as well at his or her place setting a piece of "table bread," *pain de main*, whether this was sliced or broken from a large mound-shaped loaf. Table bread was always made from a relatively fine flour, ideally a wheat flour unadultered by an admixture of other grains and as white as possible.

From the beginning of the meal through to its end each dish was presented formally to the lord first, then served to everyone else in descending order. As trenchers became too soaked in grease and sauces, they could be cleared away and replaced. Fingers were the prime instruments of eating; refined diners used their lap-cloth frequently in order to keep their fingers and mouths clean of grease. In France the invariable beverage during a banquet was wine, though cider was also drunk at normal meals in northern France and beer in eastern regions. The wine steward (*eschanson*) or butler (from the French *bouteillier*) had the sole responsibility of ensuring that drinking cups were constantly replenished.

---

[37] *Menagier de Paris*, ed. Brereton and Ferrier, p. 187/ed. Pichon, II, p. 114.

At all times it was expected that guests at a formal meal would follow a code of refined table manners whose broadly accepted injunctions were set forth in several books on the subject.[38] These rules of proper behavior, of which we have reproduced a selection in this book, covered a wide gamut of topics, from cleanliness to suitable table conversation. The authors of these collections of advice seem to aim them at young nobles whose social merit will be judged in part by their behavior at the dining table. In previous centuries chivalry and courtliness were largely ethical questions and were defined for the young noble by a sense of what he owed to the others in society, the poor, the defenceless, the needy. The original codes of chivalry gradually died in the thirteenth and fourteenth centuries, however. By the end of the Middle Ages, in these guides on table etiquette it is becoming clear that there is such a thing as noble manners and civility, that they are measured not by one's selfless service to others but by one's behavior in public, and that they are now a reliable sign of good breeding.

The banquet assumed a social significance that went much beyond the simple satisfying of appetite. For the noble it afforded a chance to demonstrate the glory of his nobility. For the guest it was an opportunity to show that he or she understood the social rules of the class to which he or she felt worthy of belonging, and that the honor of their lord's invitation was not misplaced. And for the cook, even before he began to oversee the making of the first pie or the first broth, the banquet amounted to a formidable set of logistical problems.

---

[38] See the section on Table Manners (p. 396, below).

7. The Late-Medieval Cook

In a very large French household, that of an significant aristocrat, for example, the late-medieval cook occupied a clearly defined place in the hierarchy of authority. He was responsible to the Household Steward who oversaw all activities concerned with provisioning and feeding. This latter in turn derived his authority from the Master of the Household who was directly responsible to the noble personage, the lord. The Chief Cook's work was carried on in close conjunction with the bookkeeping of the Kitchen Clerk, who received permission to dispense funds and procure foodstuffs, and who carefully documented all such expenditures. Under the authority of the Chief Cook labored all of the Kitchen personnel, including perhaps other cooks, a Roaster, a Larderer, a Poulterer, a Fruiter (who handled all fresh and dried fruit and nuts), a Pottager, a Saucer, an Ovenman, a Butcher, a Fire-Tender or Fire-Blower, a Fueler, a Potter (who scrubbed and drew water), and invariably a large crew of Scullions. Depending on the size of the household, each of the above specialized officers might be in charge of one, ten or a score of assistants; in very large households, such as that of a duke or the king himself, such Offices as that of the Larder, Bakery, Fruitery, Buttery (from the French word *bouteille*, "[wine-]bottle") or Pantry (from the French word *pain*, "bread") might be important enough to be quasi-independent from the Kitchen and responsible directly through their own respective Clerks to the Household Steward.

Within the domain of his kitchen the Cook or Chief Cook ruled with all of the authority that his responsibility invested him with. In his *Mémoires* (1473), Olivier de la Marche, Master of the Household of Charles the Bold, Duke of Burgundy—and a personage whose exalted position in this most exalted court gave him a comprehensive and perceptive breadth of view—evokes the Chief Cook's authority in a swiftly drawn vignette:

> The Cook orders, regulates and is obeyed in his Kitchen; he should have a chair between the buffet and the fireplace to sit on and rest if necessary; the chair should be so placed that he can see and survey everything that is being done in the Kitchen; he should have in his hand a large wooden spoon which has a double function: one, to test pottages and brewets, and the other, to chase the children out of the Kitchen, or to make them work, striking them if necessary.[39]

The image of authority that Olivier de la Marche sketches is reminiscent of that of kingship; with his long stirring spoon in his hand we may visualize almost a parody of a monarch posing with his royal rod of sovereignty ready to smite the lazy or the recalcitrant. There could be no sedition in the Kitchen. The cook was a ruler over a society of diverse parts which had but a single goal: the production of a good meal on time. For this it was recognized that he had to be able to exercise quasi-autocratic power within the boundaries of his realm, the Kitchen.

---

[39] Henri Beaune and J. d'Arbaumont, *Mémoires d'Olivier de la Marche, Maître d'Hôtel et Capitaine des Gardes de Charles le Téméraire*, 4 vols., Paris (Renouard), 1888; Vol. IV, p. 50.

The professional cook—then as now—had two obligations that were, in effect, absolute: to ensure that appetizing food was available when his patron wanted it, and to ensure that the food that came out of his kitchen was safe for consumption. There is no need to expound upon the first obligation, since it will be recognized as a serious concern by anyone who has ever cooked for others or who has ever ordered a meal at a greasy spoon. The second obligation calls for comment, however.

We understand today just how readily bacteria can grow in the protein of foodstuffs. We understand how to go about limiting the likelihood of infestations of harmful bacteria. But even so, every modern cook remains perpetually haunted by the spectre of a case of food poisoning that might be traced to his or her carelessness. In late-medieval France a cook's nose or palate could generally identify rancid or rotten foodstuffs, but the precise nature of this spoilage escaped the understanding of the age. To explain toxicity a cook could only fall back on the medical theories that we examined before about inappropriate humors. As we have already pointed out, it was incumbent upon the medieval cook to know the humoral qualities and complexions of all of the foods he handled, and thus to do all in his power to avoid risking the health of any persons who ate his food. And furthermore the cook could insist upon cleanliness in his kitchen, as Chiquart does constantly, even tiresomely, recognizing as he must some obscure relationship between cleanliness and healthfulness.

But what about those potential infections whose origins cannot be seen, whose reasons cannot logically be understood? What about the periodic dangers of eating rye flour ground from grain which has been contaminated by ergot. Nowadays we can identify the fungus *Claviceps purpurea*; in the Middle Ages people knew only that thousands were apt from time to time to contract "St. Anthony's Fire" and to die with horrible convulsions and madness. What about salmonella in apparently fresh chicken? What about worm-spores or pathogenic bacteria, all sorts of micro-organisms, in newly slaughtered animals whose meat certainly *looks* sound? What happens to the whole population of a castle when a feverish kitchen scullion happens to sneeze into a pot of almond milk, or another, unknowingly infected with the typhoid bacillus, does not scrub his hands as well as we today know he should? In his obsession with cleanliness Chiquart exhorts his cook never to leave baskets or platters of food, uncooked or cooked, exposed to the kitchen air but always to keep them covered them with a clean white cloth. But even Chiquart could do only so much to combat the unseen and the unknown.

In an age when accidental poisonings probably occurred far more often than paranoid grandees believed they were subject to deliberate poisonings, the cook simply *had* to earn something close to the total confidence of his master. It is true that a series of tests were normally in place to "prove" each of the dishes and each of the articles of food that would be set before a noble. If the precious unicorn horn—which was usually just a piece of narwhal tusk, though who cared, provided that it worked—failed to become discolored or to exude sweat in the presence of poisoned food, then the human taster-tester most surely would do so. This second means of testing the purity of food would undoubtedly exhibit other signs as well that the food was not altogether salubrious. In this perpetual endeavor to ensure that the master's food was safe, the cook bore the primary onus, of course. Invariably, in the formal sequence of tests that any prepared dish underwent before it was served, it was the cook who had to eat the first sample, usually in his kitchen and usually in the presence of the Master of the Household or the Steward.

But testing could go only so far; at some stage the cook had to be trusted. Happy was the cook who had won his master's trust; but very much happier indeed was the master who had secured the services of a competent and trustworthy cook.

In the same outline of household personnel that we mentioned before, the *Mémoires* of Olivier de la Marche, the author acknowledges the very high esteem that the Office of the Cook merited:

> ... It is not a common estate or office, but is a subtle and costly craft, one which is the essence of trustworthiness; and it is fundamental to the benefit of the Prince, and cannot be dispensed with. ... [40]

This is a fine summary of the craft of the professional cook in the Middle Ages, almost a definition of it. The statement recognizes the cook's knowledge, his abilities and his responsibilities; it acknowledges, too, the indispensable role the cook played in the very life of any great court at this time. A prince, or a wealthy bourgeois, could realize the pleasures and glory of his social position only with the collaboration of solid and imaginative talent in his kitchen, but this talent had always to be reinforced with learning and integrity.

---

[40] *... Ce n'est pas estat ou office commun, c'est mestier subtil et sumptueux, et qui toute seureté sent, et est le prouffit necessaire du prince, et dont on ne se peut passer. ...   Op. cit.,* Vol. IV, p. 51.

8. Advice to the Newly Medieval Cook

a. Authenticity

Medieval cookery recipes were rarely detailed or explicit. It is perhaps because of the sketch-iness of these written guides that, just like his or her modern counterpart, the medieval cook never felt entirely tied to the letter of the recipe for the dish that he or she was preparing. We may say that it was more the spirit of the recipe that provided guidance. As a matter of fact, it is much more likely that the usual professional chef of that early period never even *had* a written recipe to refer to—if indeed the chef was sufficiently literate to make use of such a written reminder of his craft. For the most part recipes existed in the cook's memory alone. This is, in fact, what the chief cook of the Duke of Savoy, Chiquart, informs us. Though he was responsible for preparing some of the most complex and gastronomically elegant dishes that were ever served to the royalty and nobility of his day, he modestly claims inadequacy as a writer of cookbooks by declaring that he has never had a recipe book of any sort even in his hand. It is not a matter of illiteracy in Chiquart's particular case, however. There can be no doubt that this exceptionally competent professional cook was nothing if not highly literate. The cookbook was simply not a necessity to the profession.

When a dish was made in the late Middle Ages, its success depended more upon the skill—and the accurate memory—of the cook than upon the availability of written recipes. In a sense the cook of five centuries ago was freer than most of us feel we are in our kitchens today. His control over heats, in the open fire or in the oven, was much less precise than we enjoy, so that he had to know, with much more certainty, the range of all his foodstuffs' tolerance to heat. Without the benefit of a little knob calibrated in fahrenheit or centigrade, he had to be able to estimate accurately for each foodstuff how much and how little heat was necessary, or dangerous. Occasionally in this regard a recipe direction will indicate to the novice cook a rule of thumb—which is literally just that: one may check on the heat of a broth, or on how much a syrup has cooked, by sticking one's thumb into the pot!

That the olden-days cook looked upon his or her craft as a skillful exercise of artistic freedom is perhaps most evident in the absence, at least in the great majority of recipes, of any exact indication of quantities. Normally neither the input nor the output for which the recipe was designed is clearly spelled out; neither the amount of the ingredients to be used nor the amount of the yield is specified. In most cases, the written recipe functioned merely as a record of the proper ingredients for any given preparation, at most an indication of which ingredients, which flavor and which color should predominate in a mixture.[41] We should remember that in all likelihood the

---

[41] Though it appears very unlikely that the recipe collections that have come down to us were ever actually used in a kitchen, even as reminders to an inexpert cook, we may imagine, with alarm, what the relative freedom they embody might have led to in the hands of a green apprentice or a total neophyte.

cookbooks that exist were copied for one of two purposes. Either they were, like Chiquart's *On Cookery*, specifically destined for the library shelf of an estate's archives, or they were intended for comparison purposes for the eyes of other professional members of the cooks' guild, for the competent individual who already knew not only *what* he was doing in preparing a dish but knew, too, what *sort* of dish he wanted. In both cases the sketchy form in which a recipe is sometimes written does not make any less adequate a document: generally speaking the recipe collection seems to have served to inform others of what was being done somewhere at some time.

Put simply, we should not rely too much upon medieval recipe collections for completely explicit directions.

In this regard we should mention, too, that the arrangement of recipes in early recipe collections is far from systematic or universal and, it goes without saying, does not anticipate the order of dishes in a formal meal today. In our book we have imposed a somewhat artificial organization upon many of these medieval dishes, feeling that our reader can more easily identify the real nature of a dish by such a modern organization, and more easily find just the sort of dish that is needed for the meal the reader has in mind. Because many early dishes are not designed to fit exclusively into one of our modern categories or to satisfy the requirements of some phase of a modern meal, we have resorted to cross-references rather frequently within recipes and regularly at the end of chapters. Naturally, early cooks, working without written recipes, managed quite well without any sort of cross-referencing; they knew how to modify their recipes, for instance how to convert a broth into a basting or serving sauce, or how to combine two preparations in order to create a new dish. Our cross-references should be understood merely as hints of a wide range of possible adaptations and uses for the basic form of these recipes. Hopefully the modern cook will come to rely upon his or her imagination just as his or her medieval counterpart did.

Another reason for the relative unimportance of written recipes in the Middle Ages had to do with the supply of ingredients. Depending on the geographical location of his master's house, or the time of year, a cook might or might not be able to obtain all of the ingredients that normally entered into a particular recipe for a dish customarily prepared in a different place at a different time. And there was too the question of economics, whether the cook had enough money in the budget allocated to the operation of kitchen activities to let him order from the local spicer or fishmonger exactly what was specified in a recipe. The cook prepared foodstuffs that he could readily get at a cost his master was willing to afford. If he followed a fixed recipe at all, he was quite naturally used to substituting ingredients as necessary or to adjusting relative quantities as appropriate.

b. Adaptations

This is what the modern cook has to do as well, when dealing with early recipes. Recipes should serve primarily to provide rough guidelines for the preparation of a type of dish. For instance, in working out each of the recipes in this book we have experimented a great deal with quantities. We believe that we have arrived at quite acceptable suggestions in every case. However, because a precise notation of the quantities of ingredients is normally lacking in the original versions of the recipes, these quantities cannot be anything more than suggestions. You too should feel free to make your own adjustments just as the medieval cook did.

And substitutions, too. In this regard what matters, of course, is the flavor, color and texture of the finished dish. In a good number of instances we have suggested alternatives, either alternative ingredients or alternative procedures. You should not consider our tentative suggestions to be the limit to which you might go and still retain some modicum of authenticity. The original cooks didn't. Their work was constantly guided by a sense that they were creating satisfying flavors, colors and textures (see above, our comments on medieval foodstuffs), but they felt free to obtain those flavors, colors and textures by many means. Once you, too, have acquired the "taste of medieval France," you should feel free to treat these recipes as mere guidelines.

As we mentioned before, the late Middle Ages were not so very long ago: twenty generations is nothing, as human societies go. And modern scholars have afforded us now the means to examine the elements of that civilization very closely. Waiting to be fully appreciated is the food and cookery from those times.

It is just such a look into this not-really-so-distant period in the history of good cooking that this book will attempt. Above all we are offering the chance to go on a delicious itinerary through the past. We have carefully chosen a number of recipes from the early French cookery manuscripts, transcribed them and set them out in a readable form. Every dish whose making is described here is not only "makable"—in terms of the supplies and equipment a modern cook has available—but really is *worth* making for the pleasure it will give to eat. Every dish, in the versions we have worked out below, has been prepared a good number of times, and has been proved—tried out on severe, but very willing, critics. Tried out successfully, we should quickly add, because those critics have kept coming back enthusiastically to volunteer as testers for each new trial.

Our criteria for the selection of recipes to be developed for inclusion in this book have always been authenticity and interest. The modernized version of the old recipe is in every case as authentically close to the original as is reasonably possible in order to produce a dish that a late-medieval diner would immediately recognize and enjoy. And each of the dishes we have chosen is interesting in and by itself, interesting *both* gastronomically and historically.

In the well known words of some anonymous but sage gastronome in the fourteenth century, "The proof of the pudding is in the eating." Medieval scribes provide you with their hand-written records, the recipes. The medieval chef invites you into the kitchen. The household steward suggests a variety of possible menus. And finally the medieval lord or bourgeois offers to lay out a sumptuous banquet for you. You have only to mix some savory herbs, to mash some chick peas, or to dip your hands into a batch of pastry dough. You have only to fill your house with the delicately rich aromas of the fourteenth- and fifteenth-century kitchen. And, finally, sit down with your guests to a sampler—or a feast—of a cuisine that few know of today, and are the poorer for that unhappy ignorance.

Chapter 1
Standard Preparations

1. *Pouldre fine* / Fine Spice Powder
2. *Ypocras* / Hypocras and *Claree* / Clarée
3. *Lait d'amandes* / Almond Milk
4. *Puree de poys* / Pea Puree
5. Stocks
6. Grease and fats
7. Breads
8. Pastry
     a. *Gauffres* / Wafers
     b. Dough for Rissoles #1
     c. Dough for Rissoles #2
9. *Dragees*
10. Handwashing Water

Chapter 1
Standard Preparations

Some food preparations are too ordinary for a place in a recipe collection. Modern cooks possess in their memory a small repertoire of simple preparations because they recur habitually in meals or enter commonly into other preparations. In just the same way it was second nature for medieval cooks to put together a range of basic mixtures that were in constant use but for which written recipes would have been quite unnecessary. In this respect the medieval counterparts of our tea-biscuit mixture, spaghetti sauce, roux paste and dry bases for soups were fine-spice powder, hypocras, almond milk and pea puree. The larger kitchens in the Middle Ages always had a supply of these mixtures on hand, pre-prepared as it were, ready for immediate use in any of a very wide variety of recipes. A dry mixture, such as the ubiquitous Spice Powder, was normally kept in a large leather pouch; for Pea Puree or Almond Milk an earthen-ware crock could be used for its storage—provided, as Chiquart cautions his cook, a clean cloth was spread over its mouth in order to keep the preparation clean of any dirt that was around in the dusty, ash-laden air of the medieval kitchen.

1. *Poudre fine*
(Menagier de Paris, p. 247/§314)*

Prenez gingembre blanc 1°.3, canelle triee *3°*, giroffle et graine de chascun demy quart d'once, et de succre en pierre *3°*, et faictes pouldre.

---

* Throughout our book all references to the *Menagier de Paris* are double and are separated by a slash (for instance, p. 225/§260): the page numbers refer to Volume II of the edition of Jérôme Pichon; the section numbers (§) refer to those given to the same material in the edition of Georgine E. Brereton and Janet M. Ferrier, pp. 191–283. Where a reference is to material in the Brereton and Ferrier edition that is printed *before* p. 191, then we show, for instance, p. 114/p. 187.

1. Fine Spice Powder

One of the definitive flavors of medieval French cookery is determined by a particular mixture of spices that entered, with variations, into many of the dishes. So common was this mixture that recipes often refer to it simply as "spice powder" or "fine spices": *pouldre fine, pouldre douce*.

In a large noble household in the late Middle Ages this was one of the ingredients the cook had always to have on hand, and in reasonably good supply. The cook would make up this powder of so-called fine spices by grinding and mixing together the proper proportions of the "big four" spices in medieval cookery—ginger, cinnamon, cloves and grains of paradise*—and keep it in a leather bag in his pantry. There the powder mixture was ready to be drawn on quickly, without the last-minute need of having to measure out variable quantities of each of these spices and grind each down into a usable powder in the mortar. Pre-prepared spice powder is an early instance of labor-saving forethought in cookery.

The practice of pre-preparation is common enough today. Cooks who want to lighten their load can purchase, or can themselves prepare in advance, combinations of spices to meet their needs. Spice mixtures for making pumpkin pies or warm spiced cider, for example, or for marinating meats are normal sights in supermarkets and bulk food stores, as are curry powders and spices like Allspice. Though this latter is really a distinct spice, whose French name is *Poivre de Jamaïque*, the term Allspice has also come to mean a combination of cloves, cinnamon, nutmeg and pepper; for this mixture the French also have a name: *Quatre Epices*. Through the ages most cultural groups have come up with their own particular combinations of spices that are complementary to their particular dishes.

In more humble medieval households, the cook or housewife habitually procured an adequate stock of fine spice powder at the local spice merchant's. This stock would be enough to satisfy the immediate need of the household. The *Menagier de Paris* (p. 190 in the Brereton & Ferrier edition; p. 122 in the Pichon edition) advises his new wife that in shopping for provisions for a wedding banquet one should plan to drop by the spicer's in order to pick up supplies of a variety of items: several sorts of *dragees*, a spice mixture for making the mulled wine (both the spice mixture and the wine being called "hypocras"), sugar, pomegranates, almonds, rice flour, wheat flour and "fine powder." Of this last item, says the *Menagier*, the conscientious cook would need and should purchase one-half pound for the purpose of a wedding banquet.

We should note the quantity that the Menagier specifies of this spice powder. For some forty wedding guests, eating more than a dozen dishes during two meals, the quantity of *pouldre fine* is by no means excessive. But it would be sufficient to secure for many of the dishes that delightfully warm aroma that so satisfied the taste of medieval diners.

The relative quantities we suggest for the ingredients in our recipe below are only very

---

* Grains of paradise are otherwise known as melegueta pepper or, scientifically, *Amomum melegueta*. Its small grey seeds resemble peppercorns and, when ground, yield a somewhat gingery flavor.

approximate. Where the quantities, relative or actual, are in fact written in early recipe collections, these vary greatly from source to source. The composition of the mixture naturally depended too upon the particular taste of the cook and of his or her master. Our recipe is found in the *Menagier de Paris* (p. 247; §314) and calls for ginger, cinnamon, grains of paradise, cloves and sugar.* The quantities indicated for each ingredient are by no means uniform even from copy to copy of the *Menagier* itself; the book's most recent editors, Brereton and Ferrier, further debate as to the sense of the abbreviations found for these quantities in the manuscript that they have chosen to follow. We would suggest that to begin with you experiment with small quantities in order to make up a batch of a fine spice powder in a mixture that you yourself find palatable.

Yield: About 1/2 cup/125 mL of spice powder

Imperial	Ingredient	Metric	Directions
3 tbsp	ground ginger	50 mL	**Mix all ingredients together. Store in**
1 1/2 tbsp	cinnamon	25 mL	**a covered container.**
1 tsp	grains of paradise	5 mL	
1 tsp	ground cloves	5 mL	
2 tbsp	sugar	30 mL	

* Later, in the middle of the sixteenth century, the *Livre fort excellent de cuysine*—a distant derivative of the *Viandier*—added nutmeg, galingale and long pepper to this mixture, but insisted that the taste of the ginger should prevail over the cinnamon.

2. *Ypocras* / Hypocras
(*Menagier de Paris*, p. 248/§317)

Claree / Clarée
(British Library, Addl. 32085, f. 119v.)

Mulled or spiced wines formed an integral part of a meal in late-medieval France. Clarée was occasionally used as an aperitif at the beginning of the meal, and hypocras was regularly served as a digestive at its end. So regular was this particular serving of hypocras that it became recognized symbolically as the ceremonial conclusion of any banquet and was followed in a limited number of cases only by the offer of "chamber candies"—candied sugar which was itself flavored with spices or a spice mixture.

The spice mixtures for making hypocras or clarée could be purchased from the local apothecary or spicer. As with "fine spice powder," the actual composition of the mixture was apt to vary according to local preference. Because of the large number of individual spices that could enter into it, hypocras in particular offered the cook or merchant a great deal of latitude in determining its nature. Undoubtedly, large households evolved mixtures for their hypocras that, because of the choice of spices or the predominence of certain spices in the mixture, became for each household a sort of gustatory tradition and perhaps affirmed the special nature of each. The *Menagier*'s recipe for hypocras (p. 248/§317) is a good standard version of the mixture.

Evidence of the high regard that hypocras enjoyed in medical lore and learning is afforded by the survival today of a recipe for a version of that drink composed by one of the most respected physicians of the thirteenth century, Arnoldus of Villanova (1235?–1313), personal doctor to three popes as well as to King Phillip the Fair of France, King James II of Aragon and King Frederic III of Sicily. Copied along with successive versions of his medical works over many generations, his treatise *On Wines* contains a recipe for a spiced beverage that was a carefully reasoned combination of wine and spices—cubebs, cloves, ginger—together with raisins, rosewater and sugar. This drink, Arnoldus argued, "fortifies the brain and the natural strength . . . . It . . . causes foods to be digested and produces good blood. It is good for flatulence of the belly, and also for ailments of the womb caused by cold or superfluous humidity which prevents women from conceiving children . . . . It strengthens all spiritual parts . . . . It is marvellously useful for the cough and for the heart."*

Though medieval physicians understood in a rational way how valuable spices were for human digestion, and particularly when mixed in moderate quantities with a good red wine, we ourselves do not need to worry about the finesse of their logic. Hypocras and clarée are in themselves tasty drinks, and provide particularly satisfying accessories to any medieval meal.

---

* Arnoldus de Villanova, *Liber de vinis*, c. 1310, trans. by H.E. Sigerist as *The Earliest Printed Book on Wine (1478)*, New York, 1943.

To make hypocras powder [to which red wine will be mixed], take four ounces of
very fine cinnamon, tested under the tooth [by biting it], and two ounces of the best
fine cinnamon powder, one ounce of fine white Mecca ginger, one ounce of grains of
paradise, six nutmegs and galingale, and grind everything together. And when you want
to make hypocras, take a generous half ounce of this mixture and eight ounces of sugar
and stir them together with a quart [Paris measure] of wine. And *nota* that this powder
mixed together with the sugar makes what is called Duke's Powder.

The *Menagier* gives a second, alternative recipe for hypocras. It calls for equal amounts of
cinnamon and white ginger, less of cloves, and less still of grains of paradise, mace, galingale,
nutmeg and spikenard. These spices are ground into a powder together with a great deal of sugar
(1 1/4 lbs for one quart of hypocras). This is heated with red wine until the sugar dissolves,
then filtered repeatedly until the drink is clear. The author notes that the tastes of the sugar and
cinnamon should predominate.

For our hypocras we are taking a simpler route, suggesting that fresh whole spices be used in
place of the powder. This may avoid the necessity of repeated strainings in order to remove fine
sediment.

Yield: Sufficient for 8–10 servings

Imperial	Ingredient	Metric	Directions
2 bottles	dry red wine	2 bottles	**Gently heat the wine.**
2/3 cup	sugar	160 mL	**Stir in sugar.**
6	sticks of cinnamon	6	**Add spices & simmer until sugar is**
12	whole cloves	12	**dissolved (10–15 min.). Remove from**
5–6 slices	fresh gingerroot	5–6 slices	**heat; let stand for 1 hr. Strain; re-**
1 tsp	crushed grains of paradise	5 mL	**heat if necessary.**
1/2 tsp	nutmeg	2 mL	**Serve warm.**
pinch	galingale	pinch	

Variation

If you wish to use powdered spices, add them, with the sugar, to one or two cups/250–500 mL
of wine and heat the mixture until the sugar is dissolved and the spices blend with the wine.
Strain until clear and then add this to the rest of the wine until you reach the strength of
spice/wine mixture that pleases you.

A note of caution: Since this drink is normally served at the conclusion of a meal, in the interests
of moderation and safe, sober driving, you may wish to dilute your hypocras with an equal amount
of a juice, such as orange juice, or of a combination of orange and lemon juice. We do, adding
the spices to one bottle of wine and one bottle of orange and lemon juices combined. Add extra
sugar to taste.

The following recipe for clarée is found in a French recipe collection that was probably copied in England toward the end of the thirteenth century. In reading its list of exotic ingredients we can perhaps understand why hypocras was a more popular cordial than clarée.

Here begins a recipe for clarée. Take cinnamon, ginger and mace in an amount making up half of your mixture; cloves, nutmeg and malabathrum to the amount of one-quarter of your mixture; fennel, anise and caraway seeds, and cardamom and squinant [camel's hay] to the amount of another quarter; and spikenard in an amount equal to one-half of all other ingredients. Reduce all this to powder and put it into a bag. And [when you want to make clarée,] take white or red wine and pour it through the powder, filtering it as you would clothes in lye, and you will have clarée. Pouring and filtering again and again will give you a stronger clarée. If you do not have all of these spices, take cinnamon, ginger and mace to the amount of two-thirds of your mixture, and one-half of that amount of cloves and spikenard, reduce them to powder and filter the wine through this as before, and you will have clarée.

London, British Library, MS Addl. 32085, p. 226

3. *Lait d'amandes* / Almond Milk

A taste for which North-American children seem to have been born is a taste for peanut butter. It has a reputation for being *the* most universally appreciated foodstuff of the smaller set, the epitome of alimentary staples among the young—and the not-so-young. Until fairly recent decades, though, the joys of peanut butter were unknown in France, except among the rare gourmet, of course.

The taste for ground peanuts is in a strange way medieval. Not that peanuts were known in medieval Europe, but other nuts certainly were, and very much appreciated when shelled and ground up. In particular almonds were very highly esteemed, affording the cook not only a means of decorating the top of his dishes (slivered, sautéed, perhaps even glazed with honey or powdered sugar) but as well, and more materially, yielding an important source of culinary oil and fat. Rich medieval kids knew the joys of almond-nut butter, a product of this grinding of almonds. Medieval cooks depended extensively upon almond-nut milk.

Milk is an important ingredient in cookery. The problem with animal milk is of course that it has a limited life. When butter is made from animal milk, salt can be added to it (as was done to the meat of the animals from which the milk came) in order to help prolong its life, but that is at best only a moderately useful measure. In warm weather milk turns quickly; consequently it is not a very common ingredient in medieval cooking. Most of the milk of the time was churned into butter and cheese. On lean days and during Lent, moreover, the Church decreed that the faithful could eat no animal products, including milk. What medieval cooks resorted to, then, as an ingredient in place of animal milk was nut milk, especially the liquid produced by grinding almonds very finely, adding a little water and filtering this mash. This was almond milk.

There is probably no single ingredient upon which late-medieval cookery depended more than almond milk. It is used in sauces (such as the White Leek Sauce), in Almond-Nut Flans, and in Cuminade of Almonds. It is a natural thickener, particularly where or whenever the use of egg yolk or liver is impossible. It lends a most delicate flavor to all preparations, a remarkably genteel flavor that is, like the spice mixtures, almost a hallmark of medieval cuisine. Looked upon by physicians as being blessed with qualities that were very close to the healthy human temperament, it is regularly prescribed as an ingredient in sickdishes; in fact almond butter is offered as a sickdish in itself by Chiquart. The clinching argument that favored almond milk over animal milk is that cooks could continue to use it in their many lean-day menus.

Almond milk, then, was *the* medieval staple. Modern French kids have largely lost this part of their heritage; they may yet discover peanut butter.

D'amandes / Almonds
(Aldobrandino, *Le regime du corps*, p. 154)*

Amandes sont de .ij. manieres, ameres et douces.

Les douces sont caudes et moistes tempereement ou premier degré, et de leur nature norrissent a le maniere de nois; mais les nois se cuisent plus legierement et se convertissent plus tost en humeurs coloriques caudes que ne font les amandes, car sachiés que les amandes sont pesans a l'estomac et demeurent moult, mais ne font pas tant de mal a l'estomac com font les nois; et s'eles sont mengiés quant eles sont verdes, a tote l'escorce, si confortent les gencives et refroident le cervele; et quant eles sont meures, et l'escorce commence a endurcir, si valent miex a user a chaux qui ont caude cervele, et qui sont malade de fievres; et jasoit ce cose qu'eles norrissent pau, cho qu'ele norrissent est boen; et li oiles qui en est fais est boens et plus legiers que ne sont les amandes.

Amandes ameres sont caudes et sekes plus que ne sont les douces, car eles sont caudes et sekes en le fin du secont degré, et valent miex por le cors delivrer de maladies que por norrir, car de leur nature eles netoient le visage de lentilles et d'autres ordures qui puent avenir, et ne laissent enivrer qui les mangue a enjun, et confortent le ventre et valent a chaus qui sont malade de viés tous, s'eles sont broiés a ewe d'orge; et de lor nature font bien oriner, et d'ouvrir les voies du fie et des rains, et destruissent le ventosité du ventrail; et user les en vin destemprees si valent en fievres longhes cotidiaines et quartaines.

"Almonds are of two sorts, bitter and sweet.

"Sweet almonds are temperately warm and moist in the first degree, and by their nature they nourish as do walnuts; but walnuts digest more easily and are more readily converted into warm bilious humors than are almonds, for you should know that almonds lie heavily and at length in the stomach but they are not as harmful to it as walnuts; if they are eaten when green, with their skin, they strengthen the gums and cool the brain; when ripe and the skin is beginning to harden, they are better eaten by those with a hot brain and those who are sick with fever; though they nourish little, their nourishment is good; the oil that is made from them is good and lighter than the almonds themselves.

"Bitter almonds are warmer and drier than sweet almonds, being warm and dry at the end of the second degree; they are better as medicine than as food, for by nature they clean the face of freckles and other possible sorts of discolorations, and they prevent intoxication when eaten on an empty stomach,† they strengthen the stomach and are useful for those who have a persistent cough if they are ground in barley water; by nature they promote urination and open the passages of the

---

* Advice that we quote from medieval pseudo-scientific sources is offered to our readers only for the sake of historical curiosity. It is never intended that the modern reader should take any of these perceptions as recommendations.

† Have you never wondered why you are given spiced roasted almonds with your alcoholic beverage on an international flight?

liver and the kidneys, and eliminate flatulence in the belly; distempered in wine they are useful in treating persistent daily and quartan fevers."

Lait d'amandes / **Almond Milk**
(*Menagier de Paris*, p. 241/§§301, 302)

Yield: About 2 1/2 cups/625 mL of almond milk.

Imperial	Ingredient	Metric	Directions
1 cup	blanched sweet almonds	250 mL	**In a mortar or blender combine almonds & ice water. Grind or blend smooth paste texture is reached.**
4 tbsp	ice water	60 mL	
2 cups	hot water	500 mL	**Add paste to hot water & let it rest for a few minutes. Strain. Grind or blend mixture again & strain. Set aside to cool.**

Variation

If the recipe that calls for almond milk also calls for meat bouillon, you may want to replace some of the water with that amount of bouillon.

If a small amount of almond milk is needed, cut this recipe in half.

4. *Puree de poys*
(*Du fait de cuisine*, §22)

Et ... fault que les escuiers de cuisine soient tresbien fournix et pourveux de grant quantité de pois blancs pour faire les potageries pour ung chescun jour de la feste partinens aux poyssons.

Et le maistre queux soit advisé du nombre des personnes qu'il ont a servir et selon le nombre si prennent la quantité des pois et les trient et nectoient et lavent bien et appoint, et mectent cuire en belles chaudieres nectes ou grandes oulles belles et cleres, et facent cuire; et, estre mis cuire, si tirés vostre puree en belles oulles ou cornues et en treysés si grant quantité que vous puissés faire la quantité de la potagerie que vous sera ordonnee a faire.

Capiteles de pois / Peas
(Aldobrandino, *Le regime du corps*, p. 141)

Peas are cold in the first degree and temperately dry; they combine two natures, for their skin by nature constipates the belly while their pulp loosens it, and when they are eaten skinned they engender good humors and are nourishing, although they cause a little flatulence—but not nearly as much as beans.

The first water in which peas are cooked is useful to treat those who are feverish or who have a cough or a pain in the chest, but the water should be unsalted and have nothing added to it that might harm the person.

4. Pea Puree

Pea puree, beef bouillon and almond milk are three of the most common liquid ingredients in medieval prepared dishes. Just as it was normal in the kitchens of the time to have quantities of ground spices and spice mixtures on hand in leather pouches, ready to be poured or spooned out as a recipe might call for them, so too a stock of the standard liquid ingredients, especially pea puree and beef bouillon, was generally available in covered tubs for immediate use as needed. Pea puree most frequently functioned as a lean alternative to meat bouillon in fish dishes. Chiquart places this fairly simple recipe for the making of pea puree right at the very beginning of his extensive section of recipes for a lean banquet, so that the cook will not have to bother setting about preparing it each time it is called for in the dishes that were to follow. It is, in fact, specified in almost all of the fish dishes of the *Du fait de cuisine*.

The variety of pea known to late-medieval cuisine was the white pea. As a result, the colors of the dishes that were made using it as a thickener (for example, the White Broth of Fish, the Pink Broth and the red Georgé Broth) should not surprise us. There is no hint of green here. According to the *Menagier*, some disagreement existed as to the source of the best water for cooking these peas—whether water from a well, a fountain or a river—but Chiquart seems to have had no such concerns; he merely advises the cook to be certain that the peas themselves have been culled through and cleaned carefully.

One is tempted to speculate here whether this Pea Puree was the antecedent of the Québecois Habitant Pea Soup. A recipe collection used in Quebec in 1775, called *La nouvelle maison rustique*, gives a recipe for *Potage à la purée* or Puree of Pea Soup.*

Yield: About 2 cups.

Imperial	Ingredient	Metric	Directions
2 cups	*cooked* fresh, frozen *or* reconstituted† dried peas *or* canned peas‡	500 ml	**Set aside the cooking liquid or liquid from the can.**
1/2–3/4 cups	liquid	125–200 mL	**In a food mill, blender, processor or sieve, puree the peas, adding sufficient of the cooking liquid to form a thick puree. Store covered in refrigerator, or in freezer if puree is to be kept more than two or three days.**

Suggestion

Use the leftover liquid in soups, gravies, etc.

---

* See Marc Lafrance and Yvon Desloges, *Goûter à l'histoire—Les origines de la gastronomie québecoise*, Montréal (La Chenelière), 1989, p. 58.

† To reconstitute dried peas, wash and cull them, discarding any discolored or withered ones. To 1 cup/250 mL dried peas, add 3 cups/750 mL warm water. Soak overnight. Bring to a boil, reduce heat and simmer until tender—about 3/4 to 2 hours. May be cooked without soaking, but cooking period will be considerably longer. Drain. Reserve liquid. Puree as above.

‡ Use white or yellow split peas. Canned peas will not need further cooking; drain and reserve the liquid.

5. Stocks

When bouillons are used in a preparation, it is bouillon of beef or chicken that late-medieval recipes call for most frequently. A stock of beef bouillon seems to have been a staple of most kitchens of the time, and was likely to have been on hand for random use much more commonly than in modern kitchens. The alternative upon which the modern cook can most easily fall back, though with a little loss of quality, is the dry bouillon cube. The beef cubes will prove to be more serviceable, although occasionally recipes need a chicken bouillon for which chicken bouillon cubes are a satisfactory substitute.

6. Fats and Grease

Authentic medieval cookery requires the cook periodically to have access to animal fat and grease, particularly of pork. If you should at some time be cooking pork (or fat mutton), consider whether you can safely put aside a quantity of the fat from this meat for the time when you will be "cooking medieval." In one recipe or another you are apt to need chunks of pork fat (pieces of fat bacon), or grease rendered from this fat.

If you are unwilling to eat such animal fats—even for the sake of authenticity—you can quite properly do what was regularly done on lean days and substitute some sort of vegetable (olive) oil or nut (almond) oil.

7. Breads

There are no recipes for the making of bread in these early French manuscripts. Baking was a separate and distinct craft in the Middle Ages. However, here and there in these and other documents we may come across a good many references to various types of bread and their uses. For an upcoming formal dinner he will be offering, the *Menagier* himself (p. 109/p. 184) advises his wife to obtain from the baker ten dozen loaves of white table bread, an unspecified quantity of day-old, flat, one-penny bread, and three dozen four-day-old brown trencher-breads measuring one-half foot (somewhat under six inches) by four fingers by four fingers. The *Menagier*'s trencher bread was made in relatively small *flat* loaves, turned over in the oven in order to smooth both sides, dense and coarse in substance, and with hard crusts; it was of a thickness that could be sliced horizontally in two so that with one of its tough crusts upwards it could become two trenchers.

Bakers' guilds were among the strongest in medieval Europe, and their shops were well established businesses. The guilds enforced rigid standards as to the quality and weight of loaves. A baker caught shortchanging a customer, either as to weight or quality, faced severe penalties. As well, street hawkers sold "bread water"—presumably yeast water or a sour-dough starter—to those who wished to make their own bread at home.

Several cereal grains were commonly used in the making of breads. The quality of bread varied according to the grain that went into the flour, or the mixture of grains, the care taken in its (their) grinding, and whether or not the bran of the grain was removed from the flour. As a plant, wheat requires a good soil to flourish, but spelt, barley, oats and rye can grow well even in relatively poor soils. Though barley and oats were employed in bread either by themselves or mixed in combinations with themselves and with such other "flours" as from ground peas or lentils or vetch, rye was really the only cereal grain that proved itself at all popular as an alternative to wheat for this purpose in the European Middle Ages. The bread of first choice was always a crusty loaf (a bellied mound—not, of course, the elongated loaf with which we are more familiar), relatively white in color (though never much more so than a fawn shade), and of fine texture because it was made from very finely ground wheat flour from which all the bran had been sieved away in the bolting cloth. On the tables of the wealthy in France the so-called *pain de main*, the small "individual-sized" table loaf that resembled a good solid bun, was made of this fine wheat flour.

From the very finest, the simnel loaf (known even in Roman times as the *siminellus* and made from the best wheaten flour, called *simila*), down to the coarsest miscellany of "unknown" grains and grasses—with chips from the millstones left in for good measure—all sorts of bread could be had in medieval France and across Europe. However, the most commonly available bread at this time was undoubtedly the large loaf that was made from a mixture of wheat and rye flours. This was *miscelin* or *meslin* bread, the bread eaten by ordinary bourgeois, and bought by the wealthy to feed to their servants. The name of this bread, deriving as it does ultimately from the Latin verb *miscere*, "to mix," points to its alloyed composition, an economical compromise between quality and cost.

The medieval reliance upon rye in bread-making entailed calamitous consequences from time to time. In damp seasons rye grain is subject to a fungus growth whose scientific name is *Claviceps purpurea* and which is more popularly known as ergot. This fungus tends to turn the rye grain dark and gives to bread baked from the flour of this grain a sweetish, musty taste. Much more seriously it can cause a fatal disease in the person eating such bread, a disease which involved horrible convulsions, a sense of all-consuming fever, and madness. In the Middle Ages the disease of ergotism was called St. Anthony's Fire, and, unfortunately, it struck quite frequently. It was just one more of the recurrent, bewildering, terrifying scourges of medieval Europe.

Nowadays, we can purchase or bake a round loaf of safe table bread that is far finer and whiter than any medieval aristocrat or baker ever dreamed of. Devoted bread makers will probably want to make their own trenchers for a medieval dinner. A whole wheat bread recipe is appropriate. You might add about 1/4 cup/60 mL of chopped fresh parsley to the dough before shaping it for the final rising. We have found it convenient to bake the bread in large, 100 fl. oz./2.84 L cans in which restaurants (and large families) buy quantities of such staples as pork and beans or catsup. It is preferable that these cans have smooth rather than corrugated sides. Made in such cans, each loaf can be cut into about 12 trenchers. Age the bread for two or three days before slicing it.

If you are buying bread, look for sales of day-old, brown, unsliced bread. Sliced into trenchers it will be slightly smaller than is proper, but will do nicely.

Six-inch round whole wheat pita bread also serves well as trenchers.

Purchase white dinner rolls for your fine table bread, or make them using a recipe for basic white rolls, or for sourdough or semi-sweet rolls. For a little variety, we have added 1 tbsp/15 mL of cinnamon, some herbs and currants to the ingredients, adding a little more liquid to compensate for these additional ingredients.

Frumentum / Wheat

(*Tacuinum sanitatis*, Vienna, Oesterreichische Nationalbibliothek
Codex Vindobonensis, 2644, f. 42v)

Nothing gladdens the heart of a farmer more than the sight of ripening grain under a cloudless sky. Wheat is life; an abundant crop means a bright future. Everyone, whatever their temperament or age, whatever the season or place, derives from wheat a food that is good for the blood, such as bread primarily, or flour. The best wheat is ripe, grown in rich soil, free of mixtures with any other cereal, its grains hard, heavy, full, smooth, shining, and of a golden color. Remember: a wheat poultice is useful to open up an abscess.

8. Pastry

In some respects pastry functioned in the Middle Ages in ways similar to the ways in which slices of bread serve today in sandwiches. An enveloping layer of pastry held something that one wanted to cook and to eat, and it held it cleanly. As a result the pie and the turnover became popular confections in the fourteenth and fifteenth centuries. In every town cooked pasties could be bought from local tradesmen. More and more dwellings had ovens built in their kitchens so that household cooks did not have to make do with setting the pastry-lined preparation in the live coals of an open fire and covering its upper crust—if there was one—directly with coals or with a metal or earthenware pot, itself covered with coals.

The pastry that pastry chefs were called upon to provide in such large quantities in the fourteenth-and fifteenth-century city shops, or in the aristocratic pastry kitchen, was not the pastry that we are used to eating today around our apple pies and meat turnovers. It was made from a simpler mix, of soft-wheat flour and water, and it was baked without the leavening, moisturizing benefit of lard or margarine. Its taste was bland; its texture and consistency were tough. It was made to fulfil a purpose—that of containing another foodstuff—and it did that quite satisfactorily. But it was not what we today would consider to be an appetizing part of the meal in itself. We may suspect that, after having conveyed the slice of flan or of fish pie to his mouth, the medieval diner may have discarded a good part of the pastry shell by which he had held the flan or fish, in much the same sort of way as he discarded his sauce-sogged trencher of bread at the end of the meal.

As is the case for bread, no actual recipes for the making of pastry have been copied in our early manucripts. From recipe to recipe there abound such phrases as, "deliver [the pie filling] to the pastry chef," "make crusts quite small and tall for deep-frying," and "order your pastry cook to make them nicely." Some mention appears of pastry whose ingredients include eggs, flour and water, with perhaps oil or butter; as well, in the making of pastry, provision is allowed for replacing water with almond milk.

We suggest using a lard-based pastry for the pies or tarts that have a meat or meat-and-fruit filling, and a butter or butter-and-oil based pastry for sweeter custard and fruit fillings. A double-crust pastry recipe is sufficient for about 24 rounds measuring 4 inch/10 cm for the rissoles we describe in this book.

Wafers can be used as an alternative to a pastry dough, although pies of them are more complicated and much more time-consuming to make. In his Parma Torte recipe (see p. 175, below), Chiquart uses sugared wafers layered four or five deep on the bottom, sides and top of the torte. His recipe calls for the use of 20,000 to 30,000 of these wafers (don't be alarmed: he *is* preparing a banquet), and directs that the inside of the torte pans be larded prior to layering the wafers.

The *Menagier* includes several recipes for making wafers. We have added the sugar mentioned in Chiquart's recipe for Parma Torte.

8a. *Gauffres*

(*Menagier de Paris*, p. 261/§343)

Gauffres sont faictes par .iiii. manieres.

L'une que l'en bat des oeufz en une jacte, et puis du sel et du vin, et gecte l'en de la fleur, et destremper l'une avec l'autre. Et puis mectre en deux fers petit a petit a chascune foiz autant de paste coomme une lesche de frommage est grande, et estraindre entre deux fers, et cuire d'une part et d'autre. Et se le fer ne se delivre bien de la paste, l'en l'oint avant d'un petit drapelet moullié en huille ou en sain.

La deuxiesme maniere si est comme la premiere, maiz l'en y met du frommage: c'est assavoir que l'en estend la paste comme pour faire tartre ou pasté, puis met l'en le frommage par lesches ou millieu, et receuvre l'en les deux bors. Ainsi demeure le frommage entre deux pastes, et ainsi est mis entre deux fers.

La tierce si est de gauffres couleisses, et sont dictes coulisses pource seulement que la paste est plus clere, et est comme boulye clere faicte comme dessus. Et gecte l'en avec du fin frommage esmyé a la gratuise et tout mesler ensemble.

La quarte maniere est de fleur pestrye a l'eaue, sel et vin, sans oeufz ne frommage.

8a. Wafers

Yield: About 30 4-inch/10-cm round wafers

Imperial	Ingredient	Metric	Directions
4	eggs	4	**Beat eggs lightly.**
1 tsp	salt	5 mL	**Whisk in salt, wine, oil & sugar.**
2 tbsp	sugar	30 mL	
4 tbsp	dessert wine	60 mL	
2–3 tsp	oil *or* fat	10–15 mL	

1/2 cup +2 tbsp	all purpose flour	150 mL	**Whisk in flour 1 tbsp/15 mL at a time until a smooth runny paste is reached.** **Drop 1 tbsp/15 mL at a time onto a hot sandwich grill or Krumcake iron. Close grill & press on lid. Cook until lightly browned—about 1 min.**
1–2 tbsp	sugar	15–30 mL	**Sprinkle with sugar. Store in airtight container in a cool, dry place until needed.** **Re-crisp in a low oven (275°F/140°C) before serving.**

Cooking variation

Add 2–3 tbsp/30–50 mL of grated hard cheese to the basic wafer mixture.

8b. Dough for Rissoles #1

For rissoles, as an alternative to the standard pastry crust you might like to try one or the other of the following pastry recipes. This first one makes a perogy-like dough. We prefer this recipe.

Yield: About 24 4-inch/10-cm rounds

Imperial	Ingredient	Metric	Directions
1/2 cup	warm water	125 mL	**Mix together water, oil, salt & saffron.**
3–4 tbsp	olive oil	50–60 mL	
1/2 tsp	salt	2 mL	
pinch	saffron *or* turmeric	pinch	
1 1/2 cup	all purpose flour	375 mL	**Stir in flour, a little at a time. Turn out onto floured surface & knead until smooth. Cover with damp cloth & let rest for 1/2 hr.**
			Roll out dough to the thickness of a dime. Cut into rounds of 4 in/10 cm diameter, & proceed to fill as for pastry rissoles. Seal edges with a mixture of flour & water.
8 cups	boiling water	2 L	**Cook rissoles, uncovered, in boiling water & oil about 5–6 min. They will rise to top of pan as they are cooking. Remove with slotted spoon to draining rack.**
1 tsp	oil	5 mL	
			Rissoles may then be pan-fried or deep-fried in oil or lard.

8c. Dough for Rissoles #2

This recipe is labor-intensive and requires experience. You might prefer to purchase egg roll wrappers, commonly found nowadays in supermarkets.

Yield: About 20–24 4-inch/10-cm rounds

Imperial	Ingredient	Metric	Directions
1/2 cup	all purpose flour	125 mL	**Sift flour and salt into bowl.**
1/2 tsp	salt	2 mL	
1	egg	1	**Beat egg slightly & stir into flour.**
about 3/4–1 cup	water	about 175–250 mL	**Gradually stir in water to make a smooth batter.**
			Grease & heat a skillet. Beat the batter again & pour about 1 tbsp/15 mL into skillet. Roll skillet to enlarge drop of batter to about 4 in/10 cm in diameter. Don't let batter brown. Turn once to cook both sides.
			Remove to plate. Cover with damp cloth until needed.
			Proceed as for rissoles. Seal edges with water/flour paste. Deep fry the rissoles until golden brown.

Another alternative

You may also wish to use your favorite pasta or egg-noodle dough to make rissoles. If so, boil the rissoles before frying them.

9. *Dragees*

When even the author of the *Menagier de Paris* advises his wife that *dragees* are bought at the spicer's at a cost of ten *sous* a pound, we may consider ourselves dispensed from the obligation of making our own.

The medieval French *dragees* were not the candy-coated almonds that are sold so commonly in France today. They were indeed a small candy, but only that: candied sugar which had been spiced and colored. The *Menagier* speaks of buying three pounds of white *dragees*, without specifying the flavor. A number of recipes call for *dragees* to be sprinkled over a dish as a decorative garnish. The *Menagier* mentions serving a White Dish of Capon with pomegranate seeds and red *dragees* on top, and baked apples sprinkled with white *dragees*; at another place he specifies that each serving of a galantine of meat and fish be garnished with white violets, pomegranate seeds, red *dragees* and four laurel leaves.

Chiquart warns his cook that for a banquet he should make sure that he has on hand *two hundred cases* of all sorts and colors of *dragees*. These appear most in use as a garnish, particularly whenever an almond-based sauce is poured over a fish dish. The rationale for the use of this garnish on fish likely derives from the perception that the nature of fish is primarily cold and moist—as is that of their habitat, the water. Though the method of cooking fish almost inevitably involved either roasting or frying, a sprinkling of *dragees* served as a final insurance that fish will be sufficiently warmed and dried for safe consumption. As he concludes his outline of a recipe, Chiquart never seems to tire of reminding his cook: "Be sure not to forget the *dragees* which should be sprinkled on top!"

Dragees were as well probably the most common form of "chamber spices" intended for serving after a meal either in the hall or, as the name implies, in the bed chamber. Physicians believed that the combination of sugar and spice could not help but be beneficial to any person's stomach, particularly any individual whose temperament tended toward the phlegmatic or melancholic because the cold humors predominated in them. These were generally, and quite naturally, the most common complexions of mature persons, and especially of the elderly.

Other varieties of these chamber spices included *Orengat* / Candied Orange Peel (see p. 284, below), candied lemon peel, red aniseed and *Sucre rosat*, white sugar clarified and cooked in rose water. In every case it was considered that the sugar—and any spices that were combined with it—acted primarily as a preservative, warming and drying the peel or seed so that they would no longer be subject to the corruption that comes from excess moisture. A number of our recipes (for instance, the Cold Sage of p. 183, below) make use of *dragees* as a presentation decoration.

Any small hard candy can be used as a medieval *dragee*, provided it is tasty and colorful. The small silver or colored candies used for cake decorating are also appropriate substitutes.

10. Handwashing Water

It is enough just to reproduce the *Menagier*'s recipe for this useful item. A bowl or two of this fragrant cleansing agent can be available not only before beginning to eat but during and after the meal—especially if you intend to have as little recourse as possible to modern cutlery.

> To make water to wash hands at table, set sage to boil, then drain the water and cool it until it is little more than warm. Or you can do the same with camomile or marjoram, or you can use rosemary. And you can boil orange peel with it. Laurel [bay] leaves are good, too.
>
> *Menagier de Paris*, p. 247/§316

The choice of scent used for handwashing water is pretty well up to the inspiration of the person who is organizing a medieval meal. Rosewater is available at druggists' and at some food stores. A ratio of 1 tbsp/15 mL of rosewater to 4 cups/1 litre of water seems appropriate.

Chapter 2
Appetizers

1. *Syseros* / Chickpea Puree
2. *Une vinaigrette* / A Vinegar Dish
3. *Menus drois* / Little Delicacies
     a. **Little Delicacies in Vinaigrette**
     b. **Little Delicacies with Egg Sauce**
4. *Pipesfarces* / Pipe Stuffings
5. *Alouyaulx* / Little Larks
6. Rissoles
     a. *Rosseolles* / Pork Rissoles (for a Meat Day)
     b. *Rissolles a jour de poisson* / Rissoles for a Fish Day
     c. *Rissolles a jour de poisson* / Fruit Rissoles : see Chapter 10, Desserts
7. [*Pastez de champignons*] / Mushroom Tarts

Soupe jacobine / **Jacobin Sops** : see Chapter 3, Sops and Soups
Moust pour hetoudeaulx / **Must Sauce for Young Chicken** : see Chapter 4, Sauces
Aulx vers / **Green Garlic Sauce** : see Chapter 4, Sauces
Pommeaulx / **Little Meatballs** : see Chapter 5, Meat Dishes
Faulx grenon (Potage party) / **Mock Meat** : see Chapter 6, Poultry Dishes
Tortres parmeysines de poyssons / **Parma Fish Pie** : see Chapter 7, Fish Dishes
Tortes of Herbs, Cheese and Eggs : see Chapter 8, Egg Dishes

Chapter 2
Appetizers

A medieval French menu would have acknowledged two particular sorts of food or food preparation as "appetizers": an aperitif whose qualities were such as quite literally to *open* the stomach in order to allow it to accept food for digestion; and an appetizer proper whose inherent properties caused it to excite the appetite of the diner, who presumably might not otherwise have been greatly interested in eating. Though in our age we tend not to distinguish any more between "appetizer" and "aperitif," the medieval physician and cook understood quite clearly the distinct nature and function of each.

In the medical lore of the late Middle Ages a number of foodstuffs were recognized as possessing one or the other, and occasionally both, of these potencies. For instance, to open the stomach and stimulate the digestive humors one should eat almonds, lettuce, mint, ginger or cinnamon: such foods were qualified as *aperitivus*. On the other hand, to stimulate the appetite one could always depend upon black cherries, mustard, rabbit meat or roast beans: these foodstuffs were valued for the peculiar properties they possess that allow them to *dare appetitum*; such foods are simply qualified as being *appetitivus*. The physician could always advise a client, or his cook, with which foods it was safest to begin a meal, which digested easiest, and therefore should be eaten relatively early in the meal, which were more difficult to digest and therefore should enter the stomach relatively late in a meal, and which, because of their faculty for promoting digestion, should ideally conclude a meal.

Nowadays we have largely lost sight of the original entirely practical functions of the aperitif and appetizer. Of the extensive body of physical doctrine in the Middle Ages that bore upon eating, what may still remain as a "common-sense" rule of thumb is the principle that in any meal lighter foods should generally precede heavier foods. The medieval doctor might well have terrified his patient with images of the gastric turmoil that would be occasioned by not adhering to this law. The stomach is little more or less than an organic stove or furnace that "cooks" the food that enters it. If a slowly digesting food were to remain overlong in the stomach it would impede the normal progress of any lighter foods that subsequently entered it, and these lighter foods, thoroughly digested but unable to move on their way out of the stomach, would inevitably become seriously over-cooked. In effect this excessive cooking would amount to a most dangerous corruption of that food, which in turn would engender the most horrible of deleterious humors. The unwary or ignorant diner would soon become painfully conscious of the egregious consequences of his error.

Our appetizers may not all fall within the authoritative canon concerning foods that open the stomach or promote its digestive virtues, but we can certainly vouch for their palatableness.

1. *Syseros*

(*Du fait de cuisine*, §76)

Pour donner entendement a celluy qui appareillera les syseros, si prenne ses syses et si les delise grain a grain en tant que il n'y demeure nulle chose que le propre grain du sise; et puis le lave en trois ou en .iiii. eaues tedes et les mecte boullir. Et, estre boullir, si les remove de celle eaue et y mecte d'autre eaue fresche, et mecte arriés boullir; et, estre boullis, si les mecte en la dicte oulle reposer jusque a l'endemain. Et, quant se viendra l'endemain, si en purés l'eaue et mectés encour d'autre eaue fresche, et mectés boullir en ung bien petit de sel, de l'oille d'amendres et de percin ensemble ses racines bien delises et nectoyees—et celles racines soient escorchiés et tresbien lavees—et ung pou de salvi. Et si n'y mectés autre chose sans l'ordonnance du medicin: et s'il ordonnoit de y mectre ung pou de cynamomy et ung pou de verjust pour lui donner aucun pou de goust, sy en y mectés; autrement non.

Capiteles de cierres / Chickpeas

(Aldobrandino, *Le regime du corps*, p. 143)

Chickpeas are cold and dry and resemble lentils, but they are better to consume than lentils because the humor that is engendered by them is not so gross nor so melancholic [*i.e.*, of cold and dry tendencies]; and it is better to consume their broth than their substance because one can use chickpea broth just as one uses that of peas.

Cicera / Chickpeas

(*Tacuinum sanitatis*, Vienna,
Oesterreichische Nationalbibliothek, Codex Vindobonensis, 2644, f. 49r)

There are white, black and red chickpeas. Large, full ones that have not been harmed or punctured by animals or insects are preferable. They heat the blood and promote strong sperm in the make (which is why the red ones are called "venereal"). Chickpeas promote urination, generate milk and open obstructions. They create flatulence in the belly, they are harmful to ulcerations of the kidneys and bladder; these disadvantages can be countered with celery, fennel and, when those are not available, with poppy seeds. Soak chickpeas in water overnight and cook them with rosemary, sage, garlic and parsley root. To the broth, which is preferable to the chickpeas themselves, add boiled must and cinnamon.

Seoir te peulz sans contredit	Your host will show you where to sit,
au lieu ou l'oste ce te dit.	for there alone is meet and fit.

1. Chickpea Puree

The Latin term for a pea, *cicer*, became the Savoyard French word, *sise*. Ultimately in French, through several phonetic deformations, the word became the epithets *"chiche"* and "chick" by which we qualify a variety of small white pea in modern French and English.

At the time of Chiquart, the *sise* was a fairly common legume that entered into various preparations on dining tables. Its particular properties had long been recognized as useful by Arab and European physicians: though "pois chiches" were in themselves considered cold and dry, the broth from their first boiling quite remarkably possessed qualities that were exactly contrary, being both warm and moist in the second degree. According to Aldobrandino, a respected physician of the time, this broth had the ability to "clarify" the blood and to give a good color or complexion to one's physiognomy. He states that this broth, called *Syseros* by Chiquart, has a special value in the diet of an invalid who is recuperating. Indeed, the *Du fait de cuisine* includes Chiquart's dish for chickpeas among those preparations that would be particularly beneficial as sickdishes, that is, as preparations whose natural digestibility and faculty to transform readily into good blood, would make them especially suitable for serving to invalids. For the same reasons this dish would be appropriate for those who, as he puts it, are finicky about what they eat.

To his recipe for *Syseros* Chiquart appends two options which would allow the cook to add either cinnamon or verjuice to the ingredients. The overriding condition that he attaches to these options, that all ingredients should be approved by the patient's doctor, is related to the subservient role a cook should play as dispenser of a doctor's culinary prescriptions. The spice cinnamon is held to be quite warm and dry in nature, and would be a useful therapeutic ingredient in food only if the patient was suffering from a malady that displaced his or her humor toward the melancholic in physiological terms, that is, toward a state that was both exceptionally cool and humid. On the other hand, verjuice is moderately cool and moderately humid in nature, and it might be prescribed therapeutically for a person who was suffering from a mildly bilious or coleric disease; by definition, this disease would have made his or her humor more warm and dry than normal.

It is moot whether either or both of these additional ingredients will restore a "good humor" to a modern diner who might be "out of temper." Either ingredient will add a very nice flavorful touch to the dish. As Chiquart knew, they are certainly worth trying.

Lovers of hummus, currently much in vogue as an appetizer in restaurants specializing in Middle Eastern foods, and at cocktail parties and other gatherings, will recognize this dish. So will those following a vegetarian lifestyle. Instead of tahini (sesame paste) used in hummus, the medieval recipe calls for almond oil. It is a delicate dip. You may wish to spice it up a bit by adding crushed garlic, to your taste, but this is a tasty dish as it stands.

Yield: About 2 cups/500 mL

Imperial	Ingredient	Metric	Directions
1–19 oz. *or* 3/4 cup	can of cooked chickpeas *or* raw chickpeas*	540 mL *or* 175 mL	**Drain chickpeas (setting aside 1/4–1/2 cup/60–125 mL of liquid if using puree recipe shown below).**
2 tbsp	almond oil	30 mL	**In a saucepan over low heat, whisk**
3 tbsp	lemon juice *or* wine vinegar	50 mL	**briskly together oil, lemon juice, salt,**
1/4 tsp	salt	1 mL	**cinnamon & sage.**
1 tsp	ground cinnamon	5 mL	**Add chickpeas, toss until well coated.**
1 1/2 tsp	fresh chopped sage (*or* 1/2 tsp/2 mL ground sage)	7 mL	
2–3 tbsp	fresh chopped parsley	30–50 mL	**Add parsley. Toss, then transfer to serving bowl.**

Garnish

2 sprigs	parsley	2 sprigs	**Serve warm, garnished with parsley sprigs.**

Serving variations

As a salad: Cool; toss with fresh salad greens and serve.

In soups: Add to soups for variety.

As a puree: Mix all ingredients, reserving a few whole peas and 1 tbsp (15 mL) of the chopped fresh parsley for garnish. Puree in food processor using steel blade, adding sufficient quantity of the reserved liquid to give a mayonnaise-like consistency. Transfer to serving bowl and garnish with whole peas and parsley. Serve as a dip for *crudités* or with small rounds of toast or on triangles of pita bread as an *hors d'œuvre* or appetizer.

---

* Wash raw chickpeas, discarding any that are discolored or withered. Soak, covered, overnight in 2 1/2–3 cups (625–750 mL) of tepid water. Drain, add fresh water and cook until tender. *Or*, alternatively: add water, bring to a boil, turn off heat, cover tightly; soak 2 hours, then cook over low heat until tender.

2. *Une vinaigrette*

(*Du fait de cuisine*, §57
also in *Viandier*, §17 and *Menagier de Paris*, p. 164/§105)

Pour donner entendement a celluy qui fera la vinagrete, si prenne des foies de porcs et si les lave et puis les mecte sur le gril sur belles brases jusques que il soit assez cuit; et quant il sera cuit si le mecte sur belles postz et puis le trenche par minuz dez. Et puis prenne des oignions grant foison et les plume et lave et trenche tresbien minuz, et tout cela souffrise tout ensemble en de bon et beau lart. Et pour le potaige de ladicte vinaigrete si prenne de tresbon vin claret du meilleur qu'il pourra avoir selon la quantité dudit potaige et y mecte du boullon du beuf ou du mouton ce qui sera necessaire; et puis prenne de beau pain blanc et le trenche par belles trenches et mecte roustir sur le gril jusques atant qu'il soit bien rousselet, et puis le mectés tremper audit vin et boullon; et quant il sera trempé, si prennés d'espices: gingibre blanc, granne de paradis, poyvre (et non pas tropt), cynamomy grant foyson de que en sera necessayre, et du sel aussi, puis tout cela passer et coler par l'estamine bien nectement et appoint, et puis le mectés bullir. Et, estre boullir, si lancés ledit grein souffrit dedans. Et puis en servés quant s'en devra servir.

2. A Vinegar Dish

All three manuscripts have copied a recipe for *Une Vinaigrette*; however, in each case the particular version offers some latitude in the choice of meat for which the *Vinaigrette* is prepared. As a consequence the modern cook may quite legitimately prepare a wide variety of meats for a medieval French *Vinaigrette*. The *Viandier* stipulates chunks of pork (unspecified cuts or offal), roasted on a spit; the *Menagier de Paris* calls for pork liver (or kidney, or spleen); and Chiquart says that if pork livers are not available then one should use loin of beef or leg of mutton.

All three sauce recipes agree in calling for wine and bouillon as the liquids, and for ginger and grains of paradise as the spices; these condiments are moistened in the vinegar whose taste will predominate and from which the dish will take its name. Saffron is included among the ingredients in the *Viandier* and the *Menagier*, whereas Chiquart does not mention saffron but does add pepper, cinnamon and salt to the ingredients list of the older sources. As a thickener for the sauce the *Viandier* omits bread—an oversight, surely—which the two later versions include. Both the *Viandier* and the *Menagier* describe the sauce as being reddish-brown in color (*brune*). While the version of the recipe that is contained in the *Du fait de cuisine* is somewhat more detailed than the others, we have felt justified in omitting the cinnamon that Chiquart put in his *Vinaigrette*—on the rather indefensible grounds that so many other sauces and dishes are flavored with cinnamon. Clearly, you may add cinnamon to taste should you wish.

Yield: Sufficient for 12–15 as appetizers, for 6 as main course or *entrée*

Imperial	Ingredient	Metric	**Directions**
Sauce			
1 1/2 cups	claret (*or* good red) wine	375 mL	**In saucepan over medium heat com-**
1 cup	beef bouillon	250 mL	**bine bouillon & wine.**
2 slices	white bread, toasted, cut into pieces *or* ground into crumbs	2 slices	**While stirring, add the toast. Whisk until well mixed with the liquid.**
2 tsp	white ginger	10 mL	**Combine the spices & the wine vine-**
1/2 tsp	salt	2 mL	**gar. Add to liquid & bread mix-**
1/4 tsp	grains of paradise	1 mL	**ture. Simmer for several minutes**
1/4 tsp	pepper	1 mL	**while stirring.**
pinch	saffron (*optional*)	pinch	**Strain mixture (*or* blend in blender**
2 tbsp	red wine vinegar	30 mL	**until there are no bread lumps). Set aside.**

Meat

1 1/2–2 lb	pork liver *or* loin of beef *or* leg of mutton, trimmed	750 g–1 kg	Broil meat in oven, or pan-broil, until cooked (time will depend upon thickness of meat). Do not overcook.
			Slice grilled meat into small pieces or strips, as desired.
4	medium-sized onions	4	Slice & chop onions. Melt lard in large skillet. Add onions & sauté until golden. Add meat slices to onions and stir while continuing to cook.
2–3 tbsp	lard *or* pork fat	30–50 mL	
			Add vinaigrette sauce mixture & continue to cook until hot.

To serve

Remove meat and onions with slotted spoon to serving plates or platter. Serve sauce in separate bowl for dipping or spooning on rice or pasta.

Serving suggestions

1. Serve with rice or buttered noodles as entrée dish.
2. Serve on small toast rounds or triangles as an appetizer.
3. Serve as an aperitif, providing toothpicks to allow dipping in sauce.

3. *Menus drois*

(*Viandier*, §62: MS Paris, Bibliothèque Nationale, fr. 19,791)

Menus doies [*sic*]: piés, foies, guisiers. Saites cuire en vin et en eaue tresbien; si metés vostre grain, quant il sera cuit, en un plat, et du percil et du vin aigre par dessus; autrement, en lieu de percil et de vin aigre, metés lait lié de moieux d'oeufs et de pain, de la poudre d'espices et un pou de saffren; et dressiés sus les escueilles sanz percil et vin aigre.

De pain, de vin, tu dois peu prendre s'autre viande doibs actendre.	Of bread and wine take only some if other foods are yet to come.

3. Little Delicacies

The old French term *drois* was associated with the hunt and specifically with the more delicate and valued parts of the slaughtered game that were cut away and reserved *by rights* (*droits*) for the hunter. Generally these morsels were small (*menu*); the whole phrase *menus drois* might in fact be well translated as "tidbits." Over time *menus drois* came to be applied to the dainty edible parts of any animal—for instance the liver, heart and lungs of a pig—but most particularly of barnyard fowl. Here by the end of the fourteenth century the precise sense of the phrase seems to have become so uncertain that both the *Viandier* and the *Menagier* feel that they must define just what constitutes *menus drois*: liver and giblets. If the modern cook wishes to follow the *Viandier*'s version quite literally, he or she will throw in chicken feet as well, although in all likelihood the word *piés* that the scribe wrote in the manuscript is merely a scribal misreading of the word *drois* itself!

The *Viandier* of Taillevent presents two methods of preparing this dish. Both are given here. The basic preparation lends itself to many types of presentation: as a luncheon or brunch menu, as an appetizer, or as tiny hors d'œuvres to serve at a cocktail party.

Yield: A quantity sufficient for appetizers for 6

Imperial	Ingredient	Metric	Directions
3/4 lb	chicken livers	375 g	**Trim membrane from chicken livers.**
1/2 cup	red wine	125 mL	**Cut livers in half. Simmer in wa-**
1/2 cup	boiling water	125 mL	**ter/wine mixture until they are ten-**
			der—about 6–8 minutes. Drain.

a. First method: Little Delicacies in *Vinaigrette*

Imperial	Ingredient	Metric	Directions
1/4 cup	red wine vinegar	60 mL	**Combine vinegar & parsley. Toss with**
1/4 cup	chopped, fresh parsley	60 mL	**livers. Transfer to serving dish.**
Garnish			
sprig	fresh parsley	sprig	**Garnish with parsley. Serve warm or**
			cold.

Serving suggestions

1. Toss warm or cold with varied greens as a salad.
2. Prepare hors d'œuvres tray with livers and *Syseros* / Chickpea Puree (see p. 77) or other appetizers. Set out with toothpicks.

b. Second method: Little Delicacies with Egg Sauce

Cook livers in wine & water as above. Drain, keep warm.

Imperial	Ingredient	Metric	Directions
1 cup	milk	250 mL	**Heat milk. Add a little of the hot milk (about 1/4 cup/60 mL) to egg yolk, stirring constantly. Return egg mixture to remaining milk. Continue stirring while cooking.**
1	egg yolk, lightly beaten	1	
1/2 tsp	cinnamon	2 mL	**Combine & add spices.**
1/4 tsp	cloves	1 mL	
1/4 tsp	ginger	1 mL	
pinch	saffron	pinch	
2 tbsp	soft breadcrumbs	30 mL	**Thicken with sufficient breadcrumbs to form a thick sauce. Toss livers in sauce to coat. Transfer to serving bowl.**

Garnish

sprig	parsley	sprig	**Garnish with parsley & serve.**

Serving suggestions

1. As a hors d'œuvre, serve warm on small melba rounds or toasts.
2. Serve on toasted bread slices for brunch.
3. Serve on a bed of lettuce as a warm salad.

4. *Pipesfarces*
(*Viandier*, §203; & *Menagier de Paris*, p. 227/§264)

Et qui veult faire des Pipesfarces, convient avoir de bon frommage de gain par grosses lesches comme le doy, et les enveloper en la paste des pettes crespes et puis les boutter en son sain chault; et les gardez d'ardoir; et quant ilz sont seiches et jaunettes les drecier, et les crespes avec.

Du fromage / Cheese
(Aldobrandino, *Le regime du corps*, p. 180)

As Isaac says, cheese is generally completely bad because it swells the belly, making it heavy and inflated, and you can see this in people who have used it for a long time that they have pains in their side, a bad head, dullness of wit, kidney and bladder stones.

But cheese is more or less bad according to the different ways of using it, for if it is eaten when it is fresh and new it will by nature cool the digestion because it is cool and moist in the first degree, and it digests well in the stomach and puts on weight and is very nourishing.

If it is eaten when it is old, and to the same extent that it is old, it is warmer and is less useful to eat because it engenders bad humors and bad, warm and dry vapors and, worse than all other sorts of cheese, it engenders gallstone. Old cheese much better as a therapeutic medicine than as a healthful food, for roasted it is very useful for those who have diarrhea, and it comforts the stomach, and it helps food go down if it is eaten after one has already eaten a great deal of food, especially if it is fat and nauseating.

Cheese that is between new and old and which has a good taste and is not too fat is best to eat and most suitable to human nature; even though it is not without harmful qualities, it is less bad than the others.

Caseus recens / Fresh Cheese
(*Tacuinum sanitatis*, Vienna,
Oesterreichische Nationalbibliothek, Codex Vindobonensis, 2644, f. 60r)

Fresh cheese. The thicker part of the milk condenses with the addition of rennet, the whey is expertly drawn off, and the cheese is formed. It is a very nourishing, substantial food which softens and fattens the body but which causes obstructions; therefore it is wise to eat cheese with walnuts or almonds. The more balanced the substances of the milk and the healthier the animal, the better the cheese will be. It is suited to those with hot temperaments, to the summer and to hot regions; however, it is suited also sometimes to the winter or cold places, given that the cheese is digested better in those circumstances.

4. Pipe Stuffings

The English name of this dish is an instance of an original having lost something in the translation. *Pipesfarces* somehow creates a more graphic image of the finished dish than the crude and cumbersome "Pipe Stuffings," as close to literal as this translation may be. When the cheese (or bone marrow) is encased in batter and deep-fried, the result is of a golden tube with a stuffing inside. *Pipesfarces*, really, rather than "Pipe Stuffings." But delightful by any name.

The *Viandier* includes this recipe after a recipe for crêpes and suggests serving them with the crêpes. A "fat" cheese (that is, a butter cheese) is suggested in the original recipe. Colby works well.

The *Menagier* suggests using bone marrow pressed into finger-sized pieces as an alternative to the cheese. *These are a bit tricky to handle*, as the bone marrow disintegrates quickly in the hot fat and makes for rather messy cooking. We have found that crumbling pieces of marrow into the coating mixture then dropping small amounts into the hot grease works better than trying to coat the longer finger-sized pieces of marrow.

Pork fat is stipulated as the cooking medium. Oil or lard can be substituted.

As for the crêpes with which the Pipe Stuffings are served, the *Viandier*'s recipe does not differ substantially from a modern one, so you may choose to prepare your favorite crêpe.

Yield: About 20 Pipes

Imperial	Ingredient	Metric	Directions
6–8 oz.	fat cheese	200–250 g	**Slice cheese into finger-sized pieces.**
2	egg yolks	2	**Beat egg yolks with fork.**
4 tbsp	all-purpose flour	60 mL	**Add flour & salt a little at a time to**
1/2 tsp	salt	2 mL	**form a smooth paste. Thin batter**
2 tbsp	wine	30 mL	**with sufficient wine to make a "drip-**
			ping" consistency.
1 cup	cooking oil or lard (pork fat)	250 mL	**Dip cheese slices into batter & fry a few at a time until golden brown. Remove with slotted spoon, drain on paper or linen towelling. Keep warm until all pieces have cooked.**

Serving Suggestion

Serve warm as appetizers.

5. *Alouyaulx*

(*Viandier*, §204)

Prenez mouelle de beuf ou de la gresse qui est ou rongnon de beuf et trenchier par morceaulx longs et gros comme le doy d'un homme, et reffaire la mouelle de beuf en eaue chaude — et ne faire que boutter et tirer, et la gresse plus largement. Et avoir ung trumeau de veau et oster la chair des os le plus emsemble qu'on pourra, et la mettre par lesches tenues comme une espesse oublee et les estandre sur ung dressouer net: et enveloper les morceaulx de mouelle en ses lesches de veau et ung petit de sel blanc et de pouldre fine ou blanche. Puis avoir une broche de fer bien gresle et les embrocher; puis avoir de la paste tele qu'il convient aux petites crespes, et les en dorer quant ilz sont bien cuitz au regart de ceulx de mouelle.

Carnes vituline / Veal

(*Le regime tresutile*, p. 67)

Sunt nutritive multum carnes vituline.   Veal is very nourishing.

In this text the author praises veal, saying that the meat of a calf is very nutritious. Avicenna mentions this opinion in the Third Distinction of his First Book in the chapter about what is eaten and drunk. He states that the nature of meat should be similar to that of the healthy person, and have a ready tendency to become blood: this is especially so of suckling kid and calf, and of one-year-old lamb. In the third Book of his *Elements* Galen praises veal highly, saying that the meat of a six- or eight-week-old suckling calf, roasted, is better than lamb, more digestible and more nourishing.

De la moieule / Marrow

(Aldobrandino, *Le regime du corps*, p. 134)

Marrow from the spine compared with that of other bones in the body is cold and moist, and it takes after the nature of the brain; the marrow of other bones is temperately between cold and warm, but it tends more to warm than to cold. Even though it causes some little nausea, marrow nourishes well when it is well digested in the stomach; by its nature it excites desire for a woman.

And the marrow which is the best is that from ruminant animals.

Le morsel mis hors de ta bouche a ton vaissel plus ne le touche.	Once of food you've had a bite to put it back is never right.

5. Little Larks

Though not explicitly designated as an *"entremets"* in the *Viandier*, these little *paupiettes de veau* could very easily satisfy the requirements of delicacy and novelty of that category. Certainly in a modest way they express the spirit of playfulness that is found at the origin of the earliest *entremets*. This genre of dish, which we shall examine more closely toward the end of the present book, was intended primarily to mark a pause between two much more earnest servings of really solid foods. The *entremets* functioned in large measure as an amusement, a *divertissement* as the French would say; the inventive, diversionary nature of this sort of dish remained with it and grew constantly even beyond the end of the Middle Ages. By the fifteenth century and the last manuscript version of the *Viandier*, the *entremets* had become a theatrical representation, both inanimate and totally *inedible*. The recipe for these Little Larks makes a dish that is both amusing and edible, however, deliciously edible.

The name of the dish derives directly from its appearance: thin slices of veal are wrapped around marrow in such a way as to suggest the form of small, light birds.

It is a relatively clean finger food which can be prepared either as an appetizer or served as a delightful incidental course in the middle of a meal—an "entremets" proper. It is preferable to cook them on an hibachi or barbecue, but they can be grilled in the oven. A variety of possible sauces enriches the appeal and the usefulness of the dish.

Yield: 6 Larks

Imperial	Ingredient	Metric	Directions
8–12 oz	piece of veal shank, bone removed & sliced thinly into 6 pieces	250–375 g	**Pound pieces of veal until of a uniform 1/8 in/ 3 mm thickness.**
	marrow from two soup bones		**With a slotted spoon, dip the marrow**
1/2 cup	water *or* beef stock (*optional*)	125 mL	**briefly (1 1/2 min.) into warm stock or water. Place equal amounts of the marrow in the centre of of each piece of veal.**

Fine Spice Powder

1/2 tsp	cinnamon	2 mL	**Sprinkle with a little spice powder.**
1 tsp	ginger	5 mL	
1/4 tsp	nutmeg	1 mL	
pinch	salt	pinch	

| 3 | bamboo or kebab skewers*
Oil to brush grill. | 3 | **Wrap the marrow in the veal & secure on the skewers or toothpicks. Dust with remaining spice powder.**
Brush grill with oil. Grill over hot coals or in oven grill for about 3–4 min. on each side. |

Crêpe Glaze

2	egg yolks	2	**Whisk eggs. Add flour & sufficient water to make a thick batter. Remove "larks" from grill. Brush with crêpe glaze & return to grill until glaze is baked on.**
2 1/2 tbsp	flour	35 mL	
1–2 tbsp	water	15–30 mL	
			For dipping serve with Tournai Cameline Sauce, in the variation with mustard (see p. 137).

Note: These glazed Larks may be prepared and cooked ahead of time and let cool. The cooling allows the crêpe glaze to adhere to the meat. When it is almost time to serve them, brush them lightly once more with batter and return them to the grill.

---

* Bamboo skewers should be soaked in cold water to cover for one hour before using.

6. Rissoles

This is another case of "What goes around, comes around." Pizza puffs, japaties and other foods encased in a pastry are very familiar items in the frozen food section of our markets. The medieval cook knew very well the value of encasing foods.

The three principal French recipe collections all contain recipes for types of fried or deep-fried tarts or turnovers called *rissoles*, *ruissoles* or *roseolles*. The name of this generic preparation derives from the rich russet color that is imparted to the pastry dough by a deep-frying process. In England the original French term degenerated into the word *risshews*.

Depending upon the ingredients chosen for their contents, rissoles could be made suitable for serving on a meat day, a fish day or a Lenten day. The author of the *Menagier de Paris* adds, as an aside, that rissoles can be simply fruit turnovers. We have prepared a selection of three possible fillings for different varieties of rissoles: 1. Pork Rissoles (for a Meat Day); 2. Rissoles for a Fish Day; and, 3. Fruit Rissoles. While this last variety is nominally designed to satisfy the requirements of a meatless dish, it makes a delightful alternative at any time. We have placed the last, the *Menagier*'s recipe for Fruit Rissoles, where it seems most appropriate, in the chapter on Desserts, p. 278, below.

The frying medium that is mentioned in late-medieval cookery manuals differed according to the "day": on fish-days and during Lent, oil, probably olive oil, was used; lard (normally clarified pork fat) could be used on meat-days. We leave the choice of frying medium to you.

Saffron was frequently included in pastry at this time, even when the pastry is to be deep-fried, in order to lend it an even richer color. Since this is today rather an expensive way merely to color pastry, you may wish to substitute a food-coloring dye or turmeric which will also give an orange-yellow color.

Ton morsel ne touche a saliere, car ce n'est pas belle maniere.	In the salt don't dip your food: this is a practice far too rude.

Yield, for all varieties of Rissoles: 24 3 in/ 7 cm rounds *or* 1 double-crust pie

Sufficient pastry *or* other pie dough for a double-crust 9 in/ 23 cm pie. See the recipe for Dough
   for Rissoles, pp. 70 & 71. Roll out pastry to a thickness of 1/8 in/ 3 mm. Cut out rounds of
   pastry about 3 in/ 7 cm in diameter.

Imperial	Ingredient	Metric	Directions
1 batch	filling of choice (see below)	1 batch	**Place 1 rounded tsp/ 5 mL of filling in centre of each pastry round. Brush edges of the rounds lightly with water. Fold the dough over into crescents. Seal firmly (tines of a fork work well), so that none of the filling escapes during frying.***
2 cups	oil *or* lard paper towelling (for draining)	500 mL	**Heat oil to 360°–375°F/180°–190°C. Fry rissoles. Remove with slotted spoon. Drain on paper towelling to remove excess oil.**

Garnish

| 1/2 cup | sugar | 125 mL | **Sprinkle with sugar. Serve warm.** |

Serving suggestions

Place on a tray around a bed of fresh parsley.

Variations

If you wish to avoid deep-fried food, these rissoles may be baked in an oven: brush with beaten
   egg, sprinkle with sugar and put in a 400°F/200°C oven for 10–12 min. or until lightly
   browned.

The pastry and filling will also make a 9 in/ 23 cm double-crust pie should you not wish individual
   rissoles.

For a different treatment of these rissoles, try a pasta recipe for the pastry; boil the rissoles in
   water, then deep-fry them briefly in oil.

---

   * Alternatively, you might use a perogy maker or a large ravioli maker.

6a. *Rosseolles*

(Du fait de cuisine, §51)

Pour donner entendement a celluy qui les fera, selon la quantité qu'il en fera si prenne la quantité de porc fres et despiece par belles pieces belles et nectes et mecte cuire; et du sel dedans. Et quant sa char sera cuicte, si la tire dehors sur belles tables belles et nectes, et si en tire la coenne et tous les ossés; et puis hasche tresbien minus. Et faictes que vous haiés de figues, prunes, dactes, pignions et raisins confitz; des raisins tirés hors les picolles, et des pignions les croises, et de toutes autres choses que ne sont nectes. Et puis tout cela lavés tresbien une ou .ii. ou .iii. foys en de bon vin blanc et puis mectés esgouter sur belles et nectes postz; et puis taillés les figues et prunes et dactes tout par minuz dez et les mescleys par vostre farce. Et puis faictes que vous haiés du meilleur fromaige que fayre se pourra; et puis prennés du percy une grant quantité qui soit defoillés par belles foilles et le lavés tresbien et le haschiés tresbien parmi vostre fromaige; et puis cela mesleés tresbien parmi vostre farce, et des oefs aussi. Et prennés vostres espices: gingibre blanc, granne (et non pas tropt), du saffran, et du succre grant foyson selon la quantité que vous ferés. Et puis delivrés vostre farce a vostre patissier, et qu'il soit pourveu de avoir fait ses beaux folliés de paste pour faire les doreures. Et quant elles seront faictes, qui les vous apporte. Et qui vous soit pourveu de beau saing blanc de porc pour le frire. Et quant elles seront frictes, que vous soiés pourveu d'or parti: pour une chescune doreure qui sera, que vous haiés ung folliet d'or pour mectre par dessus. Et quant ce viendra au drecier, si les ordonnés par beaux platz et puis lancés du succre par dessus.

6a. Pork Rissoles (for a Meat Day)

A variety of rissole is found in the collection that Chiquart made of his standard recipes. He directs that his Pork Rissoles be fried in pork fat; you may wish to use a vegetable or nut oil.

Chiquart obtained great éclat when serving his pork rissoles to his master the Duke by gilding them with finely beaten gold-leaf, and then topping this gold with sprinkled sugar. You could brush the tops with egg yolk or a saffron/milk mixture, and bake them in the oven for a few minutes. With just this sugar dressing, our rissoles must unfortunately remain a rather plain poor cousin of Chiquart's.

Imperial	Ingredient	Metric	Directions
1 lb	ground pork	500 g	**Fry ground pork, drain, set aside.**
(1 tbsp	oil *or* pork fat (lard)	15 mL)	*If necessary*, **add fat to pan.**
1 cup	white wine	250 mL	**In a large saucepan marinate wash-**
4	diced figs	4	**ed fruit (except pinenuts) in wine**
5	diced prunes	5	**for 5–10 min.**
4–5	diced dates	4–5	
2/3 cup	raisins	160 mL	
1 cup	sugar	250 mL	**Combine sugar & spices. Stir into**
1 tsp	ground ginger	5 mL	**fruit & marinade. Simmer mix-**
pinch	saffron *(optional)*	pinch	**ture on low heat until sugar is dis-**
pinch	grains of paradise	pinch	**solved & fruit is tender but not mushy.**
1	whole egg	1	**Quickly whisk in 1 slightly beaten**
1/4 cup	chopped fresh parsley	60 mL	**egg. Combine parsley & cheese,**
2 oz	cheese (cream, Brie, butter, etc.), finely diced	60 g	**& stir into hot mixture.**
			Remove from heat. Add cooked
1/4 cup	pinenuts	60 mL	**pork & pinenuts. Combine well & proceed as for Rissoles (above, p. 92).**

Garnish

Sprinkle the tops of the Pork Rissoles with sugar, and serve.

6b. *Rissolles a jour de poisson*
(*Menagier de Paris*, p. 225/§260)

Cuisiez chastaingnes a petit feu et les pelez; et aiez durs oeufs et du frommage pelé, et hachez tout bien menu; puis les arousez d'aubuns d'oeufs, et meslez parmy pouldre et bien petit de sel delié. Et faites vos rissoles; puis les frisiez en grant foison d'uille; et succrez.

Et nota, en Karesme, en lieu d'oeufs et frommage, mettez merlus et escheroys cuis, bien menu hachiés, ou char de brocherés ou d'anguilles, figues et dates hachees.

6b. Rissoles for a Fish Day

The *Menagier* offers a series of variations for the filling of his "lean" rissoles. The initial recipe, for a normal fish-day, calls for cheese and eggs, both whole eggs and egg-whites, even though the dish qualifies for serving on a day of fasting on which, in theory, no animal meats or other *animal products* were to be consumed. If this dish is to be served in Lent, however, the author suggests that hake (cod), pickerel or eel be substituted for the cheese and the eggs, along with cooked parsnips, and chopped figs and dates.

We have chosen from among the possible ingredients to present this particular version of the *Menagier*'s fish rissole.

Imperial	Ingredient	Metric	Directions
8 oz	lobster *or* other flaked cooked fish: cod, pike, eel, tuna	250 g	**Combine all ingredients. Stir to mix well.**
1 doz	sliced chestnuts* (set liquid aside)	12	
1	hard-boiled egg, chopped	1	
2 oz	cheese (cream, Brie, butter), diced	60 g	
1/4 tsp	ground ginger	1 mL	
1/8 tsp	ground cinnamon	0.5 mL	
pinch	ground cloves	pinch	
pinch	salt	pinch	
	reserved liquid from chestnuts *or* white wine		**Add sufficient reserved chestnut broth or white wine to moisten filling.**
			Proceed as for rissoles (above, p. 92).

Variation

Rather than small rissoles, you may wish to make them larger, or in tart pans, and serve with any of the sauces appropriate for fish (see page 209) as a fish course in a meal.

---

* These chestnuts may be fresh (cooked), canned or dried. To reconstitute dried chestnuts: soak in water overnight. Rinse and cull, discarding any skins or discolored nuts. Simmer, covered with water until tender. Drain and set the liquid aside.

6c. *Rissolles a jour de poisson* (cont.)
(*Menagier de Paris*, p. 225/§260;
see also the recipe for *Rosseolles, Du fait de cuisine*, §51, above.)

Item, au commun l'en les fait de figues, roisins, pommes hastees, et noix pelees pour contrefaire le pignolat, et pouldre d'espices. Et soit la paste trés bien ensaffrenee, puis soient frites en huille. S'il y convient lieure, amidon lie et ris aussi.

6c. Fruit Rissoles

For this variation on a very popular genre, see below in the chapter on Desserts (p. 278).

The fruit filling of these rissoles makes a tasty accompaniment to roast meats—especially roast pork.

7. [*Pastez de champignons*]
(*Menagier de Paris*, p. 185/§160)

Champignons d'une nuyt sont les meilleurs, et sont petits et vermeils dedans, clos dessus: et les convient peler, puis laver en eaue chaude et pourboulir; qui en veult mettre en pasté, si y mette de l'uille, du frommage et de la pouldre.

Item, mettez les entre deux plats sur charbons, et mettez un petit de sel, du frommage et de la pouldre. L'en les treuve en la fin de may et en juin.

De campaignés / Mushrooms
(Aldobrandino, *Le regime du corps*, p. 170)

Mushrooms are of various sorts and you should know that they are cold and moist in the third degree; some are even cold in the fourth degree, and those are the ones that make people suddenly die.

Know that, according to what doctors of physic say, others are not so bad, although they are to be regarded with suspicion given the dangers they pose due to vicious fumes that issue naturally from the earth.

Those that are the best engender gross, vicious, bad humors. Their harmfulness derives from the place they grow; therefore it is worth knowing that they have grown in a good place.

We shall teach you to recognize the mortal varieties: these are soft, large and viscous, and grow in a bad place. If you find them rotten, cut them in half and leave them exposed to the air a little: many people do not pay any attention to that.

Let us tell you how to prepare them for eating: they should first be cooked with calamint and pepper, then discard that water and continue cooking in fresh water; they are then eaten with pepper, ginger, caraway, calamint, oregano, cinnamon and other similar spices; and afterwards you should drink good strong old wine. Anyone of a cold temperament who eats them should take a dose of such electuaries as gyngembras, dyacorum, dyacitoniten or dyatrion pyperon, because these are useful in combatting mushrooms' harmfulness.

7. Mushroom Tarts

This dish was obviously a delicacy. According to the *Menagier*'s precise directions, it would be best to reserve for it those mushrooms usually found at the end of May or June. Again, the best of these mushrooms were those that were picked when they were only one night old.

We use tiny button mushrooms here. Should they be unavailable, tinned whole mushrooms may be substituted. The variety *"Champignons de Paris"* are preferable. We have ignored the *Menagier*'s advice to parboil the mushrooms; you may parboil them if you wish.

Yield: Serves 12 as appetizers, 6 as a vegetable dish

Imperial	Ingredient	Metric	Directions
			Preheat oven to 400°F/200°C.
	Sufficient pastry for a large single-crust pie *or* 12 medium tarlets		**Line pie plate or tartlette tins with pastry. Pre-bake blind for 5 min. Reduce oven to 350°F/180°C.**
3/4–1 lb	fresh tiny button mushrooms	375–500 g	**Clean mushrooms. Slice in half (or more if larger). Toss in oil & distribute in shells.**
1 tbsp	olive oil	15 mL	
1/2 lb	a buttery cheese (*e.g.*, Brie*)	250 g	**Slice cheese over mushrooms.**
Spices			
3/4 tsp	ginger	4 mL	**Combine spices, salt & Parmesan cheese. Sprinkle this mixture on top.**
1/2 tsp	cloves	2 mL	
1/4 tsp	cinnamon	1 mL	
1 tsp	brown sugar	5 mL	**Bake in 350°F/180°C oven for 10–15 min. or until lightly browned on top. Serve warm.**
1/2 tsp	salt	2 mL	
2–3 tbsp	grated Parmesan cheese	30–50 mL	

Cooking Variations

1. Omit the pastry. Brush oven-proof dish with oil or butter. Toss mushrooms in oil. Layer the mushrooms, cheese slices and spice/cheese mixture. Cover and bake in 375°F/190°C oven for about 20 min.
2. Sautee the mushrooms in the oil, toss with the rest of the ingredients, and prepare and cook as for Rissoles (p. 92).

---

* If you are using Brie cheese, peel the rind, chop finely and sprinkle over the pre-baked pastry shell before the mushrooms are laid in.

Other Possible Appetizers

Soupe jacobine / **Jacobin Sops**

For the complete recipe of this dish as a Soup, see p. 105, below.

As an appetizer, spread the Brie cheese on finger-sized strips of toast. Then layer strips of breast meat and dark meat, and top with a sprig of parsley. For a fondue dish, cut the bouillon recipe in half and serve it in a chafing dish or fondue pot. Let your guests serve themselves by dipping the strips into the bouillon.

Moust pour hetoudeaulx / **Must Sauce for Young Chicken**

For the complete recipe of this dish as a Sauce, see p. 130, below.

This fruity sauce makes a delicious dip for small chunks of chicken—chicken balls or fingers of chicken—or for other meat dishes such as the Little Larks (see p. 88, above).

Aulx vers / **Green Garlic Sauce**

For garlic lovers, this sauce makes a wonderful dip for *crudités* or with pita triangles (see p. 119, below). True devotees may want to increase the garlic to three cloves.

Pommeaulx / **Little Meatballs**

For the complete recipe of this dish as a Meat Dish, see p. 153, below.

As appetizers or as main course, these meatballs are delicious served with a dipping sauce such as the apple-almond sauce called *Emplumeus*: see below, p. 286.

Faulx grenon / **Mock Meat**

For the complete recipe of this dish as a Poultry Dish, see p. 202, below.

Use the same recipe. Cut the cooked meat into small pieces. Provide toothpicks and the sauce in a bowl. Alternatively, leave the sauce and meat in a chafing dish with toothpicks beside it.

Tortres parmeysines de poyssons / **Parma Fish Pie**

For the complete recipe of this dish as a Fish Pie, see p. 223, below.

Prepare the filling as for the pie but use small tartlette shells. This makes about 24 small one-crust tartlettes.

Tortes of Herbs, Cheese and Eggs

For the complete recipe of this dish as an Egg Dish, see p. 232, below.

Using your preferred pastry recipe, prepare the filling and pour into tartlette shells. Bake 15–20 minutes (or until set) in a moderate 375°F/190°C oven.

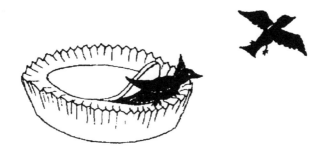

Chapter 3
Sops and Soups

1. *Potage d'oignons* / Onion-Pea Soup
2. *Soupe jacobine de chappons* / Jacobin Sops
3. *Souppe despourveue* / Quick Soups
    a. *Percil* / Parsley
    b. *Beuf froit* / Cold Beef
    c. *Poisson* / Fish
    d. *Chaudeau de la char* / Meat Bouillon
    e. *A jour de poisson* / For Fish Days
    f. *Lart et maquerel fraiz* / Fish and Bacon

Puree des poys / **Pea Puree** : see Chapter 1, Standard Preparations
Syseros / **Chickpea Puree** : see Chapter 2, Appetizers
Porriaux blancs / **Almond-Leek Sauce** : see Chapter 4, Sauces
Calimafree ou Saulse paresseuse / **Lazy Sauce** : see Chapter 4, Sauces
Civé d'oeufz (Souppe en moustarde) / **Mustard Egg Sops** : see Chapter 8, Egg Dishes

Chapter 3
Sops and Soups

Our modern word "soup" derives from the Old French word *sope* and *soupe*. The French word was used in England in the form of *sop* at the end of the Middle Ages and, fortunately, has remained in the English language in its original form and with much its original sense. We say "fortunately" because it is clear that nowdays a "sop" is not a "soup."

The distinction is important. When cooks in the Middle Ages spoke of "soup," what they and the people for whom they were cooking really understood was a dish comprising primarily a piece of bread or toast soaked in a liquid or over which a liquid had been poured. The bread or toast was an important, even vital, part of this dish. It was a means by which a diner could consume a liquid efficiently by sopping it up. The bread or toast was, in effect, an alternative to using a spoon—this latter being a very slow and labored method of ingesting soup, as any child will tell you—yet at the same time a slightly more refined, not to say elegant, way than merely picking up the soup bowl and quaffing off its liquid contents. Besides, the serving platters and bowls were usually shared among several diners at this time; to use a small sop might have been thought of as a somewhat more sanitary way to sharing the liquid contents of a bowl than drinking directly from it or dipping a used spoon in it. Bread, even more fundamental a staple on any dining board then than today, was always available at a meal. And we should remember that fingers were, after all, the primary means of carrying food to the mouth. Again, ask any child.

Soups were important in the medieval diet, but the dish that the cook prepared was often a sop that consisted of both the nutritious liquid and the means to eat it. The meal at the end of a normal day was always* the lighter of the two meals of the day, and the sop appears to have had an important place in it. In fact it was precisely because of the normal inclusion of a sop in this end-of-the-day meal that it became called *"souper"* or "supper."

The sops we give here are merely a sampling of quite a large genre. It seems likely that, beginning with a meat stock and having a selection of tasty spices on hand, the medieval cook was disposed to throw a wide range of foodstuffs into the vat. Any cook from any age will recognize this economical use of left-overs. Some of the sops found in early French recipes are not at all unfamiliar from our modern perspective; others, however, made rather unexpected use of some of their ingredients. In one of his Quick Soups the *Menagier* even combines fish and bacon.

In what follows we can see that the possibilities for creating interesting sops in the Middle Ages were endless—just as they should still be today.

---

* This is not strictly correct. Chiquart informs us that for days on which a tournament is scheduled for the afternoon, the midday dinner should be lighter than normal and the supper, following the exertions of the battlefield and tiltyard, should be correspondingly more substantial.

1. *Potage d'oignons, sans espices et non liant*
(Menagier de Paris, p. 135/§29)

A jour de poisson, quant les pois sont cuis, l'en doit avoir oignons qui aient autant cuit comme les pois en un pot et le lart en autre pot, et que de l'eaue du lart l'en paist et sert les pois; tout ainsi, a jour de poisson, quant l'en a mis ses pois au feu en un pot, l'en doit mettre a part ses ongnons mincés en un autre pot, et de l'eaue des oignons servir et mettre dedens les pois en passant; et quant tout ce est cuit, frire les oignons et en mettre la moictié es pois, et l'autre en la puree dont il sera parlé cy aprés, et lors mettre du sel. Et se a ce jour de poisson ou en Karesme il y a craspois, l'en doit faire des craspois comme de lart en jour de char.

Capiteles d'oignon / Onions
(Aldobrandino, Le regime du corps, p. 162)

Onions are warm and dry according to Rhazes, but warm in the third degree and moist in the fourth according to Avicenna. They are better to combat illness than to maintain good health or as nourishment. By their nature they create thirst and engender gross, viscous humors; but they comfort the appetite and, according to Avicenna, yield good nourishment. If they are eaten raw they cause headaches. By their fundamental nature onions produce and strengthen an impulse to have intercourse with a woman.

A poultice made with onions, rue and salt and put on the bite of a mad dog or on that of any other poisonous animal, is very useful. Onions are furthermore useful after eating in order to counter the harmfulness of bad foods that bear poisonous humors.

Cepe / Onions
(Tacuinum sanitatis, Vienna,
Oesterreichische Nationalbibliothek, Codex Vindobonensis, 2644, f. 25v)

Onions. The onion is excellent and highly suitable for old people and those with cold temperaments, because of its nature which is warm in the highest degree, sometimes moist and sometimes dry. The most desirable of the many varieties are the white ones, being rich in watery juices. They generate milk in nursing mothers and fertile semen in men. They improve the eyesight, are emollient, and stimulate the bladder. Headaches which are sometimes caused by onions can be cured with vinegar and milk. Those suffering from coughs, asthma or constrictions in the chest should eat onions that are boiled or that are baked under the coals, served with sugar and a little fresh butter.

Oultre la table ne crache point; je te diz que c'est ung lait point.	And never, ever, should you spit across the table whence you sit.

1. Onion-Pea Soup

This recipe, which appears at the end of the fifteenth century in printed versions of the *Viandier* as well as in the *Menagier de Paris*, is treated in the earlier source as a derivative or variant of a basic recipe for a *Potage de pois vielz*, that is, a stew of dried peas.

The variants of this dish that are found in the *Menagier* also distinguish between preparations appropriate for meat days and those that might be used on lean days: on meat days, for instance, *eaue de char* or meat bouillon can be an ingredient. While the *Menagier*'s onion-pea combination (the recipe for which is reproduced here) is a pottage explicitly for lean days, the equivalent of this recipe, found in the printed *Viandier* under the name *Souppe a l'oignon* (ed. Pichon and Vicaire, p. 181) contains butter and therefore must clearly have been intended for serving on a meat day. This precedent, and perhaps an heretical want of doctrinal orthodoxy on our part, have led us to include beef bouillon in our adaptation of this soup.

Yield: Serves 6

Imperial	Ingredient	Metric	Directions
1 lb	onions (about 3–4)	500 mL	**Cut onions into thin slices. Sauté in**
1/4 cup	butter	60 mL	**butter until lightly browned.**
5 cups	beef bouillon	1250 mL	**In soup pot heat beef bouillon (*or* wa-**
2 cups	pea puree (*see p.63*)	500 mL	**ter). Stir in the pea puree.**
1 cup	fresh chopped parsley (lightly packed)	250 mL	**Add parsley, lemon juice (*or* wine vinegar), salt & pepper. Continue**
2 tbsp	lemon juice *or* wine vinegar	30 mL	**cooking over low heat, stirring fre-**
1/2 tsp	salt	2 mL	**quently, for 30 min.**
1/4 tsp	freshly ground pepper	1 mL	**Serve hot in bowls.**

Serving suggestions

1. To make this "pottage" into a true medieval "sop" or soup, serve it with day-old bread which is placed on the bottom of the bowl to soak up most of the liquid.
2. For a modern garnish, put the soup in oven-proof dishes, top with slices of toasted bread sprinked with grated cheese. Heat in oven-proof dishes until the cheese is melted.

2. *Soupe jacobine de chappons*
(*Du fait de cuisine*, §18)

Et pour servir de la soupe jacobine fault que haiés voz beaulx chappons et, selon la quantité de la feste, cent ou .ii^c. chappons de haulte gresse, et d'aultre poullaille a grant foyson pour servir en deffault desdistz chappons; et si soient roustitz bien et appoint. Et quant sera au despiecer les beuffs d'aute gresse si prenne on les os miolle et les lavés bien et adroit, puis les mectés boullir en chaudieres belles et nectes, et de beau mouston parmi; et puis apprés faictes que vous ayés ung quintal de tresbon fromaige de Crampone et de Brye et du plus fin que faire se pourra et trouver, et ledit fruictz faciés parer et nectoyer bien et appoint, et puis le taflés bien minument. Et ledit queux qui est ordonné pour faire ladicte souppe jacopine si prenne deux ou .iii^c. pains de bouche et ce pain taille par belles lesches et les roustissez tresbien nectement sans bruller, et qu'il soit roussellet, et puis le mectés en belles cornues belles et nectes—et que vous aiés .ii. belles postz blanches et nectes pour tailler vostre dit pain rousti pour les souppes jacobines; et puis que vous ayés vostre platz d'or et d'argent et d'estaing a la suite, et par voz platz alloés vostre pain bien et doulcement et le fromaige par dessus. Et prennés voz chappons et les mectés par membres, c'est assavoir levés les ailles et les cuisses et levés la crouppe; et puis prennés le blanc dudit chappon et le taillés bien menuz, et ce blanc de chappon semés par dessus vostre souppe jacobine; et puis apprés prennés les membres desditz chappons, c'est assavoir les aflles, cuisses et crouppe, et mectés par dessus vostre souppe jacopine en ordonnance. Et vous prennés garde de vostre boullon des miolles de beufz et moustons qui sont bons et doulx, et coullés ce boullon en une olle grande, belle et necte; et que vous hayés une bonne—bonnete—buguete d'erbes de salvy, percy, margellayne et ysope, et qu'elles soient bien nectoyés et lavees, et mectés dedans vostre boullon. Et faictes que vers le dreceur, ou vous serés pour servir des dictes souppes jacopines, vous hayés bon feu de charbon et dessoubz vostres oulles en quoy est vostre boullon affin qu'il boulle tousjours; et dudit boullon cuisés voz dictes souppes jacopines.

Ne furge tes dens de la pointe de ton coustel, je le t'apointe.	Don't pick your teeth with your knife's point: good manners has this oft enjoined.

2. Jacobin Sops

Several generations after being detailed in the *Du fait de cuisine*, Chiquart's recipe of Jacobin Sops appears in other recipe collections of the fifteenth century, the *Fleur de toute cuysine* and the *Recueil de Riom*. In both works the name of the recipe is still *Souppe jacobine*.

The qualification "Jacobin" in the name of this dish is interesting. In Paris at this time the Dominican order had its House in the Rue St. Jacques, of which the Latin etymon is *Jacobus*; as a consequence of this association the local sobriquet for members of the Dominican order became the "Jacobins."* Because the Dominican order tended to attract its members from the aristocracy—as opposed to the Franciscans who came overwhelmingly from less exalted spheres in society—the former monks acquired a reputation for not whole-heartedly accepting a vow of poverty and for maintaining something of the life-style to which in their secular existence they had been accustomed. In particular the epithet Jacobin appears to have come to suggest a certain gourmandism or gluttony related to members of that order in Paris.† This dish, certainly a hearty one, warranted its association with reputed epicures!

The Jacobin Sops is a relatively simple preparation, using roasted capons and/or other poultry. It can easily be stretched to accommodate additional guests with the addition of extra broth and/or chicken. (See also the treatment of this dish in the Chapters on Appetizers and Poultry Dishes.) The original dish places chicken members (legs and wings), bones still intact, on top of the breast meat. Our guests prefer to have the bones removed for eating convenience.

Chiquart's recipe for *Soupe jacobine* affords us a glimpse of the quantities that, as chief cook of the Duke of Savoy, he felt were appropriate if he were preparing this dish for a banquet. Of the poultry, one needed between 100 and 200 fattened capons, and, for the slices of toast that would make up the base of each serving—properly the "sops"—between 200 and 300 loaves of table bread!

---

* The political society also called the Jacobins that was formed at the time of the French Revolution was so called because *they* regularly met in a building that belonged to the Dominican order.

† A poem that was current at the time makes the reputations of the various religious orders surprisingly clear—at least in the matter of bibulousness!

> To drink as the Capucins is to drink but poorly;
> To drink as the Celestines is to quaff amply;
> To drink as the Dominicans is to gulp by the pint;
> But to drink as the Franciscans is to empty the whole cellar.

There was undoubtedly a popular explanation just why the Dominicans could be out-guzzled by the mendicant Franciscans. It is perhaps not too surprising that there are no medieval French recipes bearing a reference to that latter order.

Yield: As a soup course, serves 6–8; as appetizers, 35–40 small pieces

Imperial	Ingredient	Metric	Directions
2 1/2–3 lb.	roasted chicken	1–1 1/2 kg	**Pick the meat from the bones & tear into strips, separating the dark meat from the breast meat.**
4–5	beef soup-bones (*or* combination of beef & lamb soup-bones)	4–5	**Combine water *or* bouillon, & bones.**
4 cups	water *or, preferably,* beef bouillon	1 litre	
	a bouquet garni (of sprigs of parsley, thyme, marjoram & hyssop) *or*		**Combine herbs in soup pot. Bring to a boil, then simmer. Taste; add more herbs if desired. Keep bouillon warm.**
3 tsp.	dried parsley flakes	15 ml	
2 tsp.	thyme	10 ml	
2 tsp	marjoram	10 ml	
1 tsp.	hyssop	5 ml	
8 oz.	Brie cheese	250 g	**Peel & discard Brie crust;* cut cheese into small pieces.**
6–8	slices of toasted bread	6–8	
			To assemble: lay pieces of toast on bottom of a flat, wide-brimmed soup bowl. Distribute cheese, then white meat and dark meat evenly on top of toast. Remove bones from bouillon. Pour bouillon over "sops," decorate with parsley sprig, and serve.

Variation

This recipe makes a very attractive and tasty appetizer or fondue dish. Spread the Brie cheese on finger-sized strips of toast. Top with strips of breast meat, then dark meat, and a sprig of parsley. Cut the bouillon recipe in half and serve it in a chafing dish or fondue pot. Let your guests serve themselves by dipping the strips into the bouillon.

---

* These peeled cheese crusts may be used in the recipe, if you wish. Chop and spread them on the toast before placing the first layer of cheese pieces.

3. *Souppe despourveue* / Quick Soups
(*Menagier de Paris*, pp. 145–46/§57)

This section in the *Menagier* presents a series of ideas for "short-notice" sops, simple supper dishes that any cook can throw together when company just happens to drop in unannounced. It seems enough here to print only a translation of the original text without converting each one to a modern recipe. In most cases a recipe is apt to be much longer than the text itself.

The modern cook should always keep in mind the meaning of the medieval dish called *souppe*. In every instance here, whether expressly mentioned or not, the *Menagier* intends that a chunk of bread or toast—the *sop* proper—should accompany the liquid mixture with which the recipe is alone concerned.

a. *Percil* / Parsley

Get parsley and fry it in butter, then pour boiling water on it and let it boil adding salt; then make up your sops as for a puree.

b. *Beuf froit* / Cold Beef

If you have any cold beef, cut it very thin; then grind a little bread soaked in verjuice and strain it onto a plate, and spice powder over top; heat over coals. It is good for three people. [The *Menagier* makes no mention of a liquid here; beef bouillon would be appropriate.]

c. *Poisson* / Fish

On a fish day, simmer water with almonds in it, then shell the almonds, grind them and dilute them with warm water, strain and set them to boil with ginger powder and saffron; serve it in bowls, and in each one put a piece of fried fish.

d. *Chaudeau de la char* / Meat Bouillon

On a meat day, get meat bouillon; take bread soaked in lean meat bouillon and grind it together with six eggs; then strain that, and put it into a pot with fat bouillon, spices, verjuice, vinegar and saffron; bring it to a boil, and serve it in bowls.

e. *A jour de poisson* / For Fish Days

On a fish day, grind up bread and moisten it with water, verjuice and vinegar, and set it on the fire; when it simmers, take it down off the fire and add egg yolks; then put it back to heat over a low fire until it boils; add in spice powder. And make your sops.

f. *Lart et maquerel fraiz* / Fish and Bacon

Boil a little fat pork in a pot, and when it has half cooked get a fresh mackerel, slice it crosswise and set the slices to cook with the pork; then remove everything; set some chopped parsley to boil briefly. And serve it.

Other Possible Soups

Puree de poys / Pea Puree

A recipe for this very common *Puree de poys*, provided by Master Chiquart in the *Du fait de cuisine*, is offered in Chapter 1 (above, p. 63) among those staple preparations that the professional cook—and probably even the apprentice cook—would have made up without having to think too much about them at all.

A puree of peas was normally prepared in medieval French kitchens as a sort of stock to be drawn upon as the need arose, and particularly as a base in sauces for meatless days. There seems to be no good reason, though, why such a tasty dish should not be used on its own, as a soup.

Syseros / Chickpea Puree

For the complete recipe of this dish as an Appetizer, see p. 77, above.
Use only the broth of this dish.

Porriaux blancs / Almond-Leek Sauce

For the complete recipe of this dish as a Sauce, see p. 132, below.

Equally adaptable as a delicious soup is another dish of Master Chiquart known as *Pors blancs*. While this is normally prepared and served as a sauce for meat, it can be prepared as a very satisfying soup merely by increasing the liquid ingredient, the meat bouillon, a little. When serving, each bowl can be garnished with a few toasted, slivered almonds.

Calimafree ou Saulse paresseuse / Lazy Sauce

For the complete recipe of this dish as a Sauce, see p. 134, below.

Civé d'oeufz (Souppe en moustarde) / Mustard Egg Sops

For the complete recipe of this dish as an Egg Dish, see p. 247, below.
Use the broth portion (the *Souppe en moustarde*) alone of this preparation.

Chapter 4
Sauces

Unboiled Sauces

1. *Cameline* / Cameline Sauce
2. *Aulx camelins* / Cameline Garlic Sauce
3. *Saulce verte* / Green Ginger Sauce
4. *Aulx blans* / White Garlic Sauce
5. *Aulx vers* / Green Garlic Sauce

Boiled Sauces

6. *Une jensse* / Jance Sauce
7. *Jance de gingembre* / Boiled Ginger Jance
8. *Jance aux aulx* / Boiled Garlic Jance
9. *Jance de lait de vache* / Cow's Milk Jance
10. *Poivre noir* / Black Pepper Sauce
11. *Saupiquet* / Saupiquet Sauce
12. *Moust pour hetoudeaulx* / Must Sauce for Young Chicken
13. *Porriaux blancs* / Almond-Leek Sauce
14. *Calimafree, ou Saulse paresseuse* / Lazy Sauce
15. *Une poitevine* / A Poitevine Sauce
16. *Saulse cameline a la guise de Tournay* / Tournai Cameline Sauce
17. *Broet camelin* / Cameline Broth or Sauce
18. *Broet georgé sur poysson frit* / Georgé Broth or Sauce
19. *Marjoliaine* / Marjoram Sauce
20. *Calaminee* / Calaminee Sauce

Froide sauge / Cold Sage Sauce : see additions to the recipe, Chapter 6,
   Poultry Dishes
Rissoles a jour de poisson / Fruit Rissoles (filling) : see Chapter 10, Desserts
Emplumeus de pomes / Almond Applesauce : see Chapter 10, Desserts

Chapter 4
Sauces

Nowadays a sauce is considered to be integral to the nature of a dish. A dish can succeed or fail merely on a nuance in the flavor of its sauce, and some cooks have become renowned primarily for their skill at elaborating exceptionally fine sauces. It was not always so.

Early cooks accepted that sauces were first invented in prehistoric times in order to stimulate the appetite. With the advent of learned Greek and Arabic medicine, however, and with increased knowledge about the physical properties of all things, sauces gradually became recognized as the principal means by which the natural properties of foodstuffs could effectively be altered. In the later Middle Ages the making of sauces and the use of them in dishes was clearly a matter based upon scientific principles. Just as the manner of cooking a meat changed its inherent characteristics, its warmth or coldness, its dryness or moisture, so the use of a sauce allowed a further modification of these characteristics. By carefully mixing another foodstuff with a liquid (vinegar, for instance, or almond milk), or with a spice or an herb—each of which ingredients had its own peculiar qualities—a cook could design exactly the sauce that was necessary for his meat. By bringing about an intimate contact of such a cleverly composed sauce with the meat, a cook could, as it were, fine-tune any changes he thought it might be advisable to effect in the temperament of the meat or or any other principal foodstuff in a dish, whether during or after its cooking. In this way any undesirable or dangerous properties in the principal foodstuff could be checked or even substantially modified. Eaten with the right sauce even the most suspect food could be rendered relatively safe.

The trick for the medieval cook was, of course, to know what was the right sauce, that is, what foods required what sauces, and how those sauces should be composed. For this the cook had to know the temperamental qualities of absolutely everything he handled, and to be familiar with all of the ways in which he could use the various liquids, herbs and spices that he had at his disposal. From them he could make basting sauces, cooking sauces, serving sauces and dipping sauces. A good number of handbooks existed to advise him what the learned physicians of the past had determined concerning the properties of all foodstuffs.

In choosing or in elaborating a sauce a cook accepted an enormously serious responsibility. At this time an ignorance of the humoral complexion of any ingredient could easily lead to a charge of inadvertently undermining someone's health, or even of murder. A cook's job was in many respects an offshoot of that of a physician; he had almost as much responsibility.

When we taste medieval dishes that incorporate a sauce of some sort, it is very easy to forget just why this sauce was ever invented and what it was intended to do. Medieval cooks worked out a very wide variety of sauces, making quite delicious use in one way or another of practically all of the herbs and spices they had in their pantries. Some sauces are thick and opaque, some are thin and runny, some hot, some cold, some very nippy with spices, some remarkably delicate and bland. Most medieval cooks would undoubtedly tell you that any given sauce had a specific range of uses: its ingredients made it specifically suitable for only certain foods that had undergone only certain cooking preparations.

In most cases we can quite cheerfully ignore the reasoning that went into this logical system of proper combinations of foodstuffs. In a sense we are very much richer in that we can combine foods and sauces on the same plate in a way that might have made a medieval cook shudder. On the other hand we should not feel guilty about such experimentation: it was after all largely by trial and error that most things were eventually understood in the Middle Ages. It was by giving the people at the dining table over the years a chance to choose among several logically feasible sauces and sauce combinations that medieval cooks also allowed a "medieval taste," a sense of gastronomic pleasure, to develop. Today we can still have a lot of pleasure out of making combinations that *even* the medieval cook might not have thought of.

The recipe collections provide lengthy catalogues of meat, fish, poultry and game meat with the boiled or unboiled sauces appropriate for each. The following list sets out some of these.

Meats (normally roasted)

Pork	Verjuice, *or* onions, wine & verjuice
Veal	Cameline Sauce
Mutton	Fine salt, *or* Cameline Sauce, *or* verjuice
Goat, kid *or* lamb	Cameline Sauce
Goose	White *or* Green Garlic Sauce, *or* Black *or* Yellow Pepper Sauce
Chicken	Cameline Sauce, Green Verjuice, Grape Mash *or* Cold Sage Sauce
Capons	Must Sauce
Rabbits & hares	Cameline Sauce *or* Saupiquet
Partridge & pheasant	Fine salt

Fish

Anchovies	Parsley, onions & vinegar, with spice powder on top
Herrings	Garlic Sauce
Lobster	Vinegar
Pickerel *or* pollack	Green Sorrel Verjuice, with white almond sops
Rayfish	Cameline Garlic Sauce, made with ray liver
Salmon	Cameline Sauce
Sole	Sorrel Verjuice with Orange Juice
Turbot	Green Sauce

In the pages below we offer an assortment of the more common, "standard" sauces, of both the unboiled (cold) and boiled (hot) varieties, as well as other slightly more complex sauces that are specific to particular dishes. You may wish to try them on plain boiled or roast meats or fish following (more or less) the outline that is tabled above. We have occasionally prepared a very interesting reception buffet consisting of six or eight of the more common sauces, presented in bowls, with a variety of nibbles (cubes or triangles of breads and meats) for dipping—a sort of medieval sampler. You should keep in mind, too, that alternative ways often existed to prepare a good many of these sauces, so that a given sauce is not limited to being used merely as a sauce: with a few suitable variations it can become, for instance, a vegetable dish.

Our choice of the quantities of spices and other ingredients in these sauces is more or less arbitrary. In most cases the guiding influence in determining the relative quantities of the various ingredients has been simply our own taste buds. You should feel free to experiment with quantities that will produce a taste you find pleasing.

Capiteles d'aus / Garlic
(Aldobrandino, *Le regime du corps*, p. 162)

Garlic is warm and dry at the beginning of the fourth degree. There are two varieties of it: wild and domestic.

Wild garlic is warmer and drier, but the domestic sort that we eat eliminates flatulence, slakes thirst and makes a man lustful. It is harmful when eaten by those who are of a warm nature because its own nature engenders warm humors and gives headaches. But when garlic is cooked and held in the mouth it assuages toothache, but it diminishes the sight and attracts bad humors to the eyes; it clears the voice, and eliminates a chronic cough brought on by cold, gross humors.

Moreover, by its nature garlic stirs an appetite to eat, is useful against the bite of a poisonous animal, and counters the harmfulness of any foods bearing poisonous humors; for these reasons it is called "the peasant's theriac."*

---

* The medieval theriac was a highly complex compound of up to 70 drugs, pulverized and mixed, normally with honey, into an electuary. In particular it seems that it was universally valued as an antidote to the poison in the bite of venomous animals. Interestingly, with some semantic shift the Old French term for theriac, *triacle*, which we read here in Aldobrandino's text, became the modern English word *treacle*.

Unboiled Sauces

1. *Cameline*
(*Du fait de cuisine*, §44)

Pour le saumon et pour la troycte, la cameline: pour donner entendement ou saulcier qui la fera, prennez son pain blanc selonc la quantité qu'il en fera et mecte roustir tresbien sur le gril, et qu'il haye de bon vin claret du meilleur qu'il pourra avoir ouquel mecte son pain tremper et du vin aigre par bonne mesure; et prenne ses espices, c'est assavoir cynamomy, gingibre, granne, giroffle, du poyvre et pou, macys, nois muscates et ung pou de succre, et cela mesler avecques son pain et ung pou de sel; et puis en drecés a vostre vouloir.

The *Viandier* (§155) also has a similar recipe for *Cameline*:

Prenez gingenbre, canelle et grant foison, girofle, grainne de paradiz, mastic, poivre long qui veult; puis coullez pain trempé en vin aigre, et passez, et sallez bien a point.

Capiteles de canele / Cinnamon
(Aldobrandino, *Le regime du corps*, p. 184)

Cinnamon is warm and dry in the second degree; there are two varieties of it, crude and fine. The crude sort is not so warm.

Cinnamon is the bark of trees that grow in India. It should be selected such that it is reddish and neither white nor black, and it should be tested in the mouth: if it has a tang and is not sweet, it is good. It can be kept twenty years, but it should not be put in too bright nor too dry a place.

By its nature it strengthens the faculties of the liver and the stomach; and in any sickness caused by cold humors that incapacitate digestion, powdered cinnamon mixed with powdered caraway is useful; it is also useful in sauces made with parsley, sage and vinegar, for such sauces stimulate the appetite. It comforts the brain and purifies the breath.

The gross sort of cinnamon is not as good or as useful for those things of which we have spoken as is the fine sort.

Garde toy bien de conseiller a table, ne de sommeiller.	Two things at table are not nice: to slumber, and to give advice.

1. Cameline Sauce

Among the standard sauces that virtually any European cook, or young housewife, mastered very early, the most commonly used was probably Cameline. Perhaps surprisingly, the name of this sauce actually does derive from what one might guess, and that is the word "camel": it is *not*, however, the smell of the camel that inspired the name but rather its color, since the cinnamon gives a characteristically brownish hue to the sauce. The sauce and its name may have originated in North Africa; some scribes, unfamiliar with the exotic camel, understood the name to reflect its principal ingredient, cinnamon (in French: *cannelle*), and consequently wrote the name of the sauce as if it were "cannelline."

Cameline Sauce is primarily an unboiled cinnamon sauce, the most common in the standard category of unboiled sauces. However, while cinnamon was the necessary foundation of Cameline and this spice always predominated no matter what the other ingredients may have been, some leeway developed allowing variations on a basic, elemental cinnamon sauce. The nature of the variations to which Cameline gave rise depended largely upon the additional ingredients that might be incorporated and upon their relative strength. Some varieties of Cameline Sauce (such as the so-called Tournai Cameline, p. 136, and the Cameline Broth, p. 138) were heated and served warm.

The *Viandier* adds salt at the end of his recipe for Cameline Sauce: *"Sallez bien a point —* Salt carefully." Chiquart specifies that only the best claret wine be used in this recipe. Claret was the name given by the English in the Middle Ages to a small territory within what is today the Bordeaux region, and the name generally designated the variety of particularly clear, light wine that was produced there. A light red wine is appropriate in this recipe.

Yield: About 4 tbsp/60 mL of sauce

Imperial	Ingredient	Metric	Directions
1/2 slice	white bread, toasted	1/2 slice	**Soak toast in wine & vinegar.**
3 tbsp	red wine	50 mL	
2 tbsp	red wine vinegar	30 mL	
2 tsp*	cinnamon	10 mL*	**Combine & add spices, & mix well us-**
1/2 tsp	ground ginger	2 mL	**ing a mortar & pestle.†**
pinch	grains of paradise	pinch	
pinch	cloves	pinch	
pinch	nutmeg	pinch	
a few grains	pepper	a few grains	
	salt		**Strain & taste. If too thick, add more wine. Correct spices & add salt to taste.**

---

* Use more cinnamon than this, if desired.

† With all four uncooked sauces a blender or food processor may be used. Take care to use only on pulse or on/off for a few seconds, or else a glutenous mass will result.

2. *Aulx camelins*
(*Viandier*, §156)

Broyez aulx, canelle et pain, et deffaictes de vin aigre.

Variant:

Broyés cannelle, pain et haulx; deffaicte de vin aigre et de verjus; et y broyés du foye de la roye avec.

2. Cameline Garlic Sauce

Both the *Viandier* and Chiquart recommend this sauce as a dressing for fish. Chiquart specifies that the sauce *aux aulx camellins* be served on ray fish and that it be made *es amendres et de son feie*— "with almonds and with the liver of the ray fish."

Even though the use of ray fish liver is confirmed by two of the *Viandier*'s manuscripts, we have omitted it in our adaptation. On the other hand, the verjuice listed in the variant recipes adds such a delightful hint of piquancy to the garlic and the cinnamon that we have decided to approximate it with a little wine and lemon juice.

Yield: About 4 tbsp/60 mL of sauce

Imperial	Ingredient	Metric	Directions
2 tbsp	soft breadcrumbs*	30 mL	**Combine breadcrumbs, wine, vinegar**
3 tbsp	red wine	50 mL	**& lemon juice.**
2 tbsp	red wine vinegar	30 mL	
1tsp	lemon juice	5 mL	
1 clove†	garlic (chopped *or* crushed fine)	1 clove†	**Combine garlic & cinnamon. Mix well with bread & wine mixture using a**
1 1/2 tsp	ground cinnamon	7 mL	**mortar & pestle.‡**
			Taste; correct spices. If too thick, add more wine.
			Strain through a sieve & serve.

---

* This is about half a slice of bread. Alternatively, you may choose to use 2 tbsp/30 mL of ground almonds.

† Use more garlic than a single clove if you wish to make sure that the people eating this Garlic Cameline Sauce understand what distinguishes it from other varieties of Cameline Sauce!

‡ See the note (†) on the previous page.

3. *Saulce verte*
(*Viandier*, §161; *Menagier de Paris*, p. 231/§276)

Grant foison de percil esfeulié sans lez tigez, gingenbre pelé, du pain blanc sans haler, broiez; destrempez de verjus et de vinaigre et collez.

3. Green Ginger Sauce

This is the first of the ginger sauces in the *Viandier*, and it is unboiled. The rest of the ginger sauces, normally given the generic name of *jance*, are boiled. This Green Ginger Sauce seems to have been used primarily on boiled fresh fish.

It may be noted in passing that one version of the *Viandier* insists that the taste of the vinegar should predominate over that of the verjuice.

Yield: About 4 tbsp/60 mL of sauce

Imperial	Ingredient	Metric	Directions
2 tbsp	soft white breadcrumbs	30 mL	**Soak breadcrumbs in vinegar, lemon**
3 tbsp	white wine vinegar	50 mL	**juice & wine.**
1 tbsp	lemon juice	15 mL	
1 tbsp	white wine	15 mL	
1/2 cup	chopped fresh parsley leaves*	125 mL	**Add parsley & ginger, grind in a mor-**
2 tsp	ground ginger	10 mL	**tar & pestle.†**
			Taste; add more ginger if desired.
			Strain & serve.

Variation

In the paragraph dealing with this Green Ginger Sauce, the *Menagier* (p. 231/§276) suggests that parsley, avens, sorrel or marjoram, or any one or two of these four, may be used to provide a adequate intensity of green color. He notes also that some people choose to use only fresh rosemary leaves. His basic recipe for Green Ginger Sauce differs from that of the *Viandier* in the inclusion of cloves and grains of paradise among its ingredients.

---

* One of the manuscript versions of the *Viandier* includes sage among the ingredients of this sauce. If desired, add in 1 tsp/5 mL of ground sage *or* 2 tsp/10 mL fresh chopped sage.

† See the note (†) on p. 116.

4. *Aulx blans*

(*Viandier*, §157)

Broyez aulx et pain et deffaittes de verjus.

5. *Aulx vers*

(*Viandier*, §158; *Menagier de Paris*, p. 231/§274)

Broiés aux et pain et verdeure, deffaites de verjus.

Variant:

Broyés pain, haulx, parressi, gigimbre; destramper de verjus.

Alea / Garlic
(*Tacuinum sanitatis*, Vienna,
Oesterreichische Nationalbibliothek, Codex Vindobonensis, 2644, f. 26r)

When selecting garlic in the garden, choose that which is moderately pungent. It generates thick, strong humors and is suited to those with cold temperaments, the elderly and the very old, and those dwelling in mountainous regions or in the north. It has many advantages: it is effective against cold poisons and the bites of scorpions and adders; it kills worms, clears the voice and soothes chronic cough. It can damage the eyes and brain; to avoid or remedy this effect, take vinegar and oil. Ground in a mortar with black olives, as the Greeks do, garlic is useful for those who suffer from dropsy.

Et se tu es servy de nois,	And if the nut bowl comes to thee,
n'en mengeüe que deux ou troys.	take only two, or at most three.

4. White Garlic Sauce

Clearly this is a simple mixture, a basic general-purpose garlic sauce.

Yield: About 3–4 tbsp/45–60 mL of sauce

Imperial	Ingredient	Metric	**Directions**
2	cloves garlic (crushed)	2	**Combine all ingredients by grinding in**
2 tbsp*	white breadcrumbs	30 mL*	**a mortar & pestle.†**
2 tbsp	white wine vinegar	30 mL	**Strain through sieve & serve.**
2 tbsp	lemon juice	30 mL	

Variation

5. Green Garlic Sauce

Green Garlic Sauce is a particularly tasty variation on the "plain" White Garlic Sauce, and is suitable for use as an appetizer along with sops made of *crudités* or pita triangles. The *Viandier* and the *Du fait de cuisine* call for it when serving goslings, beef and eels.

Add 2 tbsp/30 mL of chopped greenery to the recipe for White Garlic Sauce (above). The addition of a small amount of ginger, 1/2 tsp/5 mL of ground ginger, as specified by a manuscript variant of the *Viandier* will lend this sauce a little of the nature of the Jances.

For the green color, essential to this sauce, two of the manuscripts of the *Viandier* suggest the use of parsley among the ingredients here, while the other two manuscripts call simply—and perhaps a little vaguely, we may feel—for *verdure*, that is to say, "greenery." According to the *Menagier de Paris* (p. 231/§274) this greenery could be parsley, sorrel or rosemary, either singly or in combination. Should you want a further option for a green coloring agent, you might consider sage. The most influential medical handbook of the Middle Ages, the *Regimen Sanitatis Salernitanum*, indicates that sage can be used to produce a Green Garlic Sauce in which the bite of the garlic will be somewhat tempered.

According to the learned physician who composed a Commentary to the *Regimen Sanitatis Salernitanum*, Green Garlic Sauce is used on roast goose—although he snobbishly notes that it is normally so used only among the "common" people. After trying this combination you may be inclined to agree with us that, in this practice at least, the "common" people had quite good taste!

---

* This is about one-half a slice of bread.

† See the note (†) on p. 116.

Boiled Sauces

6. *Une jensse*
(*Du fait de cuisine*, §58)

Pour donner entendement a celluy qui fera ledit jensse si prenne de beau et bon pain de bouche grant quantité selon ce qui en vouldra fayre et si le gratuse bien et appoint sur ung beaul mantil; puis prenne une oulle belle clere et necte et coulle dedans du boullon gras du beuf et du mouston, et advise qu'il ne soit tropt salé; et puis prenne des oefs et mesle avecques ledit pain et puis cela mecte dedans ledit boullon doulcement en menant tousjours a une belle cuillier de bois; et aussy mecte ses espices dedans, c'est assavoir gingibre blanc, grane de paradis, et ung pou de poyvre, et du saffran pour luy donner couleur, et si l'agouste de verjust; et si face tout ce boullir ensemble et puis en drece.

Capiteles de gyngembre / Ginger
(Aldobrandino, *Le regime du corps*, p. 184)

Ginger is warm in the third degree and moist, although it does not seem to me to be very much so. It has the quality of strengthening a cold stomach and of softening the belly, and makes food digest well. It should be chosen white, hard and fresh.

Jance Sauces in General

The most important of the warm (boiled) sauces in the late Middle Ages were the Jances. The ingredient common to all of the Jances, and the ingredient from which the name of the sauce may have come, is ginger. As with the Cameline Sauces, there is no general agreement among cooks of different times and different places as to the composition of the basic Jance Sauce—except, of course, that it is a fairly simple mixture in which the flavor of ginger must predominate. And in most recipe collections the various basic mixtures for Jance gave rise to a number of variations according to the presence and relative importance of any secondary ingredients.

6. Jance Sauce

Chiquart's *Du fait de cuisine* offers as delicious a "basic Jance" as any of the early French collections. Though he (and other cooks of the time) include a few spices in addition to the essential ginger, these spices should always be in very modest quantities and should be present only to enhance—as Chiquart's grains of paradise will do—the fundamental gingery nature of this warm sauce. Any additional ingredients in a Jance should never be allowed to detract from the predominant ginger tang.

Yield: About 1 cup/250 mL of sauce

Imperial	Ingredient	Metric	Directions
3/4–1 cup	meat broth	175–250 mL	**Heat broth in a sauce pot.**
1	egg (lightly beaten)	1	**Stir in a small amount of hot bouillon with the egg, then add mixture to remaining bouillon.**
1–2 tbsp*	grated gingerroot (*or* 2 tsp/10 mL ground ginger)	15–30 mL*	**Combine spices & stir in. Tear bread into small pieces; whisk into broth.**
pinch	grains of paradise	pinch	**Cook, stirring continuously until slightly thickened.**
pinch	pepper	pinch	
pinch	saffron (*optional*)	pinch	
1 slice	bread	1 slice	
1–2 tbsp	lemon juice	15–30 mL	**Stir in 1 tbsp/15 mL lemon juice. If sharper taste is desired, add a second tbsp/15 mL lemon juice. Taste. Add more ginger if desired. Serve warm.**

---

* More ginger can always be used if a stronger flavor is desired.

7. *Jance de gingembre*
(*Viandier*, §168)

Prennés gingembre et almendes sans aux et deffaites de verjus, puis boullez; et aucuns y metent du vin blanc.

7. Boiled Ginger Jance

While the *Menagier* (p. 234/§288) uses a combination of almonds and breadcrumbs as a thickener for this simple ginger sauce, the *Viandier* is content to rely upon almonds alone. For some strange reason the *Menagier* includes garlic as well—an unnecessary addition since he had just copied a recipe for Garlic Jance Sauce in his book; this is the same recipe, incidentally, that was already copied in the *Viandier* (see our version of this Boiled Garlic Jance below, p. 124).

Yield: About 1/2 cup/125 mL of sauce

Imperial	Ingredient	Metric	Directions
2 tbsp	ground almonds	30 mL	**Combine almonds & ginger in sauce-**
2 tsp	ginger	10 mL	**pot.**
1/2 cup	white wine	125 mL	**Whisk in wine. Bring to a boil, then**
1–2 tbsp	lemon juice	15–30 mL	**simmer while stirring until thickened to desired consistency.**
			Stir in lemon juice. Taste; increase ginger if desired. Strain *or* blend in blender. Serve warm.

8. *Jance aux aulx*
(*Du fait de cuisine*, §43; *Viandier*, §167; *Menagier*, p. 234/§287)

La salce de l'oyson et chappon de paillier, la jance: et pour donner entendement a cellui qui fera ladicte jance si prenne ses amandres selon la quantité qu'il en vouldra faire, si les plume tresbien et nectement et si les mecte au mortier broyer tresbien nectement; et selon la quantité de ladicte saulcerie si plume des aulx selon ce qu'il en fera besoing, et qu'il n'en y mecte pas tropt; et si prenne bon vin blan et le verjust, de gingibre blanc, de granne de paradix et si la coule tout ensemble et mecte du sel dedans, et non pas tropt, et puis mectés la boullir en une belle et necte olle; et puis en drece pour servir avecques lediz pastel.

8. Boiled Garlic Jance

Similar recipes appear in the three recipe collections, although Chiquart adds a few grains of paradise (reinforcing the ginger tang a little), and salt to taste.

Yield: About 1/2 cup/125 mL of sauce

Imperial	Ingredient	Metric	**Directions**
2 tbsp	ground almonds	30 mL	**Combine almonds, ginger & garlic in**
1 1/2 tsp	ground ginger	7 mL	**saucepot.**
2 cloves	garlic (crushed)	2 cloves	
1/2 c+2 tbsp	white wine	155 mL	**Whisk in wine. Bring to a boil, then**
to taste	salt	to taste	**simmer while stirring for 2–3 min.**
a few grains	grains of paradise	a few grains	**Stir in salt, grains of paradise &**
1–2 tbsp	lemon juice	15–30 mL	**lemon juice.**
			Taste; add more ginger if desired. Strain (*or* blend in blender).
			Serve warm.

9. *Jance de lait de vache*
(*Menagier*, p. 234/§286; *Viandier*, §166)

Broyez gingembre, moyeuz d'oeufz sans la germe, et soient cruz, passez par l'estamine avec lait de vache (ou pour paour de tourner soient les moyeuz cuiz, puis broyez et passez par l'estamine), deffaictes de lait de vache et faictes bien boulir.

9. Cow's Milk Jance

Though an interesting variant upon the basic Jance, this is still a simple mixture, though nonetheless flavorful.

Yield: About 1 cup/250 mL of sauce

Imperial	Ingredient	Metric	Directions
3/4 cup	milk	175 mL	**Scald milk in a pot.**
2	egg yolks (lightly beaten)*	2	**Stir a little hot milk into lightly beaten egg yolks.**
			Add this mixture to the pot of milk.
1 tbsp	ground ginger	15 mL	**Stir in ginger. Cook, stirring continuously until slightly thickened.**
			Serve warm.

S'on sert de fruit devant lever, n'en mengeüe point sans le laver.	If fruit is served before meal's end, to wash it well always attend.

---

* The *Menagier de Paris* uses hard-boiled egg yolks here, which he passes through a sieve.

10. *Poivre noir*
(*Menagier de Paris*, p. 233/§14; also *Viandier*, §165)

Prenez clou de giroffle et ung pou de poivre, gingembre, et broyez tresbien. Puis broyez pain ars, trempé en meigre aue de char, ou en meigre eaue de chouls qui mieulx vault. Puis soit bouly en une paelle de fer, et au boulir soit mis du vinaigre. Puis mectez en ung pot au feu pour tenir chault. *Item*, pluseurs y mectent de la canelle.

Capiteles du poivres / Pepper
(Aldobrandino, *Le regime du corps*, p. 184)

Pepper is warm in the fourth degree; by its nature it strengthens a cold stomach and destroys cold, viscous humors. It should not be used by those who are of a warm nature or who have a warm temperament, especially in summer.

White pepper is of the same nature as black pepper, but it is not so warm.*

10. Black Pepper Sauce

Of all of the sauces current in medieval European cookery the one that is made from ordinary black pepper was undoubtedly the most common. For a very long time in kitchens and on dining tables from Germany to Portugal it held sway over any other condiment or dressing. Pepper ruled the spice rack; the word pepper was almost synonymous with that of sauce.

During the period from 1394 to 1405 pepper by itself accounted for an average of 75 percent of the Venetian spice trade for all of Europe. It was an expensive commodity, but no more expensive than other imported spices; as a matter of fact and significantly pepper was one of the least expensive spices and benefitted from a relatively stable price. What this stability of price indicates is, firstly, that the large quantities of pepper imported were destined for the markets of people of more or less ordinary means, the "commoners" of society; and, secondly, that by the end of the Middle Ages the importers of pepper were probably able to satisfy the demand for this exotic spice.

This is a curiosity of the medieval use of pepper: its curve of popularity declined as the Middle Ages came to a close. The growing "disaffection" for pepper is first apparent in aristocratic circles as the fourteenth century advances, and then in the overall volumes of the commodity that are

---

* It was early believed by learned Europeans that black pepper had acquired its darker color be being more exposed to the sun; as a consequence, and as Aldobrandino and other physicians and scholars regularly indicate, black pepper possessed a naturally warmer complexion than white pepper.

imported into Europe. Most interestingly we may trace in successive versions of the *Viandier* how that spice is progressively displaced by grains of paradise. It seems that as soon as aristocratic gastronomes identified the taste for pepper as being common, even vulgar, it became necessary for them to distance themselves from its use. And as aristocratic taste changed at the beginning of the fifteenth century, so eventually did popular taste. Eventually pepper lost its preeminent position as a condiment in French cuisine, entering into an eclipse that lasted right down until the seventeenth century.

The *Viandier*'s recipe for Black Pepper Sauce is the more elementary version of the two we are following here. He simply boils together ground ginger and black peppercorns with verjuice and vinegar; the *Menagier*'s directions are more specific and provide alternative ingredients. The *Menagier* omits ginger and verjuice, but adds instead cloves and a bouillon produced by the cooking of either meat or cabbage; he makes cinnamon optional.

To provide an alternative to the many spiced dishes containing the ubiquitous compound of cinnamon-ginger-cloves—*the* commonplace spice blend of the French Middle Ages—we have chosen the simpler mixture of pepper and ginger boiled in a beef bouillon. You may, of course, choose a different combination of spices, depending upon the complexity of the menu you are working on.

Yield: About 3/4 to 1 cup/175–250 mL of sauce

Imperial	Ingredient	Metric	Directions
1 1/4 cup	beef bouillon	310 mL	**Bring bouillon to a boil. Stir in ginger.**
1 tsp	ground ginger*	5 mL	**Cook, reducing quantity by about 1/4.**
5–6	crushed black peppercorns	5–6	**Whisk in peppercorns & breadcrumbs.**
2 tsp	toasted breadcrumbs	10 mL	**Simmer until desired consistency is reached.**
1 tsp	lemon juice	5 mL	**Stir in lemon juice & vinegar. Taste;**
2 tsp	red wine vinegar	10 mL	**correct spices as desired. Strain, pressing well.**
			Serve warm.

---

* Alternatively, use 2 tsp/10 mL of grated gingerroot. If you wish to experiment, rather than ginger, try cloves, or cinnamon, or a combination of any of the three.

11. *Saupiquet*
(*Du fait de cuisine*, §14)

Pour le fait du saupiquet pour mectre sur le conin, selon la quantité que l'on en fera prennés deux onnions et les taillés prin, et prennés de bel lart de porc et fondre et souffrire vostre onnions, et pource que il ne se crement en suffrizant si mectés en ung pou de boullon dedans; et puis y mectés du vin blanc a grant foyson selon la quantité du saupiquet que vouldré faire pour lesdistz connins; et prennés vostres espices, bon gingibre, granne, ung pou de poyvre qui ne passe point, et du saffran pour luy donner couleur; et aguste le de vin aigre si pour mesure qu'il ne soit pas tropt poingnant ne pou; de sel aussy.

Saupiquet
(*Viandier*, §41)

Lyevres en rost. ... Le mengez a la cameline, ou au saupiquet, c'est assavoir en la gresse qui en chiet en la lechefricte, et y mettez des ongnons menuz coppez, du vin et du verjus et ung pou de vinaigre, et le gectez sur le lievre quant il sera rosti, ou mettez par escuelles.

Saupiquet
(*Menagier*, p. 233/§284)

Le saupiquet pour connin, ou pour oiseau de riviere, ou coulon ramier. Frisiez ongnons et bon sain; ou vous les mincez et mectez cuire en la leschefricte avec eaue de beuf; et n'y mectez vertjus ne vinaigre jusques au boulir, et lors mectez moictié vertjus moictié vin et ung petit de vinaigre, et que les espices passent. Puis prenez moictié vin moictié vertjus et ung petit de vinaigre et mectez tout en la leschefricte dessoubz le connin, coulon ou oisel de riviere. Et quant ilz seront cuiz, si boulez la saulse, et ayez des tostees et mectez dedens avec l'oisel.

Acetum / Vinegar
(*Tacuinum sanitatis*, Vienna,
Oesterreichische Nationalbibliothek, Codex Vindobonensis, 2644, f. 85v)

Vinegar is by nature cold and therefore constricts and chills the body, but the very perceptive Galen maintains that it has opposing qualities—making it a so-called "mixed" substance—that incorporate both warm and cold, both to a temperate degree but with the cold predominating. The best vinegar should be made from strong wine and kept in barrels. It is useful in curbing excessive bile, it soothes the gums and stimulates the appetite. When boiled, vinegar yields vapors that are useful in treating dropsy, and relieve deafness and whistling in the ears; when distilled, it kills worms; taken hot in the mouth, it cures toothache. It has the disadvantage of harming the nerves, which action can be neutralized with water and sugar.

11. Saupiquet Sauce

This is described in various manuscripts as a sauce appropriate for roast coney (rabbit) or for any other roast meat, for river bird or pigeon (dove). The Vatican version of the *Viandier* says that Saupiquet can be used on roast hares as an alternative to Cameline Sauce.

The three manuscript sources vary in the spices they prescribe; undefined "spices" appear in the ingredients list of the *Menagier*. Chiquart has his scribe write ginger, grains of paradise, a little saffron and salt; he stipulates the use of white wine.

Because so many of the dishes and sauces of this time use ginger, cinnamon and other spices, we have chosen to present the *Viandier* (Vatican manuscript) version of this recipe: here the sauce amounts to a simple onion/wine mixture. As the compound name suggests, the essence of the sauce is its sharp bite, the *piquant* quality it derives primarily from the vinegar in it.

Yield: About 1 1/2 cups/375 mL of sauce

Imperial	Ingredient	Metric	Directions
2 tbsp	bacon drippings *or* chicken fat	30 mL	**Melt fat in saucepan.**
2	medium onions	2	**Chop onions finely & sauté in fat until soft & golden but not brown (about 2 min.).**
1 cup	hot beef bouillon	250 mL	**Pour in bouillon. Bring to a boil, then simmer for 2–3 min.**
2–3 tbsp	white wine	30–50 mL	**Stir in wine & lemon juice. Add**
1 tbsp	lemon juice	15 mL	**vinegar in small amounts, tasting for**
about 2 tsp	vinegar	about 10 mL	**sharpness.**
			Serve warm.

Variations

1. For Chiquart's Saupiquet, add 1 tsp/5 mL of ginger, a pinch of pepper, and a pinch of grains of paradise.
2. For Saupiquet on fried fish (on lean days), follow the same general recipe (above) but fry the onions in oil, and add ginger, grains of paradise, saffron, pepper and salt—all of these spices according to your taste.

12. *Moust pour hetoudeaulx*
(*Menagier de Paris*, p. 234/§290)

Þrenez roisins nouveaulx et noirs et les escachez ou mortier et boulez ung boullon. Þuis coulez par une estamine et lors gectez dessus vostre pouldre de petit gingembre et plus de canelle, ou de canelle seulement *quia melior*, et meslez ung petit a une cuillier d'argent, et gectez croustes, ou pain broyé, ou oeufz, ou chastaignes pour lyer, dedens, du succre roux, et dreciez.

... *Item*, et qui veult faire ce moust des la saint Jehan et avant que l'en treuve aucuns roisins, faire le couvient de cerises, merises, guines, vin de meures, avec pouldre de canelle sans gingembre se petit non; boulir comme dessus, puis mectre du succre dessus.

Item, et aprés ce que l'en ne treuve nulz roisins, *scilicet* en novembre, l'en fait le moust de prunelles de haye. Ostez les noyaux, puis broyez ou escachiez ou mortier, faire boulir avec les escorches, puis passer par l'estamine, mectre la pouldre, et tout comme dessus.

Vin nouveaul / Must

Impedit urinam mustum, solvit cito ventrem,	Must interferes with urination and acts as a laxative;
epatis emfraxim splenis, generat lapidemque.	it causes stoppage of the liver and spleen, and engenders kidney stone.

[*Commentary*] In this text are listed five dangerous problems in drinking must [*i.e.*, new wine]. The first is that it inhibits and prevents urination; this inhibition and obstruction can be understood in two ways: firstly, since must is gross because its lees are mixed with it, they consequently obstruct the liver and kidneys, and urine cannot flow naturally; and secondly, they prevent normal urination but cause it to occur frequently and in small quantity ... because when the lees enter the bladder they prick and irritate it and constrain it to urinate irregularly. The second problem is that it loosens the bowels because by nature it clears the bowels and stimulates their expulsive virtue, firstly because of the sharpness of the lees, secondly owing to their flatulent nature, and thirdly by lubricating the bowels through indigestion and harming the stomach, whence the stomach is the first bowel, called *portaurium*; irritated and oppressed, it relaxes. The third problem is that must harms the good complexion of the liver through obstruction, because of the great quantity of the lees which are mixed with it and engender inflammation of the liver whereby it weakens the retentive virtue of the liver. This effect is stated by Avicenna in the third distinction of the first chapter of the regimen of wine and water. It likewise gives a person dropsy and a bad coloring. The fourth problem is that must harms the spleen for the same reason as the liver, for it stops up the spleen and makes a person splenetic. The fifth problem is that must engenders stone, especially kidney stone, which is red and easy to break, because its large size creates obstructions. Here what has to be understood is very sweet new must without biting lees, because must with biting lees preserves the stone ....

Le regime tresutile, p. 63

12. Must Sauce for Young Chicken

Must is the unfermented juice obtained from pressing grapes. It is a common ingredient in medieval cookery, although naturally enough its use is restricted to the few months in the year in which fresh grape juice is available and has not yet begun to ferment thoroughly. A very common long-lasting sauce combined must and the finely ground seed of the plant whose botanic name is *Sinapis alba*. Because of the burning bite of *Sinapis*, this sauce became known as *moust ardant*, must-ard.

The *Menagier* here specifies the juice of black (or dark) grapes. Eggs, breadcrumbs or chestnuts may be used as a thickener.

For practical reasons we suggest substituting frozen concentrated *undiluted* grape juice. (You may choose to use freshly pressed grape juice.) We prefer the egg as a thickener; you may substitute breadcrumbs or cooked, ground chestnuts. This is a moderately sweet sauce.

Yield: About 1 cup/250 mL of sauce

Imperial	Ingredient	Metric	Directions
1 cup 1/4 to 1/2 cup	grape juice concentrate water	250 mL 75–125 mL	**Combine & heat grape juice & water.**
1/2–1 tsp 1/4 tsp	ground cinnamon ground ginger	2–5 mL 1 mL	**Stir in spices. Bring to a boil, then simmer for 5 min.**
1	egg	1	**In small bowl beat egg lightly. Mix a little of the hot mixture with the beaten egg; then, while stirring, pour egg mixture in a steady stream into sauce.**
1 tbsp*	brown sugar	15 mL*	**Stir in sugar. Simmer until desired consistency is reached. Taste; correct spices as desired.** **Serve warm *or* cold.**

Serving variation

This mixture could be used as a dipping sauce for appetizers of chicken or any other meat.

---

* *Or,* to taste.

13. *Porriaux blancs*
(*Du fait de cuisine*, §16)

Pour faire faire les Porriaux blancs, si face cil qui en haura la charge qu'il hait ses porriaux, et si les trenche menuz et les lavés tresbien, et mecte boullir. Et si prenne ung bon tropt d'eschine de porc salé, et si le nectoie tresbien et mecte boullir avecques; et quant ilz seront bien boullis, si les tirés hors sur tables belles et nectes—et que ilz gardent bien le boullon en quoy ilz hauront boullir. Et que il y a une bonne morterie de amendres blanches, et puis prennés du boullon en quoy ont boullir lesditz porriaux et y traysent ses amendres (et si n'a assés dudit boullon, si prenne du boullon du beuf ou du mouston); et se garde qui ne soit tropt salé. Et puis apprés mectés vostre broet boullir en oulle belle et necte. Et puis prennés deux couteaux beaus et nectz, et chapplés vostres pourreaux; et puis les prennés et broyés au mortier; et, estre broyés, si les mectés en vostre boullon, d'amendres que eaue, mi bulli. Et, elles estre bullies, quant viendra au drecier, si mectés vostre grein en beaux plateaux, et puis dudit boullon desdiz pourreaux mectés par dessus.

Pori / Leeks
(*Tacuinum sanitatis*, Vienna,
Oesterreichische Nationalbibliothek, Codex Vindobonensis, 2644, f. 25r)

By nature leeks are warm in the third degree and dry in the second. The best sort of leeks are those called *naptici*, that is those that are from the mountains and possess a sharp odor. They stimulate urination, influence coitus and, in a mixture with honey, clear up catarrh of the chest. Leeks are bad for the brain and the senses; these dangers can be countered with sesame-seed oil and with the oil of sweet almonds. Leeks cause hot blood and an acute crisis of the bile; they are principally indicated for cold temperaments, for old people, in winter and in the northern regions.

13. Almond-Leek Sauce

Leeks were one of the most common vegetables in the diet of all classes in all European countries at the end of the Middle Ages. It is therefore not surprising that a recipe for a pottage or sauce made of the white part of the leek should have made its way into cookbooks from England to Catalonia, to the greater pleasure of diners throughout Europe. In France, the *Viandier* lists a "*potaige*" of *poreaulx* among the standard, common-place preparations for which it would be useless to offer a recipe because, as the professional cook, Taillevent, notes with some condescension, "Women are experts with these and anyone knows how to do them" (§154).

It may have been true that anyone could stew leeks in medieval France, but, on the table of Duke Amadeus of Savoy, Chiquart's Almond-Leek Sauce must have been considered a treat and must surely have gladdened the taste buds of the members of the Savoyard household as well as of the Duke's guests. This sauce has a very pure flavor, is deliciously mild and delicate.

The *Menagier de Paris* confirms Chiquart's specification of pork by declaring that *only* pork grease should be used in Almond-Leek Sauce. If you wish, the almond/bouillon mixture may be strained and the lumpy residue discarded; this is not necessary if you are using a food processor or blender. Only the white portion of the leeks is used.

Chiquart suggests using beef or mutton bouillon as ingredients. If the sauce is being served with chicken, we suggest using chicken bouillon. The directions below are a simplified version of the recipe.

Yield: About 1 1/2 cups/375 mL of sauce

Imperial	Ingredient	Metric	Directions
3 or 4	leeks	3 or 4	**Wash leeks. Discard the green tops. Chop whites finely.**
1 1/2 cup 2 strips	meat bouillon bacon*	375 mL 2 strips	**Combine leeks & bacon strips with bouillon in a saucepan.** **Bring to a boil, then simmer for 8–10 minutes or until leeks are tender.** **Strain. Set leeks & bacon aside.**
1/2 cup	ground almonds	125 mL	**Return bouillon to pot & add ground almonds. Cook over low heat for 2 minutes. In electric blender process almond mixture until almonds are absorbed.** **Add leeks. (Bacon may be discarded or retained, as desired.) Continue blending until a smooth puree consistency is reached.** **Return to saucepan & re-heat. Serve.**

Serving suggestions

1. As a sauce for stuffed chicken breasts, whole roasted chickens or other meat: spoon onto the cooked meat, garnish with parsley sprigs and toasted almond slices.

2. As a serving sauce, over braised leeks or other vegetables.

3. As a base for leek soup: add sufficient bouillon to thin to the consistency of a soup. Garnish the soup with slivered, toasted almonds.

---

* Chiquart uses salt pork and discards it after the first cooking.

14. *Calimafree, ou Saulse paresseuse*
(*Menagier de Paris*, p. 233/§285)

Prenez de la moustarde et de la pouldre de gingembre et ung petit de vinaigre et de la gresse de l'eaue de la carpe, et boulez ensemble. Et se vous voulez faire pour ung chappon, ou lieu que l'en met la gresse et l'eaue de la carpe mectez vertjus, vinaigre et la gresse du chappon.

14. Lazy Sauce

In the fourteenth century just as much as today, the housewife and cook were occasionally faced with unexpected demands, one of which was the appearance of unheralded guests. The *Menagier*'s *Souppe despourvue* / Quick Soups (of p. 108, above) afforded a practical solution to the need to provide a quick light meal at very short notice; the *Saulse paresseuse* / Lazy Sauce surely owed its name to a similar need to have in one's repertoire a recipe to which one could have recourse in order to make up a sauce quickly, easily and from ingredients that were almost certain to be on hand.

In effect the *Calimafree* or Lazy Sauce is really a sort of Jance, a Mustard Jance. Chiquart does not give a recipe for *Calimafree*, but he does parallel it in the cinnamon family of sauces when he adds mustard to his Cameline Sauce (see the Calunafree of Partridge at p. 173, below), when this is to be prepared as a dressing for partridge.

The *Menagier* offers two varieties (or variations) of this sauce, one to accompany carp, the other to accompany chicken—both carp and chicken being readily available to most cooks at the end of the Middle Ages, whether in a townhouse or out in a country manor. The recipes are similar (and most elementary): carp, water and grease comprise the basis of the fish sauce; chicken bouillon and fat comprise the chicken sauce. Because carp is not all that popular a fish in North-American gastronomy, we have chosen to present the *Menagier*'s Lazy Sauce for chicken.

Yield: About 1/2 cup/125 mL of sauce

Imperial	Ingredient	Metric	Directions
1/2 cup	chicken bouillon	125 mL	**Bring chicken bouillon to a boil. Add**
2 tsp	chicken fat	10 mL	**fat & ground ginger. Simmer for 5**
2 tsp	ground ginger	10 mL	**min.**
2–3 tbsp	prepared Dijon-style mustard	30–50 mL	**Stir in mustard & vinegar.**
1 tbsp	white wine vinegar	15 mL	
			Serve warm on chicken.

15. *Une poitevine*
(*Menagier de Paris*, p. 234/§289; *Viandier*, §169)

Broyez gingembre, giroffle, graine et des foyes, puis ostez du mortier. Puis broyez pain brulé, vin et vertjus et eaue, de chasun le tiers, et faictes boulir, et de la gresse du rost dedens. Puis versez sur vostre rost ou par escuelles.

15. A Poitevine Sauce

The Poitevine is recommended in the *Viandier* either for roast capons, for hens or for cockerels; it is to be poured over the roast or served in bowls as a dipping sauce. The *Menagier*'s recipe is a little more general in intent, saying merely that the Poitevine is suitable for roast meat.

Its name indicates that this sauce enjoyed some popularity in the province of Poitou. It may be that it is this "foreign" origin that fixed the recipe, so that there is little variation between what we read in the various versions of the *Viandier* and in the *Menagier*. To the wine and verjuice of the older French versions the *Menagier* adds water, specifying that the three liquids be measured in equal quantities.

The Poitevine Sauce has a sharp taste and tends to be very granular—despite having gone through a modern blender.

Yield: About 3/4 cup/175 mL of sauce

Imperial	Ingredient	Metric	Directions
6–8	chicken livers	6–8	**Cut chicken livers in half. Remove stringy parts.**
2 tbsp	grease from roast	30 mL	**Sauté livers in grease from roast until cooked. Do not overcook.** **Press livers with tines of fork *or* grind in mortar (*or* in a processor) & return to saucepot.**
2 tbsp	toasted bread crumbs	30 mL	**Add breadcrumbs. Stir in wine. Bring to a boil, reducing wine by a quarter.**
1/2 cup	white wine	125 mL	
1/4 tsp*	ground cloves	1.2 mL*	**Add spices & simmer sauce for 10 min. until desired consistency is reached. Taste; correct spices if necessary.**
1/8 tsp	ground grains of paradise	.05 mL	
1 tbsp	lemon juice	15 mL	**Stir in lemon juice. Strain through fine sieve *or* blend in electric blender. Serve warm.**

---

* Add more cloves if a stronger flavor is desired.

The Cameline Sauces

Cameline is basically a cold cinnamon sauce. As with the ginger sauce, Jance, cooks over the years developed a range of variations on the "plain" Cameline that became established both as fundamental elements in the repertoire of kitchen professionals and as dependable, interesting garnishes for those who were responsible for determining the day's menus. The *Menagier de Paris* and the *On Cookery* each provide recipes for a standard boiled Cameline Sauce.

Recreating these boiled Cameline Sauces is a small challenge! Following the cooks' rather explicit directions produces sauces that have a sticky texture—one that is not particularly pleasant. After many trials we have found that changing the order in which ingredients are added produces a much more palatable and tasty sauce.

16. *Saulse cameline a la guise de Tournay*
(*Menagier de Paris*, p. 230/§271)

Nota que a Tournay pour faire cameline l'en broye gingembre, canelle et saffran, et demye nois muguecte, destrempé de vin, puis osté du mortier. Puis ayez mye de blanc pain, sans bruler, trempé en eaue froide, et broyez ou mortier, destrempez de vin et coulez. Puis boulez tout, et mectez au derrain du succre roux: et ce est cameline d'yver. Et en esté la font autelle, maiz elle n'est point boulye. Et a verité a mon goust celle d'iver est bonne; maiz en est trop meilleure celle qui s'ensuit: broyez ung pou de gingembre et foison canelle; puis ostez, et ayez pain hazé trempé, ou chappellures foison en vinaigre trempees et coulees.

16. Tournai Cameline Sauce

The *Menagier* advises his wife that she (and their cook, Master Jehan) could always have recourse, with satisfaction, to the variant of Cameline Sauce that was popular in the town of Tournai in Hainaut. While regular Cameline is usually an unboiled sauce, he notes that the winter version of Tournai Cameline should be boiled (in order to add a warmth that would be appropriate for the cold, damp season), and that he himself prefers this. For good measure the elderly bourgeois gentleman also appends a recipe for his own favorite, a relatively plain Cameline: lots of cinnamon, with ginger, toast and vinegar.

Yield: About 1 cup/250 mL of sauce

Imperial	Ingredient	Metric	Directions
1 1/2 cup	red wine	375 mL	**Heat wine in saucepot.**
1 tbsp	ground cinnamon	15 mL	**Combine spices & add, stirring until**
1 tsp	ground ginger	5 mL	**spices are absorbed. Simmer for 2–3**
1/2 tsp	ground nutmeg	2 mL	**min.**
pinch	saffron (*optional*)	pinch	
2–4 tbsp*	soft white breadcrumbs	30–60 mL*	**Combine the breadcrumbs & water, blending well by hand *or* (prefer-ably) in a blender. Slowly stir into the wine/ spice mixture. Add a little at a time until the desired consistency is reached. Do not over-cook.**
1/3 cup	cold water	80 mL	
2–3 tbsp	brown sugar	30–45 mL	**Add sugar. Taste; correct spices to taste. If a smoother consistency is desired, process sauce in blender *or* strain through a fine sieve.** **Pour into a sauce bowl & serve.**

Variation

Add 2 tsp/10 mL strong Dijon-style mustard to the above recipe if desired. The Mazarine manuscript of the *Viandier* provides for the addition of mustard to its Cameline Sauce. The writer further suggests that this variant, a Mustard Cameline Sauce, is suitable for roast meats—although, with seeming inconsistency, earlier in the manuscript he had said that plain Mustard Sauce should be used on *boiled* meats, especially salted pork, mutton and salted boar.

---

* This is roughly one *or* two slices of bread.

17. *Broet camelin*

(*Du fait de cuisine*, §7)

Et pour donner entendement a celluy qui fera le broet camelin, se doibt prendre selon la quantité que luy sera ordonnee de faire sa poullaille et le grein—ou de porc ou de capril ou de veaulx ou de aigneaulx—et mectre cuire bien et adroit en chaudieres ou en olles belles nectes et cleres, et aussi une bonne et grande piece de porc gros et sallé qui soit par devant bien nectoyé, lavés et brullié. Et puis faictes que vous hayés grant quantité d'amandres selon la quantité du boullon qui vous est ordonné a faire, et les nectoyés bien des croyses et de toutes autres choses que y pourroient estre, et les lavés en bonne eaue chaude bien et fermement ainsy comme est dist dessus au broet d'Alamany, et les pisés bien et adroit sans plumer et les arrousés du boullon dudit grein. Et puis soit l'on bien advisés de gouverner vostre grein qui ne soit pou ne tropt cuit; puis prennés vostres espices, c'est assavoir: grant coup de cynamomy, de gingibre blanc, grana de paradix, de poyvre par maniere qui ne poingnie pas tropt, de galinga, macis, giroffle et noix muscates; et quant serat cuit vostre grein sy le trayés et mectés en cornues belles et nectes, et puis prennés vostre boullon et le coulés bien et adroit en cornues belles et nectes. Et puis y trayés vostres dictes amandres et espices et, ce fait, mectés dedans vostre boullon de vin et de verjust ce que sera necessité pour avoir ung bon gost, et soyés tousjours bien advisés qu'il n'y ait de sel ne de nulle autre chouse ne pou ne tropt; et puis le mectés boullir en chaudiere ou en olles belles et nectes en quoy ilz puissent a aise boullir, et sy y mectés du sucre grant quantité selon le boullon que vous haurés. Et, ce fait, jusques au drecier si prennés vostre grein et le mectés en beaux platz et dudit boullon par dessus.

17. Cameline Broth or Sauce

Several of Chiquart's dishes make very little distinction between a dish that makes use of a genre of sauce in which a meat is cooked, and the sauce itself, used to accompany the dish as a presentation garnish or as a dipping relish. A case in point is the *Broet camelin* / Cameline Broth or Sauce, in which a classic Cameline Sauce is used with poultry, kid, lamb, and other meats. From the dish that Chiquart calls Cameline Broth we have extracted a recipe for what amounts to Chiquart's Cameline Sauce.

Yield: 1 1/2–2 cups/375–500 mL of sauce

Imperial	Ingredient	Metric	Directions
1 1/2 cup	meat *or* chicken bouillon	375 mL	**Heat bouillon in saucepot.**
1 tbsp	ground cinnamon	15 mL	**Combine spices & add to bouillon.**
1 tsp	ground ginger	5 mL	**Simmer until spices are absorbed—**
1/8 tsp	ground grains of paradise	.5 mL	**about 4–5 min.**
1/8 tsp	mace	.5 mL	
1/8 tsp	cloves	.5 mL	
1/8 tsp	nutmeg	.5 mL	
1/2 tsp	salt	2 mL	
pinch	grated galingale	pinch	
1/2 cup	dry red wine	125 mL	**Add wine, lemon juice & sugar, & continue to simmer.**
1 tbsp	lemon juice	15 mL	
2 tbsp	brown sugar	30 mL	
2 tbsp	ground unskinned almonds	30 mL	**Slowly stir in almonds, a little at a time, until desired consistency is reached. Taste; correct spices to taste. Adjust consistency by adding more wine *or* ground almonds. Strain *or* blend.**
			Pour into bowls & serve, *or* pour over sliced meat & serve.

Variation

When this *Broet camelin* is to be used as a fish sauce, Chiquart substitutes pea puree for the bouillon; see his recipe for Pea Puree on p. 63, above. Chiquart also reminds his cook "not to forget the candies (*dragees*) which should be sprinkled over the top" of the finished dish before serving.

18. *Broet georgé sur poysson frit*
(*Du fait de cuisine*, §37)

Et pour donner entendement a cellui qui fera le broet georgé, si prenne la quantité d'amandres selon la potagerie qui devra faire et si les face plumer tresbien et laver bien et adroit et nectement broyer, et la puree de poys blancs qui les traysoit et qu'il agouste de bon vin et de verjust blanc. Et si prenne des espices: gingibre blanc, granne de paradix, et ung pou de cynamomy et non pas tropt, noix muscates, de giroffle et de poyvre ung pou, et de saffran ung pou pour lui donner la couleur dudit broet—et qu'il n'y en ait pas tropt—et du succre grant quantité selon le boullon qui sera; et qui le gouste bien en tout, et du sel. Et quant ce viendra au drecier si le mectés sur les platz du poysson frit et si ne obliés point la dragiee que se doibt semer par dessus.

18. Georgé Broth or Sauce

Chiquart stipulates that a "great deal" of sugar should go into this sauce. He also advises us not to forget the candies (*dragees*) that should be sprinkled over the top as the dish is being presented. This spicey, sweet sauce for fish is very appetizing for those who have no particular predilection for sour things.

Yield: About 1 1/2 cups/375 mL of sauce

Imperial	Ingredient	Metric	Directions
3/4 cup	white wine	175 mL	**Heat wine in saucepot.**
1 tbsp	ground almonds	15 mL	**Combine almonds & pea puree, & add**
3 tbsp	white pea puree	45 mL	**to wine. Cook, reducing wine to 1/2 cup/125 mL.**
1/2 tsp	ground ginger	2 mL	**Combine spices & add to liquid. Sim-**
1/4 tsp	cinnamon	1 mL	**mer, stirring frequently for 5–6 min.**
pinch	grains of paradise	pinch	
pinch	nutmeg	pinch	
pinch	cloves	pinch	
pinch	pepper	pinch	
pinch	saffron*	pinch	
2 tbsp†	brown sugar	30 mL†	**Stir in brown sugar & lemon juice;**
1 tbsp	lemon juice	15 mL	**continue cooking until sugar is dis-**
to taste	salt	to taste	**solved. Taste; add salt to taste & correct spices.**
			Serve warm over fish.

* The saffron is optional. It is used here to give the "proper" color to this sauce; turmeric may be substituted.

† More brown sugar can be added, depending on your taste.

19. *Marjoliaine*
(*Viandier*, §172)

Prener jus de marjoliaine doubce, aigue et atant de vin blanc et y mecter du gigimbre et vin, ung pol de giroffle, de cannelle et de succre.

Maiorana / Marjoram

(*Tacuinum sanitatis*, Vienna,
Oesterreichische Nationalbibliothek, Codex Vindobonensis, 2644, f. 33v)

It is doubtless the delightful scent of the marjoram plant that makes it so pleasing to women, nearly all of whom grow it and care for it attentively in their garden and in pots on their balcony or loggia. One can have nothing but praise for marjoram: it appears to be in no way harmful, rather it stimulates the blood and is good for cold and moist stomachs. If a small quantity of juice is expressed from marjoram and placed in the ear, it will dispel any pain as well as any whistling, and it is useful for deafness. Inhaled through the nose, it clears the head of phlegmatic humors and purifies and comforts the brain.

19. Marjoram Sauce

This is the only instance in which marjoram is used in the *Viandier*, and it appears in only the copy of that work now catalogued in the Mazarine Library in Paris. This is a fifteenth-century copy. Along with the copy now in the Vatican Library, these two relatively late versions of the *Viandier* contain interesting additions and modifications of those recipes that were available to previous generations. Among the "novel" ingredients introduced into the renewed *Viandier* are marjoram, dittany, shallots or scallions, herb-bennet or common avens, spinach, clary, anise, pomegranate seeds, pinenut paste, currants, *tornesoc*—an orchil lichen—and alkanet (these last two being substances that are used as colorants), rice flour, wheat starch and stag testicles. In culinary matters the fifteenth century was not content to stand still!

Marjoram sauce is very thin and was probably used as a dipping sauce for chunks of roast meat. In the manuscript it is copied between a new (and interesting) Cameline Mustard Sauce for roast meat and a recipe for stewed poultry.

Yield: About 1/2 cup/125 mL of sauce

Imperial	Ingredient	Metric	Directions
1/3 cup	water	75 mL	**Bring water to a boil in small sauce-**
2 tbsp	dried marjoram	30 mL	**pot. Add marjoram. Simmer for 1–2**
	or		**min. Press through a sieve & discard**
4 tbsp	chopped fresh marjoram	60 mL	**marjoram.**

1/3 cup	white wine	75 mL	**Combine marjoram juice & wine in saucepot.**
1/2 tsp	ginger	2 mL	**Stir in spices & sugar. Cook until**
pinch	cinnamon	pinch	**sauce is reduced by about 1/4. Strain**
pinch	cloves	pinch	**through fine cheesecloth to remove**
2 tsp	sugar	10 mL	**sediment.**
			Serve warm.

20. *Calaminee*
(*Du fait de cuisine*, §48)

Þour donner entendement a celluy qui fera la calaminee et la froyde sauge si prenne sa poullaille selon la quantité que luy sera ordonnee a faire desdictes saulces, et de porcellet de lait prennés aussi, et cela prennés et appareilliés et nectoiés bien et appoint; et les poullailles mectés par cartiers et les porcellos par belles petites pieces, et de cela lavés bien et nectement, et puis le mectés cuire en une belle et necte chaudiere, et du sel selon la quantité que luy sera ordonnee a faire. Si prennés des oefs grant foyson et mectés cuire en une belle chaudiere et si les cuisés qu'ilz soient durs; et puis prennés du pain blanc qui soit bien parés et trenchiés et mis en cestes .ii. cornues selonc la quantité qui fera besoing pour lesdictes saulceries; et puis prennés les moyeux des oeufs et mectés tremper avecques le pain en la cornue en quoy ferés la calaminee. Et puis prennés vostres espices selon la quantité que ferés de la dicte saulce, c'est assavoir gingibre blanc, granne de paradis, de poyvre, de saffran et de succre, et du verjust selon la quantité de la saulserie, et du sel; et faictes la saulce bien espesse, et collés cela bien espés entant qu'elle ne se mesle point avecques l'autre.

20. Calaminee Sauce

As a dip for cold pork, this sauce is the counterpart to the *Froide sauge* / Cold Sage Sauce which is used with chicken. It should be thick, yellow and have a peppery taste. Its name seems to point to some, perhaps distant, connection with calamint, a well used medicinal herb in the Middle Ages; however, our recipe sources for Calaminee show no herbs as ingredients at all, nor do they give any other hint as to the origin of the name.

Yield: About 1/2 cup/125 mL of sauce

Imperial	Ingredient	Metric	Directions
1	large slice white bread	1	**Remove crusts, crumble bread & combine with lemon juice.**
2 tbsp	lemon juice	30 mL	
2	hard-boiled egg yolks*	2	**Mash egg yolks,**
1/8 tsp	grains of paradise	.5 mL	**& add spices. Combine with bread. Taste, add more pepper if desired.**
1/4 tsp	pepper	1 mL	
pinch	saffron	pinch	**(*Alternatively*, all ingredients may be combined in a blender *or* mortar until smooth.)**
1 tsp	sugar	5 mL	
1/4 tsp	salt	1 mL	
			Cook over low heat until thickened to desired consistency. Set out in bowl; garnish with slices of egg white.

Serving suggestion
This sauce is intended to accompany a plate of cold pork slices.

---

* Reserve the whites to be used as a garnish.

Other Possible Sauces

Froide sauge / **Cold Sage Sauce**

For the complete recipe of this preparation as a Poultry Dish, see p. 183, below.

The popular preparation known as Cold Sage is really a combination of cold pork or chicken and a sauce. This latter is quite suitable for use separately, on its own, as it were. It could be warmed and served with buttered pasta, or as a dip for *crudités* if you wish to prepare a remarkably fresh-tasting appetizer.

Rissolles a jour de poisson / **Fruit Rissoles** (filling)

For the complete recipe of this dish as a Dessert, see p. 278, below.

Omit the pastry in this recipe. Cook the other ingredients and serve as a sauce to accompany such roast meat as pork or game meat—hare, partridge, quail, pigeon, *etc.*

Emplumeus de pomes / **Almond Applesauce**

For the complete recipe of this dish as a Dessert, see p. 286, below.

Serve warm or cold as an accompaniment to meat dishes. This Almond Applesauce is very tasty when used as a dip for the *Pommeaulx* / Little Meatballs (p. 153, below).

Chapter 5
Meat Dishes

Various meats, their preparation and appropriate saucing
Game meats

    A. *Venoison de cerf fraiche* / Fresh Stag Venison
    B. *Venoison de sanglier frez* / Fresh Boar Venison
    C. *Conin ou saupiquet* / Rabbit in Saupiquet
    D. *Buchat de connins* / Buchat of Rabbits
    E. *Menus oiseaux* / Small Birds

1. *Pommeaulx* / Little Meatballs
2. *Char de porcelez en rost* / Stuffed Roast Suckling Pig
3. *Espalles de moustons, farciees et dorees* / Stuffed and Glazed Shoulder of Mutton
4. *Civé de veel* / Veal Stew
5. *Broet blanc sur chappons* / White Broth of Capons
6. *Broet de Savoye* / Savoy Broth
7. *Saulce lampree de lomblos de beuf* / Lamprey Sauce on Loin of Beef
8. *Calunafree de perdrix* / Calunafree of Partridge
9. *Tortres parmeysines* / Parma Torte

Alouyaulx / **Little Larks** : see Chapter 2, Appetizers
Rosseolles / **Pork Rissoles** : see Chapter 2, Appetizers
Calaminee / **Calaminee Sauce** : see Chapter 4, Sauces
Faulx grenon / **Mock Meat** : see Chapter 6, Poultry Dishes
Froide sauge / **Cold Sage** : see Chapter 6, Poultry Dishes

For all **Roast and Boiled Meats** : see Chapter 4, Sauces

Chapter 5
Meat Dishes

Meats could be cooked and presented in a variety of ways in the Middle Ages. The grill and the spit were used to hold meats for braising or roasting over an open flame or embers; cauldrons and pans let them be boiled or fried in some cooking medium (for instance in water or grease); sealed pots and ovens let them be baked, usually in pastry. And cooked meats arrived on the dining table in a variety of ways: the roast joint, carved at the table, was invariably accompanied by an appropriate sauce; pottages (usually *without* vegetables) consisted of chunks of meat that were served covered with their richly composed cooking bouillon, or with this bouillon transformed into a sauce; ground meats could be moulded into bite-sized shapes, deep-fried and sauced; pies were sliced and their contents (primarily meats) consumed neatly.

The recipes of both the *Viandier* and the *Menagier de Paris* are grouped in a very general way according to the nature of the dish. Boiled meats come first, then pottages (broths, civets, cuminades and the like), roast meats and fowl, fish, and finally special dishes for Lent and for the sick. Whatever cooking and serving procedures a meat underwent, the important element was the sauce that was prepared for, or with, that meat. In early cookery the definition of "sauce" was that the term designated any secondary foodstuff or condiment that was added to the principal foodstuff with the intention of changing its nature. This meant that even the liquid in which a meat was boiled was important and could properly function as a "sauce," whether this liquid was water, or wine and verjuice, or a judicious combination of, say, wine and vinegar; herbs or spices could also be present in the cooking sauce, of course.

If a meat was cut up and cooked in a pottage, then, as we have seen, the nature of the mixture of the other ingredients in the pot was just as important as the nature of the meat itself. The dish called a civet, for instance, took its name from its vital ingredient: every civet began with sautéed onions (*cepa, ciba, cive* and eventually the English *chive*), to which were added a liquid (one or all of beef bouillon, pea puree, wine, verjuice, vinegar), spices and the meat. In a pie, before the top crust went on, the meat was normally coated with a good dollop of a sauce proper for that meat; and later, when the pie was cut and served, the same or another sauce would often be available in bowls on the table for the diner's use.

In the meat recipes that follow, and in the recipes for poultry and for fish of the next two chapters, it should always be remembered that a medieval meal never contained plain ungarnished meat, poultry or fish. Even the humblest peasant or townsman could usually afford Green Sauce, purchased if necessary from a local merchant, or could make a boiled syrup-sauce by reducing sweet wine by two-thirds. More discriminating (and wealthy) households insisted upon the proper sauces for their meats, poultry and fish. The early recipe collections provide the cook with explicit directions concerning the matching of meats, fowl and fish with the appropriate sauce.

146

Various meats, their preparation and appropriate saucing

Meat	Cooking Method	Serving Sauce
veal	parboiled, roast larded	spice powder *or* Cameline
veal	baked in pie with spice powder, saffron, lard	verjuice
pork	roast	verjuice *or* drippings, onions, wine, verjuice
pork	baked in pie with saffron & spice powder	verjuice
mutton	roast	salt *or* Cameline *or* verjuice
kid, lamb	parboil, roast larded	Cameline
kid	roast	Green Verjuice
chicken	roast larded	Cameline *or* verjuice *or* Cold Sage
chicken	baked in pie, lard, spice powder	sharp verjuice
capons	boiled in water, lard, parsley, sage, hyssop, saffron, ginger	wine, verjuice
capons, hens, cockerels	roast	must *or* Poitevine *or* Jance
goose	parboiled, roast	White or Green Garlic Sauce *or* Black or Yellow Pepper Sauce
rabbit	parboiled, roast larded	Cameline
rabbit	parboiled, baked in a pie larded, with spice powder	Cameline *or* verjuice
hare	seared, roast larded	Cameline
hare	parboiled, baked in a pie larded, with spice powder	Cameline
pigeons, doves	roast	salt
small birds	roast on spit with piece of bacon between	salt
partridge	parboiled, roast larded	salt
swan	parboiled, roast (*optionally* glazed)	Yellow Pepper Sauce
peacock	parboiled in wine, roast larded, glazed	salt
pheasant	parboiled, roast	salt
mallard	roast	drippings, lard, wine, verjuice, parsley
venison	parboiled, boiled larded in water, mace, much wine	Cameline
venison	parboiled, baked larded in pie with spice powder	Cameline
fresh boar	boiled in water & wine	Cameline *or* sharp Pepper Sauce
salt boar	soak in water; boil in 50/50 water & white wine	boiled chestnuts, Mustard Sauce

It is clear that these meats, and many others, were regularly cooked by fairly simple means—boiling or roasting—and clear, too, that the cook regularly prepared a variety of sauces to accompany them. This "gross meat" course is rarely even mentioned in early cookbooks: no special recipe is needed just to boil or roast most meats. For us today what would make this type of meat course "medieval" would be the use of one of the sauces that we have outlined in Chapter 4, above. If we take into account the way in which so many of these sauces turn up, in modified form, in more complex, prepared dishes as well, it would not be too much of an exaggeration to suggest that the medieval cook was largely a master or mistress of the sauce-pot.

When we survey the meats of the medieval table, a peculiar feature that we may notice immediately, apart from the importance of the various sauces, is the uncertain role played by beef in the diet of the time. Repeatedly recipes call for the use of beef stock, beef bouillon, as if it was a very common matter to have large quantities of the liquid on hand in all kitchens. The prevalence of beef bouillon seems to indicate that people must surely have eaten a lot of boiled beef. That may be the case, but straight-forward recipes for beef as such are rare in early French cookery books. The *Menagier* enumerates the various *cuts* of beef, but in a single paragraph alone describes a sauce for a round or rump of beef—though he neglects to specify whether this cut is to be roasted as a steak or boiled as a whole joint. With our modern dependence upon roast beef, inherited apparently from Renaissance England, we are a little surprised to find that among the 220 recipes of the *Viandier* there is not a single one for beef. Among Chiquart's collection of 78 recipes we find only one for beef, specifically for loin of beef, one of the better cuts.

Some historians have suggested that at this time cows were too valuable *alive* as sources of milk, and oxen and bulls as the drawing force for ploughs on the medieval field, to abandon them to the butcher before their useful life was exhausted—by which time, we might speculate, their meat was too tough for genteel tables in any but boiled form. Physicians had already declared that the meat of cattle was, *by nature*, significantly cold and dry in its mature complexion. Despite these rather unattractive and inappropriate qualities of beef, however, in the rich pasture lands of Savoy Chiquart instructs his cook to obtain one hundred head of cattle and one hundred and thirty sheep to be cooked for a banquet. The serving of the "gross meats," along with what Chiquart terms the sauces "incumbent" to them, constitutes the first course of a formal meal:

> And let us take as the first serving the gross meats, that is to say, beef and mutton, and those who cut up the oxen should make good, big, noble pieces, and those who cut up the sheep should slice the length of the sheep without removing anything but a little of the neck.

> To serve those pieces of beef and mutton, they should be put on a great gold platter without anything else. ... And for this first serving, ... no other sauce is needed but Mustard Sauce.*

We can end this brief review of early meats and their sauces with a translation of the

---

* *On Cookery*, p. 16. The *Menagier* offers recipes for several varieties of Mustard. The basic version is made in the harvest season and uses newly pressed grape juice. With the admixture of ground mustard seed, this *must* is said to be burning hot—*ard-ant*.

Menagier's recipe for a sauce for beef (p. 155/§87).

If you wish to make a piece of beef seem like stag venison, or like bear venison if you happen to be in bear country, take the loin or round of beef and parboil it, then lard it, mount it on a spit and roast it; it is eaten with Boar's Tail Sauce [see below]. [Or, alternatively:] Parboil the piece of beef, then lard it lengthwise and slice it across; either roast these pieces, or quickly boil them because this beef is more tender than stagmeat; serve the pieces on a platter with Boar's Tail Sauce over them.

Beef prepared as Bear Venison. Round of beef. Do it in a Black Sauce made of ginger, cloves, long pepper, grains of paradise, etc. Set it out with two pieces in each bowl; and so it is eaten with a bear flavor.

Boar's Tail Sauce [p. 236/§293]. Take loin of pork, hares and river birds, mount them on a spit; collect the drippings, with good wine and vinegar. Then get grains of paradise, ginger, cloves, nutmegs, long pepper and cinnamon, and grind them; remove them from the mortar. Grind burnt bread moistened in good wine and sieve it. Filter the contents of the dripping pan with the spices and the bread into an iron pan or pot with meat bouillon, and set your roast into it, having first stuck the roast with cloves.

Veal was universally considered to be preferable to beef largely because, being from a younger animal, it was by nature more moist. The principle that aging always tended to dry the complexion of any living animal—including human beings, one might note in passing—was fundamental to medico-physical theory, and had to occupy a central place in the thinking and planning of any professional cook. This principle of the effect of aging was merely one of several similar concepts which combined to help define the nature of any given meat.

In 1256 Master Aldobrandino of Siena compiled his book of hygienic and dietetic advice at the request of the Countess of Provence, Beatrice of Savoy. This august personage was just setting out on a round trip to visit each of her four daughters—much as we might do today, spending a little time with our children. In the case of the wife of Count Raymond-Berenger IV, however, her daughters were the Queen of France, the Queen of England, the Empress of Germany (who was also the Queen of the Romans), and the Countess of Anjou (who was also the Queen of Sicily). Her physician's manual would surely help her—and her cook—to while away many a league of travel.

You should understand that every meat that is eaten is either domestic or wild, and either male or female. Know that all wild meats are warmer and drier than domestic meats and are more difficult to digest, and consequently they yield less and worse nourishment; and know, too, that all male meats are warmer than female meats, but they yield better nourishment and are easier to digest.

The meat of castrated animals takes after the nature of both male and female.

You should understand that the meats of any old animal, and of the new-born recently drawn from the belly of the mother, are completely bad, and so everyone should avoid them.*

---

* *Le regime du corps*, p. 121.

In veal, therefore, the undesirable dryness of beef was mitigated by its very youth. Some writers in the Middle Ages even go so far as to declare veal to be the most desirable of all domestic meats.

As to what constituted the best cuts of meat, Chiquart tells his chef to make sure that the butchers set aside loins of beef and the marrow from bones for the nobility at court, and to leave the animal's legs for the meals of the household staff! In all but the largest of manor houses and courts, the same kitchen would prepare food both for the head of the house and his family and guests, on the one hand, and, on the other, for all of the personnel or staff of that house: the liveried retainers, archers, grooms, gamekeepers, clerks, chamber servants, seamstresses, launderers, porters and so forth. The cooks prepared meals both for the so-called *bouche* (the mouth, that is, of the lord or master) and for the *commun* (what in another context we might call the "commons"). In the dishes and meals that were prepared for each class of person, the Kitchen Clerk and the cook or cooks working under his authority drew quite clear distinctions in quantity and quality: the household staff could expect to receive very little more than adequate provisions of food.

The *Menagier*'s recipes for pseudo-stag, -bear and -boar which we reproduced above point to another gastronomic distinction to which we also saw the physicians paying some attention. The source of a meat at the end of the Middle Ages could still be either domestic or wild. Some game meat and game fowl arrived in noble kitchens as the result of that most noble of pastimes in medieval Europe, the hunt. Whether organized as a periodic social event on the lord's estate, or enjoyed by the lord as a regular recreational activity, the hunt was an integral part of aristocratic life, just as much as warfare was, and could yield a limited quantity of stag, deer and boar, as well as of game birds such as quail and pheasant. Much more significant a source for such wild animals and wild fowl were the professional hunters and fowlers who were in the permanent employ of the noble lord or who, as independent agents, earned a livelihood from capturing this game on lands to which they had secured access.

Yet while the image of large game animals roasting on a baronial spit may satisfy our need for the romantic, meat from stag, deer and boar played a relatively small role in the diet of the time, even in the diet of royalty. The *Viandier* has very few recipes for this sort of meat. The boar's head, which traditionally led off the servings of a late-medieval banquet, enjoyed its long-standing function as a symbol of the triumph of noble courage in the face of savage ferocity only because boar itself was a relatively rare culinary phenomenon even in noble households. Taillevent, the chief cook of King Charles V, knew that, for the large quantities that he had to work with day after day, and for the security of provisioning that were for him an indispensable requirement, he could depend only upon supplies of domestic livestock and fowl. And so for the wealthy Parisian bourgeois, recipes for dishes that pretended to involve stag or bear or boar were a useful component of his cookbook. The royal or noble board might enjoy these meats from time to time; the average bourgeois could normally only simulate with substitutes.

In our day "wild" meats are becoming slightly more common than has been the case for the last century or so. We recall having seen, during a year's residence in Montpellier in the south of France, a fresh, eviscerated but otherwise intact wild boar resting on a slab outside a butcher shop at Christmastime. A processed sausage made with the meat of a *marcassin*, a young wild boar, remains a favorite delicacy in the Ardennes region of Belgium and France. In some places in

North America we can buy stag-venison, boar- and deer-meat—or at least that of moose, which can provide a modern diner with something of the gamey flavor of wild meat. For those who are real devotees of authenticity in their historic cuisine, we can offer the following recipes: Fresh Stag, Fresh Boar, Salted Stag and Salted Boar, Rabbit in Saupiquet, a *Buchat* of Rabbit and Roasted Small Game Birds.

Game meats

A. *Venoison de cerf fraiche* / Fresh Stag Venison
(*Viandier*, §6)

Venison of fresh stag or of deer. Parboiled, larded lengthwise on the inner side; then set it to cook in fresh water with mace and a good deal of wine; cook it thoroughly; serve it with Cameline Sauce. Set in a pasty: parboiled and larded; and add in fine spice powder; serve it with Cameline Sauce.

B. *Venoison de sanglier frez* / Fresh Boar Venison
(*Viandier*, §7)

Venison of fresh boar. Cooked in wine and water; serve it with Cameline Sauce or sharp Pepper Sauce.

Salted wild boar and stag. Soak your meat, then wash it and discard the first bouillon; wash the meat in fresh water and let it cool on a cloth; then slice it and boil it briefly in a mixture of equal parts of water and wine; peel the shells off roasted chestnuts, put them on a platter and set out your meat together with its broth; this is eaten with Mustard Sauce.

C. *Conin ou saupiquet* / Rabbit in Saupiquet
(*Du fait de cuisine*, §14)

To make Saupiquet to put on rabbits, depending on the quantity to be made of it, take two onions and slice them finely; then take good pork lard, melt it and sauté your onions; to prevent them from burning as they sauté, put in a little bouillon; then put in a lot of white wine depending on the amount of Saupiquet you want to make for the rabbits; and get your spices—good ginger, grains of paradise, a little pepper (which should not predominate), and saffron to give it color; add vinegar to taste so carefully that it is neither too sharp nor too bland; and the same with salt.

D. *Buchat de connins* / Buchat of Rabbits
(*Du fait de cuisine*, §20)

To instruct the chef who is to do that Buchat of Rabbits, he should take his rabbits and skin and clean them well, sear them and eviscerate them; he should take the rabbits' livers, set them aside, wash and clean them well, and put them to dry on good clean wooden tables; he should be careful to remove the bitter part, that is, the gall and anything else that is not clean; these livers should be washed in beef bouillon or in good boiling water. Also wash the rabbits, cut them up into good pieces and put them into a good clean cauldron. Then take pork backs, singe them well and cut them up into good little pieces, using a large quantity—in the amount you are ordered to make—and put them to be washed in good clean pots; then set them to dry on good wooden tables; when they have dried, put them into the cauldron with your rabbit meat. Then get beef or mutton bouillon, pour it in and set it all to cook. Then make a good big *bouquet garni* of herbs—that is, of sage, parsley, hyssop and marjoram, all cleaned and washed—and throw it in to cook. Take the rabbits' livers, which have been properly cleaned, washed and drained, put them on slender spits and set them to roast over hot coals; when they have roasted through, take them off the spits, put them in the mortar and grind them up well; get your *bouquet garni* which you have had boiling with the rabbit meat, undo it and grind the herbs in the mortar, and then mix this in with the ground rabbit livers. Then check on your meat that it is not too cooked, but take it out while it is still slightly underdone; put the rabbits to one side and the pork to another, both in good clean two-handled pots; and put the bouillon, from which you have taken the meat, into other pots which are likewise good and clean. Then get a great amount of bread, depending on the quantity of the broth, and set it to toast on the grill; then take your ground liver and herbs, put this into your broth with the toast and with spices—ginger, grains of paradise, pepper, cinnamon, nutmegs, mace and cloves—and be careful that you put in these minor spices very moderately; and add wine and verjuice, also in good measure; strain everything together into good clean two-handled pots. Then get your good clean cauldron or good big bright clean kettle and put it to boil. Get a lot of good bacon lard, chop it very small and melt it in good big pans, then strain it well into big pans and put them on the fire; fry the rabbit meat by itself, and not too much, then the other meat similarly fry a little and keep it by itself. When it is time to dress the dish, take your meat and broth to the dressing table and set out your meat on good platters of gold, silver, pewter, and so forth, and then pour your broth over the top.

E. *Menus oiseaux* / Small Birds
(*Viandier*, §45)

Roasted Small Game Birds—such as larks, quail, thrush and other sorts. Pluck them while dry, without water, then remove the gizzards and the viscera; then boil them a little (or sear them in a clear flame), mount them on a spit with their heads and feet still on, sideways and not lengthwise, putting between every two of them slices or rashers of bacon or slices of sausage (and bay leaves); fill the belly of the birds with a mixture of good rich cheese and beef marrow; they are eaten with fine salt, and they are served at table between two bowls or between two platters. Such birds may also be prepared in a pasty, their belly stuffed with a creamy cheese.

For those who are content merely to *know about* the role of game animals in medieval gastronomy, we offer nine other recipes for meats that are perhaps a little more readily available.

1. *Pommeaulx*

(*Menagier*, p. 220/§255)

Pommeaulx. Prenez d'un cuissot de mouton le meigre tout cru, et autant de la cuisse de porc meigre: soit tout ensemble hachié bien menu, puis broyez ou mortier gingembre, graine, giroffle, et mettez en pouldre sur vostre char hachée, et puis destrempez d'aubun et non pas du moyeu; puis paumoyez aux mains les espices et la char toute crue en luy donnant forme de pomme, puis quant la forme est bien faite, l'en les met cuire en l'eaue avec du sel, puis les ostez, et ayez de broches de couldre et les embrochiez et mettez rostir; et quant ils se roussiront, ayez percil broyé et passé par l'estamine et de la fleur meslée ensemble, ne trop cler ne trop espois, et ostez vos pommeaulx de dessus le feu et mettez un plat dessoubs, et en tournant la broche sur le plat, oingnez vos pommeaulx, puis mettez au feu tant de fois que les pommeaulx deviennent bien vers.

Se on met lettres en ta main,	Should someone write you, be quite modest;
mes les tantost dedens ton sein.	just slip the note into your bodice.

1. Little Meatballs

When meat wasn't served to the medieval table heaped in chunks on platters, much of it was chopped up or minced or ground, or otherwise reduced to an amorphous paste. The reasons for this treatment likely has to do with notions about the cook's proper role in preparing foods for genteel consumption. Perhaps, in adhering to the directions of medico-physical theory, the cook was attempting to correct the potentially harmful properties of a foodstuff by mixing condiments more intimately in with the foodstuff than was possible simply by incorporating them into a standard type of broth or sauce.

In any case early recipe collections abound with dishes for which the first instructions are that the meat is to be chopped or ground up finely. Often at this point in its preparation, the ground meat or meat paste is mixed with a selection of herbs or spices, and then moulded in imitation of some recognizable natural object.

While this recipe of the *Menagier*'s stipulates that the meat paste be given the shape of little apples (*pommeaulx*), large-scale *entremets* of the day frequently incorporated the forms of some variety of animal, whether this was life-size or in miniature, built up out of meat paste. For one of the *entremets* in the *Du fait de cuisine*, Chiquart does not limit himself to the static representation of such animals: a whole hunting scene involving hares, brachet hounds, stags, wild boars and huntsmen is reproduced by means of pea paste or bean paste (the lean-day alternatives to meat paste); he further specifies in this "recipe" that the curtain walls of the castle where the hunt scene is set should themselves be of meat paste. The successful medieval chef clearly had to possess some of the talents of a sculptor.

The *Pommeaulx* found in the *Menagier* are formed from a relatively simple variant on a standard procedure for making meat paste. As usual it is the choice of spices in the meat-paste mixture, and of the herb or herbs used in the glazing, that make the dish delightfully unique in its flavor and coloring. The technique that the writer of the *Menagier* proposes for cooking the meatballs, placing them gently into the boiling water, is a very efficacious one. The eggwhites coagulate almost immediately and hold the shape of the meatballs.

You can use these Little Meatballs as either an appetizer, an *entrée* or a main course, as you wish.

Yield: Appetizers for 20 or 30; *entrée* or main dish for 6

Imperial	Ingredient	Metric	Directions
			Preheat oven to 350°F/180°C.
1 lb	lean ground pork	500 g	**Combine pork & lamb.**
1 lb	lean ground lamb	500 g	
2	lightly beaten egg whites	2	**Stir in egg whites.**

1 tbsp	grated gingerroot	15 mL	**Add spices, combine well with meat**
1 tsp	grains of paradise	5 mL	**mixture.**
1 tsp	ground cloves	5 mL	**Shape into small balls for appetizers, or 1 1/2–2 in/4–5 cm balls for main course serving.**
1/2 cup	flour	125 mL	**Roll balls in flour.**
5 cups	boiling, salted water	1 1/4 L	**Drop balls into boiling water & simmer for 3–4 min. Remove from pot with slotted spoon & place on greased wire rack or tray & roast in 350°F/180°C oven for 10 min. Smaller balls will require a shorter roasting time. Remove from oven.**

Glazing

3/4 cup	ground parsley	200 mL	**Mix parsley & flour. Roll meat balls in this mixture until coated, & return to oven for about 3–5 min.**
1/2 cup	flour	125 mL	
			Serve warm.

Cooking Variations

After removing meatballs from boiling water, skewer onto bamboo skewers* or shish-kebab skewers or spit, and roast over fire or barbecue. When almost cooked, remove from fire. Roll in the parsley/flour mixture, return to spit or barbecue for a few minutes, being careful not to overcook or burn. Meatballs should remain green in color.

Serving Variations

As appetizers or as a main course, these meatballs are delicious served with a dipping sauce such as the apple-almond sauce called *Emplumeus*: see below, p. 286.

Increase the size of the meatballs and serve them with noodles, rice *or* with Almond-Leek Sauce (see p. 132, above). The meatballs could also be substituted for the cooked sausage in the dish Easter Cabbage for a Meat Day (see p. 263, below).

---

* Bamboo skewers should be soaked in cold water to cover for one hour before using.

2. *Char de porcelez en rost*
(*Enseignements*, p. 182)*

Char de porcelez: en rost, mes avant les couvient eschauder e oster la frissure e cuire tout entier; e puis cuire oués, les moués bien durs, e des chateingnes cuites en feu e du formage de mai par lesches e des peres de Saint Riulle ou de Quaillouel cuites en la brese. Puis hagiez tout ensemble e poudrez de poudre de canele, de poivre e de gingembre e des autres espices e sel, e metez en la toie du porcel ceucre, e en depechiez entre les quatre membres. E cest mes doit estre mengiez a la farsse.

Castanee / Chestnuts
(*Tacuinum sanitatis*, Vienna,
Oesterreichische Nationalbibliothek, Codex Vindobonensis, 2644, f. 17r)

Choose full, ripe chestnuts which yield a food of average goodness suited to warm temperaments, to young people and children, to the winter and to cold regions. For the most part they stimulate the appetite, alleviate nausea and vomiting, are good for the chest and for difficulties in urinating. Because of their vapors, they can weigh heavily on the brain and stomach, but this danger can be avoided if they are roasted, stirring them over a lively fire of seasoned wood, and if they are eaten along with a pinch of salt and a good, light wine.

Pira / Pears
(*Tacuinum sanitatis*, Vienna, f. 6v)

Fragrant and well ripened pears generate cold blood and are therefore suited to those with warm temperaments, in the summer, and in southern regions. They are healthful for those with weak stomachs but harmful to the production of bile; this harm can be countered by chewing cloves of garlic after a meal. We find in Dioscorides, that most diligent writer, that a drink of powdered and dissolved pear wood is effective against poisonous mushrooms; others believe that by cooking wild pears together with mushrooms you will avoid any harmful effects.

Boy sobrement a toute feste,	Drink soberly, the sage has said;
a ce que n'affolles ta teste.	take care the wine don't cloud your head.

---

* The name of this anonymous French recipe collection has come from its *incipit* which reads "Vez ci les enseingnemenz qui enseingnent a apareillier toutes manieres de viandes . . . ": "Here follow the instructions teaching how to prepare all sorts of dishes . . . ." The manuscript was published by Grégoire Lozinski, in his *La Bataille de Caresme et de Charnage*, Paris (Champion), 1933, Appendix 1, pp. 181–90. In many respects this thirteenth-century collection appears to be a contemporary or forerunner of the earliest version of the *Viandier*.

2. Stuffed Roast Suckling Pig

Though the thought of purchasing the cadaver of a piglet, lugging it home (under your arm, of course, like some young lad in a nursery rhyme), eviscerating and stuffing it may deter even the most willing modern cook, an insuperable obstacle in the preparation of this dish might well come at the moment when it is *itself* to be stuffed *into* the normal kitchen oven. Even with its tail neatly curled round on itself! It could be then that the cook is dismayed to discover that he or she has taken on a little more than the kitchen oven can handle!

In view of the limited capacity of modern ovens, to say nothing of modern cooks' arms, we propose to substitute a more manageable loin of pork for the whole carcass of a piglet. The flavor of the dish remains similar, although admittedly some of the visual effect as you serve it to your guests at the table may well be lost. Devotees of the authentic are, of course, still encouraged to make the trip to their local hog farmer or meat packer's, and to stuff the piglet and roast it on a spit over an open fire or barbecue!

Those living in farming communities where pig roasts are an annual early summer event will have no difficulty obtaining the basic ingredient for the authentic version of this dish. Local pork marketing boards can also give you practical information on "How to Barbecue a Sucking Pig." If you need further information, you might contact the local government Agricultural Office.

Pigs, domestic and wild, served frequently as *entremets* in medieval banquets. A Stuffed Roast Suckling Pig could, for instance, be mounted (astride!) by a roast chicken, in the guise of a knight riding his charger (see the *Coqz heaulmez* / Helmetted Cocks, p. 326, below). When it comes to a really striking *entremets*, of course, it is very difficult to find an substitute for the strictly authentic pig's head, roasted and decorated with leaves, fruit and glazing (see the *entremets* of the *Hures de cenglier* / Boar's Head Roasted, p. 323, below). If you are organizing just a modest, small-scale banquet you may be quite content to present a decorated piglet in the place of a fully grown boar.

The writer of the *Enseignements* specifies the use of a cheese made in the month of May, and pears that are qualified as being either St. Riulle or Quaillouel. For the first, a soft butter cheese works well; for the pears, Bartlett (Williams), a firm variety, is good.

Imperial	Ingredient	Metric	Directions
4–5 lb	boneless loin roast of pork*	2–2.5 kg	**Preheat oven to 425°F/220°C.**
	or		**Split the roast almost through, length-**
10–15 lb	suckling pig, cleaned & dressed	4.5–7 kg	**wise & flatten it out.**

---

* As well as the whole roast suckling pig mentioned here, you can substitute a shoulder roast, with the bone removed for stuffing, *or* tenderloin strips, split and flattened.

Stuffing

This gives very generous portions of stuffing; you may wish to cut this recipe in half.

6	hard-boiled egg yolks	6	**Mash egg yolks. (Chop & reserve whites for garnish).**
1/2 tsp	cinnamon powder	2 mL	**Combine spices & mix with egg yolks.**
1/4 tsp	pepper	1 mL	
1/2 tsp	ginger powder	2 mL	
1/2 tsp	salt	2 mL	
1/4tsp	ground cloves	1 mL	
1/2 tsp	ground nutmeg	2 mL	
pinch	mace	pinch	
2 tbsp	white sugar	30 mL	
4	cooked fresh *or* canned firm pears (*e.g.* Bartlett); reserve liquid	4	**Slice pears.**
1 1/2 cups (about 30 small)	cooked chestnuts;* reserve liquid	375 mL (about 30 small)	**Slice chestnuts.**
1 cup	butter cheese *or* other soft cheese	250 mL	**Cut cheese into small pieces.** **Toss pears, chestnuts & cheese with egg yolk mixture. Add sufficient (3–4 tbsp/50–60 mL) reserved liquid from pears & chestnuts to moisten dressing.**

Lay stuffing on flattened meat leaving about 1 in/ 2.5 cm on all borders. Roll & tie with butcher's string. Extra stuffing may be cooked in a greased casserole. Roast uncovered at 425°F/220°C for 10 min. Reduce heat to 350°F/180°C. Pour reserved liquid over meat. Cover and cook a total of 30 min. per lb/1 hr. per kg, basting occasionally with the broth. Remove cover for final 15 min. of cooking.

For Roast Suckling Pig: Stuff carcass & sew cavity closed. Put on spit & barbecue until done—about 4 hours.

Serving suggestion

Remove to serving platter. Garnish with the reserved egg whites. Slice and serve. Serve the cooking broth in a separate bowl.

---

* These chestnuts can be either fresh, *or* dried and reconstituted, *or* canned.

3. *Espalles de moustons, farciees et dorees*
(*Du fait de cuisine*, §64)

Encor plus, espalles de moustons farcies et dorees: et pour donner entendement a celluy qui haura la charge de faire lesdictes espalles si face qu'il hait d'espalles de bons moustons le nombre qu'il devra faire et face qu'il hait aussi autant de cuisses desditz moustons; et quant il haura ses espaules et cuisses si les refresche et lave bien et appoint et mecte cuire en bacines ou chaudieres belles et cleres et nectes, et du sel y mectés grant foison—touteffois par bonne maniere; et, estre assés cuites, si les tirés dehors sur belles et nectes postz et si en ostés toute la char et si laissés les os desdictes espalles que de une chescune espalle ilz se tieingnient tous ensemble, et si les gardés tresbien de despiecer et de dessevrer d'ensemble. Et prennés ladicte char des espalles et cuisses et aschés tresbien menuz et, estre bien aschez, si la mectés en cornue ou aise belle et necte; puis faictes qu'il hait du fromaige de Brie ou de Crampone ou de meilleur que faire se pourra et hasche tresbien menut et meslés avecques la char dessusdicte. Puis faictes que il y ait de bon percyn grant foyson et de margellayne et ung pou de ysope et salvy, et sy soient tresbien delictes, nectoyees et lavees et esgoutees de l'eaue, et tresbien haschiees menut et meslees avecques ladicte farce, et des espices aussy ce qui sera necessayre, c'est assavoir bon gingibre blanc, granne de paradix, et du giroffle entier se mecte pardessus; et face qu'il hait bons oefs fres et en mectent grant quantité par dedens jusques atant que le farce soit bien liee, et sy mecte du saffran pour lui donner couleur. Et puis aille vers les bochiers et face qu'il hait tant de toilles de moustons comme il ha d'espalles a faire, puis les mecte ung pou refreschier en belle eaue fresche et les refresche tresbien; et estre bien lavees, si les tire dehors et estende une chescune toille sur belles et nectes postz et, estre bien essuites, se froicte sur une chescune toille deux oefs fres pour la dorer. Et, estre ce fait, prennés de la farce dessus devisee et mectés ung lit et puis couchés et estandés les os d'une chascune espalle qui se tiengnent ensemble, et si n'ostent point le jangot mais ilz soient tresbien entiers et tiengnent les .iii. os d'une chescune espalle sans estre desevrés l'un de l'autre; puis mectés encor plus, par dessus, de la dicte farce et puis envoloppés cela a la dicte toille en forme et mode aussi fait et mis proprement; et qui n'y soit mise autre chose fors que les propres espalles de mouton; et soit faicte tenir la dicte toflle aynsi ployé et mise a petite brochetes de boys. Et, ce ainsy estre fait, prenne ses grilles que soient belles et nectes et mectés bien doulcement sur elles les dictes espalles et puis les aloés sur joli pitit feu jusques atant qu'elles soient reidelletes, et les virés sur le gril doulcement. Et se ainsi est qu'il luy en soit ordonné d'en faire point que soient dorees en verd si faictes qu'il hait grand coupt de percin et verdure que soit bien mondés et lavés et fort broyé tresbien et fort ou mortier, puis le traysiés et passés bien et appoint par bonne estamine; et de farine et des oefs tant qu'il en face de la dicte doreuse ce que luy en sera necessayre et le mecte en ayse que soit si large et longue que lesdictes espalles y puissent tofller et virer par mi la dicte verdure a ayse; et, estre ainsy fait, se retournent arrieres lesdictes espalles sur le gril essuyer; et soit advisé du tropt affin que ladicte doreuse ne se perde mais qu'elle soit tousjours sur le verd. Et, estre ce fait, quant vendra au drecier lesdictes espalles, si en mectés .ii. ou .iii. au plus en chescun plat et puis alés en servir.

Capiteles de char de monton / Mutton

(Aldobrandino, *Le regime du corps*, p. 124)

The meat of a young male sheep is less viscous and less moist [than that of lamb], but it is drier than that of a suckling lamb or of a ewe, and therefore it is better to eat.

For if it is well digested it nourishes somewhat better and engenders good blood, especially when the sheep is castrated [a wether], for in that case it is temperately warm and moist, and then it is by its nature one of the most suitable meats; but they should not be too old, for as they age they lose their good nature and their good nourishment with their age; yet nevertheless they are still better than any other animal at an old age.

3. Stuffed and Glazed Shoulder of Mutton

We include here two recipes for this dish. The first, with specific directions, is faithful to Chiquart's method. This recipe does, however, require that you start with a whole shoulder of lamb, bones intact, and a sheep's caul* in which to wrap both the stuffing and the bones. A custom butcher could provide this shoulder of lamb. Sausage casing may be substituted for the sheep's caul. This recipe works well on a barbecue.

We have also prepared this dish with a substitution of parchment baking paper for the caul or sausage casing; that particular variation is without any glazing and is baked in the oven. When the glazing on the shoulder is being set, whether on the grill or in the oven, the glazing and the shoulder should be exposed to only enough heat for that purpose because the meat has already been pre-cooked.

The second recipe is our own version. It calls for a boneless roast of lamb, or tenderloin, but still uses Chiquart's recipe for the stuffing.

Mutton as such is not readily available in our markets, but spring lamb can be found frozen all year round and can be ordered fresh from a custom butcher. To ensure tenderness, mutton (now understood to be the meat of a sheep over one year old) is usually cooked slowly, and for a longer period of time than lamb.

Chiquart's Directions

Cook shoulders & legs of mutton, remove the meat from the bones, leaving the bones together; chop fine. Put in bowl & add Brie cheese, chopped. Add marjoram, parsley, hyssop, sage, ginger, grains of paradise & whole cloves. Add a great number of eggs until the mixture is bound, and add saffron for color. Get sheep's cauls; wash them, spread them out, brush them with eggs to glaze them. Put a layer of stuffing on the casing; set the bones together in the proper position; spread another layer of stuffing over the top. Wrap the casing around everything & fasten it with

---

* It should be noted that for health reasons in some places a caul (or *crepinette*) cannot legally be sold as a foodstuff. You may still be able obtain a caul from an abattoir or butcher for presentation purposes, that is to say, one that is intended for showing off a dish and that is not intended to be eaten.

a wooden peg. Set this carefully on the grill over a moderate fire until set. Turn gently. Remove from the grill. Glaze with egg/flour/parsley mixture. Return coated shoulders to the grill to set the glazing. *Do not overcook.*

1. Stuffing recipe for Chiquart's directions: Serves 6

Imperial	Ingredient	Metric	Directions
4 1/2–5 lb	shoulder of lamb,* with bones	2 kg	**Simmer meat in lightly salted water to cover until tender. Remove meat from bones. Leave bones together; do not cut ligament that binds bones together. Chop meat into small pieces.**

Stuffing

1/2 lb	Brie cheese	250 gm	**Cut cheese into small pieces.**
3 tsp	fresh marjoram	15 mL	**Mix herbs & spices. Add to cheese.**
1/2 cup	fresh chopped parsley	125 mL	
1/2 tsp	fresh hyssop†	2 mL	
2 tsp	fresh sage	10 mL	
2 tsp	fresh grated ginger	10 mL	
1/4 tsp	grains of paradise	1 mL	
6	whole cloves (or grind into powder if desired)	6	
3	whole eggs	3	**Lightly beat eggs & saffron, & add to mixture.**
1/8 tsp	saffron	.5 mL	

Assemble the shoulder & cook over the grill until set.

Glaze

1/2 cup	fresh parsley	125 mL	**Glaze, then return to grill to set glaze.**
2 tbsp	flour	30 mL	
1	whole egg, lightly beaten	1	

---

* With young spring lamb this quantity may require using two smaller shoulders.

† Fresh hyssop may be difficult to obtain; if necessary, substitute a pinch of dried hyssop.

2. *Variation on Chiquart's Recipe: Serves 6–8*

This dish may be cooked on a barbecue also, medium high, 4 in/10 cm from the coals. Avoid overcooking. The meat should be crusty on the outside and pink inside.

Imperial	Ingredient	Metric	Directions
			Preheat oven to 425°F/220°C.
3–3 1/2 lb	boned shoulder of lamb *or* tenderloin strips	1.5 kg	**Slice tenderloin almost through lengthwise. Flatten, pound between sheets of wax paper to thickness of 1/4 in/5 mm.**
Stuffing			
1/2 lb	pieces of raw lamb*	250 g	**Cook lamb in boiling salted water. Drain, chop into small pieces or grind.**
1/4 lb	Brie cheese	125 g	**Cut cheese into small pieces.**
1/4 cup	fresh chopped parsley leaves (lightly packed)	60 mL	**Combine herbs & spices with the meat & cheese. Stir in eggs.**
1/8 tsp	ground hyssop	0.5 mL	**Spread the stuffing on the meat.**
1/2 tsp	ground sage	2 mL	**Roll & tie jelly roll fashion. Roast**
1/2 tsp	fresh grated ginger	2 mL	**uncovered 30–35 min. per lb/1 hr.**
1/4 tsp	grains of paradise	1 mL	**per kg. Halve the cooking time if**
1/8 tsp	ground cloves	0.5 mL	**using tenderloin.**
2	lightly beaten eggs	2	
Glaze			
1/4 cup	fresh chopped parsley leaves	60 mL	**Combine parsley, flour & egg. Remove meat from oven, glaze and**
1 tbsp	flour	15 mL	**return to oven until glaze is set.**
1	lightly beaten egg	1	
			Remove to serving platter, cut & serve.

* Or else sauté 1/2 lb/250 g of ground lamb in 1 tbsp/15 mL of lard or cooking oil.

4. *Civé de veel*

(*Menagier de Paris*, p. 168/§115)

Non lavé, non pourbouli, demy cuit en la broche ou sur le gril, puis le despeciez par pieces et friolez en sain avec grant quantité d'oignons par avant cuis. Puis prenez pain roussi seulement, ou chappelleures de pain non brulé, pour ce qu'il seroit trop noir pour civé de veel (ja soit-ce que icelluy pain roussi seroit bon civé de lievre). Et soit icelluy pain trempé ou boullon de beuf et un petit de vin ou de puree de pois; et en le trempant, broyez gingembre, cannelle, giroffle, graine de paradis, et du saffran largement pour jaunir et pour lui donner douleur, et destrempez de vertjus, vin et vinaigre; puis broyez vostre pain et coulez par l'estamine. Et mettez vos espices, le pain coulé, ou chaudeau, et faites tout boulir ensemble. Et soit plus sur le jaune que sur le brun, agu de vinaigre, et attrempé d'espices.

Et *nota* qu'il y convient largement saffran, et eschever a y mettre noix muguettes ne canelle, pour ce qu'ils roussissent.

Carnes vitulorum / Veal

(*Tacuinum sanitatis*, Vienna, Oesterreichische Nationalbibliothek, Codex Vindobonensis, 2644, f. 73v)

According to Galen—and his opinion carries considerable authority—veal is better than mutton. It provides substantial nourishment and is suited to those with warm temperaments, to the young, to springtime and to mainly southern locations. It is highly fortifying for those who exercise or who work very hard. It is harmful to splenetics, but this harm can be countered by movement and baths. Very young animals are always preferable, as are those that issue from mothers that have fed on excellent pastures. Veal should be cooked with chickens or fat capons, and with parsley.

Entre boire et ton vin tenir ne veulles long plait maintenir.	Don't pause when you have raised your cup: taste of the wine—or drink it up.

4. Veal Stew

The last sentence of the *Menagier*'s text for his *Civé de veel* / Veal Stew appears a little contradictory. After having included cinnamon as an ingredient in his recipe, the author then states that one should avoid adding either cinnamon or nutmeg! His reasoning, quite logically, is that these spices will necessarily impart a russet color to the dish, whereas according to the traditional French cookery that he is reproducing he knows that this pottage should properly be of a yellowish hue. Saffron is, consequently, one of the obligatory ingredients here. Once again we encounter a clear instance of the important role which coloration played in the prepared dishes of the period. At the same time we can again see how very greatly saffron was valued, not primarily for its flavor but for its potent properties as a colorant. Despite the *Menagier*'s cautionary note, or rather despite what he declares in his appended afterthought, we have listed cinnamon among the ingredients: we leave the choice of its use up to you.

A similar option may appear for modern cooks with regard to the preparation of the meat as well. The *Menagier* directs that the veal should *not* be washed or parboiled, but rather half-cooked (seared?) on a spit or grill, then sautéed in fat. The normal procedure at this time would indeed have called for the parboiling or frying of a meat before any subsequent cooking. Some culinary historians have seen in this procedure an influence of Arabic cookery, where the sequence of searing-and-then-boiling is fairly common. It seems extremely difficult, however, to accept the reality of such a remote, inter-cultural influence solely on the basis of a combination of cooking methods whose justification is so gastronomically reasonable.

In all likelihood the exceptional double treatment of veal, here and in the *Viandier* where the recipe is similar, is determined by the nature of this particular meat. Veal was perceived as a relatively moist meat, more moist than, say, beef which, being more mature, had dried out to become the driest of all domestic meats. Moderately warm and moderately moist, veal was in fact held to be one of the most desirable meats available for human consumption simply because these qualities approximated so very closely the temperament of the human body. Before putting veal into an essentially liquid dish, such as a *civé*, it was considered not only reasonable but prudent not to add to the natural moistness of veal by parboiling it. A quick searing over an open flame, followed by an equally rapid frying should provide an adequate preliminary treatment, and one which, by sealing the surface, would neither add to nor seriously diminish the moisture content of this ideal meat. For our part we have chosen to sear the meat in a pan.

As we pointed out earlier, a *civé, civet* or *civel* was a species of prepared dish whose essential element was its onions (*cive* in Old French). Generically the dish had many variations: for another example, see the *Civé d'oeufz* / Mustard Egg Sops in Chapter 8, below.

Yield: Serves 6–8

Imperial	Ingredient	Metric	Directions
3	large onions, quartered	3	**Sauté onions in bacon drippings in a heavy stewpot until lightly browned. Remove onions with slotted spoon & set aside.**
	or		
12	small onions, whole	12	
4 tbsp	bacon drippings *or* lard	60 mL	
1 1/2–2 lb	stewing veal	750–1000 g	**In remaining fat, sear pieces of veal until brown. Pour off all but 1 tbsp (15 mL) fat.**
2 cups	beef bouillon	500 mL	**Return onions to pot. Add bouillon & wine. Simmer, with pot tightly covered, until meat is almost tender (30 min.).**
1 cup	wine	250 mL	
3 slices	lightly toasted bread	3 slices	**Scoop out 1 1/2 cups bouillon from pot & pour over the bread slices. Let bread soak for 2–3 min., then rub it through a sieve (*or* blend in electric blender).**
1 tsp	ground cinnamon (*optional*)	5 mL	**Combine the spices & the wine, vinegar & lemon juice mixture. Stir well into the bread & bouillon, & pour all into stewpot. Simmer, covered, for a further 15 min. until stew thickens. Taste; if not tart enough, add more lemon juice to taste.**
1 tsp	ground ginger	5 mL	
1/4 tsp	ground cloves	1 mL	
1/4 tsp	saffron	1 mL	
1/4 tsp	grains of paradise	1 mL	
2 tbsp	wine	30 mL	
1 tbsp	wine vinegar	15 mL	
2 tbsp	lemon juice	30 mL	

Serving suggestions

Serve over buttered noodles *or* rice.

Ne boy pas la bouche baveuse, car la costume en est honteuse.	Nor from the cup take any sips before you've cleanly wiped your lips.

5. *Broet blanc sur chappons*
(*Du fait de cuisine*, §1)

L'on doibt prendre ses beaux chappons, et bien nectoyer le grain que on doibt mectre pour mes—ou soit porc, capril ou veaul, ou tel grein comme s'y appartient—et soit mis cuire bien et nectement en chaudieres grandes selon que on vouldra faire; et ung pou de porc meigre pourboillir dedans qui soit par devant bien lavez et nectoiez; et, selon la quantité dudit potaige que vous vouldrés faire, prennés grant quantité d'amandres et soient plumees, lavees et bien broyés, et en broyant les pour les arousés si prennés du boullion dudit chappon; et, quant voz chappons seront cuitz et le grein qui est avecques, si mectés les chappons d'une part et le grein d'autre et, selon la quantité dudit grein, prennés vostre boullon et si l'estaminés dedans une jalle ou cornue belle et necte en quoy il puisse estre; et puis prennés de bon vin blanc et de verjus et mectés dedans selon la quantité du boullon que vous avés, et de gingibre blanc et granne de paradis selonc la quantité du boullon, et soient coulees par l'estamine vostres amandres; et, selon la quantité dudit boullon, si prennés l'ayse—c'est assavoir, chaudiere belle et necte, ou olle—pour le boullir et, selon la quantité du boullon, si mectés du succre bullir dedans; et si advisés bien qui ne soit tropt ou pou salé; et puis apprés prennés vostre grein et le aloés par voz platz, et de vostre boullon par dessus.

5. White Broth of Capons

Chiquart specifies using a capon, a young cock that has been castrated and fattened to improve its flavor. For the best results, you might choose a plump, fresh chicken.

While Chiquart's cooking directions are a little imprecise—he instructs the cook only to clean the meat well and to cook it in water—we achieved best results when the veal and pork were poached first and the cut-up chicken added in the last twenty minutes of cooking time. As in other recipes, we leave to you the choice of either straining the almonds and spices after infusing them in the bouillon, or of using a blender to process the almond/bouillon mixture. There is no mention of a garnish in the original version, but our candied ginger and almond slices add a nice touch and would be quite normal.

With regard to our serving suggestion: though noodles are not mentioned in the *On Cookery*, other French recipe collections such as those written in an Anglo-Norman dialect a century earlier* do include noodles among their dishes. Generally speaking, small pasta preparations are quite common in the late Middle Ages. In Italian recipe collections of the period there are numerous references to use of ravioli, macaroni, tagliatelli, vermicelli and lasagne. One pie even has an upper crust of woven noodles! Chiquart himself refers to the way various pasta dishes, including ravioli, are prepared, as if the procedures were common enough among even mediocre cooks.

---

* The Anglo-Norman recipe for ravioli would be very popular in restaurants nowadays and is not dissimilar, in fact, to modern recipes for ravioli. "Take fine flour and sugar, and make a pasta dough. Take good cheese and butter and cream together; then take parsley, sage and shallots, chop them fine and put them in the filling. Put the boiled ravioli on a bed of grated cheese, cover with more grated cheese and reheat." The *Tacuinum sanitatis* lauds the properties of wheat pasta.

Yield: Serves 6–8

Imperial	Ingredient	Metric	Directions
1 1/2 lb	veal roast	750 g	**In a large stewing pot, cover veal & pork with boiling water. Cover & cook over medium heat for 20 min.**
1/2 lb	lean pork	250 g	
	boiling water to cover (approx. 4–6 cups/1.5–2 L)		
4–5 lb	chicken, cut into serving-sized pieces	2 kg	**Add chicken pieces (& more water if necessary). Poach until meat is tender—about 15–20 min. more. Remove meat from pot. Reserve the cooking bouillon.**
			Cut veal & pork into serving-sized pieces. Set aside with chicken to keep warm while making sauce.
			Skim *or* strain bouillon. Return to large cooking pot.

Sauce

Imperial	Ingredient	Metric	Directions
4–5 cups	reserved cooking bouillon	1.25 L	**Into 3 cups/750 mL of bouillon, stir ground almonds. Strain *or* process in a blender *or* processor. Add to the remaining bouillon …**
1 1/2 cup	freshly ground almonds	400 mL	
2 cups	dry white wine	500 mL	**… along with wine, lemon juice, spices & sugar. Return to a boil, then reduce heat & cook, stirring frequently until reduced to desired thickness.**
2 tbsp	lemon juice	30 mL	
2 tbsp	ground ginger	30 mL	
2 tsp	ground grains of paradise	10 mL	
2 tbsp	white sugar	30 mL	**Taste. Adjust spices to taste.**
			Arrange warm meat on serving platter *or* casserole dish. Pour sauce over top.

Garnish

Imperial	Ingredient	Metric	Directions
1 tbsp	slivered candied ginger	15 mL	**Garnish. Serve hot.**
1 tbsp	toasted almond slices	30 mL	

Serving suggestions

Serve over buttered noodles, accompanied by *Minces* / Brussels Sprouts in a Vinaigrette (see below, p. 262).

6. *Broet de Savoye*
(*Du fait de cuisine*, §3)

Et encour plus, ung aultre potaige, c'est assavoir ung broet de Savoye: pour donner entendement a celuy qui sera enchargié de ce broet cy, de prendre sa poullaille et le grein selon la quantité que on luy ordonnera que il en doibt faire, et appreste sa poullaille et mecte cuire nectement; et du grein selonc la quantité que on luy ordonnera faire de potaige, et mecte boullir avecque sa poullaille; et puis prenne une bonne piece de bacon meigre en bon endroit et les nectoiés bien et adroit, et puis le mectés cuire avecques la poullaille et grein dessusdit; et puis prennés de servi, pierrasi, ysope et margeleyne, et soient tresbien lavees et nectoyés, si s'en face une bugecte sans chapplez et tout ensemble, et puis se mecte boullir avecques ledit potaige et avecques le grein; et selon la quantité dudit boullon si prennés une grande quantité de persy bien nectoyé et lavé, et se broyent bien et adroit ou mortier; et, estre bien broyés, advisés vostre grein affin qu'il ne soit tropt ou pou cuit et salé, et puis selon la quantité du boullon se hait de gingibre blanc, de granne et de poivre ung pou, et mectés detramper de la mie du pain avecques ledit boullon tant que il en y ait assés pour le lier; et, estre destrampé appoint, et soit pilé et broyer avecques ledit persy et espices, et soit trait et estaminé avecques ledit boullon; et s'y mectés de vin et de verjust selon ce qui est necessayre. Et de toutes les choses dessus dictes si en mectés si appoint que il n'en y ait ne pou ne tropt. Et puis, ce fait, si mectés boullir en une grande, belle et necte oulle. Et se ainsy est que le potaige soit tropt vert, sy y mectés ung pou de saffran, si sera sur le verd gay. Et quant sera a drecier, si mectés vostre grein par les platz et dudit boullon par dessus.

Et ne rempliz pas si ta pance qu'en toy n'ait belle contenance.	Take care your belly not to stuff so much that less would be enough.

6. Savoy Broth

What appears to be a rather long, involved recipe in the *On Cookery* is really just a matter of boiling some sort of meat of your choice along with chicken and a little lean bacon; these are accompanied by a thickened parsley sauce.

For the optional meat here we prefer to use pork roast. Again, we have altered the cooking process slightly, preferring to add the chicken after the other meat has partially cooked. You can vary the amount and thickness of the sauce in this dish by increasing or decreasing the amount of bread or bouillon you use.

Yield: Serves 6–8

Imperial	Ingredient	Metric	Directions
4 1/2 lb	pork loin roast, tenderloin strips	2 kg	Place the pork in a large heavy stewpot & cover with water.
Bouquet garni			
sprigs *or* stems	parsley, sage, hyssop, marjoram *or*	sprigs *or* stems	Add the bouquet garni. Bring to a boil & then reduce heat & simmer until pork is almost done. (Allow about 30 min. to the lb/500 g).
1/2 tsp	dried herbs	5 mL	
1 1/2–2 lb	cut-up chicken	about 750 g	Add chicken & bacon. Add boiling water to cover if necessary & continue to simmer until chicken is done—about 20–30 min.
1/4 lb	lean bacon	125 g	
			Remove meat. Cut pork into serving-sized pieces. Set aside & keep warm. Skim fat from bouillon, then remove herbs (strain the bouillon if using dried herbs); reserve bouillon to use in sauce.
Sauce			
3 cups	reserved bouillon	750 mL	In a large saucepot, whisk together the bread & reserved bouillon. Bring to a boil stirring constantly to dissolve the bread.
3 slices	white bread, torn into pieces	3 slices	
3/4 cup	fresh chopped parsley, packed	175 mL	Add parsley.
1 1/2 tsp	ground ginger	7 mL	Combine spices & add to pot. Continue to cook, stirring constantly until desired consistency is reached.
1 tsp	salt	5 mL	
1/2 tsp	ground grains of paradise	2 mL	
1/4 tsp	ground pepper	1 mL	Taste; correct spices to taste.
pinch	saffron	pinch	Add saffron if you wish to alter the color.
			Set out warm meat on platters. Pour sauce over & serve hot.

Cooking variations

This sauce can also be used over roast meat should you not wish to follow Chiquart's cooking process. Roast the meat in an oven *or* on a barbecue.

Use prepared (home *or* commercial) bouillon for the sauce.

7. *Saulce lampree de lomblos de beuf*
(*Du fait de cuisine*, §4)

Encoures plus, une saulce lampree de lomblos de beuf: c'est assavoir a celluy qui haura la charge de faire la dicte saulce sy doibt prendre ses lomblos de beuf de haulte gresse et les doibt bien laver et embrochier en hastes biaus et nects; et puis doibt prendre son pain et trenchier en rouelles et roustir sur le gril tant qu'il soit bien rous, et avoir la une belle et grant cornue ou il mecte ledit pain roustir; et doibt avoir ung barral de tresbon vin rouge et, si n'en a assés d'ung, si en haye deux, et mecte dedans son pain; et gouste le boullon du beuf s'il est bon et doulx, et mecte du meigre parmy son pain ce qui sera necessité, et se y mecte du vin aygre rouge sy actrempement que il n'en y ait pas tropt affin que s'il estoit necessaire que il en y peust encor mectre; et puis prenne sa poudre de cynamomi, gingibre blanc, graynne de paradix, poyvre, noix muscates, galinga, giroffle, macy et de toutes autres espices, et les meslés avecques ledit pain et le estaminés tresbien; et advisés que vous ayés chaudieres ou olles belles et nectes selon la quantité de la saulce que vous avés faicte pour la mectre boullir. Et lesditz lomblos, quant ilz seront a leur devoir roustir, prennés les et mectés petiz trous honestes, et puis los mectés bullir dedans ladicte saulce; et, estre boullir tout ensemble, si se mecte tout en beaux platz, c'est assavoir deux tros en chascun platz, de la dicte saulce par dessus. Apprés, encor plus, patisserie de beuff d'aute gresse bien faicte: et que les patissiers soyent si bien advisiés de prendre les lomblos de beuf d'aute gresse et qu'ilz advisent celluy qui despiecera le beuf de retenir toutes les medulles des beufs pour mectre avecques les lomblos de beuf pour la bouche. Et pour le commun prennent les cuisses du beuf et sy en prennent tant grant foyson qu'il en hayent pour servir tout homme, et si soient les maistres patissiers si saiges et bien advisiés qu'ilz actremprent leur sel avecques leurs espices affin qu'il ne soit tropt salé.

Capiteles de char de buef / Beef
(Aldobrandino, *Le regime du corps*, p. 123)

Beef is cold and dry by nature, and engenders coarse and melancholic blood; when it is well digested it yields rather good nourishment; it is hardly good for anyone to eat but those whose stomach is warm and strong because it sits long in one's gut and is not at all well digested; as a result, those with a melancholic complexion ought to avoid beef since by nature it provokes quartan fever, scabies, dropsy, lentigo, a sort of leprosy that physicians call elephantiasis, ulcers and other melancholic diseases.

You should realize that beef varies according the age of the animal, so that the meat of a suckling calf yields better nourishment and is more easily digested because it is warm and moist due to its suckling, and engenders good blood, and consequently it can be eaten by those who are convalescing from bile ailments, tertian ague, double-tertian ague, and such other illnesses.

Beef from an older animal is not as estimable as that of which we have spoken, although it may be good for workingmen and for those with a strong stomach.

Beef from an aged animal is very bad, for it is cold and dry and nourishes little and poorly; therefore it is bad eaten in any way because more than any other meat it causes those maladies we referred to before.

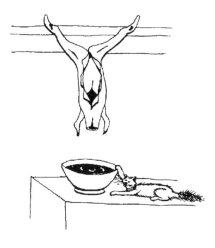

7. Lamprey Sauce on Loin of Beef

This tangy sauce provides an alternative to contemporary roast beef gravy. The beef can be barbecued on a spit or roasted in a pan, uncovered, in an oven. Make the sauce as thick or as thin as you wish by adding more bread or more bouillon. It is important to use fresh toasted bread, as commercial breadcrumbs produce a gritty texture. We encourage you to use your own judgement regarding the spices you include here since Chiquart himself, with rather surprising nonchalance, concludes *his* spice list with " . . . and all other spices"!

Despite its name, this sauce is not made of lampreys; the name comes from its original use *on* lamprey eels. Just why this sauce for lamprey should be considered appropriate for beef remains rather obscure.

The *Viandier* offers a recipe for Fresh Lamprey in a Hot Sauce, this latter being similar to the sauce here in Chiquart, although not quite so tasty. Toward the end of the *On Cookery* Chiquart describes a complex pie called a Coquart Pasty which is composed of a number of different sections containing variously meat, fish and fowl, each with an appropriate sauce; one of these sections interestingly contains lamprey which will be baked in this very Lamprey Sauce.

Yield: Serves 6–8

Imperial	Ingredient	Metric	Directions
3 lb	loin of beef	2 kg	Roast *or* barbecue beef until *almost* cooked to desired doneness. Remove & carve into serving-sized pieces. Set aside to keep warm. If roasted, reserve pan juices.

Sauce

Imperial	Ingredient	Metric	Directions
2	slices of bread, toasted	2	Place bread in large saucepot. Cover with wine, bouillon & vinegar. Cook over medium heat, stirring to break up bread.
1 1/2 cup	red wine	375 mL	
2 cups	lean beef bouillon *or* degreased pan juices & sufficient water to make 2 cups/500 mL	500 mL	
2 tbsp	red wine vinegar	30 mL	
1 tbsp	ground cinnamon	15 mL	Combine all spices & add to pot along with white vinegar. Bring sauce to a boil, stirring constantly. Reduce heat & simmer for about 5 min.
1/2 tsp	ground grains of paradise	2 mL	
1/8 tsp	pepper	.5 mL	
1/4 tsp	nutmeg	1 mL	
1 in	galingale root, grated	2 cm	Strain *or* process in blender, then strain to remove any remaining residue from galingale root, & return to pot.
1/4 tsp	cloves	2 mL	
1/8 tsp	mace	.5 mL	
1 tsp	salt	5 mL	
1 tbsp	white vinegar	15 mL	Taste; correct spices.
			Reduce to desired consistency. Add meat & cook for about 5 min. more. Set meat out on serving dishes & pour sauce over it.

Se tu es servy de froumaige, si en prens pou, non a oultraige.	If you are served with tasty cheese, take as you should, not as you please.

8. *Calunafree de perdrix*
(*Du fait de cuisine*, §47)

La calunafree de perdrix: celui qui la fera sy prenne ses perdrix et les nectoye bien et appoint et les reffaire et larde tresbien et puis les embroche et roustisse tresbien et appoint; et quant elles seront rousties si les tirés sur une belle et necte postz, et puis les prennés l'une apprés l'autre et les taillés par beaux membres et layssés les alleyrons entiers et le blanc taillés bien minut ainsi comme on le tailleroit devant le seigneur, et mectre cela en beaux platz d'argent—et sy n'avés tant de platz d'argent si les mectés en une poille belle et necte. Et prennés de la camelline grant foyson et en mectés par maniere qui se baigne tout, et y mectés de moustalde tant seulement que il luy donne gust, et y mectés de verjust qui se baigne tout. Et selon que vous avés du grein prennés des <u>rignions</u> et les chapplés tresbien minument et mectés dedans, et du succre, et si le goustés du sel par bonne maniere; et puis le mectés boullir. Et puis quant ce viendra au drecier si la despensés par beaulx platz par bonne ordonnance.

Perdices / Partridge
(*Tacuinum sanitatis*, Vienna,
Oesterreichische Nationalbibliothek, Codex Vindobonensis, 2644, f. 67v)

The partridge's meat is good for the blood, a delicate nourishment that is readily digested and suitable therefore for old and young alike, in the spring and especially for convalescents. However, it is harmful for those who do heavy work or carry heavy loads; should they wish to eat partridge, it should be cooked with slices of bread. Old partridge is tough and unappetizing and harmful to those with melancholic temperaments, so that one should choose young partridge or tenderize old partridge by hanging them one night. Partridge liver, eaten over a period of a year, is beneficial in curing epilepsy.

8. Calunafree of Partridge

Partridge was easier to obtain in Chiquart's neighborhood than it is in ours. Pheasant, however, is now raised commercially, and we have had recourse to that bird most often when we have prepared this dish. Cornish hens, more reasonably priced, are a good substitute here for the partridge as well.

The recipe for Calunafree of Partridge poses some difficulty in taste and in technique. There may be a scribal error in Chiquart's manuscript. Where the recipe says that *rignions* ("kidneys," underlined in the text above) are to be added to the sauce, the scribe *and cook* may have intended *oignions* ("onions"); both do appear in other recipes for fowl. We cook the giblets that come with our pheasant, grind them and add them to the sauce.

Chiquart directs that the cooked bird be cut into small pieces, bathed in a Cameline Sauce, then spread lightly with mustard and sprinkled with verjuice, and at last that everything be boiled together. Feel free to follow his directions if you wish, but *this cook* feels that it is a sacrilege to boil nicely roasted, succulent, astronomically priced fresh pheasant. Likewise with the sauce: rather than bathing the cut-up birds in the sauce, we present the bird on a large platter at the table, carve it there, and pass the sauce separately to our guests. The strong flavor of this sauce is not to everyone's taste.

It is likely that professional cooks referred only rarely to a manuscript copy of a cookbook. Before the days of carefully prepared printed editions of cookbooks, each hand-written copy of a recipe that was produced by a scribe was potentially marred by any of a number of factors that could interfere with its reliability: the legibility of the text *from* which the scribe was copying, the accuracy of that original copy itself, the attentiveness of the scribe that day, and even whether he had enough general knowledge in the field of cookery to allow him to correct a previous misreading or to distinguish between a reasonable reading and sheer nonsense. In the dim light at the weary end of an uncomfortable winter day, with domestic problems nagging him, many a scribe must have turned out dubious work. Fortunately, Chiquart seems to have secured the services of a remarkably reliable copyist. However, if you are inclined to think that Chiquart's normally careful scribe, Jehan de Dudens, did indeed make an error in this recipe when he wrote *rignions* rather than *ognions* or *oignions*, you may wish to try substituting a chopped, fried onion for the giblets.

Yield: Serves 6–8

Imperial	Ingredient	Metric	Directions
3 1 1/2-lb	partridge, pheasant or cornish hens	3 750-g	**Preheat oven to 400° F/200° C. Wipe birds inside & out with a damp cloth. Tie wings and legs to bodies. Place on a rack breast-side up a roasting pan.**
6	slices side bacon	6	**Lay 2 slices of bacon over each breast. Roast in oven at 400° F/200° C for 20 min. Reduce heat to 350° F/180° C & cook for about 1 1/2 hours *or* until tender.**
1 1/2 cups	Cameline Sauce	375 mL	**While birds are cooking, prepare either of the Cameline Sauces (*found on pp.115, 117 or 138*)**

Optional variations for the sauce

1	chopped cooked onion *or* giblets, cooked & ground	1	**Add onions or mustard to the hot sauce. Strain.**
1 tsp	French style mustard	5 mL	
			Transfer birds to a serving platter. Carve. Serve and pass the sauce in a sauce boat.

9. *Tortres parmeysines*
(Du fait de cuisine, §21)

Tortes parmeysines: pour lesdictes tortes parmeysines qui seront ordonnees a faire, pour vous donner entendement, prennés troys ou quatre porcs gros et, se la feste estoit plus grant que je ne pense, que on n'y mist plus, et de ces porcs ostés les testes et les jambons, et les saings metés tout apart pour fondre; et lesdiz porcs prennés et mectés par belles trenches ou pieces et les lavés tresbien et mectés cuire en belles chaudieres nectes, et y mectés du sel par mesure. Et pour lesdictes tortes parmeysines si vous fault .iii.ᶜ. pijons, .ii.ᶜ. pousins—et se ainsi estoit que la feste se feist en temps qui ne se trouvassent poussins, si hayés cent estoudeaux—.vi.ᶜ. petis oysels; et cil pijons, poullaille et oysellons soient plumés et nectoiés bien appoint et nectement; et me prennés les pijons et les fendés par le mielieu, et aussi la poullaille fendés et la mectés par cartiers; et puis les pijons, poullailles et oysellons prennés et mectés en belles jarles, lavés bien nectement et appoint troys ou .iiiiᵉ. fois en eaue belle et necte, et puis les mectés boullir en chaudieres belles et nectes, et y mectés du sel par mesure; et soit advisé qu'il ne cuie tropt; et, estre cuit soubtillement, trahés vostre grein en belles et nectes cornues et mectés voz oysellons d'une part et l'autre grein d'autre. Et puis prennés vostre saing de porc et en taillés grant foyson et mectés dedans belles et nectes casses et fondés bien et, estre bien fonduz, si le coullés en autres casses belles et nectes; et puis prennés vostres oysellons et les souffrisés dedans vostre lart legierement et non pas tropt, et aussi ensuivant l'autre grein. Et de figues .vi. livres, et .vi. livres de dactes, de pignions .vi. livres, de prunes .vi. livres, de raisins .viii. livres; et puis prennés vostres figues, prunes et dactes et les taillés menument—pour petiz des plus menuz que ne sont les raisins—et des raisins ostés les picolles et les nectoiés bien. Et puis prennés vostres pignions et les froctés tresbien, puis les vannés et espucés en beaux platz; puis les mectés sur beau mantil et les delisés et nectoiés bien et appoint qu'il n'y demoure que le grein blanc. Et puis mectés vostres figues, prunes, raisins, dactes et pinioles dedans une cornue belle, blanche et necte, et si soit bien couverte d'une belle, blanche et necte toile affin que riens qui ne fust nectz ne tombe dedans. Et puis faictes que vous ayés d'erbes, c'est assavoir salvi, persy, ysope et margellene, desquels ayés si grant quantité de persy que vous en ayés une grande pleyne selle de esgoutés et effueillés par feulles, et de la salvy, ysope et margellaynne mectés par mesure; puis les mectés en une belle et necte cornue, et les lavés bien et appoint a .iii. ou a .iiiiᵉ. eaues fresches, et puis les mectés sur belles et nectes postz et les chapplés tresbien menut. Et advisés en vostre grein du porc s'il est cuit et le mectés sur belles tables, et que vous ayés vostres belles postz grandes et bien plaines; et vous qui ferés ceste belle torte parmeysine, ensemble les compaignions que vous y mectrés, se advisent d'oster les cuenes desdistz porcs et que nuls os n'y demoure, et chapplés vostre char bien minument; et en chapplent voz dictes chars prennés herbes et les mectés parmi vostres chars; et puis ayés une grande, belle, necte et clere bacine et mectés vostres dictes chars didans—et pour vous donner entendement quelle est la bacine, je entens que ce soit une belle et grande poelle de celles en quoy on cuit les grans et gros poyssons. Et puis faictes que vous ayés ung quintal de flours de tresbon fromaige de Crampone ou de Brie ou flour de meilleur fruict que finer se pourra, et puis prennés ledit fromaige et le parés et nectoyés tresbien et appoint et le taillés minut, puis le broiés ou mortier tresbien et fort; puis prennés .vi.ᶜ. oeufs et y destrampés vostre fromaige en

broyant, et toujours arousés desdiz oez entant qu'ilz soient bien liez et destramppés et selon la
quantité des tortres parmeysines que vous sont ordonnees a faire. Et prennés moy la poelle que
dessus vous hay donné a entendre, et mectés dedans du lart en quoy l'on ha souffrit le grein
qui est affinés, et y mectés selon la quantité de la matere que vous avés, et soit mise sur beau
feu cler; et que vous ayés deux bons compaingnions fors et mennent la farce fort et fermement
a une grant poche perciee a .ii. mains, et puis descendre sur beau feu de charbon cler; et que
vostres figues, prunes, dates, raysins, pigniollas, taillés aussi comme est dist dessus, soient lavés
.ii. ou .iii. foys en belle eaue necte et clere et puis apprés lavés en de bon vin blanc et puis
les mectés esgouter et essuyer sur belle et necte postz; et puis, estre esgoutee, rués le dedans
vostre farce, et si soit tresbien menés parmy; et prennés vostre fromaiges broyés et destrampés
en oefs ainsi comme est distz dessus—la quantité que vous n'avéss fait pour ladicte farce—et
mectés dedans vostre farce en broyant tresbien et fort; et mectés ladicte poelle dehors du feu.
Et prennés vostres espices, gingibre blanc, poudre fine, granne de paradix, saffran pour donner
couleur, et y mectés par maniere de giroffle, mectés par dedans et mennés tousjours; et faictes
bactre du succre grant foyson en poudre et rués par dedans a grand foyson selonc la quantité de
la farce, et menés tousjours. Et sy faictes que vous ayés de belles casses et nectes, ou se vous
trouvés conchetes de terre belles et nectes si en prennés tant que mestier en haurés pour faire
vostres tortes parmeysines en tant grant quantité que vous en hayés de remenant; et puis quant
vous haurés vostres casses ou conchetes de terre belles et nectes si faciés que vous hayés .xx. ou
.xxx^m. de nebles ensucrees, et puis prennés vostres casses ou vostres conchetes et prennés du
lart en quoy vous avés frit vostres oysellons et la poullaille si mectés dedans vostres cassetes ou
conchetes de terre, et puis prennés vostres nebles et si mectés en chescune casse ou conchete de
terre sur les fons et en l'environ ung lit des dictes nebles en tant qu'il en ait .iiii. ou .v. l'une
sur l'autre; et sur lesdictes nebles si prennés de ladicte farce et en faictes ung lit, et puis dessus
la farce sy mectés des oysellons et les mectés cza et la et non pas ensemble; et si mectés en my
de deux oysellons ung quartier de pijons et d'autre part ung quartier de poullaflle en [my] de
deux oysellons, et face cecy en maniere que des oysellons, quartiers de pijons que de quartiers de
poullaille, soit fait bien et adroit ung lit sur le lit de la farce ja posee; et dedessus ce lit fait de
oysellons, quartiers de pijons et quartiers de poullaille si se face ung autre lit de la dicte farce, et
dedessus ce lit fait de farce si mectés nebles sus par le mode et maniere qui est dist dessus comme
elles sont mises sur le fons de la dicte casse ou conchete de terre; et, estre ce fait, qu'elle soit
couverte bien et appoint des dictes nebles. Si prennés du lart froit et mectés par dessus, et puis
mectés vostres tortes au four qui soit bien trempé; et si soyés bien advisés que quant elles cuiront
que vous ayés de feulles d'espinars et de blectes bien nectoiés et lavees affin que, se les dictes
nebles brullent riens, que vous en meisiés par dessus. Et puis traisiés vostres tortes parmeysines
et les rasclés bien et appoint en tant qui n'y demeure riens de brulé, et puis les mectés en beau
platz; et, elles estans en platz, si prennés vostre or party et le mectés par dessus vostres tortes
parmeysines en maniere d'un eschaquier, et de la poudre du succre par dessus. Et quant l'on en
servira, que sur chescune torte soit mise une banderete des armes d'un chescun seigneur qui de
cestes tortes parmeysines sera servi.

9. Parma Torte

This meat pie, whose name identifies it as originating in the central-Italian city-state of Parma, provides a tasty combination of fruit, meat, herbs and spices; the blending of flavors and textures is somewhat similar to what we associate with modern mincemeat,* although poultry as well is included here in Chiquart's recipe.

While today a *torte* is usually classified as a sweet layered cake or other dessert, this was not always the case. Many hot entrées called "tortes" or "tourtes" were made of such layered ingredients as meats, fruits, fish and vegetables, all of these contained within a pastry crust or wafers. Because of the heat of his oven, Chiquart suggests that the top crust be covered with moist spinach and chard leaves to prevent burning; even so, he directs, if there is anything burnt on the upper crust of these pies when they are withdrawn from the oven, that burnt matter should carefully be scraped away. Today we would use a piece of foil for a similar purpose.

Of particular interest, both to Chiquart and to ourselves, is the appearance of these pies when they are served. He instructs his reader to decorate the upper surface of each pie with a checkerboard pattern created out of gold leaf. When the squares of this finely beaten gold are laid out, the whole upper crust is covered with powdered sugar. Many medical treatises in the late Middle Ages discuss the various vital benefits of consuming pure gold—Chiquart gives us no reason for not assuming that those before whom these Parma Tortes are set will indeed eat the whole of the upper crust, gold leaf and all—but few of us today will ever have the means or the courage to find out whether medieval physicians propagated sound advice in this regard. The final presentation flourish for the Tortes is to be the insertion into the golden checkerboard of miniature standards or banners on which are figured the coat of arms of each noble guest before whom each Torte is set. Because of the extraordinary care that Chiquart takes with the appearance of these Tortes, we may think that they served as a distinctive *entremets* during a meal, affording the diners almost as much visual delight and gracious flattery as gastronomic pleasure.

This dish seems to have been one of the favorites of the court of Savoy in the fifteenth century. The recipe which Chiquart copies for it is particularly detailed. It is one of the rare recipes surviving from the Middle Ages that indicates the exact quantities of the principal ingredients. The care which our professional cook takes in elaborating the directions for making this pie probably reflects to some extent his concern that none of the gastronomic effect of this complex delicacy be lost when it was prepared in kitchens other than his own.

We have greatly simplified the directions for making this Torte, substituting ground pork for the pig carcasses that Chiquart causes to be boiled, chopped and fried in pork grease. As well, our fowl is limited to chicken (you may substitute whole chicken meat in place of breasts if you prefer), omitting the doves and other small birds. Raisins have been substituted for the fresh pitted grapes called for in the original recipe. Chiquart does not specify the type of grape to be used. If

---

* In fact, if you are not overly concerned with an exact duplication of the ingredients here, you could start with prepared mincemeat, add some figs, pinenuts, dates and prunes, and wine, add the eggs and cheese, and then add in the chicken; you would have a reasonable substitute without all the chopping.

you wish to substitute a fresh pitted sweet grape, such as muscat or Thompson seedless, increase the quantity of these to two cups.

Yield: Serves 6

Imperial	Ingredient	Metric	Directions
	Sufficient whole wheat pastry or wafers for 1 pie (*see pp. 67 or 68, above.*)		
1	whole large chicken breast	1	**Poach* chicken in salted water (*or chicken bouillon) to cover, until flesh turns white. Drain, tear into large pieces & set aside.**
1/2 lb	ground pork	250 g	**Fry ground pork. Drain off all but 2 tbsp/30 mL of fat.**
Herbs			
2 tsp	dried hyssop	10 mL	**Add herbs to pork & toss well to mix. Set aside.**
2 tsp	dried sage	10 mL	
3–4 tbsp	fresh parsley, chopped fine	50–60 mL	
2 tsp	marjoram	10 mL	
Fruit			
1 cup	raisins (sultana *or* muscat)	250 mL	**In a saucepan combine fruit ...**
3/4 cup	pitted dates, cut small	175 mL	
3/4 cup	prunes, cut small	175 mL	
3/4 cup	figs, cut small	175 mL	
1/4 cup	pinenuts	50 mL	
Spices			
1/2 tsp	cloves	2 mL	**& spices.**
1/2 tsp	cinnamon	2 mL	
1/2 tsp	ginger	2 mL	
1/4 tsp	grains of paradise	1 mL	
pinch	saffron	pinch	
2 cups	white wine	500 mL	**Add wine & cook over low heat for 10 minutes. Add pork mixture & continue cooking for an additional 10 minutes. Add more liquid if necessary.**

---

* Chiquart directs that the chicken first be browned in pork fat. We have eliminated this step.

4 oz	soft cream cheese (preferably Brie)	125 gm	Cut cheese into small pieces.
1	egg	1	Beat egg & sugar together to form a creamy mixture. Add cheese. Combine this mixture with the pork-and-fruit mixture.
2 tbsp	brown sugar	30 mL	
			Line a large 11–12 in/27–30 cm deep pie dish with half the pastry. Spoon half the meat/fruit mixture on the bottom. Place chicken slices on top & spread the remainder of the mixture on top.
1 1/2 tsp	butter	7 mL	Dot with small pieces of butter & cover with pastry lid. If desired, make decorative shapes out of left-over pastry & place these on lid. Brush lid with the saffron & milk mixture in a checkerboard pattern & sprinkle white sugar on top.
pinch	of saffron	pinch	
1 tsp	milk *or* cream	5 mL	
1 tsp	white sugar	5 mL	
			Bake at 425° F/220° C for 10 min. Reduce heat to 375° F/190° C & cook 35–40 min. more.
			Serve warm.

Other Possible Meat Dishes

Alouyaulx / **Little Larks**

For the complete recipe of this dish as an Appetizer, see p. 88, above.
Use larger pieces of veal and serve the Little Larks as an *entrée* dish.

Rosseolles / **Pork Rissoles**

For the complete recipe of this pastry dish as an Appetizer, see p. 93, above.

Calaminee / **Calaminee Sauce**

For the complete recipe of this dish as a Sauce, see p. 143, above.
This sauce can be used on cold pork.

Faulx grenon (Potage party) / **Mock Meat**

For the complete recipe of this dish as a Poultry Dish, see p. 202, below.
Substitute veal or pork for the poultry livers. Sear meat in fat or oil, and then follow the recipe as written.

Froide sauge / **Cold Sage**

For the complete recipe of this dish as a Poultry Dish, see p. 183, below.
Though prescribed primarily as a dressing for chicken, this sauce can also be used very satisfactorily as an accompaniment to cold slices of veal or pork.

Chapter 4, above (pp. 111–44), contains a wide variety of sauces that can be used with meats, boiled or roasted, warm or cold. We suggest that you experiment with combinations of various meats and various sauces.

Chapter 6
Poultry Dishes

Chapter 6
Poultry Dishes

In the fourteenth and fifteenth centuries, just as today, chicken, duck, goose and guinea-fowl contributed to a large proportion of the dishes in which any meat entered at all. For the modern cook, only the addition of turkey has significantly changed this list of domestic poultry. Just as today, the late-medieval cook fully recognized the great advantages of poultry, in terms both of its practical availability and of its culinary reliability. In particular, chicken could be had cheaply and throughout the year, it offered itself to a multitude of preparations, it could be—and regularly was—combined with a variety of other meats, it was relatively easy to prepare and handle, it cooked quickly and it was "gastronomically" dependable.

Almost as if to confirm all of these advantages, physicians recognized in chicken especially, but also in fowl in general, a temperament that brought them closely into accord with human temperament. Because the natural habitat of birds is the air, they were held to participate by nature in the nature of air itself: this was perceived as being moderately warm and moderately moist. Possessing, consequently, a sanguine temperament (that is, a combination of warm and moist), fowl were declared in principle to be ideally appropriate for human consumption. Of course, this medical pronouncement was most fortunate for both the cooks and their masters in late-medieval Europe.

It had furthermore long been recognized that most fowl, and again especially chicken, was good to eat cold as well as hot. And so one of the most popular dishes in medieval France was the one known as Cold Sage, the first of the recipes we have selected for this chapter.

Because physicians universally attributed desirably temperate properties to chicken, and saw it as yielding quite good nutrition to the person who consumed it, it became a staple ingredient in dishes prepared for the sick and sickly. Such a preparation as the White Dish (of which we give a couple of instances below) appeared almost invariably in the chapters on sickdishes of recipe manuscripts. These perceptions of chicken as being good for a sick person remain deeply imbedded in modern popular wisdom.

Among wildfowl only pheasant seems to have been accorded a higher rating than chicken as affording a healthful meat of all-round utility.

With such a long list of exceptional virtues attached to poultry, it is no wonder that recipe collections right across Europe at this time devote a substantial amount of their total material to recipes that call for chicken.

182

1. *Froide sauge*
(*Menagier*, p. 215/§244; also in the *Viandier*, §73)

Pour faire une froide sauge, prenez vostre poulaille et mettez par quartiers, et la mettez cuire en eaue avec du sel; puis la mettez reffroidier. Puis broyez gingembre, fleur de canelle, graine, giroffle, et broyez bien sans couler; puis broyez du pain trempé en l'eaue des poucins, percil le plus, sauge, et un pou de saffren en la verdure pour estre vertgay, et les coulez par l'estamine (et aucuns y coulent des moyeux d'oeufs durs), et deffaites de bon vinaigre. Et icelles deffaites, mettez sur vostre poulaille, et avec et pardessus icelle poulaille mettez des oeufs durs par quartiers, et gettez vostre sausse pardessus tout.

1. *Froide sauge*
(*Du fait de cuisine*, §49)

Et pour vous donner a entendre comme vous ferés la froide sauge si faictes que vous haiés grant foison de percy, grant foison de salvy, et qu'ilz soient bien deliez et lavés et esgoutés et broyés tresbien, et si en broyés tant grant quantité qu'elle soit bien verd; et quant elles seront bien broyees si les meslés et mectés avecques vostre pain. Et puis prennés voz espices, c'est assavoir gingibre blanc, granne et du poyvre et coulés tout cela, et agoustés du vin aigre et du sel et le coulés tresbien espés. Et quant vostre grein sera bien cuit si le tirés hors sur belles postz et tables belles et nectes, et puis partissés ledit grein, c'est assavoir la poullaille d'une part et d'autre part les pieces du porcellot, et tant que quant viendra au drecier si mectés en ung chescun platz quatre pieces duit grein, c'est assavoir ung quartier de poullaille et une piecete dudit porcellot sus et en la moytié d'un chescun plat, et en l'autre partie autretant; et en chescun plat en l'une part si mectés de la calaminee et l'autre part a cousté de la froide sauge. Et puis prennés du blanc des oefs et les taillés par menuz dez, puis en semés sus lesditz platz par dessus la froide sauge; et de la dragiee mectés sur la calunafree.

Salvia / Sage
(*Tacuinum sanitatis*, Vienna,
Oesterreichische Nationalbibliothek, Codex Vindobonensis, 2644, f. 37v)

The nature of sage is warm and dry, and it generates thick and sometimes warm blood. It is good for the stomach and for cold diseases of the nerves. The sage that grows in the kitchen garden is the variety that is normally used, but forest sage is better for producing warmth. It is slow to digest, but this can be speeded up with a decoction of honey. We read that if a woman who has slept alone for four days drinks this and then has sexual relations, she will immediately become pregnant; to this end, women who survived the plague in one town in Egypt were made to drink the juice of sage leaves so that the town could quickly be repopulated.

1. Cold Sage

Frugal cooks five and six hundred years ago faced much the same problems with left-overs as do economically minded cooks today. However, one difference then was the lack of refrigeration, although jelly (from natural animal sources) provided a very common means to preserve cooked meats and fish over several days. For shorter periods, when an already cooked meat or fish was to be served without reheating on the next day, or in the warmth of summer when a refreshing dish of cold meat was deemed appropriate, several cold sauces could be relied upon to lend a delectable savor to a preparation. One of the most frequently prepared of these cold sauces was a relatively straightforward unboiled green sauce in which the flavor of sage predominates.

In a sense the Cold Sage is a counterpart to Green Sauce, another very common unboiled sauce in which parsley is the basic ingredient. While the Green Sauce is more serviceable, being called upon to dress a very wide variety of meats, fowl and fish, Cold Sage retains a certain exclusivity which is undoubtedly related to the unique taste of the herb sage. This is, *par excellence*, a *cool* taste, wholly appropriate for a refreshing dish of light, easily digestible cold meat.

The *Viandier* and the *Menagier de Paris* use only boiled, cooled poultry in their versions of this recipe. Chiquart combines chicken and pork: in his *Du fait de cuisine* the cold pork is accompanied by a *Calaminee* (another cold dish whose yellow sauce is spiced with ginger and grains of paradise) and is garnished with *dragees* (see the comments at pp. 34 and 72). The Savoyard household in which Chiquart worked seems to have had a predilection for the juxtaposition of green and yellow dishes.

In the present recipe, chicken is dressed with the Cold Sage Sauce and the whole dish is garnished with quartered hard-boiled eggs. Though the directions call for an unboiled sauce, we have found it preferable to heat the sauce gently.

Both the *Viandier* and the *Menagier* include cloves among the spices for Cold Sage, although Chiquart in his *Du fait de cuisine* does not; we have chosen to follow Chiquart's lead in this omission. Along with the *Menagier*, however, we suggest saffron as an optional ingredient in the sauce. Saffron, a colorant, was often included with green herbs in early French cookery in order to lend a brighter hue to the green. This mixture produces a standard color which was universally known in French-speaking provinces as *vertgay*, "cheery green."

Yield: Makes 1 1/2–2 cups/375–500 mL of sauce, sufficient for 6

Imperial	Ingredient	Metric	**Directions**
	Sufficient cold chicken or pork pieces for 6 persons. If cooking chicken, reserve 1/2–1 cup/125–250 mL of bouillon.		
1 cup	chopped fresh parsley*	250 mL	**Process parsley & sage in blender (*or* grind in mortar) with chicken broth *or* bouillon. Blend slowly. Cook on low heat.**
1/2–3/4 cup	chopped fresh sage*	125–200 mL	
1 cup	hot chicken bouillon	250 mL	
pinch	saffron (*optional*)	pinch	**Optionally add saffron (to brighten the green color).**
1/4 cup	white wine vinegar	60 mL	**Add vinegar to mashed hard-boiled egg yolks & blend with herb mixture.**
2	hard-boiled egg yolks (set the whites aside)	2	
1/2 tsp	salt	2 mL	**Add spices.**
1/2 tsp	ginger	2 mL	
1/4 tsp	grains of paradise	1 mL	
1/4 tsp	cinnamon *or* ground cassia buds†	1 mL	
2 slices (or more)	white bread, crusts removed, torn into small pieces	2 slices (or more)	**Add bread, a little at a time, until a thick consistency is reached. Taste; correct spices as desired. Remove from heat. Cool.**

Garnish

2	sliced hard-boiled eggs (together with the chopped reserved egg whites)	2	**To serve, place chicken pieces onto serving platter, top with sliced eggs, spoon sauce over & top with reserved chopped egg whites & parsley.**
2 sprigs	parsley	2 sprigs	

Serving alternative

Try the sauce part of this recipe as a substitute for the currently popular Pesto Sauce; in this way it can be used over noodles (or wherever) instead of over just the chicken of this Cold Sage dish.

---

* When measuring, do not pack down the herbs.

† It is the most "modern" version of the *Viandier*, the one copied in the manuscript that is now in the Vatican Library in Rome, that substitutes cassia buds for the cinnamon that had been used in this recipe as it is copied in the older copies of the *Viandier*. Cassia buds are also known as Chinese cinnamon, and are known in French as *fleurs de cannelle*. They can be obtained at most health and bulk-food stores.

2. *Comminee d'almandes*
(*Viandier*, §13)

Cuisiez bien vostre poulaille en eaue, et la despeciez par quartiers et friolez en sain de lart; puis prenez amendes et les brayés, et les deffaictes de vostre boullon et mettez boullir sur vostre grain; et prenez gingenbre et commin deffait de vin et de verjus; et tousjours se lye elle mesme.

Capiteles de commim / Cumin
(Aldobrandino, *Le regime du corps*, p. 186)

Cumin is warm and dry in the second degree. It is the seed of an herb that grows very abundantly; it can be kept for five years. By nature, if cumin is consumed in powder or in a sauce, its virtue is to promote urination, to eliminate flatulence and to comfort the stomach's action.

If the wine is drunk in which cumin is cooked, along with dry figs, it is very useful for those who have a cough caused by cold humors, and for those who have belly cramps and pains; in cold weather it is valuable in making a poultice, provided it is mixed with barley flour and moistened with wine.

Moreover, for those who have blood in their eyes from having been hit, it is good to take cumin, mix it with egg yolks, set it on a warm tile and then spread it thinly on the eye; and if the face is still discolored from blows or whatever, get cumin powder and put it on it. You should note that it is not good to use cumin too much because it gives a person a pale, sickly color.

2. Almond Chicken Cuminade

In the late-medieval kitchen, cumin was common. This spice was relied upon by the professional cooks of the period to produce a category of dish and sauce, the *cuminades*, whose characteristic flavor was as distinct as those in which the predominant flavor was ginger (the *jances*) or cinnamon (the *camelines*). As a result, we find in the various early French collections a number of recipes for *cuminades* whose ingredients vary somewhat (there are, for instance, a Cuminade of Chicken and a Cuminade of Fish, as well as another of Almonds); in every case, though, a good dose of cumin is essential, the vital ingredient. These are clearly more than merely variations on some basic recipe, yet all of them belong to what we might term a family of cuminades.

Though the recipe for Almond Chicken Cuminade in the *Viandier* does not specify cooking the chicken in wine and water, the recipe which precedes it in the same collection does; this is for another variety of Cuminade, a Cuminade of Poultry. The *Menagier* likewise directs that wine and water be used to prepare the poultry for his *Comminié de poullaille* (§98). We have suggested that wine be included here. Should you not wish to cook the whole chicken first, cut it into quarters and sauté it in lard or pork fat. Substitute 1 cup of dry white wine for the equivalent amount of chicken bouillon in the sauce. Similarly chicken breasts may be substituted for the whole chicken.

Yield: Serves 6

Imperial	Ingredient	Metric	Directions
4–5 lb 1 cup 2 cups	chicken *or* capon dry white wine water	2–2.5 kg 250 mL 500 mL	**Bring water to boil. Add wine. Simmer chicken in liquid only until the flesh of the bird becomes white. Drain, cut into pieces. Set cooking liquid aside.**
4 tbsp	pork fat *or* lard	60 mL	**Sauté chicken pieces in pork fat. Set aside in warm place.**

Sauce

2 1/2 cups 1–1 1/4 cup	reserved chicken bouillon ground almonds	750 mL 250–300 mL	**In large pot, bring chicken bouillon to a boil. Add ground almonds & simmer together 5 min. (If you wish a less gritty texture for the sauce, strain the mixture *or* blend in blender 1–2 min. & return to pot.)**
2 tbsp 2 tbsp 1 tbsp	fresh grated ginger (*or* 3 tsp/15 mL ground ginger) ground cumin dry white wine lemon juice *or* wine vinegar	30 mL 30 mL 15 mL	**Infuse spices in wine & juice. Stir into sauce. Continue cooking over low heat until sauce thickens. Taste; correct seasoning.** **Heat chicken pieces in sauce slowly. Do not boil.**

Garnish

2 tbsp 3	toasted sliced almonds sprigs parsley	30 mL 3	**When heated through—about 3 min. —set out chicken on platter. Cover with the sauce & garnish with toasted almonds & parsley.**

Serving suggestion

Serve any remaining sauce in a gravy boat or bowls.

3. *Comminee de poullaille*
(*Viandier*, §12)

Cuissiez la en vin et en eaue, et puis la despeciez par quartiers et frisez en sain de lart; puis prenez ung pou de vin et en trempez vostre boullon, et le coulez et le mettez boullir avec vostre grain; puis prenez bien pou de gingenbre et de commin deffait de verjus et de vin; puis prenez moyeulx d'oeufz grant foison, et les batez bien et les fillez en vostre potaige arriere du feu; et gardez qu'il ne tourne.

Cumin & Basil
(Pliny, *Natural History*, Book 19, Ch. 36 and 47,
ed. H. Rackham, Cambridge, Mass. & London [Harvard & Heinemann], 1940, Vol. 5)

... Of all seasonings which gratify a fastidious taste, cumin is the most agreeable. It grows on the surface of the ground, hardly adhering to the soil and stretching upward, and it should be sown in the middle of spring, in crumbly and specially warm soils. ... No seed is more prolific than basil; they recommend sowing it with curses and imprecations to make it come up more abundantly; when it is sown the earth is rammed down. Also people sowing cumin pray for it not to come up. It is difficult for seeds contained in a pod to get dry, particularly basil, and consequently they are all dried artificially to make them fertile.

Il est conseillé en la Bible	The Bible urges, without cease
entre les gens estre paisible.	always strive to keep the peace.

3. Cuminade of Chicken

Cuminade of Chicken is similar to the Almond Chicken Cuminade, except that eggs are used as a thickener instead of ground almonds. This makes a dish that is slightly thicker and perhaps a little creamier. In this recipe, Taillevent stipulates that only a little ginger be added: the taste of the cumin must still predominate.

Many of these early recipes call for cooking the chicken whole rather than cut up: it was, after all, easier and almost as effective to chuck several dozen fowl into the huge cooking vats whole. A modern cook who is preparing a meal for a relatively modest number of guests may find it more convenient to cut the chicken into quarters or even smaller pieces before poaching it.

Yield: Serves 6

Imperial	Ingredient	Metric	Directions
4–5 lb	cut-up chicken *or* 6 chicken breasts	2–2.5 kg	**Poach chicken in wine & water just until the flesh becomes white. Do not**
1 cup	dry white wine	250 mL	**overcook. Drain; reserve bouillon.**
2 cups	water (to cover)	500 mL	
3–4 tbsp	lard	50–60 mL	**Sauté chicken pieces in lard. Keep warm.**
2–2 1/2 c	hot chicken bouillon	500–625 mL	**Add a chicken bouillon cube if necessary. To the hot bouillon, add bread**
2	slices of white bread in crumbs, crusts removed	2	**crumbs; combine well.**
1/2 tsp	ground ginger (*or* 1 tsp/ 5 mL fresh grated ginger)	2 mL	**Infuse spices in mixture of wine & juice. Combine with bouillon.**
1 tbsp	ground cumin	15 mL	**Remove bouillon from heat.**
2 tbsp	dry white wine	30 mL	
1 tbsp	lemon juice *or* wine vinegar	15 mL	
4	egg yolks	4	**Beat egg yolks lightly. Whisk in 1/2 cup/125 mL of hot bouillon. Add this to the rest of the bouillon, a little at a time, using a wire whisk. Return pot to heat.**
			Combine chicken with the egg sauce; on low heat (do not boil) cook until chicken is warmed through—about 3 min.

Serving suggestion & garnish

| | sprigs of parsley | | **Put chicken on platter; pour sauce over. Garnish with parsley.** |

Serve any remaining sauce in a gravy boat or in bowls for dipping.

4. *Blanc mengier*

(*Enseignements*, p. 184; & *Viandier*, §95)

Se vos volez fere blanc mengier, prenez les eles e les piez de gelines e metez cuire en eve, e prenez un poi de ris e le destrempez de cele eve, puis le fetes cuire a petit feu, e puis charpez la char bien menu eschevelee e la metez cuire ovec un poi de chucre. Si avra non Laceiz. E se vos volez, si metez cuire ris entier ovec l'eve de la geline ou ovec let d'alemandes. Si ara non Angoulee.

Another *Blanc mengier* is found also in the *Menagier de Paris*, p. 165/§107, and in the *Du fait de cuisine*, §75.

Blanc mengier d'un chappon pour ung malade. Cuisiez le en eaue tant qu'il soit bien cuit; et broiez amendes grant foison et, avec ce, de braon du chappon, et qu'il soit bien broyé et le deffaictes de vostre boullon et passez tout parmy l'estamine et puis mettez boullir tant qu'il soit bien liant comme pour le taillier, puis versez en une escuelle; et puis mettez frioler demie douzainne d'amendes pelees et les asseez sur le bout en la moictié de vostre plat, et en l'autre des pepins de pomme de grenade et les succrez par dessus.

Granata dulcia / Pomegrantes

(*Tacuinum sanitatis*, Vienna,
Oesterreichische Nationalbibliothek, Codex Vindobonensis, 2644, f. 7r)

There are two varieties of pomegranate, sweet and sour; the first is warm by nature, the second cold; both types have a peel like red leather and their inside is full of quadrangular-shaped seeds that are red and of a wine flavor. Of the sweet variety the large pomegranates are preferable and easy to peel; they provide commendable nourishment and are useful for coughs. However, they do cause swelling, which can be checked by eating sour pomegrantes. We find in some texts that whole pomegranates, roasted in a well covered pot in an oven until they are burnt, make a very effective powder for treating dysentery: take five-eighths of an ounce of this powder with red wine.

Se tu te veulx faire valoir,	If you want your praises sung,
sobre parler tu dois avoir.	always speak with sober tongue.

4. White Dish of Chicken

Practically all of the early European recipe collections contain a version of what was one of the most commonly known dishes in the late medieval period, the so-called White Dish. The ingredients of the White Dish vary only slightly: ground almonds and almond milk, rice and rice flour, chicken, sugar, a mild spice or two—some or all of these appear from version to version, from Germany right across the continent to the Hispanic peninsula. There are some grounds for thinking that in its origins the *"blanc* mengier" was originally a *"blant* or *bland* mengier": this is one of the most delicately mild dishes in all of medieval cookery. And besides, in some recipes for this preparation there are so many colored ingredients present that we might have difficulty understanding just why and how it could ever be called a *"white* dish." In its French versions the *Blanc mengier* is treated as a preparation appropriate for the sick, undoubtedly because the humors of its principal ingredients (chicken, almonds and sometimes rice) were held by physicians to be so temperately close to those of the healthy human complexion.

Significant variations are worked on the basic recipe only when colorants are added to make a Parti-Colored White Dish (see below, p. 296), and when Chiquart suggests substituting partridge for the capons of his regular White Dish.

The principal ingredients are normally chicken and almonds or almond milk. In every case the chicken is cooked in water until it is well done. The dark meat is stripped from the carcass and is ground up along with the almonds and some of the cooking liquid. The white meat is torn into striated strips and added later. Chiquart and the *Menagier* add ginger, salt and sugar; the *Menagier* further suggests that you might include coriander and grains of paradise. The *Enseignements* suggests using rice as a thickener, along with almond milk. After transferring the mixture to a serving dish we may follow the directions found in the *Viandier*: fried almonds are stuck into one half of the dish; the other half is covered with the fruit of a pomegranate, then sprinkled with sugar.

Yield: Serves 6

Imperial	Ingredient	Metric	Directions
4–5 lb	stewing chicken	2 kg	**Cut chicken into quarters. Cover with water & cook until tender. Reserve 3 c/750 mL of the *degreased* cooking liquid—add chicken bouillon if necessary. Separate white meat; tear into strips & set aside. Chop dark meat finely.**

1/2 cup	ground almonds	125 mL	**In blender, combine dark meat, almonds & 1 c/250 mL of bouillon. Add rest of bouillon; blend, then strain.**
3 cups	reserved bouillon	750 mL	
2 tbsp	white sugar	30 mL	**In pot, combine the strained mixture, sugar & ginger; bring to a boil.**
1 1/2 tbsp	fresh grated ginger	20 mL	
1 cup	long-grain rice	125 mL	**Add rice. Reduce heat, cover & cook about 20 min. or until rice is tender. Add more bouillon if necessary. Fold in white meat. Remove to serving platter.**
1 1/2 tsp	ground coriander	7 mL	**Sprinkle with coriander. Garnish one half of the dish with toasted almonds & the other half with pomegranate seeds. Sprinkle with sugar. Serve.**
2 tbsp	toasted almond slices	30 mL	
1/4 cup	pomegranate seeds	60 mL	

5. *Poullaille farcie*

(Viandier, §66; & *Menagier de Paris*, pp. 212 & 213/§§238 & 242)

Prenez vos poulles et leur couppez le gavion, puis les eschaudez et plumez, et gardez que la peau soit sainne et entiere, et ne la reffaictes point en l'eaue; puis prenez ung tuel de chaume ou autre, et le boutez entre cuir et chair et l'enflez, puis le fendez entre les espaules et n'y faites pas trop grant trou; et laissiez tenant a la peau les cuissetes, les ailles et le col atout la teste et les pietz aussi. Et pour faire la farce, prenez chair de mouton, de veel, de porc, du brun des poulletz, et hachiez tout ensemble tout cru, puis les broyez en ung mortier, et des oeulfz tous cruz avec de bon frommaige de gain et de bonne pouldre d'espices et ung bien pou de saffren; et sallez a point; puis emplez vos poullez et recousez le trou. Et du remenant de vostre farce faictes en pommez comme parciaulx de guede, et mettez cuire en boullion de beuf et en eaue boullant, et du saffran grant foison; et qu'ilz ne boullent mie trop fort, qu'ilz ne se despiecent; puis enhastez voz poulletz en une broche de fer bien deliee, et les pommes aussi. Et pour les dorer ou couvrir de vert ou de jaune: pour le jaune, prenez grant foison de moyeulx d'oeufs et les batez bien, et ung pou de saffren avec, et mettez la doreure en ung plat ou autre vaissel; et qui veult doreure verte si braye la verdure avec les oeufz; et aprés ce que vostre poulaille sera cuite et voz pommes, drecieez vostre broche ou vaissel ou vostre doreure sera et gectez tout du long vostre doreure et remettez au feu affin que vostre doreure se preigne, par deux fois ou par trois, et gardez que vostre doreure n'ait grant feu qu'elle ne arde.

5. Stuffed Poultry (Chicks or Chickens)

In both the *Viandier* and the *Menagier* a recipe for Stuffed Poultry appears among the suggestions for that special delight known as the *entremets* (see below, p. 311). If you should wish to include one relatively simple but impressive *entremets* in your medieval meal, this dish of Stuffed Poultry would be more than adequate. Even the frugal Parisian bourgeois himself, the author of the *Menagier*, copies his version of the recipe for *Poulaille farcie* into his book, though he discards several other of the *Viandier*'s *entremets* as requiring too great an effort—and, perhaps more important, entailing too great a waste of money—for a respectable bourgeois table.

The stuffed or dressed chicken recipes included in these medieval collections range from such simple outlines as the *Menagier*'s §238 for *Poucins* (small chicks) stuffed with a mixture of parsley, sage, butter, hard-boiled eggs and spice powder, to the more elaborate recipes reproduced in the *Viander*'s §66 and the *Menagier*'s §242. Ingredients common to the stuffing in these recipes include veal, pork, eggs, cheese, spice powder, salt and saffron. Depending on which manuscript version of the recipe is consulted, chestnuts and mutton, along with white and dark meat from the chicken, could also enter into the mixture. In all cases any leftover stuffing is formed into meatballs "the size of packets of woad" and cooked along with the chicken. The herb woad was a favorite blue colorant in the late Middle Ages, regularly sold in packets of about one or one-and-a-half inches in diameter.

At the end of the cooking period, the chicken and meatballs are basted with a yellow or green egg-glaze.

Recipe 195 in the *Viandier*, called *Doreures*, lists the following as ingredients for the chicken's stuffing: pork, bacon, white meat, eggs, spice powder, pinenut paste and currants. Though the manuscript says that the meatballs are of pork, the context is quite ambiguous. In light of the previous recipes, in both the *Viandier* and the *Menagier*, the meatballs were probably made of leftover stuffing which included the pork. Since this is described as a dish fit for a princely banquet, the final glaze is—literally and actually—gold leaf. The bird is first basted with egg white, enabling the gold leaf to better adhere to its skin. (See a similar decorative use of gold leaf in the Parma Torte of Chapter 5, above.)

All of these recipes designate a *boned* bird, in which the head, wings and legs remain intact with the bird's skin. The recipes provide detailed descriptions of the killing and boning process. This involves making a small incision in the neck between the shoulders and inserting a hollow straw through which air is blown to separate the skin from the carcass. For the *poucins*, the *Menagier* directs that this work be done while the chick is still alive! It is then let die and is scalded and plucked; the bones are removed through the previously made incision. The other versions indicate that the chicken is first killed before being skinned. We are sure that the laws against cruelty to animals would forbid the *Menagier*'s process today.

To find chickens with head, wings and feet intact, North Americans will likely have to visit a specialty market or give a special order to their custom butcher.

If you are not particularly adept at boning a chicken, and have no desire to experiment, we suggest that you ask your butcher to do this for you. Most large cookbooks, especially those specializing in chicken recipes, give clear directions for the operation. According to the early manuscripts, the legs are not boned. The manuscripts leave some doubt, though, as to whether the whole carcass, both skeleton and meat, is removed. We have chosen to remove only the bones. As an alternative to doing all this, you may want to buy just a regular eviscerated but unboned chicken, stuff the cavity and sew or truss it closed.

The stuffing recipe can also be used with boned chicken legs. To bone the legs, insert a sharp knife alongside the thigh bone; cut through the meat at the inner thigh and scrape the meat from the bone down to the leg joint. Cut the tendons at the joint and discard the thigh bone. Take care not to cut the skin.

The recipe works quite well also with breasts of chicken, flattened, stuffed and rolled, though of course this alternative and the previous procedure are not entirely authentic.

The *poucins* are simply skewered and roasted on a spit or in the oven. The larger birds and the meatballs are first poached in beef bouillon, then skewered and roasted on a spit or in the oven. When almost cooked they are basted two or three times with a green or yellow egg glaze, and cooking is continued only until the glaze is set.

5a. *Poucins farcies* / Stuffed Chicks (*Menagier*, p. 212/§238)

Note: *Poucins* (modern French *poussins*) are very small chickens, about 4–6 weeks old and weighing up to 2–2 1/2 lbs/1 kg. If these are unavailable, Cornish hens may be used.

Yield: Serves 4–6

Imperial	Ingredient	Metric	Directions
2	prepared chicks (1 1/2–2 lb/750–900 g)	2	**Preheat oven to 350°F/180°C**
3	hardboiled eggs	3	**Peel eggs & rub through sieve.**
1/2 cup	lightly packed fresh chopped parsley	125 mL	**Toss parsley & sage with spice powder & stir into egg mixture. Stir in**
2 tbsp	fresh chopped sage	30 mL	**melted butter.**
2 tsp	spice powder*	10 mL	**Stuff birds with mixture. Truss or sew**
2 tbsp	melted butter	30 mL	**up cavity & place in roasting pan or in oven, or skewer & roast on barbecue, for about 45 min. or until cooked.**
			Transfer to serving dish.

Serving suggestion

Transfer to serving dish. Garnish with parsley.

5b. *Poulaille farcie* / Stuffed Poultry (*Viandier*, §66; *Menagier*, p. 213/§242)

Yield: Serves 4–6

Imperial	Ingredient	Metric	Directions
1	boned prepared chicken (5–6 lb/2–3 kg)	1	
1/4 lb	ground pork	125 g	**Combine ground meat. In frying pan**
1/4 lb	ground veal	125 g	**cook meat to render fat. Pour off fat.**
1/4 lb	ground chicken	125 g	
1/4 lb	soft cheese	125 g	**Cut cheese into small pieces. Combine meat with cheese.**

---

* See the recipe for Fine Spice Powder on p. 54, above. This mixture is a medieval staple.

1 tbsp	spice powder*	30 mL	**Stir in spices, salt & chestnuts.**
1 tsp	salt	5 mL	**Stuff & truss (*or* sew) bird. Make**
pinch	saffron (*optional*)	pinch	**meatballs of leftover stuffing.**
6–8	cooked sliced chestnuts	6–8	

| 2–3 cups | beef bouillon | 500–750 mL | **In large flameproof casserole, heat beef bouillon. Place chicken & meatballs in casserole; cover. Poach chicken for 30–40 min. & meatballs for 10 min. Drain.** |
| | | | **Preheat oven to 350°F (180°C). Roast chicken & meatballs in oven until cooked (30 min.).** |

Glazing

For glazing, yellow *or* green, see below.

When almost cooked, brush with either yellow *or* green egg glaze 2 or 3 times; continue cooking just until glaze is set.

Remove to serving platter. Serve.

---

* See the recipe for Fine Spice Powder on p. 54, above. This mixture is a medieval staple.

5c. *Doreures*
(*Viandier*, §195)

Entremetz pour ung jour de feste ou pour ung convy de prince aux trois jours maslés de la sepmaine, comme dimenche, mardi et le jeudi. Pour farsiz et pommeaulx: convient, pour les pommeaulx, de la chair de porc crue — il ne peult challoir quelle — dont les poulles soient farcies. Et convient, après que la poulaille est tué, rompre ung pou de peau de la teste, et avoir ung tuyau de plume et souffler dedans tant qu'elle soit bien plaine de vent, et puis les eschauder et après les fendre par dessoubz le ventre et les escorchier; et mettre les charcois d'un costé. Et convient, pour faire la farce pour farcir la poullaille, du blanc, du lart haché avec la chair, et fault des oeufz, de bonne poudre fine, du pignolet et du roisin de Corinde, et en farsir la peau de la poulaille, et ne l'emplir pas trop qu'elle ne crieve, puis la recoudre; et convient la boullir en une paelle sur le feu et ne le fault guaire laisser cuire, et puis les brochez en broches gresles; et quant les pommeaulx seront bien faictz les convient mettre cuire avec ladicte poulaille et les tirer quant ilz seront durciz; et avoir les broches des pommeaulx plus gresles de la moittié ou plus que celles de la poullaille. Et après fault avoir de la paste batue en oeufz tellement qu'elle se puisse tenir sur la paelle, et quant la poullaille et les pommeaulx seront presque cuitz les oster et mettre sur sa paste: et prendre de la paste a une cuillier nette, en remuant tousjours, et mettre par dessus sa poulaille et ses pommeaulx tant qu'ilz en soient dorez, et les faire par ii ou par iii foiz tant qu'ilz en soient bien couvertz; et fault prendre du feul d'or ou d'argent et les enveloper — et fault avoir ung petit d'aubun d'oeuf et les arrouser affin que le fueil tiengne mieulx.

Capiteles de pin / Pinenuts
(Aldobrandino, *Le regime du corps*, p. 154)

Pinenuts are warm at the end of the second degree and dry at the beginning of the second degree; there are two varieties of them, small and large.

Both small and large pinenuts, if they are left to soak in hot water and then eaten, yield a good amount of good nourishment, and furthermore by their nature they are useful for anyone with a cough or his chest filled with gross and bad humors; ground with gourd seeds, pinenuts remove the burning back and bladder pains that come from the urine, and they do away with kidney stone, and fatten a person, and excite the sexual urge.

Ne parles point la bouche pleine, car c'est laide chose et vileine.	To talk with mouth full is, forsooth, most decidedly uncouth.

5c. *Doreures* / Glazed Stuffed Chicken (*Viandier*, §195)

While the *Viandier* describes setting the chicken carcass aside and stuffing the skin of the bird, in our recipe we use a regular *boned* chicken; extra white meat (breast) is purchased for the stuffing.

Imperial	Ingredient	Metric	Directions
1	boned prepared chicken (5–6 lb/2–3 kg)	1	
6 strips	bacon	6 strips	**Cut bacon into pieces. Lightly sauté**
1/4 lb	ground pork	125 g	**with ground pork. Drain off fat.**
1/2 lb	ground white chicken meat	250 g	**Combine with ground chicken.**
3/4 cup	pinenuts	175 mL	**Remove crust from Brie cheese.**
1/4 lb	Brie cheese (*or* other cream cheese)	125 g	**Grind *or* process pinenuts & cheese to a paste.**
1	whole egg, lightly beaten	1	**Combine spices & beaten egg with the**
3/4 tsp	ginger	4 mL	**cheese/nut mixture.**
3/4 tsp	cinnamon	4 mL	
1/2 tsp	cloves	2 mL	
1/4 tsp	salt	1 mL	
1 cup	currants	250 mL	**Stir in meat & currants. Stuff bird & truss well *or* sew closed. *Do not overstuff.* Try to retain shape of the chicken. Form the leftover stuffing into meatballs.**
2–3 cups	beef bouillon *or* white wine	500–750 mL	**On stove heat beef bouillon in pan large enough to hold bird & meatballs. Preheat oven to 350°F/180°C *or* prepare barbecue. Poach chicken over moderate heat for 30 min. Add meatballs & cook another 10 min.**
			Drain & transfer bird & balls to oven, *or* mount on barbecue spit *or* brochettes, & roast until cooked (about 30 min. for bird, 5 min. for meatballs).

<table>
<tr><td>glazing (yellow or green: see below)</td><td></td><td>When almost cooked, brush with either yellow or green egg glaze 2 or 3 times; continue cooking just until glaze is set.</td></tr>
<tr><td></td><td></td><td>Remove to serving platter. Garnish as desired & serve.</td></tr>
</table>

Variation

1. In place of meatballs, the extra stuffing may be cooked as a paté. Line a loaf pan with bacon strips. Press in the stuffing. Cover with foil and bake at 350°F/180°C in oven in a bain marie until cooked (about 1 hr.).

2. Chicken breast may be substituted for the whole chicken carcass. The quantity of stuffing prepared by this recipe would be sufficient for for 6–8 half-breasts: flatten the breasts, stuff, roll and tie. Poach or bake in white wine. Serve with Almond-Leek Sauce (see p. 132, below). Garnish with toasted almond slices and parsley.

Glazing for all three recipes

—for a golden yellow glaze:

2	egg yolks	2	**Beat.**
1/8 tsp	saffron	.5 mL	**Combine saffron (*or* turmeric) with egg yolks.**
	or		
1/4 tsp	turmeric	1 mL	

—for a green glaze:

2	egg yolks	2	**Beat.**
1/2 cup	finely chopped greens (such as spinach, parsley)	125 g	**Cook greens in small amount of water until most of water is absorbed; cool. Purée. Combine with egg yolks & strain through sieve *or* blend in blender.**
1–2 tsp	flour	5–10 mL	**If a thicker glaze is desired, whisk in flour.**

6. *Orengue de pouchins*

(*Menagier*, p. 276; not in the Brereton-Ferrier edn.)

Et pour l'orengue de pouchins, ou de perdris ou de pigons, prenés les orenges et les copés en vergus blanc et vin blanc, et mettés boullir; et du gingembre au boullir, et mettés vous chozes dedens boullir.

Cetrona, id est Narancia / Oranges

(*Tacuinum sanitatis*, Vienna,
Oesterreichische Nationalbibliothek, Codex Vindobonensis, 2644, f. 20r)

The pulp of the orange is cold and moist in the third degree; its peel is dry and warm in the second degree. The best variety of orange is that which is perfectly ripe. Its candied peel is good for the stomach. Oranges are difficult to digest, but this difficulty may be assuaged by drinking the best wine.

6. Chicken in Orange Sauce

The Arabic Near East had long been familiar with the orange tree, its fragrant blossoms and fruit, by the time these were introduced into Italy and the south of France by returning crusaders in the twelfth and thirteenth centuries. This first orange that Europeans tasted was the bitter variety, and the use of both its flower and its fruit in food preparations was generally limited to dishes for which the cook sought to provide a tart seasoning. The sweet orange with which we are more familiar was introduced into Europe from the Far East by the circumnavigator Vasco da Gama only at the beginning of the sixteenth century.

An acidulous or sour flavor became much esteemed by gastronomes in the late Middle Ages. Cooks sought out any ingredient which could lend the hint of a tart taste to a mixture. When combined with other condiments, a *soupçon* of such pungent liquids as vinegar, verjuice, sorrel juice, lemon juice, lime juice and bitter-orange juice added a piquancy which the gourmet relished. (A variation on this taste-for-the-tart was created in an increasing number of late-medieval dishes where sugar was deliberately mixed in with the acidic juice: the "bitter-sweet" flavor was born!) An exotic garnish such as pomegranate seeds, which offered the cook both a sharp tang and a strikingly distinct color, was highly prized.

In early French cookery vinegar was of course always just that, wine vinegar, "vin aigre," a bitter or soured wine. Verjuice was the juice from an unripe grape—known specifically as the verjuice grape—a variety with a high, early yield of liquid. Its characteristic flavor is tangy, even without being fermented. The qualifier *vert* in the word *vertjus* designates a juice that is both "new" and "sharp." The *Menagier* advises his wife that in July the previous year's verjuice is too old and weak, yet the current year's product is too "*vert*" to be palatable: at that time of year the best solution to the dilemma is to mix equal quantities from the two sources, old and new. Old white verjuice that is tending to become bland can also be mixed with the juice of ground sorrel leaves in order to make a sharp sorrel verjuice which was much valued for certain dishes. In modern kitchens, if we don't have access to juice from unripe grapes we can arrive at a satisfactory equivalent to verjuice by mixing lemon juice and unsweetened grape juice.

Though the present recipe for *Orange de poussins* calls for whole chicks, partridge or pigeons, we prefer to use halved chicken breasts. The result is less fatty and requires less effort to degrease.

Yield: Serves 6

Imperial	Ingredient	Metric	Directions
2 cups	white grape juice	500 mL	**Combine & heat juice & vinegar (&**
2 tbsp	wine vinegar	30 mL	**sorrel) in pot.**
1 tbsp	fresh chopped sorrel (*optional*)	15 mL	
1 1/2 cups	dry white wine	375 mL	**Add wine & ginger.**
4 tsp	grated fresh gingerroot (*or* 2 tsp/10 mL powdered ginger)	20 mL	
5–6 lb	whole chicken, cut-up chicken, *or* 6 half-breasts of chicken	2–3 kg	
3	bitter (Seville) oranges, washed, unpeeled, sliced with pits removed *or*	3	**Add chicken and oranges. Cover. Over low to medium heat, poach the chicken until cooked. Remove chicken to warm serving tray. Keep**
3	sweet oranges *with*	3	**warm.**
2 tbsp	lemon juice (*optional*)	30 mL	**Strain sauce & skim off excess fat. Taste, correct seasoning (especially the ginger) & tartness. Add lemon juice if necessary. Reduce the sauce to desired consistency. Pour some of the sauce over the chicken; serve remaining sauce in a separate dish. Garnish & serve.**

Garnish

Thin strips of orange peel, blanched and cut into julienne strips; *or* fresh orange sections and a sprig of parsley; *or* diced pieces of Candied Orange Peel (*Orengat*, see p. 284, below).

7. *Faulx grenon* (*Potage party*)
(*Menagier de Paris*, p. 216/§246)

Prenez une cuisse de mouton ou foies et jugiers de poulailles, et les mettez cuire tres bien en eaue et en vien, et les tranchez comme quarrés. Puis broyez gingembre, canelle, giroffle et un pou de saffren et graine de paradis, et deffaites de vin et de vertjus, du bouillon de char (de celluy mesmes ou de la char a cuire), et puis ostez du mortier; puis aiez pain hazé trempé en vin et vertjus, broyez tres bien, et aprés ce le passez par l'estamine, et faictes tout boulir ensemble. Puis prenez la char et la frisiez au lart et la gettez dedans; et prenez … moieux d'œufs passés par l'estamine, et gettez dedans pour lier. Et aprés dreciez par escuelles, et gettez dessus pouldre de canelle et sucre: c'est assavoir, gettez sur la moitié de l'escuelle et non sur l'autre. Et l'apelle l'en "Potage parti."

Aprés moustre toy liez tous diz ne habunde trop en vains dits.	Be always of a cheerful mien, yet never as a fool be seen.

7. Mock Meat

The dish known in French as *Faux grenon* is a standard preparation in fourteenth- and fifteenth-century French aristocratic kitchens. Versions of it are reproduced in the principal recipe collections, and indeed the *Menagier de Paris* has gone so far as to copy *Faulx grenon* twice, only a page or two apart, within the same chapter of his *Entremets*. The author's justification for this repetition lies undoubtedly in the general name, *Potage party* or "Split Dish," with which he qualifies the second appearance of the recipe (printed here), because the major variant of the second dish is in the manner of its presentation.

The term *parti* in Old French cookery was applied to a dish composed of two halves, whether the difference was purely superficial, in the appearance of the dish or its garnish, or whether it was more substantial, the dish itself being composed of two preparations served together side by side on a single platter. Literally, the term meant "parted" or "divided" as it continues to mean in the modern English *parti* as in the word *parti-colored*. Such a treatment of food was relatively common in early cookery. In an effort to enliven the meals for which they were responsible, cooks made considerable use of color, and a combination of colors in and on their dishes. For these colors a variety of herbs and spices (particularly saffron) could be used to produce a range of hues and tints, and such things as ground sugar, pomegranate seeds and slivered almonds could lend a contrastive texture to half a pie crust, to half a sop, or even to whatever could be served on one half of a platter. The *parti* presentation was a relatively simple procedure. A further variant is found in *écartelé* dishes which are split into quarters (as, for instance, Chiquart's four-colored *Blanc mengier*—which, incidentally, he still calls *parti*; see below, in Chapter 10).

Among the French recipe collections there is some disagreement about the meat that is appropriate for this dish. The *Viandier*'s recipe is for poultry livers and gizzards, or veal. The *Menagier de Paris* calls, in the first instance, for the *Viandier*'s meats as possibilities and adds to them either leg of pork or leg of mutton; then, for his later *parti* version of the dish, the *Menagier* omits the leg of pork. For Chiquart's *Faugrenon* (which he identifies by two alternative names, *Chaut mengier parti* and *Morterieulx*), only pork is specified.

Considering the range of professional practice and choice of meat among our sources, we may safely conclude that virtually any "moist" meat can be prepared in this way. In essence it is a dish of stewed meat, finely diced, then fried in order to retain its juiciness, in a thickened, slightly spicy sauce. The *parti* effect is afforded by a sugar-cinnamon garnish sprinkled on only half of each serving.

Yield: Serves 6

Imperial	Ingredient	Metric	Directions
1 1/2 lb	poultry livers *or* veal *or* pork*	750 g	**Gently cook poultry livers *or* other meat in wine & water until tender. Remove meat with slotted spoon. Set liquid aside.**
1 cup	water	250 mL	
1 cup	dry white wine	250 mL	
3 tbsp	pork fat *or* lard	50 mL	**Heat fat in skillet. Cut meat into small chunks & sauté in skillet. Pour off fat. Keep meat warm.**
2 1/2 tsp	finely grated gingerroot (*or* 1 tsp/5 mL ground ginger)	12 mL	**Combine ginger, cinnamon, cloves & grains of paradise.**
1 tsp	cinnamon	5 mL	
3/4 tsp	cloves	3 mL	
1/2 tsp	grains of paradise	2 mL	
3/4 cup	beef bouillon	175 mL	**In cooking pot, over medium heat, combine spices with the beef bouillon & reserved liquid. Whisk in bread crumbs (and *optional* saffron).**
3/4 cup	reserved cooking liquid	175 mL	
2 slices	white bread, in crumbs	2 slices	
pinch	saffron (*optional*)	pinch	
3	egg yolks	3	**Lightly whisk egg yolks in small dish, adding in the lemon juice. While stirring slowly, add in about 1 cup of the hot liquid, then return this mixture to pot.**
2 tbsp	verjuice (*or* fresh lemon juice)	30 mL	
			Simmer & stir sauce with a wire whisk until it is smooth, thickened & hot.
			Add cooked meat. Taste, correct spices as desired. Put in serving bowls.

---

* If using veal or pork, cut into bite-sized pieces, and sear in fat or oil before cooking in wine and water.

Garnish

1 tsp	ground cinnamon*	5 mL	**Combine cinnamon & sugar & sprin-**
2 tsp	sugar	10 mL	**kle over half of each serving. Serve**
			warm.

The dish called *Faulx grenon* / Mock Meat should be thick, yellowish and sharp with verjuice (*or* lemon juice).

Serving suggestions

1. Serve the *Faulx grenon* over a bed of warm buttered noodles.
2. As an appetizer. Cut meat into larger pieces. Remove meat from sauce with slotted spoon onto a serving tray. Sprinkle with ground cinnamon and sugar mixture. Pour sauce into a separate bowl. Provide toothpicks and pass sauce for dunking.

---

* The *Enseignements* garnishes its version of this dish with a mixture of ground cinnamon, ginger and cloves. If you wish, combine 1/4 tsp/1 mL of ground ginger and the same amount of ground cloves with the cinnamon.

Other Possible Poultry Dishes

Soupe jacobine / **Jacobin Sops**

For the complete recipe of this dish as a Soup, see p. 105, above.
To serve this dish as an *entrée*, increase the quantity of chicken.

Moust pour hetoudeaulx / **Must Sauce for Young Chicken**

For the complete recipe of this dish as a Sauce, see p. 130, above.
As a delicious coulis with warm or cold chicken, cover the bottom of a plate with Must Sauce and place the chicken in it.

Tuillé de char / **Chicken and Crayfish Dish**

For the complete recipe of this dish as a Fish Dish, see p. 218, below.
This is an interesting mixture of two "meats" that are not normally combined today.

Se tu fais souppes en ton verre,	If you sop your bread within the cup,
boy le vin ou le gette a terre.	pour out the wine, or drink it up.

Chapter 7
Fish Dishes

Various fish, their preparation and appropriate saucing
1. *Saumon frez* / Fresh Roasted Salmon
2. *Soles frites, ou verjust de oyselle et de orenges* /
   Fried Sole with Orange and Sorrel Verjuice
3. *Couleis de perche* / A Perch Cullis
4. *Anchoyes* / Anchovies in a Vinaigrette
5. *Moules* / Mussels
6. *Tuillé de char* / Chicken and Crayfish Dish
7. *Gravé d'escrevisses* / Gravy of Crayfish
8. *Escrevisses farcies* / Stuffed Crayfish (or Lobster or Shrimp)
9. *Tartres de poyssons* / Fish Pie
10. *Tortres parmeysines de poyssons* / Parma Fish Pie

Rissolles a jour de poisson / **Rissoles for a Fish Day** : see Chapter 2, Appetizers
Flaons de cresme de lait / **Cream Flans** : see Chapter 10, Desserts

Chapter 7
Fish Dishes

For the most part, early French recipe collections contain sections which group dishes whose ingredients allow them to be served on "fasting" days. In accord with dietary rules that had evolved in the Church, no Christian could eat the meat of animals or fowl, domestic or game, on particular days that were deemed to be penitential or purificatory. These fast days came eventually to be known as lean days or, because of the foods that people normally resorted to on those occasions, as fish days. In an ordinary week in late-medieval France some form of fasting was usually observed on Wednesday, Friday and Saturday; in the course of the ecclesiastical year, which was measured by the recurrence of a fixed series of festivals and penitential periods, roughly a third of a European Christian's meals had properly to be of the lean variety. These dietary restrictions exercised a considerable influence on the economy of European nations, particularly on the agriculture and fishery industries and on certain commercial activities.

These fasting rules clearly had an effect, as well, upon the work of the professional cook. On lean days and during lean periods he had always to be careful to avoid including any proscribed ingredients, such as animal milk or grease, in anything he prepared. He must be aware of any fine distinctions that had to be taken into account on such days: for instance, were chicken eggs currently considered to be or not to be "animal products"? He must be resourceful: he had to develop a variety of expedients that would allow him to satisfy the rigorous requirements of, say, a banquet that happened to fall on a lean day—but always to satisfy them in a gastronomically interesting manner. This additional layer of concern may have complicated the professional cook's daily task, but it enriched his repertoire enormously.

The extent to which a cook's skills and capabilities were tested by the need for lean meals depended clearly upon the strictness of his master's observance of Christian laws. For Chiquart, for example, there was never any question of fudging, even a little, by using an egg yolk to thicken a sauce, say, rather than a chunk of burnt toast ground and sieved. His master, Duke Amadeus of Savoy, was a devout Christian; he would be elected Pope, as Felix V, by the Council of Basel in 1439. Though his life-style, particularly in his youth, could not accurately be described as sober or austere, Amadeus remained throughout his life wholly faithful in all respects to the doctrine of the church. For Chiquart this devoutness meant generally that Christian dietetic rules had to be followed punctiliously, and, specifically, that all the formal ostentation of court banquets had to be expressed in *either* meat *or* meatless versions, with an equal yield of pleasure for his master's gourmet guests. Whether it fell on a meat day or a meatless day, any banquet planned by Chiquart had to contribute with unqualified glory to the prestige of his master and his master's court.

The *Du fait de cuisine* demonstrates how seriously Chiquart took this challenge to his professional skills. It shows, too, how capably he responded to the challenge, by providing not just several possible solutions to the fast-day restrictions but whole menus, two complete days of menus (that is, with both dinners, in two long servings of dishes, and suppers), suitable for an extended lean banquet. In all cases these preparations are delightfully delicious despite—perhaps even because of—the dietary constrictions placed upon Chiquart.

The importance of fish in the diet of medieval Europe can easily be imagined. The following two chapters, on Fish Dishes and on Pies and Pastry, present some of the many appetizing preparations to which early French kitchens, cooks and meal-planners could have recourse on "lean days."

Various fish, their preparation and appropriate saucing

The manner of cooking and saucing fish was as important as for meats and poultry. In its section on fish, the *Viandier* presents a remarkably full listing of fresh-water fish and sea-fish, along with crustaceans, accompanied by specifications about the appropiate cooking method and eating sauce for each. The following is a selection of the more common of the *Viandier*'s fish and crustaceans.

Fish	Cooking Method	Serving Sauce
anchovies	cut into strips, roast	Mustard Sauce *or* wine sauce
barbel	boiled in water	sharp Pepper Sauce
barbel	roast	verjuice
barbel	fried	Jance
bass	boiled in water	Green Sauce
cockles	parboiled, sauteed in oil with chopped onions & spice powder	White Garlic Sauce
crayfish	boiled in water & wine	vinegar
eels	boiled in water	Green Garlic Sauce
eels	baked in a pie with spice powder	White Garlic Sauce
gurnard	fried with salt & boiled in water	Cameline
gurnard	slit open, roast, dipped in verjuice & sprinkled with spice powder	verjuice
loach	parboiled, boiled with cheese	Mustard Sauce *or* boiled verjuice grapes *or* currants
lobsters	boiled in water & wine *or* baked in oven	vinegar
fresh mackerel	roast	Cameline *or* vinegar & spice powder
salted mackerel	boiled in water	wine & shallots (*or* scallions) *or* Mustard Sauce
mussels	boiled in water with vinegar & mint	spice powder *or* butter *or* vinegar *or* sharp verjuice *or* Green Garlic Sauce
oysters	boiled in water, then fried in oil with onions	spice powder *or* Garlic Sauce

Fish	Cooking Method	Serving Sauce
perch	boiled in water, skinned	vinegar & parsley *or* in a cullis
pickerel	roast	Chaudumé
pickerel	fried	Jance
pike	boiled in water	Green Sauce *or* a galantine whose ingredients resemble those of Cameline
ray	cut into pieces & boiled in water	Cameline Garlic Sauce
fresh salmon	larded & roast, then its layers of flesh boiled in water & wine with salt	Yellow Pepper Sauce *or* Cameline
shad	larded, salted, boiled in water	Mustard Sauce *or* shallots & wine *or* Green Sauce
shad	roast	Cameline
shad	baked in oven	Cameline *or* drippings, white wine, verjuice & spice powder
shrimp	boiled in wine & water, with a little salt	vinegar
small fry	boiled in water with chopped onion	Green Sauce *or* Garlic Sauce
smelt	baked in a pie, removed, dredged in flour & fried in oil	Jance *or* Green Garlic Sauce
sole	parboiled, boiled in water	Green Sauce
sole	roast on the grill	sorrel verjuice
sturgeon	parboiled, split, boiled in wine (with water)	vinegar & parsley
tench	parboiled	Green Sauce
tench	turned inside-out, roasted, dipped in vinegar & sprinkled with cinnamon, basted with oil	Cameline
trout	boiled in water	Cameline
whale meat	sliced, boiled in water	with peas

In 1420 Master Chiquart wrote the following summary paragraph, intended to guide cooks in the saucing of sea-fish. The similarities in this area between the *Viandier* and the *Du fait de cuisine* point to certain established gastronomic traditions.

> For turbot, Green Sauce should be provided; salmon is eaten with Cameline Sauce; ray fish, with Cameline Garlic Sauce which is made from almonds and the rayfish liver; lobsters, with vinegar; sturgeon, with parsley, onions and vinegar; fried sardines, with mustard; fried sole, with sorrel verjuice and orange juice; eel, roasted on the grill, with verjuice; anchovies, with parsley, onion and vinegar, and with spice powder on top.
>
> (*Du fait de cuisine*, f. 56v)

1. *Saumon frez*

(*Viandier*, §124)

Baconné, et gardez l'eschine pour rostir, puis le depeciez par dalles et soit cuit en eaue, et du vin et du sel au cuire; et soit mengié au poivre jaunet ou a la cameline; et le mectent aucuns ressuyer sur le grail au mengier; et en pasté, qui veult, pouldré d'espices, et soit mengié a la cameline; et s'il est sallé, soit cuit en eaue sans sel, et mengiés au vin et a la ciboule miciee; et la fresche en pasté aveques espices et sel.

Salmon

(Pliny, *Natural History*, Book 9, Ch. 32,
ed. H. Rackham, Cambridge, Mass. & London [Harvard & Heinemann], 1940, Vol. 3)

It is ... a fact of nature that different fishes hold the first rank in different places—the blackfish in Egypt, the John Dory (also called the carpenter-fish) at Cadiz, the stockfish in the neighborhood of Iviza, though elsewhere it is a disgusting fish, and everywhere it is unable to be cooked thoroughly unless it has been beaten with a rod; in Aquitaine the river salmon is preferred to all sea-fish.

S'on oste le plat devant toy,	Your still-full bowl is cleared away?
n'en faiz compte et t'en tais coy.	Try not to show the least dismay.

1. Fresh Roasted Salmon

One of the most common fish on the medieval market was salmon. The humblest retainers, as well as domestic animals, were often fed on salmon. In plentiful supply, and cheap, it was not held in very high esteem, in part because physicians' doctrine asserted that the best sea-fish must have white flesh.

We have followed the *Viandier*'s recipe for fresh salmon. He adds a note that if you are using salted salmon, it should be boiled in water and eaten with minced, fried shallots. Two of the manuscripts, with the *Menagier de Paris*, add the possibility of making a pasty of salmon with spice powder.

Yield: 6–8 servings

Imperial	Ingredient	Metric	Directions
4 lb	dressed salmon	1.5–2 kg	Make 3 diagonal slits on fish. Wrap it
5 *or* 6	strips of bacon	5 *or* 6	in bacon.
2 tsp	oil	10 mL	Brush grill with oil. Roast salmon on broiling grill for 5–6 min. for each inch/2.5 cm of thickness.
1 cup	white wine	250 mL	Pick apart cooked salmon in layers. Preheat oven to 375° F/190° C. Gently place salmon pieces in baking dish. Combine & heat wine, water & salt. Pour over salmon & bake for 10 min.
1 cup	water	250 mL	
1/2 tsp	salt	2 mL	
1 cup	Cameline Sauce*	250 mL	Serve with Cameline Sauce.

Cooking variation

If your wish to follow the *Viandier*'s and *Menagier*'s suggestions for a salmon pie, the salmon should be roasted before being baked, with spice powder, in a pastry shell. The pie is served topped with Cameline Sauce.

---

* This is the *Broet camelin* / Cameline Broth or Sauce, of p. 138, above. You may wish to use the plain *Poivre Noir* / Black Pepper Sauce of p. 126, above, or a Yellow Pepper Sauce, similar to the Black Pepper Sauce but with the addition of saffron and, optionally, cloves.

2. *Soles frites, ou verjust de oyselle et de orenges* / Fried Sole with Orange and Sorrel Verjuice

Pour le poysson de mer: ... les soles frites, ou verjust de oyselle et de orenges, ...
(Du fait de cuisine, f. 56v)

In his directions for the saucing of sea-fish, Chiquart advises that fried sole should be served with sorrel verjuice and (bitter) orange juice. Though not always available in North American supermarkets, sorrel, a perennial herb, can frequently be bought in farmers' markets. The living plant can also be had from the same source and transplanted to your garden, or grown from seed. Dried sorrel is available in bulk- and health-food stores.

The "recipe" calls for orange verjuice. The orange available for use in Chiquart's day was a bitter orange. If these are not available, the lemon juice we list in the ingredients below will give the sauce a tart taste close to that of bitter oranges.

Yield: 6 servings

Imperial	Ingredient	Metric	Directions
Sauce			
4–5	large sorrel leaves	4–5	**Blanch sorrel leaves in boiling water.**
1/2 cup	boiling water	125 mL	**Strain, reserve liquid. Chop & grind sorrel, *or* blend in blender. Add liquid. Strain.**
1–1 1/2 c	unsweetened orange juice*	250–375 mL	**Stir into orange juice. Add lemon**
1 tbsp	lemon juice	15 mL	**juice.**
Fish			
6	fillets of sole	6	**Heat 2–3 tbsp/30–50 mL of butter *or***
4 tbsp	unsalted butter *or* oil	60 mL	**oil in frypan. Fry fillets about 3 min. on each side. Remove to serving platter & keep warm.**
3 tsp	chopped sorrel leaves	15 mL	**Add remaining butter to pan. Pour in sauce. Cook, reducing by one-third. Pour hot sauce over fish. Sprinkle with chopped sorrel leaves & serve.**

Cooking variations

You may wish to try the sauce as a marinade, then continue as above.
Alternatively, bake the fish in the sauce. Preheat your oven to 425° F/220° C. Butter a baking dish. Place the fish in a single layer. Cover with the hot sauce. Cover the dish. Bake 5 minutes. Turn the fish over, and continue baking a further 5 minutes, or until done.

---

* This amounts to the juice of 3 or 4 oranges.

3. *Couleis de perche*
(*Viandier*, §94)

Cuisiez la en eaue et gardez le boullon; puis broiez amendes et de la perche avec, et deffaictes de boullion et mettez tout boullir et coullez, et y mettez du succre; et doibt estre ... claret; et y met on ung pou de vin blanc, qui veult.

3. A Perch Cullis

The culinary term *coulis* or "cullis" derives from a French word meaning "strained." The dish that had the term in its name was primarily a liquid that normally had undergone at least one straining and often repeated passing through a closely woven cloth strainer, so that the particles suspended in it were extremely fine and the mixture was of a very smooth consistency; such a genre of dish was highly suitable for the sick. Aldobrandino (pp. 72 and 78) recommends that a pregnant woman or a teething infant be fed a *coleïs* if her delicate digestive system rebelled at more substantial foods.

Even though the recipe for this dish was copied in the *Viandier* under the rubric of "Dishes for the Sick" it affords a tasty alternative to other dishes in which the concentration of spices and herbs may be rather high. A small dish of Perch Cullis is a delightful way to clean the palate, as it were, between courses.

Since the *Viandier*'s preparation is intended for the sick, the directions read that it should be "quite clear" as a result of straining. We prefer to use a strainer with a relatively open mesh.

Yield: 6 servings

Imperial	Ingredient	Metric	Directions
1 1/2–2 lb	dressed perch	1.5–2 kg	**Cook fish in water about 10 min. Reserve broth. Remove flesh from bones.**
3 cups	water to cover	750 mL	
1/4 c+2 tbsp	ground almonds	90 mL	**In a blender* combine fish, almonds & 1/2 c/125 mL of broth. Blend to a creamy paste. While continuing to blend, pour in 1–1 1/2 c/250–375 mL of broth. Strain & press through a fairly open weave strainer into cooking pot.**
2 tbsp	white sugar	30 mL	**Add sugar & white wine. Bring to a boil & reduce to desired consistency. Serve.**
1/2 cup	white wine	125 mL	

Serving variation
In a modern meal this provides a very tasty accompaniment as a cullis under a slice of vegetable pâté.

---

* Alternatively, grind the fish, almonds and a little broth in a mortar.

4. *Anchoyes* / Anchovies in a Vinaigrette

... Les anchoyes au percy, oygnions et vin aigre, et la poudre par dessus.

(Du fait de cuisine, f. 56v)

Anchovies

(Pliny, *Natural History*, Book 9, Ch. 17)

The tunny is of exceptional size; we are told of a specimen weighing a third of a ton and having a tail 3 feet 4 inches broad. Fish of no less size also occur in certain rivers: the catfish in the Nile, the pike in the Rhine, the sturgeon in the Po—a fish that grows so fat from sloth that it sometimes reaches a thousand pounds; it is caught with a hook on a chain and only drawn out of the water by teams of oxen. And this monster is killed by the bite of a very small fish called the anchovy which goes for a particular vein in its throat with remarkable voracity.

This very simple dish can be served as an aperitif for devotees of anchovies.

Yield: About 20–30 small appetizers

Imperial	Ingredient	Metric	Directions
3 tbsp	chopped onion	50 mL	**Sauté onions in oil.**
1 tbsp	olive oil	15 mL	
3–4 tbsp	red wine vinegar	50–60 mL	**Combine vinegar, parsley, spice pow-**
1 tbsp	fresh chopped parsley	15 mL	**der & onions.**
2 tsp	spice powder (see p. 54)	10 mL	
3 1/2 oz	tinned anchovies in oil*	100 g	**Chop anchovies into small pieces. Add to vinegar mixture.**
30	small pieces of toast	30	**Spread on small pieces of toast. Serve.**

---

* If you are using fresh anchovies (difficult to find even in our specialty fish stores), clean about 1/2–3/4 lb/220 g of them. Cut off the heads and cook. Add 2 tbsp/30 mL of olive oil and proceed as above.

5. *Moules*

(*Viandier*, §150)

Cuites en eaue et du vinaigre avec, et de la mente, qui veult; et puis, au drecier, de la pouldre d'espices, et aucuns y veullent du beurre; mengier au vinaigre ou au verjus vert ou aux aulx vertz; et si en fait on du civé, qui veult.

Mussels

(Pliny, *Natural History*, Book 32, Ch. 31,
ed. H. Rackham, Cambridge, Mass. & London [Harvard & Heinemann], 1940, Vol. 8)

The *myax* [mussel] ... is purgative, and in this place shall be set forth all its characteristics. These animals form clusters, as does the *murex* [purple shellfish], and live where sea-weed lies thick, for which reason they are most delicious in autumn, and from regions where much fresh water mingles with salt .... Their liquor is said to be a thorough purge of belly and bladder, cleanses the intestines, is a universal aperient, purges the kidneys, and reduces blood and fat. Hence these shellfish are very beneficial for dropsy, menstruation, jaundice, diseases of the joints, flatulence, obesity, also bilious phlegm, affections of lungs, liver, and spleen, and for catarrhs. Their only drawback is that they harm the throat and obstruct the voice. ... With honey added, they heal the bites of dogs and men, leprous sores, and freckles.

Mint

(Pliny, *Natural History*, Book 19, Ch. 47,
ed. H. Rackham, Cambridge, Mass. & London [Harvard & Heinemann], 1940, Vol. 5)

[The vernal equinox] is ... the time for planting mint, using a shoot, or if it is not yet making bud, a matted tuft. Mint is ... fond of damp ground. It is green in summer and turns yellow in winter. ... It is agreeable for stuffing cushions, and pervades the tables with its scent at country banquets. One planting lasts for a long period. It is closely related to pennyroyal, which has the property ... of flowering when it is in a larder. These other herbs, I mean mint and also pennyroyal and catmint, are kept in the same kind of way.

De ta touaille ne faiz corde, honnesteté ne s'y accorde.	The napkin in your lap to twist good manners urge you to desist.

5. Mussels

Very simple directions are given for this dish. We are advised to cook the mussels in water and vinegar with some mint (if we wish), and to eat them with vinegar or Green Verjuice or Green Garlic Sauce, or to dress them with spice powder; some add butter. The *Viandier* then says they can also be made into a stew (if we like) but does not offer us a recipe for this procedure.

We have chosen the Green Garlic Sauce. So many of the other dishes garnish or cook with the ubiquitous spice powder that this Green Garlic Sauce offers variety in a menu.

When buying mussels, buy a few more than you feel you will actually need. If this recipe is to make a main dish, count on at least 12 mussels per person (12 mussels = 1 lb/450 g).

Yield: 6 servings (about 12 mussels per person)

Imperial	Ingredient	Metric	Directions
6 lb	fresh mussels	2.7 kg	**Wash, scrub & scrape mussels.***
2 cups	boiling water	500 mL	**Add vinegar (*or* wine) & mint to wa-**
1/2 cup	white wine vinegar†	125 mL	**ter. Gently load the mussels into pot.**
8–10	mint leaves	8–10	
			Cover & heat rapidly; cook until mussels open. Drain & shell them.
1 cup	Green Garlic Sauce (see p. 119)	250 mL	**Serve on half shells with sauce.**

En plain disner ou en la fin, n'efforce l'oste de son vin.	At no time should you make a sign or ask your host to pour more wine.

---

* To clean mussels, scrape off the dirt and encrustations from the shell. Cut off the *beard*. Put mussels in a bucket or sink of cold water and rub them together to scrape off any remaining dirt. Discard any mussels that appear spoiled (they will have a strong, unpleasant odor). If you tap them when they are slightly open, fresh mussels will close. Rinse them again in a pot of cold water to cover, with 2 tbsp/30 mL of salt. Leave them for about 1 hour. Proceed with cooking.

† Alternatively, use 1 c/250 mL of white wine, if you prefer.

6–8. Shellfish Recipes

Crayfish

(Pliny, *Natural History*, Book 9, Ch. 51,
ed. H. Rackham, Cambridge, Mass. & London [Harvard & Heinemann], 1940, Vol. 3)

The kinds of crab are the *carabus*, the crayfish, the spider-crab, the hermit-crab, the Heraclean crab, the lion-crab and other inferior species.... Crabs are long-lived. They have eight feet, all curved crooked; the front foot is double in the female and single in the male. They also have two claws with denticulated nippers; the upper half of the forepart of these moves and the lower half is fixed. The right claw is the larger in every specimen. Sometimes crabs all collect together in a flock.... When alarmed, crabs can retreat backwards with equal speed. They fight duels with one another like rams, charging with horns opposed. They afford a remedy against snake-bite.

Rather than present finished recipes for the following three shellfish dishes, we have chosen to list the ingredients and to explain the processes. Our rationale is that the cooks are likely to be rare who will be experienced in cleaning and cooking the shellfish in question, and even more rare who will be comfortable with the procedure of grinding the shells that are to be included in the mixture that is cooked. Furthermore, with the high cost of lobster, langoustes and scampi, any cook would probably want to see the whole of each recipe in order to decide whether it is really worthwhile.

However, any of the recipes would no doubt enliven the proceedings of a gourmet club dinner. Similarly a group of friends might enjoy recreating the shellfish recipes found in the *Viandier*, the *Menagier de Paris* and the *Du fait de cuisine*.

6. *Tuillé de char* / Chicken and Crayfish Dish

(*Menagier de Paris*, p. 170/§118)

The generic name of the first dish, *Tuillé*, refers to its tile-like hue, a color lent by the ground-up crayfish it contains; the qualification, *de char*, indicates that, containing poultry or veal as it does, the dish must be considered appropriate for serving only on a meat day.

Ingredients

Crayfish with either poultry (capons *or* chickens *or* hens) *or* veal, almonds, toast, water, wine.
  Spices: ginger, cinnamon, cloves, long pepper (you may substitute cayenne), lemon juice (for verjuice). Oil for frying.

Directions

Boil crayfish, remove the meat of the tails and set it aside. Take all the rest (shells and body), grind it up thoroughly. Grind in unskinned almonds and toast.

Cut up into pieces the poultry *or* veal. Cook in a mixture of water, wine and salt. Reserve the bouillon.

Using some of this bouillon, moisten the ground-up mixture, strain it, then repeat the process, regrinding, restraining.

Grind ginger, cinnamon, cloves and long pepper. Moisten all these spices together with verjuice and add to the above mixture.

Fry the poultry *or* veal in lard, sit it out in a bowl. Pour the sauce over it. On top of the sauce place four or five crayfish tails in a wheel-like pattern. Sprinkle sugar on top.

7. *Gravé d'escrevisses* / Gravy of Crayfish

(*Viandier*, S190)

This second shellfish recipe resembles the *Menagier*'s Chicken and Crayfish Dish somewhat. However, the *Viandier* is a little less specific about the use of the shells.

Depending upon the optional ingredients in this dish, if it contains no animal meat it could suitably be prepared for a lean day.

Ingredients

Crayfish, almonds, thin pea puree, wine, vinegar (*optional*), lemon juice (for verjuice). Spices: ginger, fine cinnamon, grains of paradise, cloves, long pepper, sugar, salt. Butter for frying.

Directions

Wash almonds without scalding or skinning them, and grind them.

Cook fine big crayfish in a mixture of two parts water and one part wine, with a little vinegar if you wish; then drain them and let them cool. Set the claws and necks to one side and remove the shells from them. Remove the meat from the body, grind this as you would almonds, steep it in pea puree, wine and verjuice, and put all of it together through the strainer.

Get ginger, a little fine cinnamon, some grains of paradise, fewer cloves, and a little long pepper; grind these spices and infuse them in a little wine and verjuice; add in a generous amount of sugar. Boil everything together. Salt to taste.

You can put some fried meat in this if you wish.

Fry the crayfish claws and necks in a little butter—they should end up dry like fried loach—and put them to boil in a pan or in a good clean pot.

This gravy should be thick enough to cover the meat it is used on.

8. *Escrevisses farcies* / Stuffed Crayfish (or Lobster or Shrimp)
(Du fait de cuisine, S68)

Ingredients

Lobster *or* lobster tails, *or* langoustes, *or* scampi *or* large shrimps.

Directions

Wash and cook the shellfish in salted water. Clean out the meat. Choose the largest shells to be stuffed and clean these. Chop the meat up small.

Wash and drain parsley and chop it finely. Add a little ginger and saffron. Mix this with the chopped shellfish.

Fill a shell, then turn another upside down on it. Repeat with the rest of the shells. Fry in oil, remove and drain. Sprinkle with sugar.

Bonne chance!

9. *Tartres de poyssons*

(*Du fait de cuisine*, §29)

Tartres de poyssons: et pour donner a entendre a celluy qui fera ceste ouvre cy — car chescun n'en nest pas maistre — il doibt prendre son poisson, c'est assavoir bonnes ventreches de ton, bonnes grosses carpes fendisses, bonnes grosses anguilles fresches, et de tout cela prendre selon la quantité des tartres que luy sont ordonnees a faire; et prennés tout cela et mectés par belles pieces, et mectés cuire en belle et necte chaudiere selon la quantité que vous avés. Et quant il sera cuit, si tirés sur belles tables que soient belles et nctes et faictes trier tout vostre grein qu'il n'y ait nulles escailles ne arestes, et puis le chapplés tresbien. Et faictes que vous ayés de bonnes figues confictes, de prunes, de dates, et cela tailler bien primement par minuz dez; et prennés de pignions et les faciés nectoyer a leur devoir; et prennés de raisins confiz et les nectoyés tresbien qu'il n'y demoure nulz peccouz. Et de tout cecy prennés secund la quantité de la farce que avés faicte des poissons, et ce grein cy lavés tresbien en vin blanc et puis le meslés avecques vostre poysson en une belle poelle. Puis prennés une autre poille que soit belle et necte en quoy faciés affiner de bel oflle bel et cler; et quant il sera affinés, sy mectés de celluy oflle dedans vostre farce selon la quantité qu'il en y a, puis le mectés sur belle brase eschauffer, et le menés tousjours a une belle cuiller. Et puis prennés de belle poudre fine, et en y mectés par rayson, et du succre grant foyson. Et puis ordonnés a vostre patissier que les tartres vous fera ou grandes ou petites, et qu'elles soient couvertes.

9. Fish Pie

This pie, designed for serving on one of the many lean days of the Christian week or year, is one of Chiquart's "fasting" dishes. It is a remarkably rich combination of ground fish, wine, fruit, herbs, spices, and nuts. The fact that such an extensive and disparate list of ingredients can combine into such an appetizing dish is an indication of the professional skill of the chief cook of the Duke of Savoy.

Chiquart's Fish Pie is similar to the same cook's Parma Fish Pie (see below, p. 223) but comprises fewer ingredients and is of less complex a composition than the latter dish. Chiquart prescribes a fairly broad variety of fish that may be used for the major ingredient: either tuna slices, carp or fresh eel. We have prepared it here with tuna alone.

Yield: Serves 6

Imperial	Ingredient	Metric	Directions
Sufficient pastry for a large, 10 in/ 25 cm deep-dish double-crust pie.			
2 lb	flaked cooked (poached) tuna*	1 kg	**Flake the cooked tuna fillets. Set aside.**
1/2 cup	raisins	125 mL	**Wash fruit, cut the prunes, figs &**
6–8	prunes	6–8	**dates into small pieces.**
6	figs	6	
8–10	dates	8–10	
1/2 cup	pinenuts	125 mL	**Combine fruit, nuts, wine & oil in**
1 cup	dry white wine	250 mL	**cooking pot. Heat gently.**
2 tbsp	oil (olive, almond *or* walnut)	30 mL	
2 tsp	ginger	10 mL	**Combine spices & sugar, & stir into**
1 tsp	cinnamon	5 mL	**fruit mixture. Simmer over low heat**
1/2 tsp	nutmeg	2 mL	**until sugar is dissolved.**
1/2 tsp	cloves	2 mL	**Gently mix in tuna & place mixture**
1 cup	white sugar	250 mL	**into prepared pie shell. Cover with upper crust.**
			Bake at 425°F/220°C for 10 min. Reduce heat to 375°F/190°C & bake until crust is golden brown—about 20 min.

Serving suggestions

This fruit-and-fish mixture can also be served in small, individual tart shells, or in a rissole (see pp. 91 and, for the dough, 70), as an hors d'œuvre or appetizer.

Ne faiz pas ton morsel conduire a ton coustel qui te peult nuyre.	One should not eat food from his knife: he's apt to risk harm to his life!

---

* Chiquart specifies the inclusion as well of fillet of carp and good big fresh eels. Either or both may be substituted for part of the tuna. Since eel is a more gelatinous type of fish, extra wine will be necessary.

10. *Tortres parmeysines de poyssons*

(*Du fait de cuisine*, §40)

Or je, Chiquart, vueil donner a entendre a celluy qui sera ordonné a fayre les tortres parmeysines de poyssons, qui prenne les ventreches de tons s'il est en lieu ou il puisse avoir poissons de mer, et si non qu'il prenne tant plus de celluy de eaue doulce, c'est assavoir grosses carpes fendisses, grosses anguilles et lucz gros fendis, et de cela prenne tant grant quantité que il lui sera ordonné a faire desdictes tortes; et prennés de raisins confitz, prunes, figues, dactes, pignions, et de cela prennés d'une chascune ce que luy semblera de prendre selon la quantité desdictes tortes; puis, pour lesdictes tortres, qui soient despiecés, nectoiés et lavés et mis cuire bien et nectement; et, estre bien cuis, si le tirés hors sur belles et nectes tables ou postz et qui soit estaillés des ossees et des arrestes tresbien et appoint affin qu'il n'y demoure nulz ossellez, et si les chapplés bien et minument; et les raisins dessusditz soient tresbien espicollés, le pignions tresbien nectoiés, les figues, prunes, et dactes soient taillees par minuz dees; et, toutes ces choses ainsi faictes, fors le grein, soient tresbien lavees en vin blanc et esgoutees, et puis les meslees avecques le grein du poisson dessusdit. Et encour plus fault avoir, selon la quantité desdictes tortres que avés a faire, que vous hayés de percy, de margellaine et de salvi, et d'une chescune herbe et de ceste herbe la quantité selon la force d'une chescune, c'est assavoir du percy mais et des autres mains; et qu'elles soient bien nectoyees, lavees et tresbien achiees et puis les mesclés avecques le grein dessusdit. Et, estre ce fait, ayés de bel ofle cler et nect et bien affiné et puis ayeés une belle poille grande et necte et soit assise sur beau feu cler et tout cela mectés dedans, et que vous ayés ung bon compaignion atout une belle, grande et necte cuillier qui mene tresbien et fort par ladicte poile; et faictes que vous haiés vostre lait d'amendres bien espés et coulés par l'estamine, et de l'amidon grant foyson selonc la quantité des tortres que vous avés et mectés tout dedans pour le lier; et puis mectés voz espices parmy vostre grein tousjours en broiant et menant parmy la poile, c'est assavoir gingibre blanc, granne de paradis et du poyvre pou, et du saffrant qui lui donne couleur, et du giroffle entier et du succre pisié en poudre grant foyson, et du sel pour raison. Et faictes que vous partissiés ait fait bien et appoint les crotelletes desdictes tortes et, estre faictes, si prennés de la farce dussusdicte et mectés en chescune ce que s'en devra faire. Et puis faictes que vous haiés tres grande quantité de bons et beaux trençons d'anguilles belles et bonnes qui soient bien et appoint cuictes en eaue et, estre cuictes, mectés les frire et essuier en de bel ofle et necte; et, estre frit, si en tirés dehors les arestes; et puis en une chescune torte si en mectés troys ou .iiiie. tros, l'un cza et l'autre la, entant qu'ilz ne soient point ensemble; et puis couvrés les tortres et mectés ou four et, estre cuictes, mectés les par voz platz et en alés servir.

10. Parma Fish Pie

This pie is the lean counterpart to the equally rich Parma Pie for a normal meat day (see p. 175, above) whose elaboration is likewise described in great detail in the *On Cookery*. For this fish version of the Parma Pie, Chiquart advises using fillets of tuna if sea-fish are available where the cook happens to be working. Otherwise fillets of carp, eels or pike can form its basis. You may wish to follow Chiquart's directions precisely and place sliced (cooked and boned) eels over the top of the fruit/fish mixture before you lay down the pie's upper crust. In our adaptation of Chiquart's recipe, we have chosen to use tuna; we have reserved some of the tuna to form Chiquart's top layer.

Should you choose to make your pie with eel, allow extra liquid in your mixture as the eel is gelatinous.

Yield: Serves 6

Imperial	Ingredient	Metric	Directions
Sufficient pastry for a large, 10 in/ 25 cm deep-dish double-crust pie.			
2 lb	cooked, flaked fish (tuna, pike, pickerel)	1 kg	**Flake fish & set aside.**
1 cup	raisins	250 mL	**Wash fruit. Cut prunes, figs & dates**
8	prunes	8	**into small pieces.**
6	figs	6	
10	dates	10	
1/2 cup	pinenuts	125 mL	**Combine all fruit & pinenuts in bowl**
1 cup	dry white wine	250 mL	**& add white wine. Set aside.**
2 tbsp	fine oil (olive, almond *or* walnut)	30 mL	**In cooking pot, over low heat, combine oil & herbs. Add fruit & wine**
1/3 cup	chopped fresh parsley	80 mL	**mixture.**
1 tbsp	chopped fresh marjoram	15 mL	
2 tsp	chopped fresh sage	10 mL	
2 tbsp	fresh-grated ginger (*or* 2 tsp/10 mL ground ginger)	30 mL	**Combine spices & sugar. Stir into fruit mixture. Continue cooking over**
1/2 tsp	cloves	2 mL	**low heat until sugar is dissolved.**
1/2 tsp	salt	2 mL	
1/4 tsp	grains of paradise	1 mL	
pinch	saffron (*optional*)	pinch	
1 cup	white sugar	250 mL	

1 cup	almond milk*	125 mL	**Set aside 1 tbsp/15 mL almond milk, & add remainder to rice flour. Stir until smooth. Add to the fruit mixture.**
3 tbsp	rice flour	50 mL	

Gently fold in 3/4 of fish. Pour into prepared crust. Layer remaining fish on top. Cover with top pastry. Reroll any pastry scraps, cut into desired decorations & arrange on top of pie. Brush pastry lid with reserved almond milk. Sprinkle with sugar.

Bake at 425°F/220°C for 10 min. Reduce heat to 375°F/190°C. Continue to bake 20–30 min.

Serve warm.

S'entour toy a de gens grans roucte,	If not alone, you should squelch
garde que ton ventre ne roupte.	that most unseemly urge to belch.

* To make Almond Milk, see p. 60, above.

Capiteles de tous poissons / All Fish
(Aldobrandino, *Le regime du corps*, pp. 176–77)

... You should realize that, generally, sea-fish are better and more nourishing than fresh-water fish because they are not so viscous and their flesh is firmer. ... You should also know that the flesh of fish varies according to five factors. ...

The first difference lies in the scales and is of two sorts. Some fish have a lot of scales and some have none. Those that have a lot of coarse scales are better than those that have few or none at all because the scales of a fish represent the filth which nature expels, so that the flesh remains cleaner and purer; scales are to fish as feathers are to birds and hair to animals. Fish that have fine scales are not as good, and those without any scales are quite a bit worse, the reason for this being in what we have just said.

The second difference lies in the fish's feeding habits which are varied, for some fish eat good plants and good roots and good seeds and other good things; those are the ones that nourish the best and are the most healthful. But other fish eat mud and filth and dwell in tidal flats; those should not be eaten, rather they should be avoided for they make people die suddenly.

The third difference in fish lies in the winds that blow where the fish is, because northern and eastern winds, blowing on the sea or on rivers where fish dwell, make those fish healthier and better than do southern or western winds, because the northern and eastern winds are by their nature drier [as will any fish be that are under their influence], it being better that the flesh of fish be firmer and less viscous.

The fourth difference lies in winds that bear dirt, such as dust, leaves, flowers or anything else, into rivers where fish dwell and from which dirt they might feed; and, depending on the presence or absence of these things, fish are good or bad.

The fifth difference lies in the [culinary] preparation given to fish, such as salting, and eating roasted, fried, boiled in water, and so forth. Salted fish are better, provided they are eaten two or three days after being salted, because salt remedies their harmful nature and their viscosity. Roasted fish are better than fried fish because the fried takes on the viscosity of the oil in which they are fried. Fish that are boiled in water or in oil are the worst because they are viscous; they harm the stomach, they swell it and do too much damage. But fish cooked in plain salted water are better provided they are eaten with a sauce composed of ginger, pepper, cinnamon and other spices.

Other Possible Fish Dishes

Rissolles a jour de poisson / Rissoles for a Fish Day

For the complete recipe of this dish as an Appetizer, see p. 95, above.

Flaons de cresme de lait / Cream Flans

For the complete recipe of this dish as a Dessert, see p. 283, below.
A possible version of this dish contains sliced eels.

Fish were very commonly prepared in the Middle Ages by frying and then were simply presented with a sauce that was both poured over them and served in a bowl for dipping. The extensive range of sauces normally on hand in the medieval kitchen, or that could be elaborated quickly by the experienced cook, allowed quite a broad variety of "dishes" of fish. For an assortment of the principal sauces, see the introduction at the beginning of this Chapter.

Chapter 8
Egg Dishes

Chapter 8
Egg Dishes

No foodstuff was more commonly consumed in the Middle Ages than chicken eggs—with the single exception of bread. It is easy to understand the universal dependence upon eggs in the day-to-day regimens of aristocrats and bourgeois. In the first place chickens and their eggs were ubiquitous in every corner of the medieval landscape; they could be found in every farmyard, in every manor courtyard, in the backyard of every town or city dwelling, wherever there were a couple of square meters of ground, space for a flimsy leanto and a small supply of cheap feed. Those city folk who did not maintain their own poultry could always buy fresh eggs from passing peddlers in the street. To such an extent was chicken raising an intensively practised industry at this time that Chiquart could expect his noble reader—without much difficulty and wherever he happened to live—to be able to arrange for the delivery at a single time of 12,000 fresh eggs (!) for a banquet. The 4,000 head of poultry that must also appear on his order sheet for this one occasion represent an equally impressive quantity of readily available foodstuffs. Eggs in particular were vitally important in the cookery of the time in part simply *because* they were common and relatively cheap.

A second reason for the universal popularity of eggs in late-medieval cookery was probably that which accounts for their continuing popularity today, and that is their versatility. Long before the Middle Ages, cooks had explored a wide variety of ways in which eggs could be prepared for the table. In our recipe collections plain eggs are boiled, fried, scrambled (into several sorts of omelettes), roasted (on glowing embers and even transfixed on spit!), and poached. And eggs, liquid and hard-boiled, yolks and whites together or separated, entered into mixtures for a very large number of prepared dishes. We give a small selection of recipes for such dishes in this chapter. Eggs are used as a colorant (the yolk) or an adhesive for gold leaf (the white) or a basting glaze, the so-called *doreure* (both yolks and whites beaten together).

Capiteles des oes / Eggs
(Aldobrandino, *Le regime du corps*, pp. 178ff.)

You should know that eggs are of a temperate nature; but, since they are of a compound substance, that is, of white and yolk, you should know that the yolk is temperately warm and moist, which makes it suitable to man's nature; and that the white is cold and moist, is slow to digest in the stomach and engenders crude humors. To understand fully the nature of eggs, you should understand that this nature varies for four reasons. . . .

The first difference lies in the bird that lays the eggs, for when that bird is of a good complexion, is not too lean, and the hen is tread by the cock, those eggs are the best, especially those of chickens and partridge for those are the eggs that nourish the best, engender the best blood and are most suitable to human nature. Following those

230

are duck eggs, which nourish poorly, and goose eggs which, if they are well digested, nourish better than the former but are gross and heavy, and swell and inflate the belly. Then of less value are ostrich eggs; and even worse than all the others are peacock eggs, for they are the least suitable for men because they are heavy and bad smelling, and engender bad and poisonous humors. The eggs that are the warmest of all are those of a sparrow and, after them, those of a pigeon.

The second sort of difference between eggs lies in age, for eggs from a young bird are better and more nourishing than from an old bird.

The third difference lies in whether the eggs are fresh, old or half-way between. The best are fresh ones because they are temperately warm, are more nourishing and strengthen one's natural warmth. Old eggs are thoroughly bad, putrefy quickly in the stomach, engender bad humors and resemble a poison; the older an egg, the worse it is.

The fourth difference between eggs lies in the [culinary] preparation that is given them for eating. ... Those that are cooked on hot coals may be hard or soft. The hard-cooked ones are gross and heavy, digest poorly in the stomach and engender crude humors; those who have diarrhea can eat such eggs, especially the yolks. The soft-cooked ones are the opposite, for they soften the belly and stay only briefly in the stomach; they relieve a dryness of the chest and lung. Those eggs that are between hard- and soft-cooked are unlike either and are better to eat than either.

Poached eggs strengthen natural warmth, especially when they are cooked to neither hard nor soft, because the water eliminates their harmfulness, and they are better eaten that way than any other way.

Fried eggs are the worst of all sorts of preparation because they are converted into bad humors and engender vapors and nausea, and consequently are bad to eat.

Eggs that are eaten in a broth or with meat or in a similar way are to be praised or condemned depending on the substances with which they are combined: for if they are eaten with good spices, such as cinnamon, pepper and ginger, and with meat, they are digested better and nourish better, and stir a greater desire for intercourse, than if they are eaten with cheese—which does not at all correct their harmfulness but only increases it.

1a. Tortes of Herbs, Cheese and Eggs
(*Viandier*, §175)

Prener parressi, mente, bedtes, espinoches, letuees, marjolienne, basilique et pilieux, et tout soit broyer ensamble en ung mortiez et destramper d'aigue clere et espreignez le jus; et rompés oeuf grant foison avec le jus et y mecter poudre de gigimbre, de cannelle et poivre long et fin fromaige gratusiez et du sel, tout batez ensamble; et puis faicte vostre paste bien teine pour mectre en vostre bacin et la grandeur du bacin, et puis chassez bien vostre bacin et puis y mecter du sain de port dedans et puis vostre paste aprés dedans le dit bacin et mecter vostre bacin sur les charbons et remecter dedans la paste du sain de porc; et quant il sera fonduz mectez vostre grain dedans vostre paste et le couvrez de l'autre bacin et mecter du feu dessus conme dessoubz et lessez vostre tourtel ung pol sechiez, puis descouvrés le bacin dessus et mecter sur vostre torte par bone maniere .v. myeux d'euf et de la fine poudre, puis remecter vostre bacin dressez conme devant et le lessez po a pol cuire et a petit feu de charbon et regarder souvent qu'elle ne cuise tropt; puis mecter du succre dessus a dressiez.

1b. *Pour faire une tourte*
(*Menagier*, p. 218/§250)

Pour faire une tourte. Prenez .iiii. pongnees de bectes, .ii. pongnees de percil, une pongné de cherfeuil, ung brain de fanoul et deux pongnees d'espinoches, et les esliziez, et lavez en eaue froide, puis hachiez bien menu. Puis broyez de deux paires de frommage; c'est assavoir du mol et du moyen; et puis mectez des oeufz avec ce—moyeul et aubun—et les broyez parmy le frommage. Puis mectez les herbes dedens le mortier et broyez tout ensemble, et aussi mectez y de la pouldre fine; ou en lieu de ce ayez premierement ou mortier .ii. cloches de gingembre et sur ce broyez vos frommages, oeufz et herbes. Et puis gectez du vieil frommage de presse ou autre gratuisié dessus celles herbes, et portez au four, et puis faictes faire une tarte et la mengiez chaude.

1. Tortes of Herbs, Cheese and Eggs

The *Viandier* and the *Menagier de Paris* give recipes for *Tortes*, or *Tourtes*, made with herbs, cheese and eggs. However, each incorporates quite different kinds of greenery and spices for its ingredients, and each dish employs different cooking methods. The herbs in the *Viandier* are ground and infused in water, the juice is squeezed out and added to the eggs. The pastry dish is lined with pork fat (we have substituted sautéed bacon), and the Torte is baked between hot coals in a fire. When the pie is almost cooked, egg yolks are placed on its top and the surface is sprinkled with fine spice powder. When it is finally removed from the oven, the pie is garnished with a sprinkling of sugar.

The *Menagier de Paris* specifies three kinds of cheese: soft and medium as ingredients in the torte, and an old grated cheese as a topping. The herbs are ground and retained in the mixture. As an optional alternative to fine spice powder ("*pouldre douce*"), the *Menagier* lists fresh ginger root. This version also specifies oven cooking.

Adaptations of both recipes follow.

Yield: Serves 4–6

Sufficient pastry to line a 10 in/25 cm quiche pan (see Pastry, p.67, above).

a. The *Viandier*'s recipe

Imperial	Ingredient	Metric	Directions
			Preheat oven to 425°F/220°C.
5–6 leaves	Swiss chard	5–6 leaves	**Clean & wash herbs. Discard stems.**
4 tbsp	chopped fresh parsley	60 mL	**Strip green leaves of the chard from**
2 tbsp	chopped fresh basil	30 mL	**the stalks; discard stalks.**
1 tbsp	chopped fresh mint	15 mL	
2 tsp	chopped fresh marjoram	10 mL	
2 tsp	chopped fresh thyme	10 mL	
1 1/2 cups	boiling water	375 mL	**Blanch chard & herbs briefly in boiling water.**
			Grind herbs & chard in mortar. Return to pot & stir well. Strain mixture through a sieve, pressing all liquid from leaves; discard solids; use this juice in the recipe.
			Or blend the herbs, chard & water in blender, & strain: this produces a richer but stronger tasting torte.
6	eggs	6	**In medium-sized bowl beat eggs lightly. Add herb juice.**
1/2 lb	cheese (Swiss, Gruyère *or* Emmenthal)	250 g	**Grate cheese. Add to egg mixture.**
2 tsp	ground ginger	10 mL	**Stir in spices.**
1 tsp	ground cinnamon	5 mL	
1 tsp	salt	5 mL	

6 slices	bacon	6 slices	Sauté bacon.
			Grease quiche dish with bacon fat; line it with pastry & brush pastry with bacon fat. Lay bacon strips on bottom of dish. Pour in egg mixture. Bake in oven at 425°F/220°C for 5 min; reduce heat to 350°F/180°C & continue baking until almost cooked—about 20–25 min. Remove from oven.
5	egg yolks	5	Place egg yolks on top & sprinkle with spice powder. Return to oven for 3–5 min or until egg yolks are cooked.
1 tsp	spice powder (see p. 54)	5 mL	
1 tbsp	sugar	30 mL	
			Garnish with sugar. Serve warm.

b. The *Menagier de Paris*'s recipe

Imperial	Ingredient	Metric	Directions
			Preheat oven to 425°F/220°C.
1 lb	fresh chard	500 g	Pick over chard, spinach & herbs. Strip stalks from chard & stems from spinach & herbs, & discard. Wash in cold water. Chop finely.
1/2 lb	fresh young spinach leaves	250 g	
4 tbsp	parsley	60 mL	
2 tsp	chervil	10 mL	
1 tsp	fennel	5 mL	
6	eggs	6	Beat eggs. Add greens.
1/4 lb	soft cheese	125 g	Grate or grind cheese & combine with egg mixture.
1/4 lb	medium cheese	125 g	
2 tsp	spice powder (see p. 54)	10 mL	Add spice powder *or* ginger.
	or		Pour into unbaked pastry shell.
1 tbsp	peeled & grated fresh ginger root	15 mL	
1/4 cup	grated old cheese	60 mL	Sprinkle old cheese on top. Bake in oven at 425°F/220°C for 10 min. Reduce heat to 350°F/180°C & cook until done—about 25–30 min. Serve warm.

Serving variations

1. For appetizers, use small, unbaked tartlet shells instead of quiche pan. Makes about 12–14 small tarts.
2. Omit the egg-yolk garnish (of the first version).

2. *Riquemenger*

(*Menagier*, p. 268/§360)

Prenez deux pommes aussi grosses que deux oeufz ou pou plus, et les pelez et ostez les pepins. Puis les decoupez par menuz morceaulx, puis les mectez pourboulir en une paelle de fer. Puis purez l'eaue et mectez seicher le riquemenger. Puis mectre beurre pour frioler et en friolant filez deux oeufz dessus en remuant. Et quant tout sera friolé gectez pouldre fine dessus, et soit frangé de saffran, et mengiez au pain ou moiz de septembre.

Ne touche ton nez a main nue,	To touch your nose is indiscreet
dont ta viande est tenue.	with that hand with which you eat.

2. Scrambled Eggs and Apples

This simply prepared dish, combining fried apples and eggs, is topped with a spice powder and "fringed" with threads of saffron. The *Menagier de Paris* directs that the apples be of the size of eggs: use one small apple, or equivalent, for each egg. A firm apple, such as a Northern Spy, Ida Red or Granny Smith, is preferable.

The *Menagier* himself explains the proper culinary term "fringed" (*frangé*) that he writes in this recipe and elsewhere. Saffron can be either a colorant or an embellishment. If saffron is used to color a food, it should be ground finely and then dissolved in a liquid before being mixed in with other ingredients. Otherwise it is used as a decorative garnish: the threads of saffron are distributed (or laid) on the surface of the dish—which, the Menagier tells us, is then said to be *frangé*.

The qualification *rique* found in the name of this dish probably derives from the old Germanic word *rica* which meant "strong" or "powerful" (and is related to the modern German *Reich*). In this context the designation "Strong Dish" seems to be a counterpart to the name *Blanc mengier / White Dish*, a particularly mild or bland preparation. A culinary parallel may well be the French epithet found in several English dishes, *enforced* and *aforced*: this is an enriched or strengthened version of some relatively more simple dish, most likely just a plain dish of scrambled eggs.

Yield: Serves 4

Imperial	Ingredient	Metric	Directions
4–6	firm apples	4–6	**Peel, core & slice apples. In a small pot, add water to cover. Parboil for 2–3 min. Drain.**
3–4 tbsp	butter	50–60 mL	**In a large frying pan, melt butter & fry apples until golden. Remove & keep warm.**
6	eggs additional butter	6	**Beat eggs lightly. Add more butter to pan if necessary. Pour in eggs. Cook & stir eggs, folding in apple slices while cooking. Do not overcook.**

To serve

6	slices of bread *or* toast	6	**Spoon eggs onto slices of bread *or* toast. Sprinkle with spice powder & garnish with saffron threads.**
2 tsp	fine spice powder (see p. 54, above)	10 mL	
6	threads of saffron	6	

Cooking variation

The dish may also be cooked in a double boiler. Melt the butter in the top of a double boiler. Combine the lightly beaten eggs and fried apples. Cook, covered. Follow the same serving directions as above.

3. *Frasa*

(*Du fait de cuisine*, §61)

Celluy qui haura la charge de la frasa si prenne les feies de caprilz—et si n'en ha assez de celles de caprilz si prenne de celles de veaulx—et les nectoie et lave tresbien puis les mecte cuire bien et appoint; et, estre cuites, si les tire dehors sur belles et nectes postz et, estre essuytes, si les hasche bien minut et, estre bien haschiees, si face qu'il hait de beau lart bien et appoint fondu en belles et nectes poelles, puis mectés dedans friser lesditz feies hachiés et les souffrisés bien et appoint. Et puis faictes qu'il hait des oefs grant foyson et les rompés en beaulx platz et les broyés tous ensemble, et y mectés des espices, c'est assavoyr gingibre blanc, granne de paradis, du daffran et du sel par bonne guise, puis tout cela mectés esdictes poelles tout doulcement avecques le grein desdiz feies qui se frisent en menant et remenant et en mesleant tousjours a bonne cuiller parmi les casses jusques atant qu'il soit bien cuit et essuit et sur le rossellet. Et puis quant ce viendra ou drecier ordonne les testes dessusdictes en beaux platz, et en chescun plat a costé des testes mecte et ordonne de la frase dessus dicte.

Capiteles du fie / Liver

(Aldobrandino, *Le regime du corps*, p. 136)

The nature of liver is warm and moist, and more than any other type of viscera sits long in the stomach and digests reluctantly; but when it is well digested it nourishes quite well. The best sort of liver is that of suckling animals; and of those that are older, chicken liver is the best, and especially if the hen has been fed figs and wheat grain.

Ne torche de nappe tes dens et si ne la mes point dedens.	A napkin's not for rubbing teeth, or use *in* mouth, but underneath.

3. Scrambled Eggs and Liver

Like the *Menagier*'s *Riquemenger*, this dish is a variation of plain scrambled eggs. Rather than the apples of the *Riquemenger*, however, this recipe calls for fried chopped liver that is cooked with eggs. Chiquart specifies kid's liver, but also suggests calf's liver if sufficient kid's liver is not available. The spices here are explicitly named and are to be added to the egg mixture, not used just as a garnish.

Chiquart places this recipe for *Frasa* in a group of a dozen supplemental dishes to which the cook should be able to have recourse should his master's banquet turn out to last longer than the two days foreseen for it. According to Chiquart this particular preparation should be served in conjunction with a dish called Glazed Goat-Kid Heads (*On Cookery*, §60). These heads are split (but the halves are pinned together so the brains do not fall out!) and boiled, then each half is wrapped in the egg-coated caul of a kid or calf, and roasted on a grill. We are inclined to think that the *Frasa* makes quite a satisfying dish just on its own!

Yield: Serves 4

Imperial	Ingredient	Metric	Directions
approx. 1 lb	calf's liver	approx. 450 g	**Poach liver in boiling water for 3–4 min. Drain & chop finely.**
3–4 tbsp	lard *or* butter	50–60 mL	**In large frying pan fry liver pieces in melted lard *just* until tender. Remove, keep warm.**
6	eggs	6	**Beat eggs lightly. Add spices. If**
2 tsp	ground ginger	10 mL	**necessary add more lard to frying**
1/2 tsp	ground grains of paradise	2 mL	**pan. Pour in egg mixture. Cook &**
pinch	saffron (*or* turmeric)	pinch	**stir eggs, folding in liver pieces while**
1 tsp	salt	5 mL	**cooking.**
			When cooked, transfer to warm dishes & serve.

Cooking variation

This dish can be cooked in a double boiler: see the recipe for Scrambled Eggs and Apples (*Riquemenger*), p. 235, above.

4. *Lait de prouvence (Lait lyé de vache)*
(Viandier, §86)

Boullez lait de vache une onde, puis mis [hors du feu]; quant il sera ung pou froit fillez dez moiaux grant foison passés parmy l'estamine; soit [bien] liant, sur jaunete couleur [et non pas trop]; pochés dez eufs en eaue et lez metez avec sans boullir.

4. Provençal Milk (Creamed Eggs on Toast)

A very simple recipe. One wonders if it should have been included in the *Viandier*'s chapter of dishes for the sick because it is so bland. For the medieval cook, however, the dish does solve the problem of how to keep, and use, animal milk long after the time when it would have started to turn.

The *Menagier de Paris* has copied a recipe for this dish but has given it the name that is shown in later copies of the *Viandier*, "Bound Cow's Milk" (*Lait de vasche lyé*, p. 175/§133). In the *Menagier*'s version, ginger and saffron are added to the *Viandier*'s list of ingredients.

Yield: Serves 4

Imperial	Ingredient	Metric	Directions
1 1/2 cups	milk	375 mL	**In sauce pot, scald milk. Remove from heat.**
2	egg yolks	2	**Whisk egg yolks in a small bowl. Slowly, while continuing to whisk, pour about 1/4 cup of hot milk into eggs, then stir this mixture slowly into remaining milk. Cook until sauce is thickened.**
4	eggs	4	**Poach eggs in water, then gently add**
4 slices	toast	4 slices	**them to the sauce. Pour into bowls & serve with toast.**

Cooking variation

Add 1 tsp/5 mL of grated gingerroot and a pinch of saffron to the sauce.

Serving variation

Toast slices of a stick of French bread cut either lengthwise of diagonally. Place poached egg on top of each slice and spoon sauce on top. Garnish with parsley and serve.

5. *Lait lardé*

(*Menagier de Paris*, p. 224/§259 and *Viandier*, §200)

Prenez le lait de vasche ou de brebis, et mectez fremier sur le feu. Et gectez des lardons et du saffran et ayez oeufz (scilicet blanc et moyeux) bien batuz, et gectez a ung coup sans mouvoir, et faictes boulir tout ensemble. Et aprés hostez hors du feu et laissiez tourner; ou sans oeufz les fait l'en tourner de vertjus. Et quant il est reffroidié l'en le lye bien fort en une piece de toille ou estamine, et luy donne l'en quelque fourme que l'en veult, ou plate ou longue, et chargié d'une grosse pierre laissiez reffroidier sur ung dreçouer toute nuyt. Et l'endemain laiché, et frit au fer de paelle (et se frit de luy mesmes sans autre gresse, ou a gresse qui veult) et est mis en platz ou escuelles comme lesche de lart, et lardé de giroffle et de pignolet; et qui le veult faire vert, si prengne du tournesot.

5. Larded Milk

It is a refreshing change to be given a recipe which actually wants the milk to curdle! We are sure we are not the only cooks who have, through a second's lack of attention, had an egg and cream custard curdle unintentionally. Though these directions seem rather complicated, the dish is really not a difficult one to make.

The *Menagier* calls for whole eggs, and uses cloves and pinenuts pricked into the slices of larded milk before frying them. The *Viandier*'s version of this recipe calls for just cloves.

Yield: About 10 or 12 finger-sized slices

Imperial	Ingredient	Metric	Directions
3 cups	whole milk	750 mL	**Boil milk with bacon & saffron.**
3–4	strips of bacon	3–4	
pinch	saffron	pinch	
3	eggs, lightly beaten	3	**Add eggs & wine, & cook until cur-**
1/4 cup	white wine	60 mL	**dled.**

Remove bacon & set aside. Line a sieve with muslin *or* cheescloth. Pour mixture into sieve, draining off as much of liquid as possible. Line a loaf pan with cheesecloth. Place bacon strips on bottom. Add egg mixture & flatten down evenly with the back of a spoon. On top place several layers of absorbant towelling, then a heavy object* to squeeze out liquid. Repeat process until most of moisture has been absorbed & mixture is firm. Turn out onto a slicing board. Slice.

10–12	cloves	10–12	**Prick with cloves & pinenuts. Fry on a**
10–12	pinenuts (*optional*)	10–12	**griddle. Garnish with sugar & serve.**
1–2 tsp	sugar	5–10 mL	

---

* We use another loaf pan and press down with our weight.

6. *Brouet vert d'oeufs et de fromage*

(*Viandier*, §87)

Prenez persil et ung pou de sauge, et bien pou de saffren en la verdeur, et pain trempé, et deffaictes de puree ou d'eaue boullie, et puis gingenbre deffait de vin, et mettez boullir; puis mettez le frommage dedans et les oeufz quant ilz seront pochiez en eaue; et soit lyant, vertgay; et aucuns n'y mettent point de pain, mais y mettent layt d'amendes.

Ne offre a nully, se tu es saige,	To pass your neighbour surplus stew
le demourant de ton potaige.	is not the proper thing to do.

6. Green Brewet of Eggs and Cheese

The *Viandier* offers two options in this easy recipe. The herbs may be steeped in either pea puree or boiled water, and either moistened bread crumbs or almond milk may be used as a thickener. The pea puree gives a much richer dish. We have chosen to use bread crumbs. If substituting almond milk, use 1/2 cup / 125 mL of it as a thickener (see p. 60).

This brewet should be thick. With the addition of the yellow saffron (or turmeric) to the chopped parsley, the end color would have been the bright green hue which French cooks called *vertgay* ("cheery green") and their English counterparts *gawdy green*.

Yield: Serves 4

Imperial	Ingredient	Metric	Directions
2 cups	pea puree (see p. 63)	500 mL	**Heat pea puree & water.**
1 cup	water	250 mL	
1/2 cup	fresh chopped parsley, lightly packed	125 mL	**Add parsley, sage & saffron (*or* turmeric).**
1 tbsp	fresh chopped sage	15 mL	**Cook over low heat, stirring frequently**
pinch	saffron* (*or* turmeric)	pinch	**until herbs are well infused into the base.**
1/2 cup	moistened white bread crumbs	125 mL	**Add bread crumbs & cheese. Con-**
1/4 lb	grated cheese (parmesan *or* other firm cheese)	125 g	**tinue cooking, stirring constantly until the cheese has melted & a thick consistency is reached.**
4	eggs	4	**Keep sauce warm while poaching eggs**
2 tbsp	water	30 mL	**in water & vinegar solution. Add salt**
1 tsp	vinegar	5 mL	**to taste.**
	salt		

To serve

| 4 sprigs | parsley | 4 | **Divide the brewet into four soup bowls. Place a poached egg on each. Garnish with parsley sprigs.** |

---

* Saffron is used here in order to intensify the color. Turmeric is much less expensive and works almost as well.

7. *Une arboulaste ou deux de oeufz*
(*Menagier de Paris*, p. 206/§225)

Une arboulaste ou deux de oeufz. Prenez du coq .ii. feuilles seulement, et de rue moins la moictié ou neant—car sachiez qu'il est fort et amer—de l'ache, tenoise, mente et sauge, de chascun au regard de quatre feuilles ou moins—car chascun est fort—marjolaine ung petit plus, fenoul plus, et percil encores plus. Mais de poree: bectes, feuilles de violectes, espinars et laictues, orvale, autant de l'un comme de l'autre, tant que de tout vous ayez deux pongnees largement. Eslisiez et lavez en eaue froide, puis les espraignez et ostez toute l'eaue. Et broyez deux cloches de gingembre, puis mectez ou mortier a deux ou troiz foiz vos herbes avec ledit gingembre broyé, et broyez l'un avec l'autre. Et puis ayez seize oeufz bien batuz ensemble—moyeulx et aubuns—et broyez et meslez ou mortier avec ce que dit est. Puis partez en deux, et faictes deux allumelles espesses qui seront frictes par la maniere qui s'ensuit: premierement vous chaufferez tresbien vostre paelle a huille, beurre, ou autre gresse que vous vouldrez; et quant elle sera bien chaude de toutes pars, et par especial devers la queue, meslez et espandez vos oeufz parmy la paelle, et tournez a une [palecte] souvent ce dessus dessoubz; puis gectez de bon frommage gratuisé pardessus. Et sachez que ce est ainsi fait pour ce, qui brayeroit le frommage avec les herbes et oeufz, quant l'en cuideroit frire son alumelle, le frommage qui seroit dessoubz se tendroit a la paelle. Et ainsi fait il d'une alemelle de oeufz, qui mesle les oeufz avec le frommage. Et pour ce l'en doit premierement mectre les oeufz en la paelle, et mectre le frommage dessus, et puis couvrir des bors des oeufz; et autrement se prendroient a la paelle. Et quant vos herbes seront frictes en la paelle, si donnez fourme quarree ou ronde a vostre arboulastre, et la mengiez ne trop chaude ne trop froide.

Ruta / Rue
(*Tacuinum sanitatis*, Vienna,
Oesterreichische Nationalbibliothek, Codex Vindobonensis, 2644, f. 35r)

Rue is an antidote for poisons and helps epileptics, yet it causes headaches. The best place to grow it is in the shade of a fig tree; a green, fresh plant is preferable. Its virtues as an antidote are well known by the weasel which, it is said, prepares itself with rue before it goes out snake-hunting. Some believe that it has powers against spirits, referring to a passage by Aristotle in which the Stagyrite discusses its fascinations or enchantments. But everyone knows, on Galen's authority, that rue "extinguishes the flames of Venus."

Feniculus / Fennel
(*Tacuinum sanitatis*, Vienna, f. 41v)

Pliny testifies that the health-giving qualities of fennel were discovered by observing snakes which, on eating it, threw off all signs of age and clouded vision and became sharp-sighted; but not only is it good for the eyes, purifying the eyesight, but it increases the milk of nursing mothers, acts as a diuretic for everyone and clears away flatulence. Choose the domestic plant, fresh and flavorful, verging on the pungent. Since it is digested slowly, take care to chew and grind it up carefully. It generates bilious humors.

Spinachie / Spinach

(*Tacuinum sanitatis*, Vienna, f. 27r)

The usual way to cook spinach is in a pan without any water, especially when it is tender: spinach is so full of juice, which is drawn out by the heat, that it cooks in its own liquid. Garden spinach is best when bedewed with rain. It is fairly nourishing and good for coughs and the chest. It is true that it spoils the digestion, and if you normally suffer from this sort of problem the spinach should be fried with salted water or with vinegar and spices. When drunk, the water from spinach is useful against spider and scorpion bites, and it is also helpful if sprinkled directly onto the bites.

7. An Herb Omelette

The French name for this omelette, *arboulaste*, is merely a combination of the words "herb" and "*aloumaste*." This latter part of the name, which ends up as the modern "omelette" (with the *l* and *m* exchanged), derived from the word *lamina* or *lamella*, meaning a thin plate; the word is descriptive, evoking the appearance of a thin, plate-like omelette.

Though the *Menagier* lists many ingredients for this dish, it is really just a simple herb and cheese omelette. Some of the herbs specified by the old recipe are no longer in common usage. Because of their bitterness and strength, the *Menagier* warns the cook to use very small amounts of dittany (a plant in the mint family) and of rue (so strong and bitter, the author says, that it may even be omitted). Smallage (wild celery), tansy, mint and sage are also to be included only in small amounts because of their strength. Marjoram, fennel and parsley are used in increasing amounts. The salad greens—chard, spinach, clary (a variety of sage) and violet leaves—the author directs to be used in about equal portions.

If you are able to locate the less well-known herbs and greens, and are familiar with their properties and with just how safe each is, you may wish to create your own combination according to the *Menagier*'s directions. Some of the ingredients, such as tansy, can be procured at a health food store. We have chosen those items that are more readily available.

Typical of the practical concerns of the *Menagier* is his advice that the cheese be sprinkled on top of the egg/herb mixture *after* it has been poured into the pan, in order to avoid having the cheese stick to the bottom of the pan.

Yield: Serves 4–6

Imperial	Ingredient	Metric	Directions
1 1/2 cups	a combination of chopped spinach & chard leaves	750 mL	**Remove ribs & stems from chard & spinach.**
1/2 tsp	fresh chopped mint	2 mL	**Wash all greens & herbs, & press**
1/2 tsp	chopped tansy	2 mL	**out all moisture, before chopping &**
1 tsp	fresh chopped marjoram	5 mL	**measuring.**
1 tsp	fresh chopped fennel	5 mL	
1 tbsp	fresh chopped parsley	15 mL	
2 tsp	fresh chopped sage	10 ml	
1 tbsp	finely grated fresh ginger root	15 mL	**Combine blanched greens, herbs & grated ginger in a mortar or in a processer. Grind or process together.**
8	eggs	8	**In a large bowl beat eggs lightly. Add in the herb/greenery/ginger mixture, mixing well.**
4–6 tbsp	butter	60–90 mL	**In a large skillet melt butter over medium heat. Pour in eggs. (You may wish to divide the mixture: use a smaller skillet & cook 4 separate omelettes). When partially set, sprinkle cheese on top. Shake pan occasionally to allow even cooking.**
1/4 lb	grated Emmenthal *or* Gruyère cheese	125 g	
			When cooked, fold over once & turn upside down onto a warmed plate & serve.

Cooking variation

Though not called for in the recipe, a smoother blend of greenery mixture is obtained if the herbs are blanched briefly in boiling water, and then all moisture pressed out, before they are ground and mixed with the eggs.

8. *Civé d'oeufz* (*Souppe en moustarde*)
(*Viandier*, §§83 & 84; *Menagier de Paris*, pp.174–75/§§131 & 132)

Civé ð'oeufz. Poschez oeufz a l'uille. Puis ayez ongnons par rouelles cuiz, et les friolez a l'uille, puis mettez boulir en vin, vertjus et vinaigre, et faictes boulir tout ensemble. Puiz mectez en chascune escuelle .iii. ou .iiii. oeufz, et gectez vostre brouet dessus; et soit non lyant.

Souppe en moustarde. Prenez de l'uille en quoy vous avez pochez vos oeufz, ðu vin, ðe l'eaue, et tout boulir en une paelle ðe fer. Puiz prenez les croustes ðu pain et le mettez harler sur le gril; puiz en faictes souppes quarrees et mectez boulir. Puiz retrayez vostre souppe, et mettez en ung plat ressuier. Et dedans le boullon mectez ðe la moustarde, et faictes boulir. Puis faictes vos souppes par escuelles, et versez vostre boullon dessus.

Sinapi / Mustard
(*Tacuinum sanitatis*, Vienna,
Oesterreichische Nationalbibliothek, Codex Vindobonensis, 2644, f.24r)

The seeds of the mustard plant are used to make the sauce that is served with food and stimulates the appetite wonderfully. Because of its vaporous nature it sometimes penetrates the nose unpleasantly, rising to the brain and causing sneezing. Mustard, which thins the blood, is useful mainly against gout. It is also useful against sciatica if mixed with figs and applied to the affected area until it turns red owing to the very hot nature of mustard. The harm that it may do to the brain can be avoided by preparing it with almonds and vinegar.

Capiteles de senevés / Mustard
(Aldobrandino, *Le regime du corps*, p.163)

Mustard is warm and dry in the fourth [*i.e.*, the mortal or very dangerous] degree; by its nature it dries up the gross, moist humors of the head and stomach, especially in those people in whom they are cold.

However, for those whose complexion is warm and dry, mustard is harmful in the summer. You should understand that its warmth is reduced if it is distempered with vinegar; and if it is distempered with new wine, it is not so dry, but rather is more kindly to the stomach because of the sweetness of the new wine.

Ciens ðevant toy le tablier net; en ung vaissel ton relief met.	From cleanliness try not to lapse but use a dish for all your scraps.

8. Mustard Egg Sops

Among the various genres of dish in early French cookery the *civé* or *civet* is one of the more common. The generic name derives from the vegetable now known as "chive"; in the Middle Ages the Latin word *cepa* and its French counterpart *cive* designated any variety of onion in general. As a consequence, any pottage that incorporated onions as a basic ingredient could normally given the name of *civet*.

Both the *Viandier* and the *Menagier de Paris* indicate in the wording of their recipes for these two dishes, Egg Civet and Mustard Sops, that they should be prepared and served together. In both books the recipes are copied together, although the order in which they are copied varies. Because the earliest copy of the *Viandier* (the manuscript roll now in the Archives of the Canton of the Valais at Sion, Switzerland) happens to have been cut at this point and neither of these recipes appears in what remains, we do not know what the "original" order may have been for Egg Civet and Mustard Sops. However, it is quite clear that the dishes are related because one of the later versions of the *Viandier* begins the recipe for Mustard Sops by saying, "Take the oil in which you have fried or poached your eggs . . . ."

Unfortunately, all three of these later copies invert the order of the recipes. Because the Mustard Sops is supposed to use the oil in which the eggs of the Egg Civet are initially poached, the inversion of the order of the recipes can lead to a little confusion about the nature of each of the dishes. In a futile attempt to straighten out some of this confusion, one later copyist, seeing the reference to "oil in which you have poached your eggs," even went so far as to begin *his* copy of Mustard Sops by writing, "Take eggs poached in oil . . . then take that oil and wine and water . . . ." This blunder is but a small example of the vicissitudes of food recipes from one manuscript copy to the next over a century of copying. The dish called Mustard Sops obviously has nothing to do with eggs, or at least with eggs as ingredients, but rather is simply to be served in conjunction with the eggs that are the basis of the dish called Egg Civet.

The *Menagier de Paris* (whose text is reproduced here) retains what must surely have been early versions of the two recipes, including a sensible order that makes the relation between the two dishes much clearer.

Our hybrid, which we have baptized with the composite name "Mustard Egg Sops," is served as a single dish.

Yield: Sauce sufficient to serve 4–6

Imperial	Ingredient	Metric	Directions
4–6 tbsp	olive oil	60–90 mL	**In large skillet, heat oil & fry eggs to desired consistency. Set eggs aside & keep warm.***
4–6	eggs	4–6	
1	large onion	1	**Slice onion thinly & sauté in the oil over low heat for 2–3 min.**
1 cup	red wine	250 mL	**Increase the heat & stir in wine, water, vinegar & lemon juice.**
1/2 cup	water	125 mL	
2 tbsp	red wine vinegar	30 mL	
2 tbsp	lemon juice	30 mL	
4–6 slices	bread	4–6 slices	**Toast bread. Cut each slice into 4 & add them very gently to the sauce. Leave them for 30 sec. Remove these sops with slotted spoon & drain. Distribute them equally among 4–6 soup bowls.**
2 tbsp	Dijon-style mustard	30 mL	**Stir mustard into sauce, then gently add eggs. Simmer until eggs have heated through.**
			Place one egg† on sops in each bowl & spoon sauce evenly over top.
			Serve warm.

---

* The *Viandier*'s directions may imply that the fried eggs be incorporated into the sauce from the beginning. We have found that adding the eggs just before serving is preferable. You may wish to delay cooking the eggs until after the sauce has cooked, adding them just before serving.

† The *Menagier* suggests allotting three or four eggs per bowl. It should be remembered, though, that at this time the contents of a serving bowl were supposed to be shared, normally between two persons although occasionally among three or four.

9. *Brouet d'Alemaigne d'oeufz*

(*Viandier*, §85; *Menagier de Paris*, p. 172/§125)

Pochez en huille, layt d'amendes boully et oingnons par rouelles friz en huille, et mettez boullir ensemble; puis affinez gingenbre, canelle, girofle, grainne de paradiz et ung pou de saffren deffait de verjus, et mettez avec sans trop boullir; et soit bien lyant et non pas trop jaune. Et la souppe en la moustarde, qui veult.

9. German Egg Broth

This recipe for *Brouet d'Alemaigne d'oeufz* is somewhat similar to the *Civet d'oeufz* that both the *Viandier* and the *Menagier de Paris* include, along with this Broth itself, in their collections. There are two significant differences, though, between the two dishes: this present recipe for German Egg Broth contains a good assortment of spices that are totally absent from the *Civet*; and almond milk is called for instead of the wine that is the basis of the *Civet*.

This second difference, the use of almond milk, may actually have something to do with the name of this present *Brouet d'Alemaigne d'oeufz*. The *Viandier*'s version of the name (which has *Almengne* in the Bibliothèque Nationale manuscript) points to a German origin for the recipe—an assumption confirmed by the *Menagier*'s later spelling of the name as "*Alemaigne*." However, a few English recipes of the time, derived from the French, write the word as if it were "almonds." Almonds are in fact the characteristic ingredient of both this lean dish and its meat-day counterpart, the so-called German Meat Broth (*Brouet d'Alemaigne de char*) that appears in the chapter of "Thick Broths for Meat Days" in both recipe collections.

Otherwise the affinity between the two preparations, the Egg Civet and the present German Egg Broth, is underscored by their proximity in the two recipe collections. Both are copied in the chapter entitled "Thick Meatless Pottages." And both conclude in the same way, with a suggestion that each could appropriately be served along with the dish called Mustard Sops. In dealing with the Egg Civet recipe we suggested making a hybrid dish which combined the eggs *with* mustard sops: Mustard Egg Sops. Here for the German Egg Broth we would suggest one of two possible procedures. Either you may turn back to the recipe for *Souppe en moustarde* / Mustard Egg Sops and make up a batch of toast flavored with onion and covered with a mustard sauce—this is indeed what both of our sources suggest is appropriate. Or, alternatively, and perhaps more simply, you may take merely the "sops" part of the other recipe and serve the German Egg Broth over toast.

All of the manuscript versions of this recipe insist that the sauce should be thick and only slightly yellow in color.

Yield: Sauce sufficient to serve 4

Imperial	Ingredient	Metric	Directions
4–6 tbsp	olive oil *or* almond oil	60–90 mL	**In a large skillet, heat oil & fry eggs**
4	eggs	4	**to desired consistency. Set eggs aside & keep warm.***
1	large onion	1	**Slice onion thinly & sauté in the oil over low heat for 2–3 min.**
2 cups	almond milk (see p. 60)	500 mL	**Slowly stir in almond milk.**
2 tsp	ground ginger	10 mL	**Infuse spices in lemon juice & add to**
1 tsp	cinnamon	5 mL	**sauce.**
1/2 tsp	cloves	2 mL	**Cook over low heat, stirring constantly**
1/4 tsp	grains of paradise	1 mL	**until sauce is of desired consistency.**
pinch	saffron *or* turmeric (for color)	pinch	
2 tbsp	lemon juice	30 mL	
			Gently add eggs. Simmer until eggs are heated through. Divide eggs & sauce among 4 bowls. Serve.

Serving variation

Place slices of toast on the bottom of each bowl and serve the eggs and sauce over this toast.

---

* The recipe indicates that the eggs should be incorporated into the sauce from the beginning. Alternatively, you may wish to add them to the sauce *after* it is cooked. To do this, reserve 2–3 tbsp/30–50 mL of the oil in order to fry the eggs later. You may feel that this gives a better texture to the dish.

Another Possible Egg Dish

Lait lardé / Larded Milk

For the complete recipe of this dish as an *Entremets*, see p. 327, below.

Chapter 9
Vegetables

Preparation of vegetables
1. *Poree de cresson* / Stewed Cress
2. *Navaiz* / Turnips
3. *Ris engoullé* / Ruddy Rice Pudding
4. *Minces* / Brussels Sprouts in a Vinaigrette
5. *Choulx pasquerés* / Easter Cabbage for a Meat Day
6. *Escheroys* / Parsnips
7. *Courges* / Fried Squash
8. *Poreaulx* / Leeks in a White Leek Sauce
9. *Champignons* / Baked Mushrooms
10. *Composte* / Honey-Glazed Vegetables

Puree de poys / **Pea Puree** : see Chapter 1, Standard Preparations
Syseros / **Chickpea Puree** : see Chapter 2, Appetizers
[*Pastez de champignons*] / **Mushroom Tarts** : see Chapter 2, Appetizers
Porriaux blancs / **Almond-Leek Sauce** : see Chapter 4, Sauces

Chapter 9
Vegetables

It is clear that the recipes found in existing cookbooks from the late Middle Ages cannot be taken as a reliably complete indication of all the foods that were served on the dining tables of the period. For instance, in contemporary descriptions of what might be planted in a good domestic garden* we find lists of vegetables whose number and variety suggest that the diet of the time was not nearly as dominated by meats and pasties as those recipes in the cookery manuals would seem to suggest.

In a chapter of the *Menagier de Paris* just previous to the series of food recipes, the Bourgeois author offers detailed directions on the planting, transplanting, fertilizing, pruning, grafting, pest-control and general maintenance of his garden—the one that he expects his wife to manage, with the help, of course, of their gardener. In this seemingly typical urban plot will be grown the following: peas, *poix perciés*, field beans, marsh beans, savory, marjoram, stock-gillyflower (*giroflee*), parsley, fennel, basil, hyssop, violet (of several sorts), sage, lavender, dittany (*coq, cost*), mint, herb bennet (*toutebonne*), clary (two sorts: *orvale* and *sclaree*), poppy, sorrel, rosemary, borage, orach, leeks (and *les porees* generically), houseleek (*joubarde*), spinach, lettuce (common and romaine), squash, chard (*bettes*), cabbage (of several sorts) and Brussels sprouts, turnip (*raves*), peony, snake-wood (*serpentine*), lily bulb (*oignons de lis*), roses (whose petals were used, among other purposes, to make rosewater), raspberries, gooseberries, grapes (several sorts), cherries and plums. Just as common on fourteenth-century tables, and cultivated widely in France, were the produce of other fruit and nut trees that the *Menagier*'s gardener has overlooked: apples, pears, medlars, quince, peaches, figs, chestnuts, walnuts, filberts.

Even more revealing of the fresh fruits and vegetables that were included in the normal diet of ordinary people at the end of the Middle Ages are the poems that reproduce the cries of street hawkers. These itinerants sold their groceries daily to the good housewives of French towns and cities. Their cries advertised the availability, in good quantity and freshness, of a surprisingly wide variety of produce. Included in peddlers' stocks were carrots, fresh peas in their shells, fresh beans in their shells, puree of peas, puree of beans, turnips, several varieties of mushrooms, garlic, onions, scallions, water cress and garden cress, chervil, lettuce, leeks and other mixed leafy vegetables known as *poree*; peaches, several varieties of pears, apples, sorbapples (serviceberries), cherries

---

* In Jean de Garlande's *Dictionarius* (ed. Wright, *A Volume of Vocabularies*, 2 vols., London (n. publ.), n.d., Vol. I, p. 136), we read that the Parisian garden of even as early as the middle of the thirteenth century could contain a very good variety of vegetables and herbs: "Master John gathers in his garden vegetables called cabbage, borage, chard, leeks, garlic, mustard, *poreta*, chives, scallions, for in his park grow pimpernel, pilosella, sanicle, bugloss, *lancea*, and other herbs of value to the human body."

(sweet and sour), plums, medlars, walnuts, Lombardy chestnuts, figs and imported grapes.†

To these vegetables and fruits should be added aparagus, cucumbers, celery, aubergines, truffles, dill, vetchling, lupines, acorns, hazelnuts, swedes, capers, melons and watermelons, oranges (bitter), pomegranates, apricots and dates: all are relatively well known in late-medieval kitchens.

Clearly, vegetables and fruits that were grown domestically or that were sold by itinerant vendors in urban streets must generally have been consumed as foodstuffs. And consumed in quantities that would warrant these vegetables and fruits being cultivated on very scarce urban land or carried and peddled by individuals who depended on such sales for their livelihood. The problem is that most contemporary cookbooks make only slight and passing reference to such vegetables and fruits.

The relative absence at this time of recipes for vegetables has led some people to think that people in the fourteenth century must have eaten little other than meat and fish: roast meat and fish, fried meat and fish, boiled meat and fish, pottages of meat and fish, pies of meat and fish. When we glance through the medieval recipe collections, though, we should bear in mind that recipes are written only for preparations that were out of the ordinary or tending to be complex. The ordinary, trivial sort of preparation does not need a recipe. And even less so the fruit or vegetable that was normally eaten raw. It is very likely that the cooks of the time would never have dreamed of looking into a cookbook to find out how to prepare vegetables for the table. You boiled them or you cut and ground them—or you did both—and that was that. But vegetables were undoubtedly eaten, in quantity and in variety.

Even such a work as the *Viandier* of Taillevent, destined as it was for the kitchens of the royalty and aristocracy of France, mentions (albeit briefly) dishes made from vegetables. And this mention has a clearly condescending tone. At the very end of his list of substantial dishes Taillevent adds a paragraph (§154) that he heads, somewhat dismissively, "Other lesser pottages":

> Other lesser pottages, such as stewed chard, cabbage, turnip greens, leeks, ... plain shallot pottage, peas, frenched beans, mashed beans, sieved beans or beans in the shell, ... *women are experts with these and anyone knows how to do them*; as for tripe, which I have not put in my recipe book, it is common knowledge how it is to be prepared. [My italics.]

When Taillevent writes that the preparation of tripe is such "common knowledge" that it does not need a recipe, and that even, says he, *women* can handle the making of stewed chard—presumably because it is a perfectly normal procedure—we have to assume that vegetables in one form or another were more or less commonplace on the dinner tables of the late Middle Ages.

---

† As well as the "standard" vegetables and fruits, these hawkers peddled a great variety of other foods, including wine, vinegar, mustard vinegar, verjuice (both the liquid alone and with the crushed verjuice grape), garlic sauce, honey, anise, pepper, fresh butter, several varieties of cheese, wheat flour, oatmeal, sour dough starter, bread, pasties, rissoles, tarts, simnel and other cakes, several varieties of wafers and biscuits (*oublées, galettes, eschaudez*) and flans. A few of these travelling vendors and some specialized shops sold semi-prepared foods, such as almond oil, meat pies, roast geese and theriac, so that their stock-in-trade might be reminiscent of that of our delicatessens or "fast-food" outlets today. The fourteenth-century housewife had ready access to a broad choice of fresh foods for the dining board.

Our selection of recipes for vegetables is gleaned from the scanty offerings of our French cookbooks.

To our prepared dishes for vegetables the modern cook should feel perfectly free to add—and still remain quite medievally authentic—any of the following, whether raw or boiled, whether whole or chopped, minced, mashed, ground and strained: any leafy green vegetable (this is the standard dish known in the early French menu as the *poree*); any root vegetable, including carrots and parsnips but excluding potatoes; tomatoes (provided your definition of the Middle Ages stretches far enough to include the sixteenth century); white peas and any beans other than green string beans.

Preparation of vegetables

While few actual recipes for vegetables are included in most of the recipe collections, the *Menagier de Paris*, with his typical encyclopedic thoroughness, has roughly drafted a section on vegetables and provides some direction regarding the proper procedures for cooking them.

Undoubtedly plain boiled vegetables were served, but a popular alternative appears to have been vegetables prepared as a *poree*, that is, stewed or pureed, with the addition of a thickener as necessary. Virtually any vegetable available in medieval times could have been cooked in this manner. However, three types of *poree* are mentioned specifically in the *Menagier*.

1. *Poree blanche*, a White Poree: a variety of white vegetables may enter this, including the white part of leeks, the white stems and veins of chard, beans, peas, onions and shallots.
2. *Poree verte*, or Green Poree: chard leaves or other green leafy vegetables such as spinach or brussels sprouts, garden cress or water cress, were used for this *poree*.
3. *Poree noire*, or Black Poree: the *Menagier* lists no specific vegetables here; presumably any of the above could be used. The dark color appears to have come from the cooking process, during which the frying of the vegetable in bacon fat or beef grease produced a characteristic hue. The finished dish had pieces of cooked bacon or lardons on top.

The cooking process for *poree* was similar in all cases, but the ingredients used to cook the vegetables varied as to whether it was a meat day or a fish (lean) day. The vegetable was culled, washed and cut into smaller pieces (with occasional exceptions). If it was an old or tough vegetable it was first parboiled; otherwise it was cooked in a meat bouillon or in milk (on lean days, in almond milk or water), then chopped finely or mashed, fried in beef or pork fat or butter (in oil on lean days), and served. Bread crumbs, oatmeal or almond milk functioned as a thickening agent if needed.

The *Menagier* suggests that the dietary rules of the ecclesiastical calendar were not strictly adhered to because, where butter ought to be proscribed for a lean dish, he simply notes, "Some people do." He also states that while vegetables cooked in bouillon were to be strained through a sieve or boulting cloth, those cooked in almond milk were not.

For a poree

Cook the prepared vegetable in meat bouillon, milk, water or almond milk (see p. 60, above), adding any desired additional ingredients (see the choice below), until tender. Strain, chop finely and run through a sieve (or use a blender or processor). Fry in meat fat, butter or oil. Serve.

Specific vegetables: notes in the Menagier de Paris

beans *(feves)*—usually broad white *(haricot)* beans which in medieval times were harvested in August and kept dried for use out of season. New bean puree was enhanced by the addition of much parsley, some sage and hyssop, and thickened with bread crumbs. Oil or butter was used for frying. Old beans would be reconstituted—parboiled, then cooked with onions in meat bouillon and fried in lard.

brussels sprouts *(petiz choulx* or *minces)*—available from January to Easter. They were cooked whole in a small amount of water, drained and tossed with a vinaigrette composed of olive oil, vinegar, salt and raw herbs (see the recipe for *Minces*, p. 262).

cabbage *(choulx)*—the *Menagier* advises his wife that the best cabbages are those that have been picked just after a frost; there is no need to parboil these before cooking. Older cabbages were to be parboiled; these were called Roman *(romaine)* cabbage and were eaten in winter. Only beef fat, butter or oil was to be used in the frying. Oatmeal was added as a thickener if necessary. Some meat could be added (see recipe, p. 263).

carrots *(garroictes)*—available on about All Saints Day (November 1) at a market in Paris that the *Menagier* calls Les Halles. The author directs that they be cooked in the same way as turnips (see the recipe for *Navaiz* / Turnips, p. 260, below).

chard *(bectes)*—the white stems and veins, and the green leaves were used in different *porees*. The whites were cooked in beef or mutton bouillon (*never* in pork bouillon), or in cow's milk or almond milk, then fried in butter, fat or oil. The green leaves were cooked in beef bouillon, with parsley added, then fried in fat. If they were very young and tender chard leaves could be cooked in verjuice (we may substitute lemon juice) with a little water added, drained and fried in butter. Cheese could be added during the frying process (see the recipe for *Poree de cresson* / Stewed Cress, below, p. 259).

chickpeas *(sises)*—washed, (if dried, they should be reconstituted), cooked in salted water with almond oil, whole parsley (leaf and root, cleaned and peeled) and sage. Cinnamon and verjuice could be added (see the recipe for *Syseros* / Chickpea Puree, p. 77).

water cress *(cresson)*—in Lent, cooked in almond milk (see recipe, p. 259).

fennel root *(fanoil)*—cleaned, scraped and cut into small pieces. The hard centre core was discarded. It was cooked as other vegetables.

leeks *(poireaulx)*—require parboiling if not young and fresh. On meat days they were cooked in meat bouillon and always fried in pork fat. Minced onions, chives, sausages and ham could be added. On lean days the cooking liquid was almond milk (see the recipes for *Porriaux blancs* / Almond-Leek Sauce, p. 132, below).

onions (*oingnons*)—cooked in water or bouillon, and fried in oil. Ginger, cloves, grains of paradise, wine, vinegar and saffron were added.

parsley root (*racines de percil*)—cleaned, scraped, cut into small pieces and cooked in the same manner as other vegetables.

parsnips (*escheroys*)—scraped, cut into slices, washed two or three times in hot water. They were then dipped in flour and fried in oil. If parsnips were used in a pie, onions, spice powder and fish were added (see recipe, p. 266).

peas (*pois*)—cooked in meat bouillon or almond milk. Onions could be added.

spinach (*espinards*)—if the spinach were young and tender, it could be fried raw along with some parsley in olive or almond oil with a very small amount of water added to the pan. Otherwise, it was cooked in boiling salted water, drained, chopped and then fried in olive oil. A little verjuice (or lemon juice) could be added.

squash (*courges*)—always seeded. The *Menagier* preferred peeling the skin and discarding it, though he acknowledged that if the skin were tender it could be left on. The squash was cut into pieces, cooked in bouillon and mashed; when serving, the top was garnished with strands of saffron.

turnips (*navaiz*)—peeled, cut into pieces, cooked in bouillon (either pork, beef or mutton), fried and sprinkled with spice powder (see the recipe, p. 260, below). Alternatively, turnips could be sliced, cooked in water, drained and cooked in a bit of honey.

Rape / Turnip

(*Tacuinum sanitatis*, Vienna,
Oesterreichische Nationalbibliothek, Codex Vindobonensis, 2644, f. 52v)

Like the leek, the nature of the turnip tends to warmth, but to a much more temperate degree; and whereas leeks are dry, the turnip is moist, sometimes to a very high degree. Turnips can be kept for a whole year if they are prepared in vinegar or brine. The best turnips are sweet-tasting and thin-skinned. They are beneficial to the stomach and to dry intestines and as a diuretic. They need to be cooked for a long time or, better still, twice; if not properly cooked, they are difficult to digest and cause flatulence and a swelling of the belly. If these problems are encountered, take an emetic or vinegar and salt.

Tiens toy nettement et regarde comment a toy chacun prent garde.	Take care you be at no time sloppy: all watch—for them a model be to copy.

1. *Poree de cresson*
(*Viandier*, §153)

Prenez vostre cresson et le faictes boullir et une pongnee de bettes et mettés avec, puis la miciez et friolés en huille; et puis la mettez boullir en lait si vous la voulez telle, ou, en charnage, en l'eaue de la chair, ou au frommage, ou toute crue sans riens y mettre, se vous la voulez ainsi. Et est bonne contre la gravelle.

1. Stewed Cress

The *Viandier* suggests that cress is a good remedy for gallstones! The *Regime tresutile* recommends that anyone eating gross meats such as beef, pork or stagmeat should eat only one meal a day and should often eat "things that are laxative and appetitive such as parsley, cress and wild celery."* Although the *Viandier*'s recipe calls specifically for garden cress, it works equally well with the watercress variety. Medieval cooks parboiled the greens (a treatment advisable in principle because products of the earth tended naturally to partake of the earth's cold and dry temperament), chopped them, sauteed them in butter or animal fat, then boiled them again in meat broth, adding cheese.

The *Menagier* adds a recipe to be used on meatless days. Oil was substituted for butter or meat fat; almond milk was used instead of meat broth, and the cheese was omitted.

Yield: Serves 6

Imperial	Ingredient	Metric	Directions
1 lb	cress	450 g	**Choose greens that are young & tender. Cull & rinse the greens thoroughly. Trim stem ends of cress & remove white ribs from chard. (Discard, *or* reserve for another dish.)**
1/2 lb	Swiss chard	250 g	
3 cups	boiling, salted water	750 mL	**Blanch rapidly in (*or* steam over) boiling water. Drain & chop fine.**
3 tbsp	butter *or* oil	50 mL	**In heavy skillet, sauté the greens in butter *or* oil. Add broth & cheese. Simmer about 5 minutes. Stir & serve.**
1/2 cup	beef *or* chicken broth	125 mL	
1/2 cup	grated cheese	125 mL	
	Salt—to taste.		

Variation

Substitute vegetable or nut oil for the butter, and replace cheese and broth with 1/2 cup of almond milk (see the recipe for almond milk, p. 60, above).

---

* Patricia Willett Cummins, *A Critical Edition of Le Regime tresutile et tresproufitable pour conserver et garder la santé du corps humain*, Chapel Hill (University of North Carolina), 1976, p. 56.

2. Navaiz

(Menagier de Paris, p. 144/§54)

Navaiz sont durs et mal cuisans jusques a ce qu'ilz aient esté au froit et a la gellee. L'en leur oste la teste, la queue et autres barbillons ou racines. Puis sont rez, puis lavez en deux ou en troiz paires d'eaue chaudes (bien chaudes); puis cuire en chaude eaue de char, soit porc, beuf ou mouton. Item, en Beausse, puis qu'ilz sont cuiz, l'en les tronçonne et les frit en la paelle, et gecte l'en pouldre pardessus.

2. Turnips

The *Menagier de Paris* offers two simple recipes for the humble turnip. He tells us that people from the Beauce region—a flat plain to the south and west of Paris, including the town of Chartres—liked their turnips fried. Young, small fresh turnips, picked after the first frost, are preferable.

Because turnips can absorb large amounts of fat, it is customary to serve them with fatty meats such as mutton, pork and duck.

Yield: Serves 4–6

Imperial	Ingredient	Metric	Directions
2–2 1/4 lb	turnips	1 kg	**Peel & quarter turnips.**
2–3 cups	pork *or* beef bouillon (to cover)	500–750 mL	**Cook in boiling bouillon until tender —about 30 min. Drain & serve.**

Garnish (optional)

Sprinkle top with 2 tsp/10 mL of Fine Spice Powder (see p. 54, above).

Serving variation

Mash, then press cooked turnips through a sieve or puree them in a blender. Sprinkle with spice powder and serve.

Cooking variation

Turnips *à la Beauce* (according to the *Menagier*): Cook turnips as above either in salted water or bouillon until tender but still firm. Slice into pieces 1/4 inch/5 mm thick. Melt 2–3 tbsp/30–50 mL of butter or fat in a skillet. Fry the slices of turnip briefly, sprinkling with 2–3 tbsp/30–50 mL of spice powder while frying.

3. *Ris engoullé*
(*Viandier*, §71)

Rix engoullé a jour de mengier chair. Eslisiez le rix et le lavez tres bien en eaue chaude et le mettez essuyer contre le feu, puis le mettez cuire en lait de vache fremiant; puis broyez du saffren pour le roussir, et qu'il soit deffait de vostre lait, et puis mettez dedans du gras boullon du pot.

Capiteles du ris / Rice
(Aldobrandino, *Le regime du corps*, p.113)

Rice is warm in the first degree and dry in the second, and its warmth is temperate. By nature it is heavy, and remains at length in the digestive system, and constipates; consequently, those who are subject to flatulence or who have a weak digestion should not consume it.

Yet for those who must eat rice, in order to counteract its harmfulness, to make it quite nourishing and to generate a great abundance of blood, it should be eaten in almond milk, with sugar, and with anything greasy.

3. Ruddy Rice Pudding

Because this dish was prepared with meat broth and milk, it could be served only on days when the consumption of meat was permitted. On meatless days, the rice would be cooked in almond milk or water.

The qualification *engoullé* refers to the red color of the dish. Those readers familiar with heraldic terminology will recognize the word *goules* or *gules* which defines a bright red color in the description of armorial bearings.

Yield: Serves 4

Imperial	Ingredient	Metric	Directions
1 cup	uncooked rice	250 mL	**Rinse rice. Dissolve saffron in hot**
1/4 tsp	saffron *or* turmeric	250 mL	**milk. Stir in rice.**
1 cup	hot milk	125 mL	
1 cup	hot beef bouillon	250 mL	**Add beef bouillon & grease. Cover &**
2 tbsp	beef grease or butter	30 mL	**cook on low heat until liquid is absorbed & rice is cooked. Add more bouillon during cooking if necessary.**

Cooking variation
Replace milk and beef bouillon with 2 cups/500 mL of almond milk (see p.60, above). Omit grease.

Serving variation
Ruddy Rice can be prepared also as a dessert. In that case garnish with pomegranate seeds, candied orange peel (*Orengat*, see p.284, below), *or* sliced browned almonds.

4. *Minces*
(*Menagier de Paris*, p. 143 f./§53)

... Et des troncs [des choulx Rommains], se ils sont replantés, yssent de petits choulx que l'en appelle minces, que l'en mengue avec les herbes crues en vinaigre; et qui en a foison, ils sont bons esleus, lavés en eaue chaude, et tous entiers mis cuire avec un petit d'eaue; et puis quant ils sont cuis, mettre du sel et du l'uile, et dreciés bien espois sans eaue, et mettre de l'uille d'olive dessus en Karesme.

4. Brussels Sprouts in a Vinaigrette

Brussels sprouts seem to have been quite a commonly eaten vegetable in the late Middle Ages. The *Menagier* advises his young wife how to go about growing them in their kitchen garden, giving her (or their gardener) quite detailed directions on how and when to cultivate and harvest them.

Yield: Serves 6

Imperial	Ingredient	Metric	Directions
1 lb	small tender Brussels sprouts	500 g	**Trim & rinse sprouts. Cook in boiling**
to cover	salted water	to cover	**salted water 10 min. Drain.**

Vinaigrette

3–4 tbsp	olive oil	50–60 mL	**Warm oil & add vinegar and salt.**
1 tbsp	wine vinegar	15 mL	
1/2 tsp	salt	2 mL	
1 tbsp	mixed chopped herbs*	15 mL	**Add herbs.**
			Toss with Brussels sprouts & serve.

Serving variation

Add 2 tbsp/30 mL of chopped walnuts.

---

* Choose from parsley, chives, tarragon, chervil and sorrel.

5. *Choulx pasquerés*

(Menagier de Paris, p. 143 f./§53)

Et premierement des pommes est assavoir que quant icelles pommes sont effeullees, eslites et mincees, il les couvient tresbien pourboulir et longuement, plus que les autres choux. Car les choulx romains se veullent le vert des feulles dessirer par pesches, et le jaune, c'est assavoir les arrestes ou veines, eschachees ou mortier; puis tout ensemble esverder en l'eaue chaude, puis espraindre et mectre en ung pot, et de l'eaue tiede qui n'a assez eaue de char. Et puis servir du plus gras et de l'eaue de la char; et plusieurs y broient du pain.

Et sachiez que choulz veullent estre mis au feu des bien matin, et cuire treslonguement, et plus longuement que nul autre potage, et a bon feu et fort; et doivent tremper en gresse de beuf, et non autre—soient pommes ou choulx, ou quelz qu'ilz soient, exeptez minces. Sachez aussi que eaue grasse de beuf et de mouton y est propre, maiz non mye de porc—celle de porc n'est pas bonne fors pour poreaulx.

Aprés ce, l'en fait choulx a jour de poisson, aprés ce qu'ilz sont parbouliz, cuire en eaue tiede et mecte de l'uille et du sel. Item, avec ce aucuns y mectent du grumiau. Item, en lieu d'uille aucuns y mectent beuree. A jour de char l'en y met pigons, saulcisses et lievre, fourques et foison lart.

Capiteles de colés / Cabbage

(Aldobrandino, *Le regime du corps*, p. 161)

Cabbage is of two sorts, wild and domestic. Domestic cabbage is of two sorts, young cabbage and red cabbage.

Wild cabbage is warm in the first degree and dry in the second, but domestic cabbage is cold and dry, and the red more so than the white. You should know that in any case by their nature they engender gross and melancholic blood and cause bad breath; but if they are eaten with fat meat and their first cooking water is discarded, this limits their harmfulness; and when thus prepared, their cooking water softens the belly and the cabbage itself toughens it.

Cabbage is better to combat disease than to maintain health, for in the former it promotes urination, drinking its juice mixed with wine is useful against the bite of a mad dog, and its seed, boiled and drunk on an empty stomach, prevents intoxication; a poultice made of it, especially when boiled in water, is useful for many bodily pains.

Headed cabbage has the same nature except that it is stronger and harder to digest in the stomach.

Caules onati / Cabbage
(*Tacuinum sanitatis*, Vienna,
Oesterreichische Nationalbibliothek, Codex Vindobonensis, 2644, f. 23r)

Some people think that cabbage is very useful against any sort of illness; among these is certainly Chrysippus, the skillful Roman physician who wrote an entire book on the cabbage. Ellbochasim records only that cabbages are bad for the blood and that their only virtue is that they open obstructions. In Dioscorides we read that if cabbage leaves are chewed and the juice swallowed, this will restore a lost voice; elsewhere we read that cabbage juice, cooked with honey and used very sparingly as eyedrops, clears the eyesight. The grape vine hates cabbage; Theophrastes, Varro and Pliny all say that if you plant a vine nearby, a cabbage will move away.

5. Easter Cabbage for a Meat Day

We may note in passing that in the *Menagier*'s day the most commonly used cabbage was harvested with long, open leaves. A "head" of cabbage such as we know it was rare, and Aldo-brandino (quoted above) does not think too highly of its natural properties.

There are several possible combinations in the *Menagier*'s section pertaining to cabbage dishes. The cabbage eaten around Easter time, since it was not freshly picked, was always parboiled then shredded and cooked either in water, salt and oil on a lean day, or in beef bouillon with butter or lard on a meat day. Bread crumbs were added to thicken the mixture; however, the *Menagier* notes that some people use oatmeal instead for this purpose. On meat days sausage meat, pigeons (doves), hares or the river bird called a coot could be included in the dish.

Using the designated ingredients, we have changed the cooking process a little, preferring to make this an oven casserole dish rather than to boil everything together in a pot.

Yield: Serves 6

Imperial	Ingredient	Metric	Directions
			Preheat oven to 350°F/180°C.
1	small- to medium-sized green cabbage	1	**Peel off & discard outer leaves of cabbage. Cut cabbage into quarters. In a large pot of boiling salted water, parboil cabbage for 10–15 min.; drain. Cut out creamy, firm sections; puree these by grinding *or* rubbing through a sieve; set aside. Cut rest of cabbage into strips.**
4 tbsp	melted butter *or* beef fat	60 mL	**Brush a medium-sized casserole dish with butter & sprinkle with 2 tbsp/30 mL bread crumbs.**
1/2 cup	toasted bread crumbs*	125 mL	
1/2 lb	cooked sausage, diced *or* thinly sliced	250 g	**Layer half the cabbage strips, half the sausage & half the puree. Dot with half the butter & half the bread crumbs. Repeat procedure.**
1/2–3/4 cup	beef bouillon *or* beef stock	125–200 mL	**Heat beef bouillon & pour gently over casserole. Cover.**
			Bake in 400°F/200°C oven for 40 min. Remove cover & bake further 15 min. Serve.

> Ne mouche hault ton nez a table,
> car c'est ung fait peu aggreable.

> Don't blow your nose out loud at table
> unless of 'lout' you want the label.

---

* *Or else* substitute 1 cup/250 mL quick cooking oatmeal for the bread crumbs.

6. *Escheroys*
(*Menagier de Paris*, p. 185/§161)

Lavez en deux ou trois paires d'eaues chaudes, puis les enfarinez et frisiez en huille. Item, aprés ce, aucuns les mectent en pasté avec grant foison de ongnons, et tronçons de harenc ou d'anguille, et pouldre.

Pastinace / Parsnips
(*Tacuinum sanitatis*, Vienna,
Oesterreichische Nationalbibliothek, Codex Vindobonensis, 2644, f. 28r)

Parsnips are a very white, tasty root vegetable; certain varieties [probably carrots] are red. They are grown in gardens for eating on lean days, as directed by the Church, when fish is not available. This is a curious custom, in that meatless days are supposed to be an opportunity to mortify the flesh, and yet the main property of parsnips, as the best authors tell us, is to excite in no small measure the fires of lust. The red, sweet ones are to be preferred and should be boiled for some time as they tend to slow down the digestion.

6. Parsnips

While this recipe for *Escheroys* appears in a section devoted to *pastez* or pastry coated dishes, the *Menagier* says that parsnips could also be prepared as a simple vegetable dish by dipping them in flour and frying them in oil. As a pasty, they could form the basis of a more substantial dish that would include as well onions, spice powder and fish, enclosed in pastry and fried.

We present the recipe here with two choices: the first omits the fish and pastry; the second is prepared as a pasty with fish and vegetables.

Yield: Serves 4

a. As a vegetable dish

Imperial	Ingredient	Metric	Directions
1 lb	parsnips	500 g	**Scrape parsnips. Cut lengthwise into 3 or 4 pieces. Parboil (*or* steam) until tender but still crisp (about 10 min.). Drain.**
1	large onion	1	**Slice onion thinly.**
4 tbsp	all-purpose flour	60 mL	**Combine flour & spice powder.**
1 tbsp	spice powder (see p. 54)	15 mL	
3–4 tbsp	olive oil	50–60 mL	**Heat oil in frying pan. Sauté onion for 5–10 min. stirring frequently. Do not brown. Set aside & keep warm. Dip parsnips in flour mixture & fry, a few at a time, transferring the cooked pieces to the centre of a large warmed serving plate. When all are fried, reheat onions if necessary & surround parsnips with a circle of onions.**

Garnish

1 tsp	spice powder	5 mL	**Sprinkle surface of plate with spice powder & serve.**

b. As a pasty

Prepare the above mixture and add 1 lb/500 g of cooked sliced herrring or eel. Fry or bake as for Rissoles (p. 91, above), using either our pasta or pastry recipe (see pp. 70 and 71, above) or a recipe of your own choice. Fry in oil and serve warm.

7. *Courges*
(*Menagier de Paris*, p. 148/§63)

Courges. Soit pelee l'escorche, car c'est le meilleur. Et toutesvoyes, qui vouldra mectre ce dedans, soint ostez les grains; ja soit ce que l'escorche seule vault mieulx. Puis couvient tranchier l'escorche pilee par morceaulx, puis pourboulir, puis hacher longuement, puis mectre cuire en gresse de beuf; a la parfin jaunir de saffren, ou jecter dessus du saffren par filectz, l'un ça, l'autre la, ce que les queulx dient frangié de saffran.

Cucurbite / Squash
(*Tacuinum sanitatis*, Vienna, f. 22v)

Squash is cold and moist in the second degree. The best sort is that which is fresh and green. Squash are useful in quenching thirst, but are dangerous in that by nature they are a swift laxative; this danger can by countered with salted water and mustard. They offer a moderate and cold nourishment, and are good for choleric temperament, for the young, in summer, in all regions but especially in those of the south.

7. Fried Squash

The variety of squash (*courge*) that is shown in illuminated manuscripts of the period is green and resembles the present-day butternut, spaghetti squash or large zucchini in shape. The *Menagier* says they are best peeled, but, he adds, "if you want to put in the peel, the seeds should be removed even though the fruit itself is better."

Powdered saffron may be incorporated into the dish, or saffron threads garnishing the squash may be substituted. Our choice is to peel and seed the larger squash such as the acorn squash and other firmer varieties. The entire young tender zucchini is used.

Yield: Serves 4

Imperial	Ingredient	Metric	Directions
1	large squash (*or* 4–5 small zucchini)	1	**Slice peeled, seeded squash *or* whole zucchini.**
	boiling salted water		**Parboil in water to cover (*or* steam) for 5 min. or until tender. Drain & chop finely.**
3 tbsp	beef grease *or* bacon fat	50 mL	**Fry in grease.**
1/8 tsp	powdered saffron	1 mL	**Stir in saffron & serve, *or* spoon into serving dish & garnish with saffron threads.**
	or		
5–6	threads of saffron	5–6	

Cooking variation

Rather than chop the squash, you may prefer to slice it and to fry the slices.

8. *Poreaulx*

(*Viandier*, §154)

D'autres menuz potaiges come poree de bettes, chouz, navetz, poreaulx, veel au jaunet, et potaiges de ciboulles sans autre chose, poys, feves frasees, pillez ou coullez ou atout le haubert, chaudun de porc, brouet aux yssues de porc—femmes en sont maistresses et chascun le sçait faire; et des trippes, que je n'ay pas mises en mon Viandier, sçait on bien comment elles se doibvent mengier.

Pori / Leeks

(*Tacuinum sanitatis*, Vienna,
Oesterreichische Nationalbibliothek, Codex Vindobonensis, 2644, f. 25r)

Choose pungent-smelling leeks from the mountains. They act as a diuretic and an aphrodisiac; cooked and mixed with honey and swallowed slowly, they help to cure chest problems and get rid of catarrh by cleansing the passages of the lungs. Cooked under the coals they can, according to some authorities, overcome the poisonous effects of fungi and act as a remedy against overeating and excessive drinking. They may be harmful to the brain and the senses, but this may be countered by taking sesame oil or sweet almond oil. Leeks heat the blood.

8. Leeks in a White Leek Sauce

The leek was probably one of the most commonly served vegetables on the tables of every social class during the Middle Ages. For this dish we have taken Taillevent, the author of the *Viandier*, at his word when he says that "everyone knows how to prepare leeks." We may find this assertion either reassuring or rather intimidating. In the same way, the only advice the *Menagier* gives us about leeks is that the young, tender plants do not need to be parboiled!

The basis for the dish that follows, then, is simply sautéed leeks. It is, however, delicious topped with Chiquart's recipe for *Porriaux blancs* / Almond-Leek Sauce.

Yield: Serves 4–6

Imperial	Ingredient	Metric	Directions
1 1/2 cups	prepared Almond-Leek Sauce	375 mL	**(See p. 132, above.)**
8	medium-sized leeks	8	**Wash, trim leeks, leaving only the white part. Cut each leek in half, vertically.**
3–4 tbsp	melted butter (*or* bacon fat)	50–60 mL	**In large frying pan sauté leeks in butter.**
1/4 cup	water *or* meat stock	60 mL	**Add water *or* meat stock, cover & simmer until tender.**
			In small pot heat Almond-Leek Sauce. Transfer leeks to serving bowl. Pour hot sauce over.

Garnish

1/4 cup	toasted almonds	60 mL	**Garnish with almonds & parsley.**
4 sprigs	parsley	4 sprigs	**Serve.**

Cooking variation

Transfer sautéed leeks to a greased casserole dish. Pour the Almond-Leek Sauce over them, cover and bake in an oven at 350°F/180°C for 20 min. Sprinkle toasted almonds on top and garnish with parsley sprigs. Serve.

9. *Champignons*
(*Menagier de Paris*, p. 185/§160)

Champignons d'une nuyt sont les meilleurs, et sont petiz, vermeilz dedens, cloz dessus; et les couvient peler, puis laver en eaue chaude et pourboulir. Qui en veult mectre en pasté, si y mecte de l'uille, du frommage et de la pouldre.

Item, mectez les entre deux plats sur charbons et mectez ung petit de sel, du frommage et de la pouldre. L'en les treuve en la fin de may et en juing.

9. Baked Mushrooms

The *Menagier*'s recipe for Mushroom Tarts forms an excellent appetizer and can be found above in that chapter at p. 96. One of the variations that the Parisian author himself suggests lends itself to being served as a vegetable dish, so we include it here.

Yield: Serves 6

Imperial	Ingredient	Metric	Directions
3/4–1 lb	fresh, tiny button mushrooms	375–500 g	**Gently brush-clean mushrooms & snip stems.**
1/2 lb	Brie cheese (*or* other soft cheese)	250 g	**Peel rind of Brie cheese & set rind aside. Cut cheese into small pieces.**
3 tbsp	olive oil	50 mL	**In a processor, blender or by hand, combine cheese, oil & spices.**
2 tsp	spice powder (see p. 54)	10 mL	**Gently fold in mushrooms.**
1/2 tsp	salt	2.5 mL	**Brush oven-proof casserole dish with oil. Place mushroom/cheese mixture in dish. Cover & bake in 375°F/190°C oven for about 15–20 min.**
2–3 tbsp	ground parmesan cheese	30–50 mL	**Sprinkle with parmesan cheese. Bake in 400°F/200°C oven for 10 min.** **Serve warm.**

10. *La maniere de faire composte*
(*Menagier de Paris*, p. 243/§312)

Prendrez environ la Toussains des gros navetz et les pelez, et fendez en .iiii. quartiers, et puis mectez cuire en eaue. Et quant ilz seront ung petit cuiz, si les ostez et mectez en eaue froide pour attendrir. Et puis les mectez esgouter et prenez du miel et fondez ainsi comme celluy des nois; et gardez que vous ne cuisiez trop vos navetz.

Item, a la Toussains vous prendrez des garroictes tant que vous y vouldrez mectre, et qu'elles soient bien raclees et decouppees par morceaulx, et qu'elles soient cuictes comme les navetz. (Carroictes sont racines rouges que l'en vent es halles par pongnees, et chascune pongnee ung blanc.)

Item, prenez des poires d'angoisse et les fendez en .iiii. quartiers et les cuisiez aussi comme les navetz, et ne les pelez point, et les faictes ne plus ne moins comme les navetz.

Item, quant les courges sont en saison, si en prenez ne des plus dures ne des plus tendres, et les pelez, et ostez ce dedens, et mectez en quartiers; et faictes tout ainsi comme des navetz.

Item, quant les pesches sont en saison, si en prenez des plus dures, et les pelez et fendez.

Item, quant les courges sont en saison si en prenez et fendez par .iiii. quartiers, et ostez le cuer de dedens, et les gouvernez tout ainsi comme les navetz.

Item, environ la saint Andry prenez des racines de percil et de fanoul, et les rasez pardessus, et en mectez par petites pieces; et fendez le fanoul parmy et ostez le dureillon de dedens et n'ostez pas celluy du percil. Et les gouvernez tout ainsi comme les choses dessusdictes, ne plus ne moins.

Capiteles du miel / Honey
(Aldobrandino, *Le regime du corps*, p. 159)

Honey is warm and dry in the second degree, and by its nature it rids and purges the body of its bad humors; it is therefore better for those who are of a cold and moist nature, such as old people and phlegmatics, for it is not suitable for those who are of a warm temperament because it heats too much and gives them no nourishment.

Honey varies according to the season, because the bees that make the honey feed variously. So you should understand that there are three sorts of honey, that of the spring, of September and of the winter: the best sort is spring honey, September honey is worse, and winter honey still worse again.

Not only the seasons account for varieties of honey but also the flowers on which the bees feed, for instance on almond blossoms, and on apple, cherry and peach blossoms: these give honey the most temperate and best flavor of all. For you should know that honey that is made when bees are nourished on flowers of oregano, calamint, thyme, hyssop and other such herbs is unlike the honey we mentioned before because this latter honey is warmer and drier and is not temperate. In short, honey takes on the nature of that from which it is made.

10. Honey-Glazed Vegetables

In the section of his food recipes that the *Menagier de Paris* entitles "Other Incidental, Minor Things" (*Autres menues choses qui ne sont de nécessité*), the bourgeois author provides directions for preserving nuts in honey and spices, and lists other edibles that can be preserved in the same way. Among these is a series of vegetables: turnips, carrots, squash, parsley root and fennel root. The recipes he gives here call for cooking these vegetables in water and honey; they contain a warning to avoid overcooking. The author describes these honeyed vegetables as *confiture*, and states that you *may* make a sauce of them (rather like a compote) for which he offers a very long, procedurally complicated and time-consuming recipe. This combines as ingredients twelve different spices (!), nuts, raisins, honey, horseradish root, red cedar, wine, and vinegar or grape juice. Preparing this sauce would be a chore indeed for a fifteen-year-old novice housewife.

While it is unclear whether these vegetables were used *as* vegetable accompanying a meal or as a sweet with the sauce, the *Menagier*'s recipe does afford us an alternative way of preparing the vegetables.

Imperial	Ingredient	Metric	Directions
1 lb	choice of vegetables:	500 g	
	turnips		**Peel turnips, cut into smaller pieces.**
	carrots		**Preferably new baby carrots, scrubbed; *or* larger carrots, pared & sliced.**
	squash		**Slice squash in half, remove seeds & peel; cut into slices.**
	fennel root		**Peel outer skin of fennel root, slice; remove hard centre core.**
	parsley root		**Peel parsley root & cut into slices.**

Cook all vegetables in a medium pot in as little water as possible: bring to a boil & cook until *almost* tender.

4 tbsp	honey	60 mL	**Stir in honey & reduce heat. Simmer until liquid has almost evaporated. Shake pan to ensure the honey has coated all the vegetables.**
Garnish			
	sprigs of parsley *or* fennel *or* saffron threads		**Garnish & serve.**

Other Possible Vegetable Dishes

Puree de poys / Pea Puree

For the complete recipe of this Standard Preparation, see p. 63, above.

Though this purée is used primarily as a thickener in stews and brewets, it may also be served as a vegetable accompaniment to other dishes.

Syseros / Chickpea Puree

For the complete recipe of this dish as an Appetizer, see p. 77, above.

Syseros / Chickpea Puree may also be served as a puréed vegetable along with an *entrée* dish.

[*Pastez de champignons*] / Mushroom Tarts

For the complete recipe of this dish as an Appetizer, see p. 96, above.

These tarts can be made as a vegetable dish to be served with an *entrée*.

Porriaux blancs / Almond-Leek Sauce

For the complete recipe of this dish as a Sauce, see p. 132, above.

Although the Almond-Leek Sauce is very tasty with a wide variety of meat, poulty and fish dishes, you can make a particularly delicious dish by combining it with any of the versions of *Poullaille farcie* / Stuffed Poultry on p. 193 f., above.

Chapter 10
Desserts

Chapter 10
Desserts

The category of the recipes that have been placed in this chapter, "desserts," is a relatively modern invention. As far as the word itself is concerned, it does derive directly from medieval usage in which the successive courses of a meal are *served*, and at the end of a meal the scraps of these *servings* are "cleared away": a French verb is a literal rendition of this idea, *desservir*. Of course, the end of a meal was marked most forcefully, too, when the board and trestles of the table were themselves "cleared away." The *dessert*, or "un-serving," "clearing-away," just signaled the conclusion of eating.

In its most popularly accepted sense today a "dessert" refers to a serving whose most significant element is its sugar, whether this is a cane sugar or a fruit sugar. In Britain it is now called simply the sweet course. Despite the name of our chapter, and despite the artificial grouping of dishes that it contains, we have to point out clearly that the Middle Ages had developed no such understanding of a dessert.

The *Menagier de Paris* sets out a series of 23 suggested menus, for both dinners and suppers and for both meat- and fish-days. He carefully defines in each menu the sequence of the various servings, from the beginning of the meal to its conclusion, and lists the various dishes which could make up each serving. Clearly what the *Menagier* was trying to do was to provide his young wife with practical guidelines on menu-planning for their household, guidelines which, given the girl's inexperience as mistress of an affluent bourgeois domestic establishment, were probably of good use to her.

What these menus show us in the twentieth century is that our modern notions (even though they are by no means fixed universally) of the proper dishes for the various parts of a meal—appetizer, soup, fish, salad, meat, cheese, dessert—cannot be linked wholly to any system current in medieval France. Some dishes, such as pasties of various sorts, appear in the *Menagier*'s menus variously at the beginning of a meal, in the middle of a meal, or at the end of a meal. The dishes that turn up most frequently in the latter courses of the menus are, surprisingly perhaps, a dish of wheat porridge called Furmenty or Frumenty and served with either venison or porpoise (meat or fish, that is, depending upon whether the day is meat or lean) and deep-fried pasties including rissoles and crepes, among more than half a dozen possibilities in this genre.

The closest the *Menagier* comes to identifying a "dessert" in our modern sense is not in the regular courses of his meals but in a conclusion of certain meals (and by no means all of them) where he suggests what he calls an *Yssue*. A rough translation for this term might be "end" or "close." According to the *Menagier* one way appropriately to close a meal is to serve bowls of fruit (he mentions specifically baked apples or pears, roasted figs, grapes, medlars, walnuts or simply some sort of "fruit"), plates of spiced candies called *dragees*, and goblets of a standard spiced wine called hypocras. In the cases where the meal did not end with this trio of fruit, candies and mulled wine, the preferred conclusion seems to have been the Furmenty or the pasties.

Our selection here of desserts is perhaps too influenced by modern tastes. The modern cook will, however, find the staples of the medieval *yssue* in the fruit (cooked) and the pasties—in a couple of instances our recipes are for pasties of fruit—and will generally recognize the late-medieval love of sweetened spices. We don't offer a recipe here for hypocras, though, mainly because on the medieval table and in the medieval house it is more than just a dessert beverage; its recipe has been incorporated into the more important section of regular, stock preparations we have outlined in Chapter 1, Standard Preparations (see p. 57, above).

1. *Rissolles a jour de poisson*

(*Menagier de Paris*, p. 225/§260)

Item, au commun l'en les fait de figues, roisins, pommes hastees, et noix pelees pour contrefaire le pignolat, et pouldre d'espices. Et soit la paste trés bien ensaffrenee, puis soient frites en huille. S'il y convient lieure, amidon lie et ris aussi.

1. Fruit Rissoles

A variety of rissole—a preparation of which the *Menagier* seems exceptionally fond—makes use of what is basically a fruit filling. Should you feel that a binding agent would be useful to give this filling a good consistency, you may add a little cooked rice or rice flour; we have not really found it necessary.

The starch referred to in the manuscript is a common enough ingredient. Recipes elsewhere advise a cook how to prepare his own supply of starch:

> To make starch for a year, to last as long as you wish, get clean wheat at about St. John's day and let it sit nine days in a vessel with a good amount of clear water, each day stirring thoroughly and changing the water; then grind up the wheat fully, put it back overnight with clear water, and then strain out the water; set it out on a cloth in the sun until dry, then put it into a clean vessel. Keep it as long as you wish, well covered; cut it up into pieces, or whatever. (*Viande e claree*, §21.)

Yield: 30–40 small rissoles

Imperial	Ingredient	Metric	Directions
3–4	medium-sized cooking apples	3–4	**Peel & slice apples. Chop figs small. Simmer fruit in water & wine mixture several minutes until fruit is soft but not mushy. Do not overcook.**
8	figs	8	
1 cup	raisins	250 mL	
1 cup	water	250 mL	
1/2 cup	white wine	125 mL	

1/2 cup	sugar	125 mL
1 tsp	ground ginger	5 mL
3/4 tsp	ground cinnamon	4 mL
1/4 tsp	ground cloves	1 mL
1/4 tsp	grains of paradise *(optional)*	1 mL
1/3 cup	pinenuts *or* chopped walnuts	80 mL

Combine sugar & spices. Add to fruit; if mixture appears dry, stir in white wine by the teaspoonful/5 mL to correct. Taste; adjust spices to taste.

Stir in nuts.

Proceed as for Rissoles (pp. 91 and, for the dough, 70).

Cooking Variation

Use the fruit rissole mixture as a filling for a double-crust pie.

Serving Variation

This filling is a tasty accompaniment to roast meats—especially roast pork.

2. [*Fritelles d'orvale*]
(*Viandier*, §177)

Prener harbe qui se appelle orvale et la broyer et deffaicte de aigue clere, et y mecter et bater avec farine bien buretelee; et y mecter du miel avec et ung pol de vin blanc et le batez ensamble tant qu'il soit cleret; puis frissiez en huille per petites cuillerez conme l'on fait buignés; et mecter bien de romany sur chacun fritel; et espreignés vous fritelles entre deux tranchens pour esgoutez l'uille, puis les mecter en ung bel pout neuf pres du feu; et mecter du succre a dressiez sur vous plat.

2. Clary Fritters

As with the wafers outlined in Chapter 1 (above, p. 68), making the *Viandier*'s Clary Fritters requires a lot of labor. They can, however, be made in advance of the time they will be needed and then stored in an airtight container.

Clary is a variety of sage, *Salvia sclarea*. Should this herb prove difficult to obtain in your local grocery store, you might wish to try growing it yourself: seeds and seedlings are available from specialty herb markets. The leaves of clary sage are much larger than those of common sage. We have substituted ordinary sage here.

Yield: 16 small (2"/5 cm) diameter fritters

Imperial	Ingredient	Metric	Directions
6 or 7	medium-sized sage leaves*	6 or 7	**In a blender combine sage, water, wine**
4 tbsp	hot water	60 mL	**& honey. Blend until sage is puréed.**
4 tbsp	white wine	60 mL	
1 tbsp	honey	15 mL	
6–7 tbsp	flour	90–105 mL	**Add flour a little at a time until mixture has pancake-batter consistency.**
1/4 cup	cooking oil	60 mL	**In frying pan heat cooking oil. Drop a teaspoonful of mixture at a time, keeping fritters separated. Turn over once. Fry until golden brown. Place on paper towelling.**
1 tsp	finely chopped fresh rosemary	5 mL	**Sprinkle with rosemary. Cover with paper towelling & press to squeeze out oil.**
2 tbsp	sugar	30 mL	**Sprinkle with sugar.**

Store in an airtight container until needed.

---

* This amounts to about 3 tbsp/60 mL of chopped sage leaves.

3. *Flons de lait d'amendres*

(*Du fait de cuisine*, §28)

Selon la quantité des flons que ferés, si prennés la quantité des amendres, si les faictes bien plumer nectement et laver, et puis les faciés tresbien broyer; et prennés de belle eaue bien necte et colle son lait d'amendres en celluy [seille] ou en cornue que soit belle et necte, selon la quantité des flons qu'il doibt faire. Et puis prennés de bel amidon et le lavés de belle eaue fresche et le mectés en une belle seille quant il sera lavés; et puis prennés vostre lait d'amendres et puis le mectés dedans son amidon trempé, et si mectés un petit de saffran pour lui donner couleur; et puis coulés cela a une belle estamine dedans une belle et necte seille, et mectés ung petit de sel dedans et de succre grant foyson. Et quant cecy est fait si appellés vostre patissier que on face les crostes, et qu'il les mecte dedans le four ung petit enroydir; et que puis ledit patissier hait une belle cuillier ou de boys ou de fer estachiee a bon bastonnet bauc pour emplir dedans le four les cortelletes dudit flons.

Amigdale dulces / Sweet Almonds

(*Tacuinum sanitatis*, Vienna,
Oesterreichische Nationalbibliothek, Codex Vindobonensis, 2644, f. 18v)

In the month of August, when the outer shell begins to break open, almonds are knocked down from their trees. The large sweet ones are the best and they have singular qualities: they overcome anxiety, remove freckles and, eaten before drinking, they prevent drunkenness. They stimulate the body's digestive humors, but are harmful to the intestine. An excellent remedy for this danger is sugar mixed with poppy seed. Various authorities advise that almonds should be ground in a mortar along with the water in which vervain has been boiled, and then applied to the temples with a bandage: this will relieve headaches and induce sleep.

Quant ta bouche tu laveras,	When rinsing mouth, to table quit,
ou bacin point ne cracheras.	into the basin never spit.

3. Almond Milk Flans

The use of almond milk in these flans makes them a lean-day counterpart for standard medieval milk or cream flans which would incorporate animal milk, eggs and butter, as well as spices and saffron, on non-fasting days. The *Menagier* lists *Flaons de cresme* / Cream Flans as part of the *issue* or dessert of a meal, although neither he nor the various copiers of the *Viandier* have thought it worthwhile to provide a recipe for this preparation.

The variety of flan that Chiquart has left us is a delectable use of almonds. Despite the absence of ingredients that we might nowadays think necessary for a custard, baking a combination of almond milk and rice flour produces highly palatable results that are not greatly different in texture from the modern flan, but perhaps more interesting in flavor.

Imperial	Ingredient	Metric	Directions
Prepare sufficient pâte brisée *or* other pie dough for a single-crust 9 in/ 23 cm pie *or* 10–12 tartlet shells. Pre-bake blind, *or* prick with fork, and bake for 10 min. at 375°F/190°C.			
1 cup 1 1/4 cups	ground almonds water	250 mL 300 mL	**Combine almonds & water well (blender may be used). Strain through several layers of damp muslin *or* cheesecloth to obtain almond milk. In a sauce pot bring almond milk just to boiling point.**
1 1/2 cups pinch pinch	sugar salt saffron	375 mL pinch pinch	**Add sugar & dissolve. Add salt & saffron.**
1/4 cup	rice flour	60 mL	**Add 1/2 of this hot mixture to rice flour, while stirring. Combine with remaining hot almond milk.** **Pour custard mixture into prepared pastry. Bake 20–25 min. at 375°F/ 190°C until light crust appears on surface.**
Garnish			
2 tbsp	blanched sliced almonds *or* fresh fruit *or* pomegranate seeds *or* candied orange peel (*Orengat*, p. 284)*	30 mL	**Sprinkle with sliced almonds & return to oven until almonds are toasted.**

To Serve

Serve warm, garnished with fruit, *or* with fruit and almonds.

To add extra richness to this flan, add 1/4 cup/60 mL ground almonds to the pastry.

---

* Our preference is for *Orengat* and toasted almonds.

4. *Flaons de cresme de lait* / Cream Flans

(Menagier de Paris, p. 99/p. 179; *Du fait de cuisine*, f. 26v)

Both the *Menagier* and the *Du fait de cuisine* mention Cream Flans, but unfortunately neither the bourgeois gastronome nor the Duke's chef provides us with a recipe. The *Menagier* refers to them as part of the *issue* or dessert of a meat dinner; for Chiquart they are merely part of the second serving of a meat dinner, and their counterpart in a lean dinner would be the Almond Milk Flans of our previous recipe. Presumably these Cream Flans were a standard flan well known to all cooks over a number of generations.

We have given a standard custard recipe below. Should you wish to lend this flan a more medieval flavor, add pieces of cooked eel and a little ginger to the pie before baking. This variant produces the dish known as *Flaons cochus* / Rich Flans, for which a recipe turns up in the fifteenth-century *Viandier* (§194). A sugar garnish was used on this latter flan.

Yield: Serves 6

Imperial	Ingredient	Metric	**Directions**
Prepare a 10"/25 cm unbaked pie shell. Prick the pastry with a fork. Partially pre-bake in 450°F/220°C oven for 10 min. Let shell cool. Reduce oven heat to 350°F/180°C.			
6	egg yolks (*or* 3 whole eggs)	6	**In bowl, lightly beat eggs.**
1 cup	sugar	250 mL	**Add rest of ingredients, mixing well.**
1/4 tsp	salt	1 mL	**Pour into prepared shell. Bake for 15**
2 cups	light (15%) cream	500 mL	**min. *or* until knife inserted comes out clean. Serve.**

Serving suggestion

You might wish to garnish your flan with *Orengat* / Candied Orange Peel (see the next recipe).

5. *Orengat*

(Menagier de Paris, p. 265/§352)

Pour faire Orengat, mettez en cinq quartiers les peleures d'une orenge et raclez a un coustel la mousse qui est dedans, puis les mettez tremper en bonne eaue doulce par neuf jours, et changez l'eaue chascun jour; puis les boulez en eaue doulce une seule onde. Et, ce fait, les faictes estendre sur une nappe et les laissiez essuier tres bien; puis les mettez en un pot, et du miel tant qu'ils soient tous couvers, et faites boulir a petit feu et escumer. Et quant vous croirez que le miel soit cuit—pour essaier s'il est cuit, ayez de l'eaue en une escuelle, et faites degouter en icelle eaue une goutte d'icelluy miel, et s'il s'espant, il n'est pas cuit; et se icelle goute de miel se tient en l'eau sans espandre, il est cuit—et lors devez traire vos peleures d'orenge. Et d'icelles faites par ordre un lit, et gettez pouldre de gingembre dessus, puis un autre, et getter etc., usque in infinitum; et laissier un mois ou plus, puis mengier.

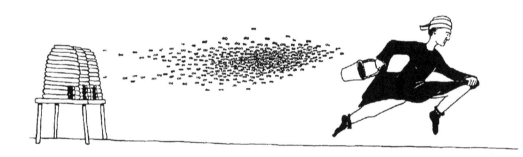

Of Orenges / Oranges

(Andrew Boorde, *A Dyetary of Helth*, p. 286)

Orenges doth make a man to have a good appetyde, and so doth the ryndes, yf they be in succade [candied], & they doth comforte the stomacke; the Juce is a good sauce, and dothe provoke an appetyde.

A ton hoste dois mercy rendre,	Those guests are blamable the most
de t'en aler dois congié prendre.	who, when leaving, thank not their host.

5. Candied Orange Peel

The *Menagier de Paris* makes the preparation of *Orengat* / Candied Orange Peel a nine-day operation, soaking the strips of orange peel, changing the water, then, after boiling the peel, draining the strips before setting them once again to boil in the honey sauce. The following recipe reduces the time substantially! The *Menagier* also suggests storing the candied peel for one month before eating; the members of the bourgeois's household must have had more patience than ours!

Imperial	Ingredient	Metric	Directions
2 cups	sliced orange peel	500 mL	**Cut orange peel into quarters. Scrape**
1 1/2–2 cups	cold water	375–500 mL	**pulp from inside with a spoon or knife & slice peel into thin strips. Cover with cold water in a pot. Bring slowly to a boil. Simmer 10 min. Repeat 2 or 3 times. Drain & dry.**
1/2 cup	water	125 mL	**Make a syrup of honey & water. Add**
3/4 cup	honey	175 mL	**peel. Boil until syrup is absorbed & the peel becomes transparent.**
2–3 tsp	powdered ginger	10–15 mL	**Lay individual strips of peel on waxed**
2 tsp	sugar	10 mL	**paper. Sprinkle on both sides with powdered ginger & sugar mixture. Expose to air until cold & surface moisture has evaporated.**
			Store in airtight container until needed.

Cooking variation

Instead of dressing the mixture with ginger, include small thin strips of gingerroot in with the orange peel and cook them together. Sprinkle with sugar.

Serving suggestions

As an after-dinner confection along with Honey-Nut Conserve (see the recipe for this, p. 290). *Orengat* can also be used as a garnish on chicken dishes (as in the Chicken in Orange Sauce, p. 200, above), or on Cream or Almond Milk Flans (see pp. 282 or 281).

6. *Emplumeus de pomes*
(*Du fait de cuisine*, §73)

Emplumeus de pomes: pour donner entendement a celluy qui le fera, sy prennés de bonnes pomes barberines selon la quantité que l'on en vouldra faire, et puis les parés bien et appoint et les taillés en beaulx platz d'or ou d'argent. Et qu'il hait ung beau pot de terre bon et nect, et y mecte de belle eaue necte et mecte boullir sur brase belle et clere, et mecte boullir ses pomes dedans. Et face qu'il ait de bonnes amendres doulces grant quantité selon la quantité des pomes qu'il ha mis cuire; et les plume, nectoie et lave tresbien et mectes broyer au mortier qui ne sante point les aulx; et si les broie tresbien et les arouse du boullon en quoy cuisent lesdictes pomes. Et quant lesdictes pomes seront assés cuictes, si les tirés dehors sur belle et necte postz; et de celle eaue colle ses amendres et en face lait qui soit bon et espés, et le remecte boullir sur brase clere et necte sans fumee; et bien petit de sel. Et entretant que il bouldra, si hache bien menut ses dictes pomes a ung petit et nect coutel; et puis, estre hachiés, si les mecte dedans son lait, et y mecte du succre grant foison selon ce que il y a desditz emplumeus de pomes. Et puis, quant le medicin le demandera, si le mectés en belles escuelles ou casses d'or ou d'argent.

Capiteles des pumes / Apples
(Aldobrandino, *Le regime du corps*, p. 147)

By their nature apples are cold and moist—we mean those that are ripe and have little flavor. The nature of all apples, and the way in which they work on the human body, varies according to the season of the year.

It they are eaten when green and with a sharp flavor, they comfort the stomach and are useful for those who have a cold digestion because of the nature of their juice; the nature of the pulp engenders flegmatic, rotting humors from which fevers, worms and cramps in the side may arise. Ripe apples cool the digestive system and engender cold, bad blood; over long use they cause pain in the nerves, especially if eaten in winter.

But apples are beneficial for those who have drunk an overly large amount of pure cold wine because they absorb the vapors of the wine which might fill the brain and intoxicate a person.

Zucharum / Sugar
(*Tacuinum sanitatis*, Vienna,
Oesterreichische Nationalbibliothek, Codex Vindobonensis, 2644, f. 92r)

Ask the grocer for refined sugar which is hard, as white as salt and brittle. It has a cleansing action on the body and is beneficial to the chest, kidneys and bladder. It arouses thirst and stimulates the bilious humors; these effects can be countered with unripe pomegranates. Sugar is good for the blood and therefore suitable for every temperament, age, season and place. Artificially white, it is very effective for tightness in the chest and when the tongue is unusually dry.

6. Almond Applesauce

In fourteenth- and fifteenth-century French recipe collections, a good number of the dishes that do *not* involve meat or fish are to be found placed in a chapter of preparations for the sick (or sickly). Sickdishes containing chicken or veal are occasional exceptions, these two being foodstuffs whose properties are considered to be close to those of the human nature. The rationale for this discrimination probably has to do with a reluctance on the part of physicians to expose a particular patient to the risk of having to digest a meat whose properties might run contrary to the actual needs of the patient. Cookbooks were, after all, designed to be useful in a general way to the average healthy assortment of appetites as well as to the average sickly assortment of people. The chapters containing foods for the sick or sickly normally contain suggestions for dishes whose nourishing ingredients are considered temperate in their natural qualities and that should of themselves pose no danger if they are offered for the sustenance of an invalid.

One might be tempted to overlook the contents of the various chapters entitled *Pour Malades*, on the assumption that such preparations are likely to be either medicinal in intention and effect, or about as appetizing as a watery gruel, were it not for the very good reason that most French sickdishes of this period are neither. Chiquart's chapter of sickdishes, on which he bestows the rather pretentious Latin title of *Pro Infirmis*, consists of a relatively large (fourteen recipes) and broadly varied selection of dishes. None of them is merely banale; each clearly benefits from the inspired touch of a master cook in its ingredients, even though these ingredients had necessarily to pass the critical assessment of the court physician.

Because the *Emplumeus de pomes* / Almond Applesauce is intended for serving to a person in ill-health, a variety of precautions must be observed which would not otherwise preoccupy the cook. Dishware, for both cooking and serving, should be made of precious metals (gold or silver are specifically mentioned) not only because these can be trusted not to contribute inadvertently to the patient's illness but because they were believed in themselves to possess curative properties. (One of the interesting sickdishes of the *Du fait de cuisine* has capons cooked in contact with an impressive array of precious metals and jewels. The curative virtue of these metals and jewels was believed likely to pass into the foodstuff.) Chiquart attempts to avoid contaminating this preparation with the slightest trace of any garlic that might linger in an imperfectly scoured mortar: garlic was universally recognized as being both dangerously warm and dangerously dry in its natural qualities—its warm and dry complexions being ranked at the relatively high and exceptionally dangerous grade of 4 by early physicians.* Even the slightest pollution of a sick person's food with garlic might prove fatal to him.

And finally, Chiquart's direction about the use of sugar here is worth observing. Like chicken and veal, sugar is of a nature which closely resembles that of human beings, that is, moderately warm and moderately moist. Because of these qualities, sugar had long enjoyed a prominent position among medieval pharmaceuticals. In fact, until the fourteenth century sugar was considered to be more a drug than a foodstuff. With the increase in trade with the Arab near-East in the fourteenth century, loaves or cones of cane sugar became a relatively common commodity along with such "exotic" spices as cloves and ginger which were themselves originally therapeutic in use. The after-dinner cordial known in Old French as a *dragee* was merely a clever medicinal combination of sugar-and-spice.

---

* Among vegetables only aubergine (eggplant) and onions are regularly recognized as being so extremely warm. Prudent doctrine required that as foodstuffs they should be avoided by a person of normal or warm temperament; at the very least they should be prepared with vinegar, a "cool" liquid.

Though sugar was handled by household cooks at first only on a physician's prescription, by the beginning of the fifteenth century it made its way into a rapidly increasing number of ordinary culinary preparations. The wealthy in France were gradually acquiring a sweet tooth.

And if, like the Savoyard, you possess gold or silver dishes, serve them forth!

Yield: Serves 6

Imperial	Ingredient	Metric	Directions
6–8	cooking apples	6–8	**Wash & pare apples, slice & cook in**
2–3 cups	water	500–750 mL	**salted water until almost tender.**
1/4 tsp	salt	1 mL	
1/2 cup	ground almonds	125 mL	**Remove apples from liquid. To this liquid add ground almonds & cook for several minutes to extract almond milk. Strain & discard almond residue, *or* blend almond milk in an electric blender.**
			Return to pot, add apples & cook until tender.
1 cup	sugar	250 mL	**Stir in sugar. Cook gently for an additional 3 min. Taste; add more sugar if desired. Serve.**

Serving suggestions

Serve warm or cold as a dessert or an accompaniment to meat dishes. This Almond Applesauce is very tasty when used as a dip for the Little Meatballs (above, p. 153) or other meats.

Se on te fait boire après graces,
soit en hanap, ou verre, ou tasses,   If, after Grace, your final thirst
laisse premier boire ton hoste   is slaked, your host should drink the first.
et boy après quant on lui oste.

7. *Confiture de noiz*

(*Menagier de Paris*, p. 270/§315)

Prenez avant la saint Jehan noiz nouvelles et les pelez et perciez et mectez en eaue fresche tremper par .ix. jours, et chascun jour renouvellez l'eaue, puis les laissier secher et emplez les pertuiz de cloz de giroffle et de gingembre et mectez boulir en miel et illec les laissiez en conserve.

7. Honey-Nut Conserve

The directions given by the *Menagier* to peel, pierce, then soak the nuts in fresh water for nine days, changing the water each day, suggest that the nuts that the Parisian author had in mind were green walnuts. If you can obtain green nuts, you may wish to follow this procedure. The nuts were pierced in order to insert whole cloves and fresh ginger slivers into them before boiling them in the honey. When this procedure is followed, the flavor of the cloves tends to predominate, but it is worth trying. The following version of the recipe simplifies it and allows for the use of walnut halves or large pieces of walnut.

Yield: About 2 cups/500 mL

Imperial	Ingredient	Metric	Directions
1 cup	liquid honey	250 mL	**On low heat in small cooking pot, combine honey & spices. Let spices marinate in warm honey for 5–10 min.**
10–15	whole cloves*	10–15	
2 tbsp	finely sliced slivers of fresh ginger*	30 mL	
8 oz	whole *or* halved walnuts *or* large walnut pieces	250 mL	**Add walnuts & bring to a boil. Cook, stirring occasionally until honey reaches soft ball stage (approx. 10 min.).**
			Spoon out walnuts (& include some cloves & ginger), & set them to cool & harden on a piece of tinfoil *or* marble slab.
			Store in tightly sealed container.

---

* Powdered cloves (1 tsp/5 mL) and powdered ginger (1 tbsp/15 mL) may be substituted if necessary, but they are a poor substitute.

8. *Poires d'angoisse*
(*Menagier de Paris*, pp. 244–45/§312)

Prenez des poires d'angoisse et les fendez en .iiii. quartiers et les cuisiez aussi comme les navetz, et ne les pelez point, et les faictes ne plus ne moins comme les navetz. . . .

[Prendrez environ la Toussains des gros navetz et les pelez, et fendez en .iiii. quartiers, et puis mectez cuire en eaue. Et quant ilz seront ung petit cuiz, si les ostez et mectez en eaue froide pour attendrir. Et puis les mectez esgouter et prenez du miel et fondez ainsi comme celluy des nois; et gardez que vous ne cuisiez trop vos navetz.]

8. Pears in Syrup

This paragraph on preparing pears in a honey syrup appears among a number of similar directions for fruits and vegetables in a "recipe" whose general theme is the preserving, or rather conserving, of these fruits and vegetables. The *Menagier* assimilates pears and turnips; except that turnips should be "peeled" and pears should not, he indicates an identical treatment for each.

The variety of pear known in the *Menagier*'s day as *poires d'angoisse* were probably rather hard when ripe, a good cooking pear.

A few pages after writing this recipe, the author copies another one for pears cooked in a waterless pot—likely a clay baking pot similar to those available today. These pears he garnishes with fennel seeds cooked in red wine. We have combined the two recipes.

Yield: Serves 6

Imperial	Ingredient	Metric	Directions
2 tsp	fennel seeds	10 mL	**In a small sauce pot soak fennel seeds in red wine. Bring to a boil, then reduce heat. Cook, stirring occasionally until wine is absorbed or evaporated. Set seeds aside on a tray to dry.**
2 tbsp	sweet red wine	30 mL	
6–8	cooking pears	6–8	**Cut pears into quarters & core. Bring water to a boil; add pears. Cover, reduce heat & simmer until pears are tender but not soft (about 10–15 min.).**
3 cups	water (*or* a combination of red wine & water)	750 mL	
1 cup	honey	250 mL	**Add honey & cook 10 min. more. Strain pears & place in serving dishes.**
			Return sauce to heat & reduce to desired consistency. Pour over pears. Garnish with fennel seeds & serve.

9. *Condoignac*

(*Menagier de Paris*, pp. 247/§313)

Prenez les coings et les pelez. Puis fendez par quartiers et ostez l'ueil et les pepins. Puis les cuisiez en bon vin rouge et puis soient coulez parmy une estamine. Puis prenez du miel et le faictes longuement boulir et escumer, et aprés mectez vos coings dedens et remuez tresbien, et le faictes tant boulir que le miel se reviengne a moins la moictié. Puis gectez dedens pouldre d'ypocras et remuez tant qu'il soit tout froit. Puis tailliez par morceaulx et les garde.

Citonia / Quince

(*Tacuinum sanitatis*, Vienna,
Oesterreichische Nationalbibliothek, Codex Vindobonensis, 2644, f. 8r)

The best quince are large and full; they cheer the heart and stimulate the appetite. They can also cause colic; this effect can be remedied with dates sweetened with honey. Quince, which are prepared in a variety of ways, are not only suitable for the sick but useful and pleasant for the healthy. When preserving quince for over the winter, avoid putting them near grapes because their strong odor will contaminate the grapes and cause them to rot. It is said that pregnant women who eat a lot of quince will give birth to industrious and hightly intelligent children.

9. Quince Confection

Quince was a relatively popular fruit in the *Menagier*'s day, perhaps because of the positive qualities attributed to it in the *Tacuina sanitatis* or Health Handbooks of the period. The Italian, French and German handbooks reassure us that quince were useful for both the sick and the well. The *Regimine sanitatis* tend to warn physicians of the dangers of foodstuffs, and with regard to quince very usefully point out that, eaten before a meal, quince stir the appetite and constrict the bowels; eaten after other foods, however, they loosen the bowels. So much of the advice in these handbooks seems to fit into the category of "things our mothers told us." Maybe Mom was right!

We rarely come upon quince in our local markets, although we have seen this golden colored fruit growing in abundance in southern France and neighboring countries. It was brought very early to France in pre-Christian times by the Romans who had in turn been given it by the Greeks. Occasionally quince are found at farmers' markets and in specialty fruit and vegetable stores. Nowdays they are classified as exotic fruit (with the concomitant exotic price!).

Cotignac—the confection—had a long history in France, especially in Orleans where it was purportedly given to "the Maid of Orleans," Joan of Arc, when she entered that city. Quince have a tart flavor. They are not eaten raw.

A recent gift of quince jam and a tasting of quince wine, made by medieval cooking enthusiasts and brought to a medieval food conference, confirmed our original decision to have this recipe in the book. Both items were delicious.

Yield: 2 cups/500 mL

Imperial	Ingredient	Metric	Directions
6–8	quince	6–8	**Peel & core quince. Cut into quarters.**
1–1 1/2 cups	red wine	250–375 mL	**Cook quince, covered in red wine, until soft. Drain. Press through sieve.**
1/2 cup	honey	125 mL	**Add honey to any remaining wine & bring to a boil. Add strained quince.**
1/4 tsp	cinnamon	1 mL	**Add spices. Boil until honey is reduced**
1/4 tsp	ginger	1 mL	**by a half; it should be thick & gelatinous.**
pinch	grains of paradise	pinch	**nous.**
pinch	nutmeg	pinch	**Pour into greased 8"/20 cm cake pan.**
pinch	galingale	pinch	**Let cool. Cut into bite-sized pieces.**
1 tbsp	sugar	15 mL	
3–4 tbsp	white sugar	45–60 mL	**Dip pieces into sugar.**
			Store in tightly closed tin.

Variation

Chiquart's *On Cookery* offers an interesting recipe for Quince in Pastry (§§70 and 70a). Before being placed whole in pie shells, the quince are cored, cooked and filled with sugar. Optionally—in the version of this pie that is to be prepared for a noble's plate—the quince can be packed around with a mixture of bone marrow, ginger and cinnamon. The pies are covered with a top crust.

10. *Tailliz de Karesme*
(*Viandier*, §207)

Prenez amendez pellees et broyez tres bien en ung mortier, puis ayez eaue boullue et reffroidiee comme tiedde et deffaictes les amendes et coulez parmy l'estamine, et faictes boullir vostre lait sur ung petit de charbon; puis prenez des eschaudez cuitz de ung jour ou de deux et les tailliez en menuz morceaulx come gros dez; puis prenez figues, dates, et raysins de Daigne et trenchez lesdictes figues et dates comme les eschaudez et puis y gettez tout et le laissiez especir comme frommentee; et mettre du succre boullir avec; et fault mettre boullir une onde ou deux ledit lait d'amendes; et pour luy donner coulleur convient avoir du saffren pour le coulourer comme fromentee; et qu'il soit doulx salé.

10. Lenten Slices

The title that the *Viandier* has copied for this confection assures the reader that it contains nothing that might be considered a proscribed foodstuff during the penitential season of Lent. Christians must surely have appreciated such delicious dishes as this as a delightful means to vary the strictly controled regimen during their forty-day "fast."

The recipe calls for dried or preserved fruits only. All of the ingredients of the Lenten Slices would be available at this time in the year when a dearth of fresh foods might begin to weigh upon gourmets' spirits.

This dish can be served as a warm pudding, as cold slices, as squares or as ball-shaped cookies.

Yield: Serves 8–10

Imperial	Ingredient	Metric	Directions
1 cup	ground almonds	250 mL	**Combine almonds and water. Steep for 5 minutes, stirring occasionally. Sieve the mixture to remove coarse grains *or* (preferably) blend mixture in electric blender until grains are absorbed. Yield—2 cups/500 mL almond milk.**
2 cups	boiling water	500 mL	

1/2 cup	granulated sugar	125 mL	**In pot, over low heat, combine almond**
pinch	salt	pinch	**milk, sugar and salt. When dissolved, add**
2–3 cups	diced bread (crusts removed) or biscuit pieces or stale cake pieces	500–750 mL	**bread, *or* biscuits, *or* stale cake. Stir well.**
pinch	saffron	pinch	**Add saffron for color if desired.**
3/4 cup	raisins	175 mL	**Add raisins, dates and figs. Cook while**
3/4 cup	dates, cut into 3/4 in/ 2 cm pieces	175 mL	**stirring over low heat—about 15 min. —until a thick, porridge-like consis-**
6–8	large figs, cut into 3/4 in/ 2 cm pieces	6–8	**tency is obtained.**
			Taste; add more sugar if desired.

For garnish

| 2 tsp | granulated sugar | 10 mL | **See below.** |

Serving suggestions

Pudding: Divide mixture into desired number of portions. Sprinkle with sugar. Serve.

Slices: Line a loaf pan with plastic wrap *or* waxed paper. Grease very lightly. Pack the mixture firmly into pan. Sprinkle with sugar. Refrigerate. When cool, remove from pan, slice and serve.

Squares: Grease a cake pan. Layer broken biscuit (*e.g.* vanilla wafers) on bottom of pan. Turn mixture into pan. Sprinkle with sugar. Cool. Cut into squares and serve.

Cookies: Use 1 tbsp/15 mL of mixture. Roll into a ball. Roll balls in sugar, coating thoroughly, tapping off excess sugar. Place in small paper candy cups. Cool. Store in tightly sealed container.

Cooking variations

If desired, after adding the sugar and the bread, biscuits or cake to the almond milk mixture, add the remaining ingredients, pour into prepared baking dish. Set the dish in a pan of hot water and bake in a 350°F/180°C oven for 30–40 min. Serve.

The *Menagier de Paris*, written at about the end of Taillevent's life, adds chopped apples to the mixture and omits the dates and figs. It is a tasty variation of this dish. More bread/biscuits/ cake pieces should be added to absorb the moisture from the apples.

11. *Blanc mengier parti*

(Du fait de cuisine, §33;
and also, Viandier, §199; Du fait de cuisine, §9)

Et, encour plus, ung blanc mangier parti de quatre couleurs tout en ung plat, c'est assavoir d'or, d'azur, de goules et d'argent: et pour donner entendre ceste potagerie, celui qui la fera doibt prendre des amendres grant foyson et les faire plumer nectement et laver et les faire tresbien broyer et les arouser de belle eaue tede et les trayés en une belle et necte cornue, et en faictes selon la quantité que vous voulés faire dudit blanc mangier parti; et mectés dedans ledit boullon que vous faictes de poudre de gingibre blanc et de granne; et puis de ladicte eaue tede traysiés voz amandres et en faictes lait, et puis ledit lait partissiés en quatre oulles belles et cleres et nectes, et tant en l'une comme en l'autre, et du succre aussi en chascun a grant foysson, et du sel par rayson y mectés; et puis les mectés sur gracieux feu eschauffer.

Et puis prennés grant quantité d'amidon et puis le nectoiés et lavés tresbien et adroit et puis en mectés en ung beaulx platz nect pour chescune des dictes quatre oulles; et puis prennés du lait de l'olle que vous lier et si l'estaminés a bonne estamine et puis le mectés tout plan en ladicte olle tousjours en broiant jusques atant que vous verrés qu'il soit bien liés fermement en tant que quant on mectra de l'une au cousté de l'autre sur ung plat que l'une ne se melle avecques l'autre; et aussi faictes de toutes les quatre olles.

Et pour donner entendement a cellui qui fera cestes couleurs pour faire ce mangier parti en quatre couleurs: pour faire la premiere couleur, c'est d'or, si prennés de saffran batu selon la quantité que voulés faire et le destrampés ou lait de l'oelle que avés ordonné pour faire le mangier d'or; et puis le mectés tout plan en broiant a une bonne cuillier en la dicte olle que voulés qu'il a couleur d'or.

Et a cellui de l'azur si prennés vostre tournesaut et le mectés destramper ou lait de l'olle en quoy voulés faire de la couleur d'azur, et puis l'estaminés a une belle et necte seflly bien fort en tant que la couleur n'y demeure point, et puis le mectés dedans l'olle que avés retenue pour porter ladicte couleur d'azur; et destrampés et coulés vostre amidons en la seille audit boullon ou avés coulé vostre couleur d'azur, et puis le mectés en l'olle en fillant et broiant tousjours a une bonne coullier jusques atant qu'il soit bien lyés; et puis quant il sera bien liés si le tirés arriere du feu.

Pour faire cellui de goulles prennés de ofle cler et bien affiné et le mectés en belle casse eschauffer bien et fort; et puis prennés vostre or cannete et lancés par dedans et le menés a une belle cuiller perciee et puis le coullés a ung canton d'estamine dedans ung beau plat; et prennés vostre amidon et le coulés avecques le boullon en quoy devés faire le mangier de goulles, et puis filer en vostre lait en broyant tousjours ou pot en quoy faictes vostre mengier de goulles; et quant il sera bien liés si prennés vostre couleur et y mectés de la diste couleur par bonne maniere tant qu'il soit sur la couleur de goules.

Ou blanc mangier parti d'argent si prennés vostre amydon et le desfaictes ou lait et le coulés a l'estamine et puis le liés bien fort et ferme.

Et, ainsi fait, lesdiz quatre mengiers partir, pour en servir si mectés en ung chescun plat desdiz quatre mengiers, c'est assavoir le mengier d'or, puis celluy de goulles de costez, dessoubz celluy d'azur, et apprés celluy de l'argent; et quant il sera ainssi parti et mis par beaulx platz ainsi comme est devisé, sy ayés vostre dragiee et sur chescune coulleur dudit mangier parti si mectés la dragiee que lui appartient.

11. Parti-Colored White Dish

Though they share the same name, this dish differs from the one found in the section on poultry in that chicken is not included here, and the whole rice of the standard White Dish becomes rice flour or starch. The Parti-Colored White Dish is, in fact, similar to the modern French Blancmange, gelatine having in turn replaced the rice flour as a thickener in more modern times.

The word "parti" refers to the way the dish is "divided" into distinctly colored parts. It illustrates a late-medieval love of cheerful, variegated hues in what was set on the dining table.

This dish was clearly meant to impress the eye as well as the taste buds! Chiquart provides two complete recipes for a *Blanc mengier parti*. In the first recipe (§9 in the *Du fait de cuisine*), almond milk is prepared using mutton or beef bouillon as the liquid. In the second recipe (§33), grains of paradise are added along with the ginger. The *Viandier* calls for neither ginger nor grains of paradise in his version of the dish.

A simple almond pudding is made and divided into four parts. Each part is suitably colored using certain specified colorants: saffron for the gold, nothing for the silver, orchil lichen for the blue, and alkanet for the red. The three colorants are first to be soaked in bacon grease in order to draw out the respective pigments, and then this colored grease is added to a portion of the almond-milk and rice-flour preparation. Different colored sugar candies garnish each section of the dish.

Our efforts to locate orchil lichen and alkanet have proven futile. As well, we are not certain about the properties of these pigments, or their safety when they are ingested. If you are comfortable using food dyes, by all means make the dish using two, three or four such colorants.

The recipe below is for just two colors. The pudding should be thick enough that the colors do not run into each other. This is easier said than done! We have found a trick to help keep the colors separate in the serving dish: before pouring out the colored batches of the pudding, we divide the dish into sections with a stiff piece of cardboard wrapped in plastic; then we remove this divider when the pudding has settled and cooled. Alternatively, you might pour the first pudding into the dish or lightly greased jelly mold and put it to settle and cool in the refrigerator; then add the other(s) in turn.

Yield: Serves 6

Imperial	Ingredient	Metric	Directions
2 cups	almond milk (see p. 60)	500 mL	**Heat 1 1/2 cups/375 mL of the almond milk in a pot.**
2–3 tsp pinch pinch	powdered ginger grains of paradise (*optional*) salt	10–15 mL pinch pinch	**Stir in spices & salt.**
2 tbsp	rice flour	30 mL	**Combine rice flour with remaining milk. Pour this into the warm milk in a steady stream, stirring constantly.**
1/2–3/4 cup	sugar	125–200 mL	**Stir in sugar. Taste. Add more ginger if desired.** **Cook until a thick pudding consistency is reached.**
pinch	saffron (*or* turmeric)	pinch	**Divide into 2 pots. Add saffron to one pot, stirring until color is blended. Pour each pot into one half of serving dish. Cool.**

Serving suggestions

Garnish with colored candies before serving.

If using jelly mold, turn out onto serving dish. Garnish and serve.

Aprés peulx dire a haulte voix: "A Dieu vous commans, je m'en vois."	Then tell your host, in voice not low, "God keep you, Sir: I must now go."

Other possible desserts

Riquemenger / Scrambled Eggs and Apples

For the complete recipe of this dish as an Egg Dish, see p. 235, above.

Ris engoullé / Ruddy Rice Pudding

For the complete recipe of this dish as a Vegetable Dish, see p. 261, above.
As a dessert, omit the grease and replace the milk and beef bouillon with 2 cups/500 mL of almond milk (for the making of which see Chapter 1, Standard Preparations, p. 60, above). When serving, garnish each serving with pomegranate seeds, candied orange or sliced browned almonds.

Menu Suggestions and Meals

1. Menus for a Reception
2. Menus for a Barbecue
3. Menus for Small Dinner Parties
4. A Banquet
    a. Menus
    b. *Entremets*
    c. Room and decor/decorations
    d. Table arrangement and table setting
    e. Personnel and their responsibilitites
    f. Costumes
    g. Ceremonial and etiquette
    h. Entertainment
5. *Entremets* and Culinary *Divertissements*
    a. *Hures de cenglier* / Boar's Head Roasted
    b. *Lucz cuitz de troys manieres* / A Pike Cooked in Three Ways
    c. *Coqz heaumez* / Helmetted Cocks
    d. *Herissons et Potz d'Espaigne* / Hedgehogs and Spanish Pots
    e. *Layt lardé* / Larded Milk
    f. *Entremetz plus legiers* / Easier Entremets
    g. *Alouyaulx* / Little Larks
    h. *Faulx grenon (Potage party)* / Mock Meat
    i. *Tortes parmeysines* / Parma Torte and Parma Fish Pies
6. Table Manners

Menu Suggestions and Meals

In the French cookery collections from the end of the Middle Ages the complexity of the recipes varies widely. A few of the longer, more difficult recipes describe dishes whose use was most likely limited to feasts, banquets or other exceptional occasions. However, fortunately for us, by far the larger number of the recipes we find in these manuscript collections lend themselves to an extensive range of possible uses in the ordinary, day-to-day meals of the period; these are generally the "easier" dishes, though by no means are they generally any less satisfying to eat today.

What is, furthermore, rather reassuring for the modern cook of limited time, energy or funds is that the apparently "ordinary" dishes that compose 95 percent of a late-medieval cookbook are just the ones that make up 95 percent of a late-medieval banquet. A close study of banquet menus in the fourteenth and fifteenth centuries shows that these grand, formal meals relied for the most part upon standard fare. A banquet menu seems to have been defined on the one hand merely by quantity—the profusion of such standard dishes, prepared and served in a series of courses that was itself more numerous than normal—and on the other hand by the phenomenal—the presence during the banquet of exceptional productions such as an *entremets* or other entertainment.

We heartily encourage you to organize a medieval banquet, with as much of the attendant splendor as you can manage to furnish. Later in this section we shall provide hints and details for organizing such a banquet. Medieval recipe collections offer a good number of quite manageable dishes that are unusual and suitably impressive for your banquet guests; we shall look at a few of those, too.

Should a formal banquet be beyond your scope for the moment, or if you want to gain some practical experience before embarking on preparations for a large event, why not use some of the recipes of this book as refreshments for a reception instead of the usual wine and cheese? Many of the dishes here are more authentically prepared on the open fire of a barbecue; you might try giving a medieval flavor to your summer barbecue parties. Perhaps a few friends would like to get together for a medieval brunch or a gourmet dinner; again, there is plenty of scope here. Or you may wish to share a more intimate dinner with a good friend.

In every case, whether it's a matter of one or two dishes for a simple medieval brunch or the ambitious undertaking of a fully developed banquet, the late-medieval recipe collections offer the modern cook a broad range of possibilities from which to put together an appetizing menu.

Whatever the occasion, we would suggest that it will always be enhanced if you take care to set the proper mood. A few banners, invitations and menus drafted in a "medieval" style and scripted on parchment paper, a brief historical commentary to highlight the menu, appropriate live entertainment or tapes of early music, white linen cloths, and candles—*et voilà!* a merely unusual event is transformed into a memorable one.

For those wanting initial assistance in choosing menus, the following pages provide suggestions on how to use some of the recipes that work particularly well for specific occasions. We shall propose as well a sample menu for each type of occasion.

Please check the Yield in each individual recipe, and *revise the quantities to correspond with your guest list*.

What is offered throughout this section is, we repeat, only by way of suggestion. Delightful menus composed of many other recipe combinations are of course possible.

1. Menus for a Reception

Many of the recipes of this book can be adapted to make smaller bite-sized finger-foods for a reception; particularly versatile for this purpose are the meat/fruit pies, the rissoles, the egg tortes and various tarts. Other dishes are easily adapted for serving at a reception if you furnish toothpicks. You might also consider providing small pieces of toast (authentic medieval sops!) or pita triangles, together with bowls of one or several medieval sauces for dipping.

Check the recipes for quantities.

Menu Nº 1

A tray of anchovies in vinaigrette on small pieces of toast
Anchoyes / **Anchovies** (p. 215)

Assorted small rissoles: lobster/rice, pork/fruit, fruit
Rissolles a jour de poisson / **Rissoles for a Fish Day, Fruit Rissoles** (p. 95)

A tray of cold chicken & pork slices, folded & speared with a toothpick
along with an assortment of sauces:
Aulx vers / **Green Garlic Sauce** (p. 119)
Saulce verte / **Green Ginger Sauce** (p. 118)
Froide sauge / **Cold Sage Sauce** (p. 183)
Moust / **Must Sauce** (p. 130)

A tray of pureed chickpeas
Syseros / **Chickpea Puree** (p. 77)

Pipe the puree onto a plate; garnish with parsley & whole chickpeas; accompany this dish with pita triangles.

Menu Nº 2

Assortment of tartlettes
[*Pastez de champignons*] / **Mushroom Tarts** (p. 96)
Tortes of Herbs, Cheese & Eggs (p. 232)

A chafing dish of meatballs in applesauce
Pommeaulx / **Little Meatballs** (p. 153)
Emplumeus de pomes / **Almond Applesauce** (p. 286)

A chafing dish of small pieces of sole with orange/sorrel sauce
Soles frites / **Fried Sole with Orange & Sorrel Verjuice** (p. 213)

Menus drois / **Little Delicacies** (p. 83)

Soupe jacobine de chappons / **Jacobin Sops** (p. 105)

Bowls of candied orange and nuts
Orengat / **Candied Orange Peel** (p. 284)
Confiture de noiz / **Honey-Nut Conserve** (p. 290)

2. Menus for a Barbecue

The roasting spit and grill were commonplace implements in a medieval kitchen, and their products, roast and grilled meats and fish, constituted an integral part of most meals. A barbecue is, in fact, a very natural place at which to begin to recreate medieval foods.

The choice of meat or fish that you can prepare on a barbecue is almost limitless. Given that beef was rarely roasted (no pun intended!), it might make sense to take this chance to break out of the North-American barbecued-beefsteak habit and to consider looking at the broad range of other possibilities. Another important decision you will have to make concerns the sauce that is appropriate for serving with your meat or fish. We would suggest that you consider the following combinations:

Veal with *Cameline* / Cameline Sauce (pp. 115, 117 or 138)

Chicken with *Moust pour hetoudeaulx* / Must Sauce for Young Chicken (p. 130)

Rabbit with *Saupiquet* / Saupiquet Sauce (p. 128)

Goose with *Aulx vers* / Green Garlic Sauce (p. 119)

or Goose with *Poivre noir* / Black Pepper Sauce (p. 126)

Salmon with *Cameline* / Cameline Sauce (p. 138)

Sole with *Verjust de oyselle et de orenges* / Orange and Sorrel Verjuice (p. 213)

Certain of the recipes lend themselves particularly well to preparation on a barbecue:

Pommeaulx / **Little Meatballs** (p. 153)

Alouyaulx / **Little Larks** (p. 88)

Char de porcelez en rost / **Stuffed Roast Suckling Pig** (p. 156)

Espalles de mouston, farciees et dorees / **Shoulder of Mutton, Stuffed & Glazed** (p. 159)

3. Menus for Small Dinner Parties

Many hosts and hostesses favor smaller, more intimate dinner parties of four to six persons. The following menus provide dishes that will entice not only the appetites but the curiosity of your guests. Armed with the history and manuscript sources for *Poullaille farcie* or *Soupe jacobine de chappons*, the host or hostess has the basis for stimulating dinner conversation!

Menu N⁰ 3

Couleis de perche / **Perch Cullis** (p. 214)

Salad of greens tossed with warm *Menus drois* /
Little Delicacies in Vinaigrette (p. 84)

Poullaille farcie / **Stuffed Chicken Breasts** (p. 197)
with
Porriaux blancs / **Almond-Leek Sauce** (p. 132)

Ris engoullé / **Ruddy Rice Pudding** (p. 261)

Poree de cresson / **Stewed Cress** (p. 259)

Rissoles a jour de poisson / **Fruit Rissoles** (p. 278)

Ypocras / **Hypocras** (p. 57)

Menu N⁰ 4

Chicken & Brie Cheese Soup
Soupe jacobine de chappons / **Jacobin Sops** (p. 105)

Escrevisses farcies / **Stuffed Shrimp** (p. 220)

Tossed green salad with toasted pinenuts

Tortres parmeysines / **Parma Torte** (p. 175)

Escheroys / **Parsnips** (p. 266)

Flons de lait d'amendres / **Almond Milk Flans** (p. 281)

Ypocras / **Hypocras** (p. 57)

4. A Banquet

Today, as cooks, we have things a little easier than those who prepared banquets at the end of the Middle Ages. This is, in part, because few of us will be called upon, or will volunteer, to prepare some 40 dishes of exceptionally fine food for 500 people. And things are easier, in part too, because we are working with kitchen equipment which is ever so much more efficient and less wearing than that of A.D. 1400, and with foodstuffs which often come to us in a more convenient state than our counterparts formerly had. Our banquets nowadays can be quite a bit less onerous than for the medieval cook—provided we can keep the guest list somewhere well below the number of 500. A modern banquet can even provide quite a lot of fun for the cook as well as for the banquetters.

Our experience has been that, unless you have exceptionally generous amounts of space, staffing, cooking equipment and financial resources, or are working within the framework of an organization such as a service club, church or school, and can enjoy the sponsorship of this organization, it is wise to limit the number of guests to under fifty participants. This "manageable maximum" includes all the entertainers and servers who will eventually be receiving their just desserts somewhere at your banquet board.

Assuming, then, that you are willing to have about fifty guests, we would make the following suggestions.

The first requisite, as for any successful cooking job, is organization. Divide your arrangements into a series of categories:

     a. menu
     b. *entremets*
     c. room and decor/decorations
     d. table arrangement and table settings
     e. personnel and their responsibilities
     f. costumes
     g. ceremonial and etiquette
     h. entertainment.

a. Menus

For your banquet it is important to choose a menu that you can work with easily, and have sufficient time and help to prepare. Experience has taught us that it is helpful to invite a few critical and willing friends over ahead of time for a "trial run" of dishes in order to ensure that the banquet menu is workable. Such experimentation is useful as well to refine the recipes to your taste. As you gain experience you can enlarge the scope of your menu and include such dishes as the *Char de porcelez en rost* / Stuffed Roast Suckling Pig and the more complicated Tortes. We prefer a menu in which most of the dishes can be at least partially prepared in advance. Should you, like the chief cook in some affluent medieval household, be blessed with a small army of talented and eager cooks, your menu and the variety of dishes served could always be enlarged, of course.

Menu N⁰ 5

Mead or Cider

Potage d'oignons / **Onion-Pea Soup** (see p. 103)

Tartres de poyssons / **Fish Pie** (see p. 221)

Une vinaigrette / **A Vinegar Dish** (see p. 80)

Salad   Bread

Blanc mengier / **White Dish of Chicken** (see p. 190)

Composte / **Honey-Glazed Vegetables** (see p. 272)

[*Fritelles d'orvale*] / **Clary Fritters** (see p. 280) *Poires d'angoisse* / **Pears in Syrup** (see p. 291)

Tailliz de Karesme / **Lenten Slices** (see p. 294)

Ypocras / **Hypocras** (see p. 57)

Menu N⁰ 6

Mead or Cider

Porriaux blancs / **Almond-Leek Sauce** (as a soup: see p. 132)

Tortes of Herbs, Cheese & Eggs (see p. 232)

Syseros / **Chickpeas** (in a green salad: see p. 77)   Rolls

Char de porcelez en rost / **Stuffed Roast Suckling Pig** (see p. 156)
on toast

Minces / **Brussels Sprouts in a Vinaigrette** (see p. 262)
with walnuts

Rissoles a jour de poisson / **Fruit Rissoles** (see p. 278)

Confiture de noiz / **Honey-Nut Conserve** (see p. 290)
with
Orengat / **Candied Orange Peel** (see p. 284)

Ypocras / **Hypocras** (see p. 57)

Having chosen the date, time, place and menu for your banquet, you should prepare an information sheet for each of your guests. This sheet should present the menu and any historical data you believe interesting about the food or dishes, or, by way of practical guidance, about the protocol you intend to follow in the course of your banquet—hierarchical seating order, handwashing, fanfares, entertainment, even the proper etiquette and manners you hope your honorable guests will display. The information sheet can be as simple or elaborate as you wish, depending of course upon your time, artistic talents and financial resources. Our practice has been to number each sheet and to use it as an entry ticket to the banquet. These may be handwritten effectively on sheets of parchment. Parchment is available at craft shops or art supply stores. If your caligraphy skills are not adequate, Letraset has a nice Gothic Script set; you can make up one master invitation or menu and then photocopy or print it onto sheets of parchment. Scorching the edges of the paper adds an "aged" effect to the menu.

Assuming you are having a relatively small banquet for some thirty guests (plus six musicians/entertainers), and that you are using the first of the Banquet Menus above (Menu N⁰ 5), we would offer the following suggestions.

Quantities: If you are planning to feed the serving and kitchen help, you can adjust the quantities of all the ingredients. However, we have found that in most cases—what with incidental nibbling during the meal and everyone's exhaustion by the end of it—there were enough leftovers to satisfy all of the help.

Potage d'oignons / Onion-Pea Soup: Make five or six times the recipe. It can be made in the early afternoon and reheated.

Tartres de poyssons / Fish Pie: Substitute the *Tortres parmeysines de poyssons* / Parma Fish Pie if you wish. Make six times the recipe. These recipes can be made either as six pies or as 40–45 individual tartlettes. Prepare them in the morning before the banquet and reheat. Prepared well in advance, they may be frozen but only if absolutely necessary; allow sufficient time for them to thaw, and then reheat them.

Une vinaigrette / A Vinegar Dish: Make two or three times the recipe. This can be made earlier in the day and reheated.

Salad greens: Cleaned earlier in the day. Toss them with dressing at serving time.

Blanc mengier / White Dish of Chicken: Best made just before dinner, but the chickens can be cooked earlier in the day. Prepare almond milk, toasted almonds and pomegranate seeds earlier, ready to be used.

Composte / Honey-Glazed Vegetables: Make six times the recipe. Clean the vegetables; have them ready to cook just before dinner.

Clary Fritters: Make two times the recipe. They are made ahead and stored in an air-tight container. If necessary, crisp them in the oven before serving.

Fennel Pears: Six times the recipe. Made ahead and stored in the refrigerator.

Tailliz de Karesme / Lenten Slices: Three times the recipe. Made ahead.

Your banquet must always conclude with a serving of the mulled wine, hypocras (see its recipe at p. 57, above). If you can find or make spiced candies (called *dragees* in medieval France, but not to be confused with the modern candied almond of the same name), serve them with the hypocras.

b. *Entremets*

The provision of some sort of *entremets* during your banquet can add much both to the richness of your menu and the delight of your guests. A selection of such a "dish" is possible from a wide assortment of actual, historically documented *entremets*, ranging from the most elementary and edible to the more complex type whose purpose is only to evoke the wonderment of the banquetters. We refer you to the section devoted entirely to *entremets* at p. 321, below. You should keep in mind, though, that you are under no obligation to make only those dishes described there; the hallmark of a cook's genius is imagination, in the creating of amusing and appropriate *entremets* as in most other things.

c. Room and decor/decorations

Choose a room in which you can set enough chairs to only one side of your table(s) but still have space enough to allow your guests to assemble and your servers to move freely. Ideally, of course, this room should have something of the air of a medieval hall—that is, a high ceiling, gothic-style architectural detailing, with some structural wood or wood panelling.

Around the walls hang plain colored banners or anything suggestive of tapestries. Banners can be made from brightly colored felt and suspended from poles. An impressive touch is to determine your family's or institution's coat of arms and repeat either its motif or simply its colors around the room. Simple but effective banners can be made by using a "magic lantern," an overhead projector using transparencies made from a photocopy, or a child's "magnajector" in order to project an image from a book; one can also enlarge any drawing by the use of a graph. Dover Books publish a good assortment of both medieval lettering and medieval images; for this material you can also usefully consult books on early heraldry. Trace your image in outline on a sheet of paper on a wall and enlarge it; then use this as a pattern to cut out odd-sized mosaic-shaped pieces of felt, of the same or different colors, and glue these to a banner of canvas in order to make up the whole image. New commercial products such as *Heat & Bond* are very easy to use, quicker and more effective than glue. Another new product is an iron-on clear protective coating which is very useful in preserving the banners or if you should want a leaded-glass window effect. (For an idea of several possiblities for this latter type of banner, see the adjoining pictures.)

You can also trace the whole outline of the image you have chosen and cut out the larger shapes—that is, a head and neck, shoulders, body, and so forth—and glue or appliqué them onto felt or a stiff canvas.

For tapestry, a simple substitute that avoids a costly visit to your local tapestry weaver is to mount some sort of patterned or scenic gift wrap on a stiff board, and hang several of these around the walls. Similarly, prints of medieval scenes can be enlarged from picture books, traced and mounted the same way on panels.

If an open flame is allowed by the fire regulations governing your banquet hall, consider burning large candles to provide some of the light for your banquet. Candles of a church-office style, 3 in/8 cm in diameter and 18 in/45 cm long, placed at each end of the head table, for instance, can contribute to the atmosphere.

d. Table arrangement and table settings

A banquet for thirty guests and six musicians/entertainers will require the following dishware and miscellaneous hardware.

For the kitchen

Kitchen utensils as needed for the cooking:
        soup cauldrons, pots, pie plates, carving knives, 2 soup ladles
        an extra table for dressing platters of food

For serving

serving platters	12	Blanc mengier & Composte are presented on platters holding 6 servings each
small bowls	6	same serving arrangement for the Vinaigrette
small plates	6	same serving arrangement for the Clary Fritters
serving spoons	18–20	

For the table settings

tables & chairs (or benches)	for 36 places	
tablecloths	8–10 large white	
napkins	36	plus perhaps a few extra
finger bowls	10	or one for the Guest of Honor & one between every 4 guests
salt bowls	9	
soup bowls	36	
fruit nappies	36	for dessert
sherry glasses	36	or 18, if sharing; for the mead or cider
wine glasses	36	or 18, if sharing
mugs	36	or 18, if sharing; for the hypocras
knives	36	
spoons	36	
soup spoons	36	

If possible, use several tables and arrange them in an open, square U configuration. This allows an open area in the centre of the room from which servers can present the succession of dishes formally, and clear them away efficiently. Besides, this open arrangement seats your guests in such a way that all guests can see each other, as well as their host and the Guest of Honor at the head of the room, and to enjoy any entertainment (including the parade of the *entremets*) that can take place before them. Long benches should be preferred over individual chairs.

Again if possible, raise the head table a little on a dais of 6–9 inches/15–25 cm. The host, hostess and Guest(s) of Honor should be seated on high-backed chairs suggestive of thrones. For a final touch of nobility in this setting, a rough carpenter in your family can fashion the framework for a fabric baldequin over these chairs; this baldequin can perhaps be hung with the coat of arms of the family represented beneath it.

Tables have a plain white tablecloth. Because inevitably these will become soiled in the course of the banquet, probably between the time your guests are dipping meat into the brimming sauce bowls and the time you clear away the sop-of-the-day, it might be wise not to bring out your best damask. You may choose to provide your guests with napkins—in which case the same *caveat* applies—or simply allow enough of the table cloth to overhang the guests' side of the table that it covers their knees; this "lap-runner" serves as a useful safeguard against greasy drips and as a most necessary and handy finger-wipe.

The table-setting is plain: a spoon, a knife and a bread trencher (see the recipe for this bread, p. 65, above) per guest, one goblet between two guests[1] (or individual goblets, if you prefer; the Guest of Honor will have one to himself or herself in any case, of course), and salt in a small decorative container. For the greatest authenticity, the container for the salt should be in the shape of a boat and made of something that at least looks like silver or gold. (Here's a good chance to bring out those silver model gondolas you bought in Venice!)

Non-essential items for your table setting—but touches which enhance the mood considerably—are flowers, candles and finger-bowls. (For the simple mixture of rosewater with which to fill the finger bowls, see p. 73, above.) Table candles that are set in colored glasses or jars are very attractive, and pose less of a risk of fire.

e. Personnel and their responsibilities

Unless you were born on the planet Krypton and can leap tall buildings at a single bound, you will need competent, willing help to put on your banquet. We would suggest that spreading the work among nine people, each of whom has his or her own jobs and knows clearly what is expected, will keep the presentation of a banquet from becoming too onerous a chore for the person who is responsible.

---

[1] The enforced intimacy of the medieval meal, in which guests not only share the same goblet but dip into the same bowl of sops, imposes an obligation upon the host or hostess to ensure that partners are compatible. Don't let *your* banquet flounder on the friction of poorly matched pairs!

The following seems a good, efficient division of labor.

Personnel	Their Responsibilities	
Total: 9		
	Before the Banquet	During the Banquet
Chief Steward & 2 Helpers	Decorate the hall. Set up dinner tables & table for wine & bread. Set tables: glasses, cutlery, salt, etc. Welcome guests. Serve mead.	**Chief Steward.** Calls guests to table & directs seating. Organizes handwashing. Directs fanfares & serving. **Helper 1.** Assists Steward & acts as Wine Steward, filling glasses & replenishing as necessary. Serves hypocras. **Helper 2.** Assists Steward & acts as pantler, replacing trenchers & bread rolls as necessary.
Chief Server & 2 Helpers	Assist Steward (in hall) or Cook (in kitchen), as needed.	**Chief Server.** Serves the Guest of Honor & head table. **Helpers 1 & 2.** Serve guests all dishes in each course. Assist Cooks in dressing & garnishing platters as necessary. Clear tables at end of meal before hypocras is served.
Chief Cook & 2 Helpers	Prepare dishes & hypocras.	**Chief Cook.** Oversees final food preparations, dressing & garnishing of platters & dishes. **Helpers 1 & 2.** Dish out into bowls & onto plates & platters. Garnish these as directed by Chief Cook.

After the Banquet: **everybody** helps to clean up!

f. Costumes

One of the most effective ways of lending a medieval atmosphere to a banquet is by inviting your guests to "dress medieval." In some cases for women this may mean a simple long shift-type dress in plain fabric with long sleeves. In others it could mean something more historically accurate, perhaps with slashed sleeves and veil-draped henin millinery.

Your servers should be dressed in medieval style.

If you are willing to tackle costume-making, from scratch as it were, a number of books on historic costumes can be consulted to see the main features of late-medieval dress. If your time or talent is not quite up to the detailed reproduction of a robe-with-surcoat or a doublet, you might try a simple shortcut such as the following.

For a lady's dress:

For average 5'2"–5'6"/163 cm–168 cm height. (For other sizes, measure width from tip to tip of outstretched arms; measure length from floor to shoulders, and double.) Prepare a rectangular piece of fabric, 72"/180 cm wide and 10 1/2–11'/3.3 m long. (You will probably have to join fabric to obtain this width. If so, the seam should be in the centre of the fabric.) Cut and hem a 12"/30 cm opening in the centre of the fabric. Round off the ends of fabric and hem all the outside edges. Make a belt of the same fabric about 3"/8 cm wide and long enough to be tied or pinned at its back.

To assemble, centre the gown on shoulders. Pick up fabric at centre 2"/5 cm below waistline and pin this just below centre breast line at bottom of sternum. Cover with belt, passing the belt under armpits and fastening at back; back of gown is left flowing freely.

An attractive hat can be fashioned by covering a cone-shaped cardboard or plastic bucket (such as fried chicken pieces are delivered in) with fabric; sheer fabric sewn to the brim of the hat further provides an effective veil. The dress neckline, as well as the belt and the brim of the hat may be decorated with wide braid (found in drapery notions departments). Craft stores now stock many new items that can be used to decorate: glass beads, studs, fabric paints, gold and silver iron-on trim. The choice is limited only by your pocketbook and imagination.

For a man's tabard:

For average 5'9"/175 cm. (For other sizes, measure width across shoulders; measure length from shoulder to desired length, and double.) Cut a 6' X 2'/180 cm X 60 cm rectangle of plain or simple-patterned upholstery fabric. In the centre of this cut, trim and edge a head-hole; a key- hole shape works well. Hem at knee or thigh-height back and front; round off the hem back and front, if desired. Encase the edges in bias tape or fancy braid. Cut and sew a belt of the same material or use a plain leather belt to hold either the back or front of the tabard, or both. Alternatively, tie the back to the front at each side and let the tabard hang free (as in the diagram).

The tabard is worn over a long-sleeved tee-shirt and tights.

If you are energetic you might like to appliqué the family crest onto the front of the tabard. This repeated emblem is very effective on the servers' tabards, and makes it clear that they are wearing the House's livery.

Silks and other fabrics from the East were brought back to Europe by pilgrims and crusaders and by the wives of those crusaders who remained in the East. By the later Middle Ages the Mediterranean ports had regained mastery in maritime trade. Chroniclers of the time speak of a growing taste for luxury cloths imported by merchants operating through these ports.

Important textile industries were located in Flanders, France and Italy. A new social class of merchants and craftsmen was emerging at this time. The *Book of Crafts* of Etienne Boileau[2] lists at least nineteen guilds in the city of Paris alone which were concerned with the fabrication and embroidery of cloth, especially silks, wools, linens and cottons. Fairs in major French cities such as Troyes, Reims, Chartres and Provins were well stocked with fabrics along with other goods. Fabrics from certain sources were considered superior: Flemish fabrics, for instance, were much in demand. Italians, especially those from Florence and Lucca, became well known for the methods they employed to embellish and embroider the fabrics purchased in Flanders or France.

With the rise of this new class of wealthy merchants and tradespeople, the rulers and nobility sought to reserve certain fabrics and types of clothing for themselves. Sable and ermine (called "Babylonian skin") were reserved for royalty. Interdicts were promulgated against the wearing of certain luxury garments in the streets. Even the number of new garments which an individual could purchase in one year was regulated, as was the average price of the materials used in those garments. Needless to say, these rules were neither universally adhered to nor successfully enforced. Human nature and the competitive spirit of the day frequently found ways around the rules.

You may not be able to afford to trim your garments with ermine, or to purchase fine silks or damasks, fabrics that were relatively common among the wealthy in medieval times, but nowadays we have also the option of cheaper man-made fabrics which can be embellished with fabric paint and assorted bindings and trim. Check out theatre companies that may rent out costumes. Occasionally theatre costume designers will have a sale to get rid of odd pieces of fabric, or even sell used costumes to make room for more stock. Nor are you obliged to adhere to the rigid social restrictions of class. With your banquet you can choose to be whomever you wish, and to plan your costume accordingly.

A good variety of books on historic dress is available in bookstores and libraries. For period costumes designed specifically for the do-it-yourselfer, you may consult (for example):

- Iris Brooke, *Medieval Theatre Costume. A practical guide to the construction of garments*, London (Adam & Charles Black), 1967. (Contains very useful patterns.)
- Lynn Edelman Schnurnberger, *Kings, Queens, Knights & Jesters. Making Medieval Costumes*, New York, Hagerstown, San Francisco, London (Harper & Row, in association with the Metropolitan Museum of Art, New York), 1978. This book gives simple and clear instructions for a variety of costumes and their decoration.
- Margaret Scott, *History of Dress. Late Gothic Europe, 1400–1500*, Atlantic Highlands, New Jersey (Humanities Press), 1980.

For a short history of medieval costume, a useful source is:

- François Boucher, *2000 Years of Fashion — The History of Costume and Personal Adornment*, New York (Harry Abrams), 1965; repr. 1983. Chapters VI and VII are of specific interest.

---

[2] Etienne Boileau, *Le livre des mestiers (XIIIe siècle)*, ed. René de Lespinasse et François Bonnardot, Paris, 1879; repr. Geneva (Slatkine), 1980.

Two further works may prove of practical usefulness, though they present costumes of the Renaissance period in Britain:

- Janet Arnold, *Patterns of Fashion*, London (Macmillan), 1985.
- Janet Winter and Carolyn Schultz, *Elizabethan Costuming for the Years 1550–1580*, Oakland, California (Other Times Publications), 1983.

In addition to these detailed monographs on the dress of the period, you might leaf through modern reproductions of late-medieval illuminated manuscripts. In the illustrations painted in these books— particularly in the ornate books of liturgical Hours commanded by wealthy patrons—you will find very careful depictions of garments and dress accessories worn by all contemporary segments of society.

g. Ceremonial and etiquette

Observance of a minimal number of formal procedures is *de rigueur* in the reproduction of a medieval banquet. A finely detailed outline of the day-to-day operation of a noble household is afforded in the *Mémoires* of Olivier de la Marche[3] who was the *Maître d'Hôtel*—the person in charge of the Household—of Charles the Bold, Duke of Burgundy (1433–1477). The following brief extracts will give an idea of the rigid formality that obtained in the late Middle Ages when food was served to "the Prince."

> The Duke has a Grand Master of the Household (*grant maistre d'ostel*). ... He must lead in the Prince's food, with his staff held upward. He does not do any food assays in the kitchen, but rather it is the First Master of the Household who does them, or else in his absence one of the other Masters of the Household. When food is set in front of the Prince, the Grand Master of the Household takes all of the covers off every dish served to the Prince, of both the first course and the second, and generally of everything served during the dinner. ...
>
> The Duke has six Medical Doctors, and these serve to oversee the person and the health of the Prince. And when the Duke is at table, these Doctors are behind the bench, and they see what dishes and foods are served to the Prince and they advise him which foods in their opinion are the most beneficial to him. ...
>
> The Duke has two Spicers and two Helpers. ... The Spicer brings the Prince's *dragee* box before him, whatever may be the great feast or affair of state; the First Chamberlain takes the *dragee* box and hands its assay to the Spicer, and then hands the box to the senior person of the Duke's Household present; this person presents the box to the Prince, then returns it to the First Chamberlain, and the First Chamberlain returns it to the Spicer. This Spicer supplies all sorts of *dragees* and candied fruits; he makes and supplies the hypocras. ...
>
> I shall describe how the Pantler should conduct himself in serving the mouth of the Prince. When the Prince wishes to dine and the table is set, the Hall Usher goes to get the

---

[3] *Mémoires d'Olivier de la Marche, maître d'hôtel et capitaine des gardes de Charles le Téméraire*, ed. Henri Beaune and J. d'Arbaumont (Paris, 1888); vol. 4, pp. 13–27.

Pantler who is to serve that day, and brings him to the Pantry. The Pantry Porter hands a napkin to the Pantler, and kisses it as an assay; the Pantler puts it on his left shoulder, the two ends hanging front and back. Then the Porter hands him the covered salt dish which the Pantler is to carry holding it in his fingers between its foot and its bowl—as distinct from the goblet which is to be carried by its foot. And, bare-headed, the Pantler follows the Hall Usher; following him comes the Porter, who bears the silver boat that serves for alms: within this boat are the silver trenchers and the small salt dish and another little boat, along with the stick and the unicorn horn with which the assay of the Prince's food is made.

When they have come into the hall and are before the table, the Porter should set the boat where the Pantler directs him, and it should be at the lower end of the table; and the Pantler opens the salt dish and with the lid takes some salt and hands it to the Porter who makes the assay in the presence of the Pantler; then the Pantler sets down his salt dish and his trenchers, the small salt dish, the small boat and the tester; then he hangs his napkin from the boat. When the Prince wishes to wash, the Pantler hands the napkin to the First Master of the Household who is serving at that time; the First Master of the Household hands it to the First Chamberlain, and the First Chamberlain hands it, at his discretion, to anyone superior to him, if he should be present, and gives it back to the Master of the Household. After the Prince has dried his hands, the Master of the Household gives the napkin back to the Pantler who refolds it and replaces it on his shoulder, and who then follows the Master of the Household into the kitchen. When dishes are taken up from the dresser, the Pantler takes off the covers and the Master of the Household makes the assays of these dishes; when this is done, the Pantler re-covers the dishes and hands the covered dishes one after another to the Gentlemen of the four Offices who have followed along to bear the Prince's food, as well as to the Prince's Pages and Serving Valets. These persons are marshalled to bear the Prince's food, and are bare-headed. When the food is taken up, the Saucer presents verjuice to Pantler, and the Pantler takes a sample of each sauce and passes it to the Saucer to make an assay of it; the Pantler carries these sauces. . . . So, with the food taken up, the Usher goes ahead of the Master of the Household, and after him the Pantler, then the dishes after him; and the great dish should come first; the Clerk of the Kitchen comes after the food. In front of the Prince, the Usher kneels clearing room and way, and then the Master of the Household, who stands at the end of the table where he remains until the food is set down and the assays made, and he should keep his eye closely on the food. The Pantler sets the food on the table, then he takes his sample and passes it one after the other. The Pantler in turn places himself at the end of the table in front of the boat. He serves the Duke in two servings, each time with twelve or thirteen dishes; supper is served in one serving. . . .

And so forth. The dining-hall protocol elaborated in noble courts during the Middle Ages was highly detailed and rigid.

At your banquet, then, the guests have to be summoned to table: have your musicians prepare and sound a fanfare; or play a record or tape of some appropriate trumpet or bugle call; or blow a flourish on a kazoo if you have to—but do it ceremoniously, of course! You or one of your servers must then offer a wash basin (with scented water: see p. 73, above) and a towel to each guest, in hierarchical order (if you dare!) beginning with the Guest of Honor or Lord/Lady of the House. Then you or your Master/Mistress of Ceremonies (the modern incarnation of the Herald) assigns seats.

A loaf of fine table bread is served to the head table, the upper crust is cut and properly set before the most senior dignitary. After another fanfare the banquet begins as the first dish is paraded about the room by the whole corps of servitors, and in stately style the first platter or bowl of it is solemnly offered to the same most senior dignitary; subsequent bowls or platters are then distributed to all of your other guests. Several different dishes can make up any one serving (see the suggested banquet menus, p. 307, above), but each serving should be heralded by a fanfare.

If an *entremets* is prepared, it should likewise be shown off in a solemn parade about the room so that everyone present may examine and admire it.

Under the general rubric of etiquette (as we outline in our section on "Table Manners," below): impress on your guests that they are *not* boorish louts rounded in off the streets and visiting a genteel banquet hall for the first time. They are debonair—literally *de bon air*, they have been well brought up—and they know that they pick up their meat with only the tips of the finger and thumb of their right hand (and *never* their left!). They will wipe these fingers carefully before they take a pinch of salt from the salt boat. They will wipe all trace of grease from their lips before they sip from the wine-cup that they may be sharing with their neighbor. They will not speak, nor take another bite of anything, while unswallowed food remains in their mouth. They will refrain from belching, breaking wind, spitting or scratching themselves (anywhere!) while at table. Their conversation should turn on dignified topics only, and eschew religion, politics or any matter that might be thought indecent or that might lead to dissention. And when leaving the table at the end of the banquet, their good breeding and training should impel them to thank their host as graciously as possible for his/her generosity.

h. Entertainment

The most desirable sort of medieval divertissement that you can offer your banquet guests is almost certainly music. Naturally this can be recorded, on disks or long-playing tapes, but if you happen know a singer, a viol player, a recorder player or a lutenist of even modest competence, by all means prevail upon him/her/them to come and present several fanfares and musical interludes in the course of your meal. Perhaps these entertainers will be willing to play/sing/dance for their supper.

It goes without saying that the music at your banquet (whether live or recorded) must date from before 1500 A.D. Dance tunes and rhythms are always a sure hit.

Other forms of entertainment can be solicited from jugglers, acrobats and dancers. It is surprising how many closet jugglers exist among your friends when you mention that you would like to find one for a banquet. And almost every town has its gymnastic club, a few of whose younger members would be only too flattered by a request to perform a routine or two on a mat between your banquet tables.

Serious dancers (as distinct from the amateur variety, of which you are bound to have several among your guests) may be harder to come by, although they likely have costumes that everyone can at least pretend are medieval. It may not be too difficult to find among your acquaintances an individual with some knowledge of old dances and old dancing style who would be willing to teach your entire company a step or two from the fifteenth (or even sixteenth) century: the *basse-danse*, the *branle*, the *estampie*, the *carole*. In our experience, having sat for close to two hours banquetters appreciate the chance to stand and stretch (a little) and to join in one of the slower-paced dance steps of the early period. They may even become so carried away with the music and movement that they dance right out of the banquet hall and snake their way hand-in-hand throughout the entire building; this did indeed happen at one of our banquets as our guests merrily farandoled after our Pied Piper musicians!

Branches of the Society for Creative Anachronism have multiplied into many towns: while their *re*-creations occasionally tend toward armor and mock battles, you may be able to justify such martial displays in the midst of your genteel banquet; they will certainly add color and life to your party.

Don't disdain entertainment of the home-made variety. Medieval banquetters loved games, too. Under each of your guests' trenchers place a slip of paper with instructions that the person compose a rhyming couplet on some theme and then recite it, or sing a song, or read a dramatic passage or poem copied on the paper, or invent an Arthurian tale out of a short list of (fictitious) characters provided, or through a charade identify some medieval personnage, or ... whatever you think might be amusing. You may be surprised how willing people are at the end of a banquet to make their own fun out of the simplest of ideas or materials.

That, after all, is the purpose of putting together a medieval banquet. You will want to reproduce, with a fair degree of authenticy, the food and conditions of a formal meal in the late Middle Ages, but even more than that you will want your guests to feel that the experience has not been merely a dry, academic exercise, albeit an historically accurate one. You and they should have fun. In the late Middle Ages a banquet, with all of its delightful wealth of savor and color and sound, was the supreme entertainment, and as much as possible it should continue to be so today.

5. *Entremets* and Culinary *Divertissements*

In modern meals the *hors d'œuvre* is served at the beginning—"finger foods," offered before guests settle down to the really serious eating. In the Middle Ages there was no polite gastronomic shilly-shallying, no dainty appetizer to awaken a desire for the good solid stuff when, in due course and almost coyly, it would be served. Or, perhaps to put it another way, in the Middle Ages almost everything was "finger foods." After the guests had washed their hands and been invited to take their allotted seats, they had all the natural appetite they needed to dispose of the first course as it was immediately served; presumably they dealt in the same way with all of the subsequent courses in their due order. The meal began right off with platters mounded with chunks of roast and boiled meats (or fish): these were the so-called *grosses viandes*, whose qualification indicated that this serving was not of culinarily complex preparations such as pies or broths. These meats (or fish) constituted in effect what we today call the "entry" (or *entrée*) course.

At the medieval table the real *hors d'œuvre* was introduced *between* courses. In the medieval meal this dish served not so much as a stimulant to the appetite but as a rest from appetite. Called in French, quite appropriately, the *entremets* (literally, the "between-dish" course), this preparation was originally a lighter food or a dish which claimed the interest of guests because it was somehow prepared with art, and was not simply a "gross" cooked meat in a sauce, or some variety of stewed meat. In time "with art" became "artificial," and the *entremets* became an "artefact." The *Viandier* of Taillevent contains thirteen dishes called *entremets*. Central among these are humble porridges of wheat, millet grain and rice; they are dishes in which "gross" or stewed meats or fish are totally absent. But in this category of dish we also find at early times several quite striking delicacies, such as chicken livers cooked in wine and served dressed in parsley and vinegar, or fish in a delightfully spiced jelly.

While it originated as a light pause that refreshed, over the years the *entremets*, this course between other courses, became used increasingly to provide a point of interest in a prolonged formal banquet. It came to function as a focus for the guests' attention among the series of more or less standard preparations. It offered a very welcome means to amuse them, or even to amaze them.

The desire to entertain one's guests is evident already in the *Viandier* where the section of *entremets* contains a recipe for a swan "re-dressed in its skin with all its feathers" (Recipe 72): the swan is to be served *cooked*, but complete and "natural," resplendent in its white feathered coat, with all of its limbs still in place, and its head still on its neck which is shaped in the well known graceful curves. The secret of this amazing trick of re-dressing the swan appears not to have become established yet in the universal professional repertoire of chefs because Taillevent, around the middle of the fourteenth century, feels it necessary to detail the technique: after the swan is killed, a small hole is made through the skin on its breast, a hollow straw is inserted and the skin is "inflated" in such a way that it separates from the carcass; the skin, with all of its feathers, is then slit along the swan's belly and carefully removed, together with the bird's neck and wings, from the body. After the carcass is roasted, it is re-dressed in its skin (together with the wings and neck—this latter being held in proper position with small wooden pins, the *Viandier* directs very precisely), and the whole marvellous artifact is paraded before the Lord and his guests to the great delight of all.

Following the time of Taillevent, this particular procedure for skinned, roasted and re-dressed fowl seems to have remained a standard one for more than a century in preparing *entremets* for aristocratic banquets. It satisfied the banquet's demand for novelty and ostentation. The same process was followed for serving a chicken (as we have shown among our recipes, above) and particularly for a peacock. With its tail spread out and displaying all its glory, a re-dressed peacock produced a truly magnificent impression.

Despite the glorious visual effect of these particular re-dressed *entremets*, they both shared one rather serious drawback. Neither the swan nor the peacock has a particularly palatable flesh. Rather—and undoubtedly to the chagrin of those chefs who first elaborated the technique of re-dressing these magnificent birds—they have an exceptionally tough meat. Solicitous hosts were naturally reluctant to offer such unappetizing fare to their honored guests. To this admittedly grave culinary problem Taillevent provides his own straightforward solution: just let the roasted swan or peacock sit for a month, he says; after scraping away the mould which will have formed on the surface of the carcass, the meat beneath will be found now to be quite edible! In the fifteenth century Chiquart's master must have been a little more fastidious. What the chef of the Duke of Savoy advises in the *Du fait de cuisine* is that the canny cook be prepared to practise a little deceit: simply discard the inedible carcass of your peacock and substitute for it a succulent roast goose, which will be re-dressed in the peacock's skin and splendid feathers. One imagines the added delight of each guest, ready to gnaw at a sample slice of this classic *entremets*, who discovers beneath the gorgeous plumage the tasty tenderness of steaming goose-meat!

But Chiquart was a master of the *entremets*. By the beginning of the fifteenth century the courts of Europe vied with one another to present at least an air of sumptuousness. At the height of a lavish feast an *entremets* called for all the skill and ingenuity that a chef, or a whole corps of chefs, could muster. The *entremets* became quite literally the *pièce de résistance* of any banquet, the creation by which the nobleness, the munificence, and hence the glory, of the host could be measured.

Chiquart describes a particularly prodigious production for which he was responsible at one time, an invention whose basic structure was a battlemented Castle of Love borne from beneath by four concealed servants. In each of the castle's four towers—each lit from within by a torch—was a different culinary marvel: a fire-breathing boar's head, a great pike in three sections, each cooked differently, a fire-breathing roast suckling pig, and our old friend, a re-dressed swan, this one likewise breathing flames. In the courtyard was fashioned a fountain (from which spouted wine for the guests) and a dove-cot containing every variety of cooked game-bird; beside the well stood a re-dressed peacock in brilliant array. The courtyard with its central fountain represented the Garden of Love; concealed under the castle, musicians, both instrumentalists and singers, charmed the audience with appropriate love-songs. Around the outer walls of the courtyard a series of other marvels—a hunting scene moulded out of meat- and bean-paste—provided an endless source of wonderment for those before whom the platform was paraded. Incidentally, this was to be no idealistic fairy castle: beyond its walls was painted a rough sea from which an army in ships was in the process of attempting to storm the fortress— shooting arrows, scaling the walls on ladders, and being violently repulsed by defenders on the towers—all of which with as much realism as could be imagined! What a pleasure for the guests themselves to demolish such a castle by actually consuming it, one succulent morsel at a time!

For Chiquart the *entremets* was a matter of food at the service of drama. In later centuries the *entremets* actually did become a sort of dinner theatre with an elaborate setting and actors (both of which were, alas, inedible).

Such extravagance, architectural, visual and gastronomical, was highly esteemed in the banquet halls of fifteenth-century aristocracy, but it enjoyed no place in the mundane menus of that Parisian bourgeois, the author of the *Menagier*. His *entremets* are entirely practical—modest descendants of the earlier, traditional, even incidental dishes which demanded of the chef only a slightly greater degree of thought and perhaps skill than was regularly required by the ordinary dishes of a meal. *His* suggestions for this sort of preparation include frogs' legs, snails, summer sausage, fried parsnips, flans, rissoles and crepes, as well as the various porridges found in the *Viandier*.

In producing your medieval meal you are of course perfectly free to adopt any *entremets* you wish. Using meat-paste, or on lean days bean- or pea-paste, these being the clay, bricks and mortar of the medieval culinary sculptor, you can shape virtually any object you can imagine—subject only to the limitations of your imagination and your budget. Or you may want to make use of one of the more colorful appetizers (such as the Boar's Head or the Pike in Three Ways). Or you may feel inclined to take your inspiration from Chiquart's Castle of Love and attempt a scene that combines both sculptured figures and more conventional *entremets* dishes, all within some sort of inclusive framework. The only rules to the game are that your creation should be largely edible. And deliciously so! Remember: there is no record that medieval cooks ever had any difficulty disposing of the uneaten portions of their *entremets*!

Here are two of Chiquart's *entremets* from his Castle of Love.

a. *Hures de cenglier*
(*Du fait de cuisine*, §10)

En la basse cour aura au pié de chescune tour: en l'une de les tours, une hure de cenglier armee et doree lanczant feu; d'autre part ung grant lucz, et ce lucz sera cuitz de troys manieres: le tiers du lucz sera frit devers la queue, et l'autre tier du mielieu sera boullir, et l'autre tier de la teste sera rusti sur le gril; et lediz lucz sera assiz au pié de l'autre tour en regardant dehors de la beste gectant feu. Or fault adviser le saucery dudit lucz a quoy il se douibt mangier, c'est assavoir: le frit avecques orenges, le boully a une bone sauce verd que soit aygrete d'un pou de vinaigre, et le roustz dudit lucz se doibt mengier a verjust verd qui soit fait de oyseille.

a. Boar's Head Roasted

Chiquart does not provide his reader with instructions for preparing a boar's head as an *entremets*. The procedure must have been relatively commonplace; even the neophyte chef having to consult the *Du fait de cuisine / On Cookery* would undoubtedly have been familiar with the various steps to follow in its preparation. He would have been aware of precautions to take, for instance to prevent the animal's ears from burning (wrap them in wet cabbage leaves). Our "recipe" here, though modern, comes in part from the very long tradition from which Chiquart himself and his immediate successors benefitted; in part, too, our recipe benefits from our own somewhat more modern experience.

Chiquart directs that his Boar's Head should be *armée et dorée lanczant feu*, that is, with it tusks still intact, glazed and breathing fire. We can fulfil one of his requirements: an all-purpose recipe for glazing is printed below. The other two stipulations are certainly not impossible nowadays, but may take you a little more time if you really want to keep Chiquart happy: the method of endowing an animal with fire-breathing capabilities is outlined among Taillevent's later (and largely inedible) *entremets*. Clearly you will have to decide whether you want a classic apple-in-the-mouth style of boar's head, or a more modern, not to say high-tech, version of the *entremets* in which the boar's maw will spout flames!

There is some chance you may encounter difficulty in finding a boar's head to begin with. Of course an artificial Boar's Head can be fashioned out of papier maché or self-firing clay. We have settled for a pig's head, generously donated by a local meat-processing plant. If you go with the pig, the fabrication of the boar's tusks is your own affair! You might try making them, as well, out of papier maché—just as the author of the *Viandier* suggests for the fearsome fangs of a lion in another of his *entremets*.

General directions

1. Wrap ears in foil with dull side in.
2. Remove eyes, close lids.
3. Prop jaw open with a stick.
4. Sit head on its neck on baking sheet while roasting.
5. Bake at 250°F/120°C for 2 1/2 to 3 hours. Cool.

Glazing

Imperial	Ingredient	Metric	Directions
2 tins	consommé (20 oz/ 545 mL tins)	2 tins	**Heat consommé.**
3 tbsp	unflavored gelatin	45 mL	**Dissolve gelatin in cold water. Add**
3 tbsp	cold water	45 mL	**to the consommé.**
			Bring mixture to a boil & cool.

Pour the mixture slowly over the top of the cooked boar's (pig's) head, covering all parts of the head. If necessary, brush the glaze on with a soft pastry brush.

Use cherries or olives in the eye-sockets if you wish. Remove the stick from the mouth and insert either an apple—the classic presentation—or a cloth soaked in camphor which may be lit at the appropriate moment. (In the case of this latter presentation, it would be prudent to have a fire extinguisher discreetly on hand!) Decorate with bay (laurel) leaves, parsley, or other natural herbs so as to suggest the boar's existence in the wild. Give free rein to your imagination—and to that of your guests.

You may wish to add a final touch of humiliation to your ferocious animal by piping around its ears and snout, and wherever you wish to create a highlight. Take 1/2 lb/250 g of shortening, beat it and spoon it into a piping bag.

b. *Lucz cuitz de troys manieres* / A Pike Cooked in Three Ways
(*Du fait de cuisine*, §10)

One of the principal *entremets* that Chiquart incorporates both into his Castle of Love and into a "lean" banquet that his master, Count Amadeus, offered in 1400 to his father-in-law, the Duke of Burgundy, was the interesting trisected fish whose parts are prepared differently, then assembled and served on a single platter. With the fish Chiquart serves three different sauces, each intended respectively for a particular third of the fish.

The pike was a favorite fish on medieval French tables. Its size and the firmness of its flesh made it very suitable for this *entremets*, though the modern cook would have a fair amount of leeway in choosing a substitute for Chiquart's pike. The fish should be eviscerated and washed, but its head and tail should be left on, of course.

Chiquart's threefold treatment is as follows:

The Head Third: Roasted on the grill; sauced with Green Sorrel Verjuice. This is made by crushing three or four large sorrel leaves in a mortar; mix with 1/2 cup/125 mL of water, and strain.

The Middle Third: Boiled; sauced with Green Sauce which is tangy with a dash of vinegar. A recipe for standard Green Sauce is presented on p. 118, above.

The Tail Third: Fried; sauced with oranges. Chiquart serves another fried fish, sole, with a sauce made of sorrel verjuice made with orange juice. It seems reasonable to propose that the fried one-third of our pike is served with either sliced oranges or an Orange and Sorrel Verjuice (see p. 213).

When the cooked fish is reassembled on a serving platter, some of each sauce is poured over the part for which it was made, and the remainder is served in separate bowls for dipping.

From the *Viandier* come several other interesting possibilities for various *entremets*. A few of these, in particular the older and simpler ones, are copied into the *Menagier*. The frugal bourgeois, however, has a very clear idea of those preparations that are so complex or expensive that he does not consider them even feasible; it would not be appropriate to transcribe them into this cookery guide he is drafting for his young wife. At one place, he writes only several lines of the *entremets* called Stuffed Chickens, Colored and Glazed, then he gives it up, saying, "But there is too much work in all this, and it's not the proper job for the cook of a bourgeois or even the cook of a modest knight." Similarly, after writing only its title he dismisses the following *entremets*, for Stuffed Shoulder of Mutton, with the comment (in Latin), "The same thing here, because all they amount to is effort and labor." For the *entremets* of *Herissons* / Hedgehogs (recipe "**d.**" below), made with mutton rennet, he writes that the dish involves "great expense and great work" but that it results in "little honor and little benefit. Therefore, there shall be no recipe for them here."

Taillevent had another class of consumer for his imaginative work, though. Working for the King and Queen of France, he was furthermore privileged to enjoy relatively unlimited funds. Some of his *entremets* anticipate the elaborate architectural structures that Chiquart would undertake for the Duke of Savoy a generation later; but some are entirely practicable by any modern cook with means that are just as modest as those of the *Menagier*'s author.

c. *Coqz heaumez* / Helmetted Cocks
(*Viandier*, §196)

Toward the end of the Middle Ages, there developed a love of playful subterfuge in the kitchen and dining hall. In directing the cook how to prepare his re-dressed swan, Chiquart draws great relish from advising him to substitute a roasted goose for the tough carcass of the swan. This sort of food game, making the prepared dish seem to be something other than what it was, became a popular source of inspiration for the *entremets*. Ground meat-paste was modelled into the shapes of birds and animals. Thin slices of veal were given the form of larks.

In the "dish" known as *Coqz heaulmez* / Helmetted Cocks, a cock is set upon a piglet, representing a galant knight astride his graceful charger. For the preparation of the piglet, see the recipe for *Char de porcelez en rost* / Stuffed Roast Suckling Pig in the chapter on Meats, p. 156, above. For the upper part of this *entremets*, the proud and plumed knight, it is enough to read a translation of the *Viandier*'s text:

> [Get] roast piglets and such poultry as cocks and old hens. ... The poultry should be stuffed—without skinning it, if you wish; it should be [glazed] with an egg batter. And when it is glazed it should be seated astride the piglet; and it needs a helmet of glued paper and a lance couched at the breast of the bird, and these should be covered with gold- or silver-leaf for [*that is,* if the dish is to be set before] lords, or with white, red or green tin-leaf.

For the glazing on the chicken we suggest whisked egg yolks.

The distinction in the choice of decorative materials between those for dishes to be served to aristocratic diners on the one hand, and those intended for consumption by persons of a lower social status on the other, is seen constantly in medieval *entremets*. Here, as usual, gold and silver are reserved for the most exalted in society; tin-leaf, painted in cheerful colors, is good enough for everyone else. For your knight's helmet and lance, to be added after the bird is stuffed, roasted and glazed, you can pick up colored foil at any craft store.

d. *Herissons et Potz d'Espaigne* / Hedgehogs and Spanish Pots
(*Viandier,* §§210 and 211)

Chop raw meat as small as possible; mix seedless grapes and crumbled rich cheese together with fine spice powder; get sheep cauls, scald them and wash them thoroughly— though not in water hot enough to shrink them—and fill them with the chopped meat, and then sew them up with a little wooden skewer.

If you wish to make Spanish Pots, you must get little jugs such as earthenware water pitchers, and moisten them on the inside with egg white so that the filling will stick better; then fill them and set them to boil on the fire in a pan or cauldron; when they are well cooked, take them out and let them drain; when they are cool, break the pots and do not disturb anything. Then get slender spits—not so small as for the Hedgehogs; and you should make little meatballs and put them on skewers in rows of two or three; then glaze them with a flour batter.

These two *entremets* are copied one after the other in the *Viandier* because they use the same minced-meat mixture. Generically, they belong to the category that we might call "meat-paste artifacts," although a little more technique is involved in making them than simply sculpting or molding the paste by hand.

For the Hedgehogs, the *Viandier* uses sheep cauls (stomach linings) which are stuffed with a meat-paste in order to create simulations of the animals in the dish's name. We suggest that you use sausage casing. The small animals are then mounted on a spit, glazed and roasted. Any left-over meat-paste will be formed into meatballs and likewise roasted on the spit.

A detail overlooked by the *Viandier* is the important touch which will give the hedgehogs their characteristic appearance: the animals' skin should be pricked with slivers of almonds before they are set to roast. An English version of the preparation supplies the missing step: "Take blaunchid Almaundys, & kerf hem long, smal, & scharpe, & frye hem in grece & sugre; take a litel prycke, & prykke the yrchons [French *herissons*: 'hedgehogs'], An putte in the holes the Almaundys, every hole half, & eche fro other; ley hem then to the fyre . . . ."[4]

An *entremets* in the *On Cookery* (f. 36r) consists of these small animals (which have become marmots in the Savoyard collection) served with a Almond-Leek Sauce (see p. 132, above).

e. *Lait lardé* / Larded Milk
(*Viandier,* §200 and *Menagier,* p. 224; §259)

Set milk to boil on the fire; get beaten egg yolks, then take the milk down off the fire, place it on some coals and pour the eggs into it. Should you wish it for a meat-day, take rashers of bacon, cut them into two or three pieces and put them with the milk to boil; and should you wish it for a fish-day, you should not put any bacon into it; but add in wine or verjuice before it is taken down in order to make it curdle. Then take it off

---

[4] Thomas Austin, *Two Fifteenth-Century Cookery-Books*, London (Oxford University Press), 1888, p. 38.

the fire and put it in a clean cloth and let it drain, and wrap it in two or three layers of
the cloth and squeeze it until it is as hard as beef liver. Then put it on a table and cut
it into slices the size of the palm of your hand or of three fingers; interlard them with
cloves, then fry them until they are russet-colored. Set them out garnished with sugar.

This preparation is fairly common in early recipe collections. Although they seem bland, fried
slices of Larded Milk qualified as a satisfactory *entremets*. The dish does indeed become quite
tasty with the cloves and sugar. See the full recipe for this dish in the chapter on Egg Dishes,
p. 240.

Further possibilities for *entremets*

f. *Entremetz plus legiers* / Easier Entremets
(*Viandier,* §219)

You could make platforms of coarse bread, and represent a damsel sitting on the
platform, which platform should be covered with tin-leaf painted to look green and
grassy; and you need a lion that will have its two front paws and its head in the lap
of the damsel. And you can make it with a brass-lined mouth and a thin brass tongue,
and with paper teeth glued in the mouth; and put camphor and a little cotton in the
mouth and, when it is about to be served before the lords, set fire to this. If you wish
to represent a wolf, a bear, a zebra, a serpent or any other animal, whether domestic or
wild, they can be done in the same way as the lion, each in its own fashion.

g. *Alouyaulx* / Little Larks

For the full recipe of this dish as an Appetizer, see p. 88, above.

h. *Faulx grenon* (*Potage party*) / Mock Meat

For the full recipe of this dish as a Poultry Dish, see p. 202, above.

i. *Tortres parmeysines* / Parma Torte and Parma Fish Pie

For the full recipe of these dishes, see pp. 175 and 223, above.
The manner of presentation chosen by a cook often transforms a more or less standard dish
into an *entremets*. What matters here above all is the decoration of the top of either Parma pie.
With the proper colorants and metal foils, an artist could represent the coat of arms of an honored
guest on the pie's surface (as Chiquart suggests), or implant a miniature heraldic banner in that
top crust (as the *Viandier* suggests).
The side crust of the Parma pie should be extended vertically by 2–3 in/5–8 cm and crenel-
lations cut out in order to give the appearance of a battlemented tower. This makes an impressive
display when paraded into the banquet hall on the shoulders of costumed servitors.

6. Table Manners

"Sit up straight!" "Don't talk with your mouth full!" "Wipe your lips before you drink!" Such commands are common enough in households with young children nowadays, but we should not assume that the behavior of previous generations of children escaped the attention of their elders at mealtimes. The modern code of table manners has been many years in the evolving.

During the late Middle Ages a number of authors tried to define proper behavior at table by compiling lists of such injunctions. Most of the "rules" in these lists would be quite familiar to anyone in the twentieth century—and the need for them would certainly be apparent to any modern parent.

It was an age then in which young members of aristocratic families were often sent to spend several years in the household of a noble, normally someone who was a more powerful member of the clan to which the parent himself belonged, or even the parent's liege lord. There an adolescent would observe proper social behavior, would practise it and, one way or another, would become acculturated by serving the lord according to the courtly rules of this model household. This was a period of aristocratic apprenticeship during which the youngster was expected to learn the skills and graces of the class into which he had been born. An important part of this class training consisted of what he learned about civility at the dining table.

The oldest French behavior manual was composed early in the twelfth century by Hugh of Saint Victor (in Latin and translated into French in the fifteenth century). It is perhaps not strange that this work was intended for cloistered monks, those individuals whose isolated society required rules to ensure that every aspect of their daily existence be rigidly set. Very soon after this, other "educators" addressed their treatises to aristocratic lay readers who might be anxious to learn the proper ways of behaving at a royal or noble table. And soon after that, it is clear that copies of these code-books were being bought by members of the literate bourgeoisie who were apt to want it to appear that they possessed the refinements and social poise of classes ordained to be superior to them in rank.

Several books of manners became relatively well known and well read in the French Middle Ages and Renaissance: *Les Contenances de table / Behavior at Table*, Rabbi Moïse Sephardi's *Chastoiement que li peres ensaigne a son fils / Admonition of a Father Instructing his Son*, Erasmus' *De civilitate morum puerilium / On Good Manners for Boys*, and a succession of Latin and French works each called simply *Civility*. An English variation on the theme is contained in a work called *Stans puer ad mensem / The Youth at Table*. To a large extent, whether in Latin, French or English, the books tended generally to repeat much the same injunctions; in this way they built from generation to generation upon previous works and created the corpus of a true code of social behavior.

In an effort to ensure that the guests at your medieval meals will behave themselves in the best of a very long-standing tradition, we have provided at various points throughout our medieval cookbook translations of the couplets found in the fifteenth-century *Behavior at Table*.[5] You may of course take them as a practical resource—and a useful one, we hope.

One of the best thirteenth-century French writers, Jean of Meung, instructs a bourgeois house-wife on her duties when she will have the occasion to offer a formal dinner.

It is proper that her behavior at table be fitting. But before coming to sit, she should be seen moving throughout her household so that everyone is aware that she is attending to all matters: let her come and go busily, then sit down last. She should even have everyone wait for her a little. And when she is seated she should, if possible, serve everyone; she should be the first to cut the bread and to pass it around her, beginning with her tablemate with whom she will share a bowl. In front of him she should set the thigh or wing of fowl, or in front of him carve beef or pork depending on what is served, whether it is meat or fish. She should not be chary in this serving, if she is able. She should be careful not to moisten her fingers up to the knuckles with the broths, and that her lips not get smeared with sops, garlic or grease; nor should she stuff her mouth too full, nor take too large bites. Only with the tip of her fingers should she pick up the morsel she dips into the Green Sauce or the Cameline or Jance; and then she should bear it carefully to her mouth so that not a drop of the broth or sauce drips down her front. Likewise she should drink carefully so that not a drop falls, else she will be looked upon as vulgar and piggish. She should refrain from reaching for her goblet while she has a morsel in her mouth, and she should always wipe any grease from her mouth—at least from the upper lip, because if there is any grease there, drops of it will show up on the wine, which isn't very pretty.

She should take only small sips; even if she is thirsty, she should not guzzle in a single gulp from her goblet or cup, but rather in small sips, and often, so that others will not say she is swilling down greedily. She should not swallow the rim of her goblet as many wet-nurses do who are so simple-minded and gluttonous that they pour their wine into their belly as if they were filling an empty boot. She should avoid becoming drunk, because neither a drunk man nor a drunk woman can keep private counsel; besides, when a woman is drunk she can no longer protect herself; she prattles her thoughts and is open to everyone's advances. She should keep herself from falling asleep at the table: it is really improper, and too many indecent things happen to those who let that happen. It doesn't make sense to doze where you should be awake; many who do so end up falling to one side or the other, or backwards, and break their arm or ribs or crack their head. Let her always bear in mind Palinurus, who when he was awake steered Aeneas's ship well, but when he fell asleep he dropped overboard into the sea and was lamented by his companions.

(*Romance of the Rose*, ll. 13,355–444)

In the thirteenth century also, Robert of Blois, a courtly, didactic poet, wrote a more general

---

[5] Stefan Glixelli, "Les contenances de table," *Romania*, 47 (1921), pp. 1–40; specifically pp. 33–40.

book a manners intended specifically for ladies, the *Chastoiement des dames / An Admonition to Ladies*. The work amounts to a sort of code of worldly etiquette for the guidance of proper ladies seeking a dignified place in refined society. Among its far-ranging counsels we find, for instance, recommendations that proper ladies avoid both intemperance of speech, at the one extreme, and mute silence (which might be mistaken for haughtiness), at the other, that they speak with a clear, mellow voice, and that they not swear (or at least not in public). The author thoughtfully inserts several hints of a personal, beauty-care sort: cut finger nails closely, correct a pale complexion by eating and by drinking wine early in the day, correct bad breath by eating anise, cumin, fennel or coriander; and so forth. Then he passes on to the the following durable pieces of advice which fall into the conventional category of table manners. Most of them clearly derive from earlier sources:

> don't laugh too much at table
> don't speak too much at table
> don't take the best pieces
> don't take too large pieces
> don't take too hot pieces
> don't dip your food into the salt cellar
> don't pick your teeth with your knife
> keep your elbows off the table
> wipe your mouth before drinking
> wipe your nose before drinking
> don't let your nose drip
> don't blow your nose noisily
> don't scratch yourself
> wash any fruit before eating it
> don't hasten to swallow your bread before the first course is served
> don't speak or drink with your mouth full
> don't reach across in front of your neighbour to serve yourself

In reading these early books on table manners we become aware just how long a tradition has shaped modern notions of table etiquette. The modern concern with *proper* behavior in civilized society is not a recent phenomenon. We can glimpse in the Middle Ages a growing consciousness among some people that one's behavior in public reflects one's worth. Refined manners are a sign of refined breeding. The dining table afforded the wealthy host an opportunity to display generosity and hospitality. But it also placed an obligation upon the guest to demonstrate, by following the rules of proper manners, that he or she was worthy of partaking of the host's generosity and hospitality.

Appendix

A Day in the Life of Master Chiquart Amiczo, Chef to the Duke of Savoy (1416 A.D.)

1. Morning and Dinner
2. Afternoon and Supper
3. Evening

1. Morning and Dinner

Master Chiquart Amiczo[1] normally rose at about 6 A.M. The little Chapel bell on the far side of the castle courtyard rang prime at that hour a little more persistently than it rang the previous hours, perhaps just to remind the sluggards that no further delay in their rising could be tolerated.

Since he had received his appointment as Chief Cook of the Duke's Kitchens Chiquart had, in unconscious stages, allowed himself to lapse into habits that in his younger years he (or his master) would have called slovenly. Nowadays he would certainly not have tolerated such lax behavior in anyone who occupied less exalted a position in the Duke's household than that of Chief Cook. Yet, even so, for that very evidence in himself of a double standard he felt an even more acute pang of guilt.

By now in his long and wholly venerable career Chiquart had, by any really objective assessment, earned the right to roll over in bed at least once after prime had rung. Through years of faithfully striving to warrant the trust of the Grand Master of the Household, the Chamberlain and the Duke himself, he had surely earned the right in turn to put a little trust in those who worked under his authority in the kitchen's hierarchy. It was this handful of individuals whom he had carefully instructed in their duties the night before, and who—he had every right to expect—had awoken and risen this morning a good half hour earlier than Chiquart himself.

Through the thick boards and beams of the floor under his bare feet came the reassuring murmurs of voices and occasional muffled clatter of pots and heavy kitchen cutlery. Oliver, Young Jean and Martin would already have chopped the lamb shanks that had been selected and brought from the larder last evening. The boy Fernand would be fanning a small handful of heather in the large fireplace, the ritually minute beginning of a fire that would blaze, with greater or less intensity as required, for the remainder of that day. As soon as he had the first logs carefully placed and ignited in that fireplace, Fernand would turn his attention to the fire under the great

---

[1] In this fictional "day-in-the-life-of" a late-medieval court cook, we call our principal character "Chiquart." We do this primarily because the cookery manual of that eminently historical figure affords us more in the way of concrete historical evidence about a cook and cookery at this time than any other contemporary document. Unfortunately the physical site of Chiquart's day-to-day activities between roughly 1400 and 1435, the castle kitchens at Chambéry in Savoy, can no longer furnish us with as authentic evidence about the actual circumstances of his life and work. The imaginary "home" castle where *our* fictional Chiquart works in the narrative that follows is modelled after Villandraut Castle constructed by Pope Clement V (1305–1314) on his estate near Bordeaux, or (if you will) Bodiam Castle in East Sussex, England, which was begun in 1385 and was being built probably during the very years of Chiquart's professional apprenticeship. Likewise, much of the relationship here between Chiquart and those with whom he must have had daily contact is speculative; the persons themselves are entirely imaginary.

brick-lined wall oven, and then to the two lesser pottage fires in the split fireplace directly across the great kitchen floor from the large fireplace. In the cant of the Kitchen these smaller pits had from time immemorial been called the pottage fires even though in recent generations they had been more used for frying and grilling operations than for heating stew-pots. Such was the force of habit: names became so attached to things that no one ever questioned their pertinence.

Bernard, his second-in-command and the person responsible for all the kitchen activities—along with its discipline—whenever Master Chiquart was absent, would be slicing onions for one of the large flat-bottomed pots. Two of the scullions would later hoist it onto a trammel-hook and swing it in over a pottage fire when that fire was ready. And so the day's dinner would have begun.

Chiquart gave his torso a hasty wash, then drew on his rough cotton shirt. It fell loosely over the trousers that he had bound with a favorite colorful braided cord about his waist. Later he would bind his apron about him; it still hung, down there in the kitchen, on its peg above his chair. He caught himself almost thinking "his throne," knowing full well that the scullions, with some sarcasm—their own private in-joke—had given that name to his chair, raised as it was on a minuscule dais in a corner. But despite the august popular designation, that chair rarely felt the weight of Chiquart's bottom in the busy course of a day. The freshly washed apron would probably continue to hang above it until he set about the work he had reserved for himself, the great Parmesan Pies.

Before leaving his chamber he stepped into its narrow window embrasure to glance out the open, unglazed slit. On the eastern horizon an orangy pink glow promised a bright day. The rich color gleamed on the calm mirror of the moat's surface. He promised himself he would find an excuse, when the twenty-six dishes of dinner had safely been taken care of, to walk the circuit of the castle's moat. Spring had made itself be waited for long this year. With bright new flowers sprouting more and more in the fields, with the cheery chirping of early-morning birds, Chiquart felt the need these days to get away from the incessant smoke, heat and bustle of his kitchen, if only for a brief moment. He needed to hear, feel and smell the cool clean freshness that was being brought by Spring.

While his was certainly one of the most important positions to which a person could be appointed in the Duke's service—and he was very aware of the enormous dignity, and the even greater responsibility, of his office—there were still times at which Chiquart longed to take a break from all the supply contracts, receipts, reports, accounts, inventories, discipline, regulations, obligations, pressures and tensions. That's what this most exalted post of his sometimes seemed really to be: smoke, sweat, stress and all too frequent frustration. But only sometimes did he feel overwhelmed by it all. Most often he experienced a great satisfaction when he finally made it through to the moment when all of his planning for a meal had brought about the satisfactory conclusion of its last dish. At such times he thought he enjoyed a dim insight into the satisfaction experienced by God Himself when He considered His six-days' labor and realized that it was good. Of course those absolutely perfect meals, those moments of profound satisfaction, did not come as often as Chiquart might have wished; but even so, when they did they were good.

And most particularly gratifying, of course, were those times when the Duke made a point of complimenting him on his work. In the last couple of years he seemed to enjoy more and more of the Duke's personal attention, and this was certainly flattering. Yet even though his position at present might be considered exalted among the large body of those who wore the Duke's livery, he was still very much aware that, just like the very least of all of them, he lived only for the Duke's pleasure and, in a real sense, only *at* the Duke's pleasure.

Chiquart left his chamber, crossed through the small dormitory of a few of the kitchen retainers, littered still with dishevelled pallets, and descended the narrow wooden stair into the Pantry below. Immediately, automatically, he was aware of the absence of Albert, the Pantler. Albert, a fussy, self-important ancient, should normally have been busy at the buffet there, checking through the stacks of fabrics or the six or seven thousand serving vessels in pewter, silver and gold with the keeping of which he was entrusted. The innumerable bolts of cloth had a wide variety of uses in the kitchen and on the serving and dining boards; the metal platters and bowls "belonged" in the realm of the Kitchen because they received the cooked food first, though this might later be transferred to more suitable table vessels. One of Chiquart's duties in the course of the day would bring him back officially to the Pantry in order to receive from Albert a statement on all its current stocks. He knew from long experience that Albert's reckoning would be meticulously accurate. Now, where Ricardo was concerned, ...

The Pantry was empty. Chiquart's sense of responsibility was tweaked, both for Albert's sake and, vicariously because this apparent fault lay with his underling, for his own. He checked Albert's work. The lead-lined bins along one wall seemed amply supplied with the three types of bread: good white table-bread, coarse trencher bread and dry cooking bread. The candle racks had a good stock of stubby tallow candles, suet tapers, and pure wax tapers; and a glance told Chiquart that Albert had replenished the stand of torches so that it now held fifty or sixty of the tarry reed fabrications. With the increase in daylight, candles and torches were less in demand throughout the castle. Albert could afford to take things a little more easy in the matter of candles until next September. But that still didn't explain what had happened to him at that moment.

From the Pantry, with its dull glint of silver plate and its confused scents of fresh yeast breads and pork fat in the tallow, Chiquart passed into the kitchen proper. This was a large, very-high-ceilinged room of almost square dimensions. It lay across the full width of that wing of the Duke's castle. Along its right wall, as Chiquart came from the Pantry, and really dominating the whole room, lay the magnificent great fireplace, a fifteen-foot-wide recess in the wall, lined with heat-resistent red brick laid on edge. Its generously deep hearth was paved with the same brick. Over the opening, its massive stone hood was borne on corbelled projections on each side. A good fire was beginning to blaze there in three split logs set across the massive andirons. A dozen or more logs, each the height of a man and the thickness of his thigh, had been stacked neatly out of the way to one side.

Two very tall windows, too narrow to contain mullions, reached high up, almost to the wall-tops on each side of this great chimney. Across the room, opposite the great fireplace, another pair of tall windows framed its much lesser counterparts. A fifth window, hardly more than a hatch, was located at waist-height in the outer wall opposite the Pantry; it did indeed function less as a window for light than as a hatch for the disposal of "clean" garbage into the moat. The four lofty window-openings, unstoppered except during the bitterest winter storms, would later admit a good light throughout the whole room. And, very much more to the point, the good supply of fresh air that usually flowed in through them would be appreciated by everyone who would be laboring there. Right now the kitchen was still chilly with the cross-flow of night air; but, as the natural rule of thumb had it, the cooler any day began in the kitchen the less hot it was apt to become during the day's work. Besides, all cooks and kitchen workers learned very early in their careers to put up with extremes in their working environment: it was usually very smoky, very hot, very humid, very noisy and very busy—through a very long day.

Chiquart's kitchen was still dim. Only the newly-set fire in the large fireplace and the flicker of a stout tallow candle in an iron dish suspended on a chain from the murky rafter peak illuminated the four or five figures grouped about two of the three big tables in the centre of the room. The third table was the serving table, always kept scrupulously bare and clean under Chiquart's rule except when in actual use for the dishing-up of preparations.

At a small leather bucket on a peg by the door he filled a leather cup with wine and slaked his morning thirst. It was a mixed local red and, Chiquart thought, long past its prime. It was probably Vernetello, the thrifty Kitchen Clerk, who had had Robert use it up in this way. But it was still cool from the cellar, and certainly better than the vinegary white the lads had been given last week. During the day every worker in the kitchen would come to the bucket over a dozen times to replace what was lost in running sweat. Before the day was out Robert would attentively refill the bucket five times with cool wines from his underground domain—even if they were very far from among the best there. With the coming of summer's heat and increasing thirst among all of the kitchen help, he had better remind Robert that a discrete watering of the supply would be apropos.

Albert was not among those semi-ghostly figures chopping and slicing at the tables—and Chiquart would have been very surprised to see him there. A Kitchen Pantler does not labor with the scullions, whether under the direction of the Butcher, the Poulterer or the Larderer, let alone frequent them. Though he and Chiquart could clearly remember the days when Albert did chop, grind and stir as vigorously as any of those scullions, as Kitchen Pantler Albert had earned with his title a certain dignity that removed him from anything as menial as actually *working* at cooking. So much the worse, Chiquart thought, when anyone attached to a kitchen didn't know when to pick up a pestle or to put his hand into a warm stewpot to keep a mixture from settling.

He stopped Bernard who was carrying a large shallow basket of onion rounds to one of the kitchen's iron kettles that were set out on the edge of the great hearth.

"Good morning, Master," Bernard greeted him.

"Where's Albert?" Chiquart croaked hoarsely, then cleared his throat and repeated his question: "Where's Albert? He's not in the Pantry."

"He was earlier," Bernard replied, carefully layering onion slices across the bottom of the pot. A deliciously sapid odor permeated the air around him like a pungent cloud. To the onions Bernard added a ladleful of clarified pork fat from an old battered vat that had been installed almost permanently on a low stone step to one side of the fireplace. "I didn't see him go out. Maybe he's in the Buttery."

On the face of it the proposal seemed unlikely in the extreme. Animosities were as common in kitchens as elsewhere, and Albert the Kitchen Pantler was not apt to share any more time with the Kitchen Butler than he strictly had to.

Chiquart moved over to the twin hearths in the opposite wall of the kitchen. The slight figure of the twelve-year-old Fernand was squatted in front of a small heap of tinder heather and twigs. By striking a light bar of iron against a piece of flint the boy managed to ignite a dry fern that projected from the heap; he then blew gently on the feeble glow until a dainty flame grew out of the glow. Suddenly he became aware of Chiquart standing behind him and jumped up with embarrassment.

"It was only for practice, sir. Mr. Bernard said there wouldn't be any rush for these pottage fires this morning, sir. I'll replace the tinder."

Chiquart smiled. The boy's anxious apology reminded him of a long-forgotten episode from the time of his apprenticeship when he had "borrowed" a yard of filter-cloth to try the effect of its coarse weave with potash in a scouring basin. "Replace it, then, before tomorrow morning," he said to the boy, consciously trying to insert a patient, gentle tone into his voice. "And make sure there are enough spills in the box, or speak to Bernard about it. Did your flint work well?"

The boy beamed, having lost his timidity. "Oh, yes sir. I've been working at my striking the flint—just in case I should ever have a chance to go with the kitchen crew to one of our Lord's outer castles, or go out on campaign. I want to be able to strike fire smartly and surely, so all the cooking fires can be ready when they're needed, sir."

"That's fine, boy," Chiquart approved. "You may have your chance sooner than you think. But see that the flint and iron go back in their box. The oven fire is drawing well?"

"Yes, sir. Master Schroeder told me he would need it by terce for empty pie shells. I did it first, and used a spill from the chapel candle to do it."

"Fine. See to the fuel next. And for these pottage fires no damp wood, mind. It must all be well-seasoned and burn evenly without any smoke. No smoke at all."

"Yes sir. No sir."

Chiquart turned just as the sought-for Albert came into the kitchen from the Buttery. A very long, plain towel draped from his left shoulder, back and front, a cherished symbol of his Pantry responsibilities among the Duke's silver plate. The white towel made Chiquart think of an ecclesiastical stole, and beside Albert's gaunt, sanctimonious visage the comparison was strangely not out of place. Before Chiquart could open his mouth Albert, seeing him, launched into an angry, breathy protest.

"Robert took a length of boulting cloth again! Just took it! I've just spent half an hour trying to make my count tally. I knew my stock was out a length and I just couldn't find it and I've looked high and low and recounted twenty times. Then I remembered light-fingered Rob there and came to check and what do I find but my missing length all befouled with ropy Burgundy. You've got to have the Seneschal punish him. He can't go on making off with goods that other offices are responsible for. What am I supposed to do now? There's no way my lads can clean all that wine stain from the cloth. And, Master, you yourself keep harping on how filter cloth has to be absolutely white. It's enough to make a man do murder. And I'd gladly dump his body into one of his precious vats in his cellar!" Then, a peroration in a paroxism of outrage: "My boulting cloth!"

At the back of his mind Chiquart sighed about the prospects for the day when it began thus—a day whose dawning, as he had seen it from his chamber window, had seemed so promising. The only feature that saved the moment for Chiquart was the fleeting image in his mind of grave, feeble Albert actually "doing murder" somehow to the strappingly muscular Robert, Robert who spent his day wrestling with tuns of wine and casks of cider and stacking them in his gloomy cellar as if they were a child's building blocks.

"I'll speak to him about it later. If he was in the wrong I'll speak to the Seneschal. But there are other things to take care of first."

"But the missing length on my inventory," Albert persisted. "What am I to do about my count?"

Chiquart felt like blurting an expression of his frustration with Albert's petty worries, but thought better of it. Albert's strutting self-importance and the magnified sense of responsibility that he was forever brandishing like a banner were often too much for Chiquart. But on the other hand he would be the last to denigrate any sign of fidelity to one's task. His kitchen itself could not operate without every single worker in it having some similar sense of responsibility. Nor could any office in the whole of the Duke's household. Every individual in that household, all those who wore the Duke's livery, those who wore the Duchess's livery and those whose nobility had given them a sinecure appointment to their various positions of authority—everyone accepted along with his position an obligation to carry out the responsibilities of that position to the best of his or her ability. The word "duty" had often interested Chiquart; its Latin etymology related it to what was "owed," and it was clear that everyone, retainer or noble, owed the Duke his or her very existence. Any question of work inevitably came down to a matter of responsibility. Albert could not be seriously faulted *just* for being too responsible.

In a sense, too, Albert had been right with his invocation of Chiquart's insistence on clean linen—even though Chiquart had initially been miffed at the terms Albert had used. Chiquart did set out rigorous rules that governed the conduct of the affairs of his kitchen. The same rules held for all of the offices that pertained to the Kitchen: Pantry, Buttery, Bakery, Spicery and Larder. Everyone knew that his standing orders and regulations were strict and that in the case of any serious infringement of them the Master Cook would not hesitate to seek severe punishment for the culprit at the hand of the Duke's Seneschal. If there was anything Chiquart would not tolerate, it was shoddy, dishonest behavior. He *could* not tolerate it. His kitchen fed the Duke, his family, his guests, all of the numerous personnel of his court and household. Chiquart had on several occasions prepared meals for the King himself, and princes of the realm, and the Duke and Duchess of Burgundy, his Master's in-laws, whom many claimed were more important potentates than the mere King and Queen of France! Someday he might even be required to cook for the Pope; more wonderful things had happened than that.

When his responsibilities included the safety, the pleasure and the glory of the Duke of Savoy, no chief cook could put up, among his own workers, with less than absolute integrity and an absolute devotion to their duty. A pilferer, an apprentice-butcher, long-suspected but only recently caught in the act with a leg of lamb he thought he could smuggle past Chiquart's chair by the door, was summarily traduced to the Seneschal, accused, condemned, imprisoned, relieved of three fingers by the Duke's Captain, and ejected from the Castle. The poor fellow's young family, whom Chiquart had met, would be even hungrier now. But surely any organization required such authoritative management. People like Albert, with a keen (if keenly proclaimed) sense of their responsibility toward their office were vital to the welfare of any organization. Chiquart, too, fully accepted his very important link in the chain of authority-with-responsibility in this household. If only Albert wasn't so tedious in exulting in his own responsibility.

Barely hiding his exasperation he finally said to him, "Oh, mark that length on your inventory as having gone to the service of the Kitchen. We'll get it back from Robert in time and use it to bundle alms at the end of the day."

Albert was only partly appeased. His animus toward the Kitchen Butler had been robbed of a clear-cut chance of satisfaction. There was little more that he could do, though, because Master Chiquart's word was more or less final here in the kitchen, no matter what the offence or the circumstances. With a grumbling he crossed the broad flagged floor and disappeared into his realm of bread, candles, plate and cloth.

Much later, in the lull between dinner and supper, Chiquart would have the job of examining Albert's daily inventory, along with those of each of the other Kitchen offices. Albert's, he knew, would be an exemplar of neatness and precision, but the others, each different in the way of the chief of that office, would have their own virtues and flaws. Their reports would contain a financial schedule of expenses approved and incurred for each office as well as submissions for projected future costs. Chiquart would spend his normal hour examining all these reports and accounts, judge their accuracy and respective merits, combine them into one, on behalf of the whole Kitchen, then along with Vernetello take them off to the Clerk of Accounts Office. Although this rendering of the Kitchen accounts, and the subsequent defence of the statement and proposals in the presence of the Duke's Master of the Treasury, used to intimidate Chiquart when he was young and a novice at his post, he now knew that his honesty and meticulousness had earned him a certain respect among the supreme officials in the Duke's household. And even, he felt sure, with the Duke himself.

Such respect did warrant a little egotistical pride, perhaps. Provided he kept the thought of Albert's sort of arrogance as a reminder of the sinful dangers of any excess. In fact Chiquart *was* proud, but hoped that he always managed somehow to turn this pride back into his work, into the conscientious efforts that his craft as cook demanded. To be the Chief Cook of the Duke of Savoy called for supreme and unflagging exertions in order always to deserve that very honor with which he had been privileged. Above all Chiquart strove to be an honorable and worthy Chief Cook.

At the main mortar, a two-foot cube of granite hollowed of most of its volume, Hervé paused to scoop a mush of almonds onto a filter cloth whose corners were tied to four cords. When the bottom of the mortar was clear of the mush, he wiped his hands on the cloth, filled a wooden measure of shelled almonds from a sack, and set to once more with a hardwood pestle that was the size of a man's leg and many times more solid. Chiquart noted that the almonds still had their skins.

"You have finished with the two hundred pounds for the Parmesan Fish Pies for Dinner?" he asked Hervé.

"Yes, Master, over there." He nodded to the near end of the central table where Chiquart would supervise the composition of the pies' filling. "This is the one hundred and fifty for Supper. For German Broth, I think." Hervé was a squat, muscular man who always made Chiquart think that some compressive force had transformed a normal man's height into powerful arms, a sturdy torso and tree-trunk-sized legs. He wielded his large pestle as if it were of unspun wool rather than of the densest elm, and would continue throughout most of each day to pound, up and down, up and down, with a sustained regularity that awed everyone else in the kitchen. If it wasn't almonds, it would be walnuts or some other nuts, or leeks for *poree*, or chunks of meat or fish. The light was still too dim to see Hervé's face but Chiquart knew there was probably the beginnings of a smile there. He had often speculated on that smile which, as the day wore on, became more and more fixed like a rictus on a half-wit. Yet no one ever saw him passionate about anything, either happy or angry. And most amazingly, even on the hottest days of summer, with all the fires blazing for a great dinner, and for all his straining arms and back, Hervé never sweated. The pestle persisted in its rhythmic, unhurried, unbroken pounding, yet Hervé never sweated.

"The Larder was short on its pinenuts," Hervé said.

"Short?"

"They brought only four-score pounds—two sacks. You had said six-score."

Chiquart checked under the centre table and found the two sacks. Then he came back to the mortar. "I'll see about the rest. Don't do any onions or garlic until all the nuts are finished. You'll contaminate the milk." He knew that a more sensitive worker would be thinking, "Yes, yes. You've told me that a hundred times before!" He could never tell what Hervé might have going on behind his smile.

It occurred to Chiquart that before leaving Hervé he might still venture another general directive, a practical hint he remembered his old Master Antonio passing on to him when he was still just a beginner. "And when you are told to grind bread and spices in your small mortar for a sauce, always remember to do the spices first and empty them out, and then grind the breadcrumbs after so they'll pick up any residue of the spices." Hervé may have nodded as he hoisted the pestle and let it fall. Chiquart had turned away.

An irregular chopping started up in the far corner of the kitchen where Oliver butchered with his half-dozen youths. Chiquart had noticed that Oliver's help tended to be young, in their teens or twenties. He worked them hard to make up the orders that Chiquart had calculated the day before for his department, and whenever the current job was done he would immediately set them to other interim chores such as sharpening their great knives and cleavers or rasping and scrubbing the surfaces of the edge-laminated tables and blocks on which they carved and hacked. Chiquart always thought of that corner of the room as being a model of efficiency for the rest of the kitchen. Yet the butchery help were a cheerful lot. In an organization that was composed of smaller organizations, the Office of the Butchery showed perhaps the most cohesion of all those composite parts, its members the most playful among themselves and possessing the most *esprit de corps*. The joking and playfulness didn't seem to hurt the work of that Office at all. Provided, Chiquart thought, that it was kept under control.

Oliver himself was a tall stooped figure of a man, only a little younger than Chiquart, surprisingly taciturn, firm with his lads but knowing when to turn a blind eye to their practical jokes. He always gave them a model of dedication to work, rising with them and working just as hard with them throughout the day. In the growing light of the room Chiquart could not mistake the huge hump of his rounded back over the butchers' worktable.

"Do you and your lads not need a torch, Master Oliver?" Chiquart asked from the end of the table. A mound of skinned hares was perceptible in the centre of the table. Everyone was engaged in the next stage of preparing the meat: eviscerating, cutting and chopping. From all around the table the offal was flung with surprising accuracy into the dim rim of a basket on the floor to one side. It would be incorporated into a Hastelette before the end of the day. "The summer daylight hasn't come yet to our mornings."

"No, that's true enough, Master. But no man who knows which end of a knife to hold" —Oliver clearly meant no competent butcher— "needs good light to skin a hare, which was our job 'til now. Let Albert keep his torches."

"When you get to deboning the salmon and pike . . . ."

"There'll be daylight enough by then."

As if to prove the point, a cleaver pounded, a hare's head and feet arched rapidly through the air and plunked softly into the basket; more sharp thuds and four legs and two half-breasts of a hare were scooped into another basket in the middle of the table. The mound of whole, skinned hares was shrinking.

"You wanted only half an ox with the two sheep?" Oliver inquired.

Chiquart had been thinking of Oliver's long-standing worry about the supply of hares. He wrenched his mind back to the roast and boiled joints of meat which would begin the day's dinner. "Yes," he finally said. "That should do. Sir Thomas said the two lords of Madoc and Marmora were leaving this morning, so that means ten fewer at the Lord's Dinner. Probably a total of 30 to 35 if no one else shows up. With the commons. Say 140 in all. The half-ox and two sheep should be safe for the first serving, particularly with the game fowl of the second."

Oliver said nothing. He seemed busy with the hare he was currently gutting. With his Butcher, Chiquart always felt inclined to justify his estimated needs of meats, ready for some questioning of his guesses but rarely getting any from Oliver. He never had any idea whether Oliver agreed with his estimates or whether he simply was content to shrug his massive misshapen shoulders, to get on with his butchering and leave such guesswork to his superiors.

"I'll still need herons with the partridge and pheasants for the second serving. Can you give me maybe ten herons at the same time?"

"That's after the capons?" Chiquart nodded. "Yes, I have dozen hanging. No heads?"

"No heads."

"That's faster. You'll have them."

As Chiquart turned to leave, a scullion panted to the table bearing a wicker basket filled with thick sausage coils.

The imperturbable Oliver was clearly irritated. "No, not yet, boy. Tell Hugh I don't have room here. Bring them later. I'll call for them."

"Mr. Hugh says he doesn't have room either, sir," the boy puffed. "Something about the new bacon, sir."

Oliver's heavy knife clattered to the table. He straightened up, partially. "Well you just tell that master of yours ... ." Chiquart intervened. "I have to go in there. I'll see what the trouble is. Set your basket on the floor there, boy. And cover it with a cloth. You know you're not to carry anything around the kitchen without a cloth over it."

"It's happening more and more, you know," Oliver protested to Chiquart. Hugh doesn't have space for his stores and he tries to move them out before they're needed. And we don't have space here. Just where are we to put things we're not working on?" He appealed to Chiquart with a gesture around his corner of the kitchen. Shelves laden with baskets, bowls and colanders rose up the two walls out of sight; pegs and hooks at eye-level were hung with cleavers and saws and rasps. On the floor the offal baskets were beginning to encroach on the passage to the corner tower and its well. "If Hugh needs space, we need it more."

First Robert, now Hugh, Chiquart thought. Both problems were long-standing, and had been calling for some sort of resolution for some time. He realized he had not dealt effectively with either in the past. Well, he might as well tackle Hugh now; the proper movement of supplies was much more crucial to his kitchen than merely a petty misuse of those supplies.

From the high-ceilinged cavern of the kitchen, its cool overhead space sparking now with motes of dust stirred into the earliest beams of sunlight that penetrated its eastern windows, Chiquart ducked through a broad low doorway that led to the Larder. If there was a design flaw in the Duke's newly completed castle, it was certainly here in the Larder. When Richard the Mason laid out his sketches on parchment twenty years ago, Chiquart's elderly predecessor could not have noticed how little room had been reserved for this function—or else he had simply lost out in a competition for space with the hostelry. The stable wall had compressed the Larder to little more than a dead-end hallway. Chiquart could imagine old Antoine, with or without Vernet who was the Kitchen Clerk at the time, stooped in front of the Master of the Household, trying to argue against the demands of the Marshal. By that time in his life Antoine was much racked by the lung sickness and could barely utter two words without coughing. He had become a sad shadow of the robust chief under whom Chiquart had learned most of the craft of cookery.

The Larder measured perhaps four arm-spans by ten arm-spans, and its ceiling was at the same modest height of the stables which lay beyond the partition. The room's two longer walls were lined with laden shelves; stacked bales and bundles left only the most constricted passage down its middle. Beyond the far narrow end was the Bakery where much the same amount of space seemed almost generous for Schroeder and his two assistants. Compounding the space shortage in the Larder, between the two offices the oven backed part of its warm rounded rear hump between the kegs of salted herring and the crates of stockfish. The domain of the Larderer was choked, incredibly packed with all sorts of vegetables, fruits, cheeses, herbs, grains, spices; it seemed only Hugh could ever hope to dig out the variety of items that a cook might call for in a day.

A single window sat low in the wall of the narrow courtyard end of this room. This window admitted some light and virtually all of the foodstuffs that would eventually make their way into the kitchen. Hugh was forever complaining about the relative awkwardness of passing sacks and bundles and carcasses in through the window, but Chiquart knew that questions of security always dominated the thinking of any Master of the Treasury or Master of the Household: this access had been designed as it was because such a window could be more securely barred than a doorway.

Hugh was not among the bales and bundles of this cramped room, but the Larder extended below ground as well. Immediately inside the window, tackle hung from a beam over an open trap in the floor. Chiquart swung onto the rungs of a ladder there and descended into the murk of the castle's cellars.

At the foot of the ladder the rough stone wall on his right again delimited the realm of the Marshal and his stables: Richard the Mason had rightly insisted that the Larder should have absolutely no communication with any other part of the castle. A small torch lit the doorway from the first small chamber into a series of low, massively vaulted rooms that ran back under the kitchen proper. A diminutive terrier appeared out of the gloom, sniffed at Chiquart's leg, whined quietly and disappeared again. To one side in a very cool chamber, hung innumerable clutches of game birds and domestic fowl along with the skinned carcasses of freshly killed animals. Ahead, to each side of a narrow passageway, was where the bulky sacks of grains were stacked. And here, with a lad holding a brighter torch for him, was where Hugh the Larderer was presently occupied with his inventories. A minute mound of wheat lay beside a stack of bags.

"Still the rat problem, Hugh?"

"Worse than ever, Master," Hugh grunted, as he leaned in to peer behind a heap of bags of milled oat flour. "The Kitchen Clerk may be right, it may be the late spring has driven them all indoors. Though it's beyond my ken how they ever get across that moat. All we need is swimming rats!"

"They swear by hemlock over in Dijon, I hear. Put hemlock bows between bags. And even burn some from time to time: just dampen them and let them smoulder. They say they don't have nearly the number of rats now."

"Then they don't have the same rats as I do. These bastards would chew on the hemlock and cast spells in the midst of the smoke. Even our terriers are afraid of them and cower off to a corner when they smell one. I lost the better part of a sack of semolina grain last week." Then, with a sharp voice that revealed his frustration: "Hey, you, get out of there. You'll get yourself wedged back there and nipped by one of my fine rats. *Then* I'll hear from her Ladyship."

Chiquart knew immediately whom it was that Hugh was addressing in such tones. The Duke's four-year-old Phillip had recently made a habit of wandering into all of the areas of the Kitchen, just to watch the men at work or to see whatever it was he could find. Other small children in the castle had the same curiosity, but Chiquart and officers like Hugh hesitated to swing a switch at Phillip's bottom as they regularly did with the others who were constantly getting underfoot.

"Can you not at least persuade the Master of the Household not to store grain in the castle," Hugh was asking him. "I'm spending half my labors nourishing the healthiest colony of rats between Rome and Uppsala!"

"No, he's still adamant. We have to maintain supplies in case of any attack. It's a matter of policy, he says, and I don't dare push him on it. He has already made it clear it's none of my business."

"So it's just between him and the rats, then? I wish he'd speak with them himself. I'm tired of all the one-sided conversations I've been having with them." And Hugh added in outrage: "And they *bite* my dogs—as if they didn't get enough to eat without dog-meat, too!"

Chiquart could see no solution to the eternal, insoluble problems of rats and defence policy, so he passed to the more practical problems at hand.

"What about pinenuts?" he called out, because Hugh was pursuing his other concerns of inventory. "Hervé is short. He found only two bags. Is the third still coming?"

"I'm out. I told you last week I was low. That's the last." Hugh's voice, from somewhere behind a boarded bin of loose wheat, seemed to express a shrug of indifference that Chiquart found a little annoying. All the more annoying because Hugh was right; he did remember now that Hugh had warned him to look into a shipment that was past due. Other worries had displaced that one from his consciousness.

"The order still hasn't been delivered?"

Hugh came into the torchlight again squeezing around the far corner of the bin. His hand was firmly on the shoulder of a lean little urchin in a grubby yellow silk smock. "It was for one thousand pounds. To be delivered two weeks ago. I cleared a space upstairs."

"Who is the merchant? Still Nardoccio?"

"He's done well for us in the past. On time, exact amounts, fairly good quality. I haven't seen him or his men recently to ask about the pinenuts. And he hasn't made good on his promise to get pomegranates, either."

"I'll try and find out what's gone wrong."

"Tell him to watch the filberts he handles. The last lot had a mould on the shells. Maybe you didn't see the shells then."

"He may not be supplying the Duke with anything at all if he doesn't have a good excuse for the pinenuts." Then a thought occurred to Chiquart. "It might be better to speak to Vernetello yourself when something isn't delivered at the time it should have been. He can look into the matter better than I can." Vernetello was the Kitchen Clerk, the person who bore the responsibility of maintaining all the accounts and handled orders for the Kitchen; officially and formally he was the link between Chiquart and, on the one hand, the Accounts Office and Treasury, and, on the other, the Master of the Household. Because of the respect Chiquart had earned over the years, though, the latter link had become much less formal and both the Chief Cook and the Master of the Household were content to have it so. "I'll tell Vernetello about Nardoccio this time."

"Well, I mentioned to him our problem getting sea-fish—you know, the cod and turbot you needed. And I haven't seen any improvement there. Better luck with the nuts." Then, an afterthought as Chiquart turned, "Here," said Hugh, "you can have our Prince."

With Phillip's tiny hand in his own Chiquart made his way in semi-darkness back to the chamber at the foot of the ladder. His Parmesan Pies would have to do with two-thirds of the pinenuts they should have had, it looked like that's all there was to it. He hoisted the child ahead of him on the ladder, then, in the Larder, lifted him into his arms in order to step over the low window sill into the bright courtyard.

"So what is your nursemaid doing this morning?" he asked the bright young face. "As little as normal, is she?"

"Annie didn't want to come see the doggie. I came when she was busy with Catherine. Catherine doesn't like doggies either."

That, thought Chiquart, was likely, Phillip's sister Catherine being barely at the toddling stage. Anne de Beaumont, the young ones' nursemaid, was hardly the most conscientious of persons. As a daughter of nobility herself, her position at court of Savoy was surprisingly humble, not the sort of job to which a person of some aristocratic rank, and a distant relative of the Duke to boot, would be expected to be assigned. But all of the household's liveried retainers speculated, if they couldn't outrightly see, that the poor girl was lacking more than half the intelligence that should by rights be allotted any normal person. In taking on the Duchess's three youngest as her charges, Anne de Beaumont became in turn in a certain sense herself a charge of the Duchess her mistress. The noble clan thus took care of its own.

"See, there's Anne and mummy and Catherine." From the far side of the quadrangle, the sunlight glimmering on its rounded paving stones, the first two called out to Phillip with something that may have been relief.

Chiquart set Phillip down on his feet and with a pat on his bottom sent him scampering off toward the women.

The Chapel bell clanged for terce: nine o'clock.

In the kitchen there was much more activity. The central tables were now heaped high with cloth-covered mounds of pieces of hare, legs and breasts of capons, the rounded lumps of pheasants, partridge and herons; around them a dozen men worked with skewers and spits. The two pottage fires blazed brilliantly. There two large pots, each with a capacity for thirty chickens and water, were suspended at a height such that the tallest flickering flames were just bending around their curved bottoms. Bernard was directing the addition of red wine to the boiling water. At the end of the table closest to him he had a man chopping the herbs (sage, parsley, hyssop, marjoram) which would be added to one pot as soon as the capons went in. At the other side of the room Old Jean with two others was lifting the first spit of the day and seating it securely into the spit-mounts standing in the great fireplace. A muscular youngster squatting at one end began immediately to crank the spit with steady regularity. The long wrought-iron rod held a dozen joints of mutton which caused it sag slightly in its middle.

Old Jean, who was perhaps 40 years of age, had been so baptized by the Kitchen in order to distinguish him from the other Jean who worked under Oliver the butcher and who may have been five years younger. The Older Jean was Chiquart's roaster, the man whose experience had taught him exactly how much heat was necessary to cook every sort of meat, whether on a spit or on a grill, that had to be cooked over an open flame. He now stood back and studied the sag in the spit with a critical eye. His helpers set a second spit behind the first.

"It's the moisture gives the weight, you know," he said to his chief at his elbow, by way of explanation. "As they dry the spit straightens."

"It's still too much, Jean. Where will we be if our long spits get weak in the middle from bending back and forth? Take off a piece or two and spread the rest away from the middle." The helpers left their work of loading two other long spits and came to make the adjustments Chiquart had suggested.

Fernand, stripped now to his waist, had spread the logs the full length of the spits, keeping them separated just enough that their burning never gave out an intense, leaping flame that would sear or burn the meat, and adding fresh logs in time to keep the fire going at the proper constant heat. By the end of the day Fernand's young face would be blackened and his eyes red almost with the glow of one of his fires. Now he was forever threading his way back and forth across the kitchen to feed each of the blazes he was responsible for. A battered bellows of two thin planks joined by a membrane of supple leather helped persuade a denser length of wood to give off just the right heat of flame the cook needed. When the lad could spare a moment he checked that the more sedate conflagration under the oven was getting all the fuel it needed to reach around to its flue. The brick encasing the oven would have to be thoroughly heated to full temperature by quinte, an hour before the first preparations of dinner would be dished up and leave the kitchen.

Chiquart went to the middle of the central table. There he quickly checked across the baskets of herbs and various fruits that were stacked there and found that Bernard had directed the Larder well. He went to one of the pottage fires and peered through the steam at the bubbling brew of fish in a cauldron; tuna, carp, pike and eels, half a dozen of each, they swirled to the surface and disappeared like some densely packed piscine school in frothy agony. There would be very many more vats of those tomorrow, a lean day. Using a long two-tined fork he speared a whole pike, laid it on a board, chopped its head off with a cleaver and examined its flesh: if the pike was almost done, which it was, then the others should be right. He called to two of his apprentices, Andrew and Jeannet, to swing the fish out from the fire and to place them on his table; the fish broth should be skimmed and half of it put into an earthenware jar for the supper brewet.

He called Martin over from Oliver's corner and together they set to on the fish and eels, skinning, filleting, slicing. He knew that he could have entrusted the Parmesan Fish Pies to Bernard, who as his Assistant had in fact made both them and their meat equivalent on occasions when the Chief Cook had to be away. But Chiquart felt he still needed to be involved in the actual cooking in his kitchen. To become simply a director was somehow to become less of a cook, to be only a sort of authoritative advisor only slightly different from Vernetello, the Kitchen Clerk. A cook had skills as well as knowledge, but he kept those skills only by using them.

And so he strapped his fresh apron around him, stood with Martin at the massive oaken table in the very centre of the room and chopped off fish-heads and tails. Then he set the raisins, prunes, figs and dates to soak in large pot of red wine; he chopped the herbs—parsley, marjoram and sage—and called on Hugh's lad, Valerian, to fetch more parsley. Meanwhile Martin worked on the pinenuts, which had to be culled and chopped coarsely, the almonds which Hervé ground and which Martin then sieved and strained with thin pea puree to make three jugs of almond milk, and the sugar, which he rasped coarsely from its cone and then pulverized. Chiquart sliced the eight thick boiled eels lengthwise into four score slabs which he laid in a very little oil in large two-handled pans to fry over one of the pottage fires, watching them and flipping them himself. As each panful was done he emptied them into a flat basket and called for a clean cloth to cover them. When he was finished with the pan he had the scullion boys take it off to scour at the stone sink in the tower scrub-room.

Chiquart himself meticulously poured the powdered spices from their leather bags and combined them—the beige of ginger, grey grains of paradise, black pepper, reddish-yellow saffron, russet cloves—each according to its strength and nature and according to the final effect Chiquart knew the mixture should have. Then he added a flask of clear well-water and white wine to the large bowl, stirred with his hand until all but the coarsest particles had dissolved, and poured the tawny, runny paste through a boulting cloth into another bowl.

In an hour all the ingredients for the Parmesan Fish Pies were ready and incorporated in four large earthen bowls: the pieces of fish fillet, broken small, the chopped, wine-soaked fruit and pinenuts, the savory herbs, the steeped spices, the three flasks of almond milk, wheaten starch, oil and sugar; a small sack of finely-ground salt sat near at hand. Chiquart sent Martin to Schroeder for the pie shells.

The shells came immediately, still warm and laid out snugly on four broad planks, each shell a fore-arm in diameter, five to a plank. Since they were only a hand's width in depth they did not need to be in a pan: Schroeder was skilled in making a very sturdy dough that only rarely burst apart in the oven. A pair at a time, the planks were suspended just over the middle of the table where Martin and Chiquart filled them, scooping handfuls of the mixture from the bowls and adding a little salt. Then on top of the mixture in each pie they laid four slices of the fried eel. The bakery assistants brought the score of top pastry rounds which they and Martin proceeded to fix neatly in place on each shell. Then Chiquart passed a cloth soaked in almond milk over each top surface; when they were damp, he sprinkled half of each pie top with sugar while Martin sprinkled the other half with ground cinnamon. He resorted to this Italian practice of garnishing a pie with cinnamon and sugar because he had discovered yesterday that the Larder had not been able to procure pomegranates—or their seeds. Again that merchant Nardoccio, who tended to promise more than he could deliver.

Still on their planks the pies were draped with fresh cloths from the Pantry and borne over to shelves alongside the oven. They would have less than an hour more to wait until it was time for them to bake.

At his worktable Chiquart called to the scullery lads to clean up. Three of them gathered up the used linens, the various bowls and knives and the baskets. Whatever was dirty was carried off to the scrub-room in the corner tower. One lad scrubbed the table with a rasp and a brush and bucket, removing any trace whatsoever of fish or fruit. The Chief was extremely fussy about cleanliness, and woe be it to anyone who did a less than thorough job of cleaning up.

Every single worker in the kitchen complement, all 37 of those who had a right to wear the Duke's livery, was busy at quarte. By quinte, with an hour to go until the first course of dinner was due to begin being dished up, their activity had become brisk and vigorous. Bustling would be too mild a word for the pace of their labor because, though very busy, it was above all efficient. The roasters tending the joints, mounting them on spits, turning them, removing them, had stripped to the waist and were now running in sweat that glistened in the gleaming flames. But sweat, after all, was merely the costume of the roaster, the intense heat of living fire his very life. This heat radiated throughout the kitchen and smoke from the wood and from dripping mutton fat swirled from under the hearth hood and billowed toward the vent at the rafters' peak. Oliver's crew were now working on chicken livers and the sausage—finally delivered—chopping and grinding. At the main tables in the middle of the floor men still sliced salted bacon and bread for the Savoy Broth. Youths carried shallow baskets of chopped meats to the tables, and deep baskets of ground herbs to pots that had been swung to simmer over the pottage fires. Fernand continued to lug chunks of firewood that looked to weigh half his own weight, and to place them just where their flames would be needed when they fully caught.

Chiquart checked on the Frumenty as it bubbled sedately in a bronze kettle to one side of a pottage fire. The deer venison, cut into small slabs, had boiled directly over the same fire; Bernard had been seeing to that. The men chopping leeks, beet tops, spinach and other greens for the Green Poree were nearly finished and about to dump their mounds of brayed leaves into a stew pot along with vinegar and water. He saw Albert the Pantler with great dignity deliver his precious plate to the various Offices, then he visited the Bakery to make sure that the wafers were indeed being put out on their two dozen silver platters, ready to be brought to the dressing tables when he called for them; he looked in on Hugh in the Larder to check that the assortment of fresh nuts was in the proper pewter bowls; he made sure that the spiced candies and the candied sesame seeds were already in their gold boxes on the kitchen buffet. He would have been happier if he could have provided fresh fruit for Albert's deep silver bowls, but even the Duke conceded that April was an awkward time of year for fresh fruit.

Finally he went into the Buttery to confirm that the various wines and hypocras were all ready to be delivered to the Hall Butler and his men at the moment they were required. This room, Robert's Buttery, was the counterpart to Albert's Pantry which lay on the other side of the main kitchen alley, though it was slightly smaller because it had to share the space with the fuel depot. Where in the Pantry a range of responsibilities was ministered to, here only one predominated, immediately obvious by the pungent, musty odor of wine. Around its walls were shelves and pegs holding a vast array of leather pots and dippers, of pewter flagons and long-handled spoons, of thick sheets of cork, wooden bungs of all sizes and squares of brown- and purple-stained fabric, small skins of tanned leather, sets of funnels, strainers, mallets, dozens of spigots of all models, and mysterious supple leather bags of assorted powders. Along the foot of the wall opposite the window lay a row of kegs on a pair of sturdy sills, their spigot cocks occasionally dripping into earthenware saucers as if, like some liquid hour-glass, they were measuring the languid time of vintage.

Squatting forlornly in a dusty corner was an apparatus consisting of a large pot-bellied copper kettle on stubby legs, with large and narrow tubing twisting and bending from its top. A merchant could now supply a better quality of distilled wines for both kitchen and pharmacy, and at no much greater price than the cost of the best wines themselves that had to be used. If Chiquart had had the keeping of the Duke's disused alembic he would have shrouded it decently with an old cloth for the inefficient, superannuated servant that it was.

Robert, the Kitchen Butler, was on a three-legged stool at the rickety table that he used as a desk whenever he brought his inventory up to date. The other chiefs of the various Kitchen Offices,

Albert in particular in his orderly Pantry, managed to keep all of the details of their respective inventories in their memories; that skill was merely part of their work. Robert, a fairly young, squat, muscular man who looked as if he might have been a professional wrestler if he hadn't chosen instead like his elder brother before him to wrestle the Duke's huge tuns of wine, had a peculiar flaw in that he could not remember from day to day exactly what stocks of which wines, vinegars, musts, verjuices, ciders and juices he had on hand. His memory had not always been so faulty. But Chiquart had seen from month to month that Robert was depending increasingly on the little scraps of paste paper that he scavenged from the Duke's Secretariat and on which he inked out a private shorthand of squiggles and codes.

Only rarely yet, though, did Robert err in his accounts. But Chiquart noticed that, though formerly the most placid and cheerful of young men, Robert was showing signs of greater impatience with himself, and a growing tendency to outbreaks of frustration. Chiquart noticed, too, that he was spending more and more time down in his cellar reviewing the row after row of stacked barrels and casks.

The mullion-free window, affording the same means of stock delivery as for the Larder, located just across the angle of the castle courtyard from the other, admitted the bright beams of the full mid-morning sun. Robert wore his usual heavy leather apron that reached to his knees. In the direct sunlight his gleaming blond hair, tied back in a knot, framed a creased brow.

He cast a bewildered, almost frantic look on his Master. "According to my last count I should have a total of seventy-three and a half tuns of special reds, Monterosso, Vernaccio, Osey, Rochelle, Malmsey, Teorduijn and Rinische. What with the partial casks I have counted only sixty-nine. Yet I *know* I haven't drawn that much of those reds since last week. There were barely two score flagons delivered to the Hall Butler on Wednesday, and he confirmed that this morning. I'm short and I'm going mad. I'm ready to believe it's leaking out of the casks and into the moat."

"You've allowed for the smaller measures, the Brugge *loth* and the Paris *sestiere?*"

Robert was too preoccupied with his mystery to take offence. "Yes. And the *mezeruola* that the rest of the Monterosso is in. It just doesn't add up any more." He shook his head plaintively.

Chiquart decided that his own concerns of the moment had precedence over Robert's worries, which he was inclined to think were apt to be imaginary in any case. "You're still alright with the Romania and the Spanish Bastard for dinner tomorrow, and with the Greek Moscatello for supper, tonight and tomorrow?"

"Oh, yes. No problem there. ... I think." He leafed quickly through several layers of crumpled slips of coarse yellowish paper. "Yes, I was sure: there are still fourteen *mistatos* of Cretan Moscatello. But I'll put it on the re-order list with Mondiglia for November. We should have it again by March. You wanted Bastard for tomorrow?"

The Italian wine distributors, Mondiglia & Speroni, had a local agent who tended to be offensively obsequious in his dealings with the Duke's Buttery, but that company was on the whole efficient and had always managed to get the wines the Duke favored.

Chiquart tried to be patient with Robert. "Yes. You marked it down yesterday. There, on that sheet." Robert saw his notation and had a vague recollection of having calculated the possibility of treating two tuns of Spanish red that was beginning to go ropy, and, hopefully, of eventually mixing it with something else to make an ersatz Bastard.

"Boiled wheat, eggwhites and laser-wort, and don't disturb the dregs," he said, rather obscurely, but Chiquart understood what he was talking about. "It seems to work well. The ginger and zedoary mixture needs a richer wine than the Barcelona reds. It had better work: at the rate the Duke is having Bastard served, and not just to his own table, I'll need more by the end of next month."

Suddenly he jumped to his feet. "The Romania!" In one sudden move his sinuous short body dropped gracefully down through the hole of the trap as if the ladder there had no rungs. Chiquart followed, somewhat more sedately.

If the smell of wine was strong in the Butler's office, in his cellar it was overpowering. Robert was no longer in sight, but Chiquart was familiar enough with the tortuous alleys among the racked barrels that he could follow the receding sound of Robert's passage. Everywhere he could sense nothing but barrels stacked on their side to the ceiling with neat regularity, barrels, kegs, casks, firkins and butts that varied in size from two-gallon caskets to 64-gallon tuns whose two-hundred-and-fifty-pound mass the Kitchen Butler and his occasional lad manhandled with block and tackle through the trap door and rolled into place on their racks in this cellar. At the far end of the wide room Chiquart knew there bulked the two enormous upright vats of local reds, each capable of containing some 1600 gallons. They had been constructed of the best oak by master coopers twelve years ago where they stood and, because of the weight of their volume, they had to be cinched about with iron bands that Chiquart remembered being bent around and rivetted by the Duke's blacksmiths. The making of those vats, floors, staves, top and bands, had been the work of seven weeks for the coopers and smiths and their apprentices.

Few of the casks or barrels in the cellar had been broached, yet the evaporation of wine that had perspired through wood was such that Chiquart habitually expected to splash blindly into a puddle at every step. But the beaten earth of the floor felt dry. He knew that Robert had conscientiously placed leather-lined wooden trays beneath any defective barrels; he knew, too, that when it was Robert who tapped a barrel, the spigot rarely leaked. Yet the organic mildew of the wines was palpable in the air. Though the castle could still be called new, the stone walls, columns and low, arched ceiling of its cellar were already ripe with a dark growth of vinic fungus. It was almost as if the vaulted stone room held the wine just as directly as all the cylindrical wooden barrels that were in it.

He caught up to Robert in a back corner as he bent peering by the flicker of a small torch at charcoal figures written on one barrel-end. The Butler straightened and tapped on the barrel in several places with a short hammer. His face bore a look of bewildered dismay.

"I thought .... I'm sure there were eighty *mezeruole* of Romania. Eight barrels. They *were* here!" He looked at the solitary, half-empty cask in front of him, as if it could be accused of having consumed seven of its fellows. Then slowly he turned a full circle, seeming to will his eyes to penetrate all the stacked barrels about him and to carry his sight into the most distant blackness of the room. "Unless .... I think we may have moved them .... When the Burgundy came in ... there were forty barrels of it and we .... Yes, ..." With sudden alacrity Robert's short strong frame darted off down a side alleyway and disappeared between stacks of barrels. Since he still had the torch, Chiqart was left in darkness. A dim dancing gleam on the broken vaults of the ceiling traced Robert's tortuous route across the room. Chiquart was beginning to lose patience with the young Butler.

"Look, Robert," he called after him. "It's just the Moscatello I was concerned about, for tonight." "No, that's fine. I've set out enough in two-gallon leather bottles for Sir Geoffrey." His voice, from under a dim glow on the far side of the ceiling, had a peculiar hollow echo to it, the effects of all the wood that was enclosed under the stone arches. "He likes it kept cool down here until the last moment." Then: "I've found them," he announced triumphantly.

"Good," Chiquart muttered under his breath. And louder, as he groped slowly toward the light, "There's another thing. Albert's upset that you're taking linen without accounting for it with him."

"Linen? Oh, yes. For looking at my white Tadesco. It's going off somehow. The best thing is to run some through a cloth and look at it."

Chiquart knocked his knee against a projecting support and cursed silently. "Albert was peeved."

"Albert is always peeved. It was only two aunes of the plainest thing I could find on his shelf. He wasn't around," he added, as if the Pantler's absence from his office were grounds to legitimize the filching. "And I needed it right then."

"He said it was a full length, and it was soaked with Burgundy."

Silence. "Burgundy? Oh, that was earlier." Chiquart came up to him. "It's not as if it was cloth-of-gold! And anyway, I think I gave that piece back to him. I don't have any way to wash filter cloth," he added innocently, a sort of partial apology.

"Ask him in the future. Vernetello can transfer the cost of it against the Buttery. Albert likes his accounts to balance." But Robert was already mumbling something about six tuns of Grenache and had scurried away like one of Hugh's rats, taking the torch-light with him. Chiquart felt his way toward the bright spot that marked the foot of the ladder.

Back in the kitchen he dipped himself another cupful from the wine bucket and mounted his "throne" between the Buttery and the great fireplace. From there he could survey the entire room and study the progress being made in the preparation of each of the dishes for the dinner's two courses. The last of the fowl were being turned over the flames to his right. The ten-year-old at the end of the spit was the son of Jeannet; he was a lad with a spirited imagination, forever seeing his crank as some hunting or jousting weapon in a game. At that moment it seemed to be a shield protecting him from Saracen arrows. Beyond the main fireplace Schroeder's men were arranging the lumps of a batch of trencher bread dough on a trestle in front of the oven. And again beyond them Oliver and his assistants were still trimming roasted meats, heaping their work into huge mounds on basket trays.

Across on the far side of the kitchen Bernard had assembled all of the ingredients for the hare civet and was seeing it through its last cooking beside one of the pottage fires. A big kettle sat on a hearth trivet opposite Bernard, covered; Chiquart knew that it held the hot mess of Frumenty with which the cooked venison would be served. Sharing the other pottage fire were two cauldrons of the Savoy Broth; Old Jean had just filtered a bowl of the spice mixture, tempered with wine and verjuice, and was adding it into everything else. Billows of steam rose from the cauldrons, mixed in an swirl with the woodsmoke and was drawn back into the chimney hood. Chiquart checked the tell-tale ribbon he had fixed high in the window opening above him, and noted that a good flow of air was entering from the courtyard side of the kitchen. He saw too, with approval, that Bernard had closed the long board windows on the moat side; the kitchen would be warmer, but the fires would draw better and smoke and steam would be taken more directly up the chimneys. Though the sun had swung now to the south and its beams no longer entered the kitchen directly, there was still much more light to work by at midday than during the pale noon of mid-winter.

Old Jean came over to him and asked, "Is the Savoy Broth to be gaudy green?"

Chiquart told him, Yes. He knew he did not have to instruct Old Jean on the amount of saffron to grind, or how to allay it for the Savoy Broth. That Broth now in the cauldrons would already be a bubbling rich green from ground parsley and sage; Old Jean could be trusted to handle the saffron properly. Chiquart could imagine its deep hue brightening to the attractive, fresh yellow-green for which the Duke seemed to have such a predilection.

As slight Fernand, soot-smeared and sweaty, passed in front of his "throne," a log escaped his grip and clunked to the flagstone floor. With his young muscles straining, he retrieved it, realized the Master was there watching him, paused in a moment of embarrassment, then lugged his never-ending load off across to the pottage fires.

In the middle of the floor Andrew and Jeannet were clearing off the tables from the last dish that had been prepared there, three different sauces for the roast wildfowl. A sense of duty lifted Chiquart onto his feet again. Picking up a long-handled iron spoon from the rack of utensils on the fireplace hood beside him, he hooked it around the swivelling arm that held a pot over the fire just by the end of the rear spit. With a deft gesture he caught its lid handle with the curved end of the spoon and dipped the spoon itself into the pot's contents. He tasted. He knew that the sauce should have been Cameline, and it was, almost. He called to Valerian, who had made the three sauces; he came from the far side of the great fireplace where he was tending two other one-gallon pots similarly warming at a safe distance from the flames. Valerian took the proferred spoon, still with the iron lid swinging from its handle, and tasted.

"More ginger?" he asked.

Chiquart nodded. "The cinnamon is distinct enough but there's not enough bite there. Just a bit more ginger. The color is right, though."

A impatient shout of "Take it back! I've no room here!" cut across the kitchen. It was Oliver shouting at the hapless Larder boy and it reminded Chiquart that he was still to talk to Hugh about sending in supplies before they were called for. Well, the problem certainly wasn't new that day, and it wouldn't go away before he saw Hugh again. Maybe that afternoon, when the work of dinner was over.

Standing reminded him that his bladder was full. Either that or the rough red he and others had been drinking from the bucket was irritating something. He shuddered to think of his entire workforce writhing and lined up at the two-seat latrine by the Well Tower. It had been a horrendous day last September when some phlegmatic influence had smitten all of the kitchen help at one time. The debilitated few who had been able to remain standing at the tables and stewpots were utterly incapable of finishing the dishes on time. They made Chiquart think of an army of feeble heroes who were getting the worst of a battle fought with knives and spoons and lengths of boulting cloth against a ghostly enemy.

Could his bladder wait? Yes. He had to see the dishing up begun, at least for the first course. He checked the sandclock on its shelf by the wine bucket. It wasn't all that accurate, but was adequate in the short run. The top vessel had been refilled at the quarte bell of the Chapel; a little better than half of the sand had now run out into the lower pan. The Hall Marshal, Sir William, would be here in a third of an hour, and with him would come the Hall Pantler and the Hall Butler with their dozen servers. Dishing out of the first course must have finished by the time the chapel's sexte bell rang, in half an hour at the most.

Andrew and Jeannet had cleared and scrubbed the central table. Then they scrubbed the two tables that framed the opening of the long passage between Pantry and Buttery and that led directly into the Duke's Hall. Their brushes and rasps stood in buckets of hot water. Albert brought fine linen cloths and spread them on these two tables; together they would become the Kitchen Buffet on which the various dishes of each course would be assembled. A formal, if invisible, line was drawn between the worktables in the centre of the kitchen and what was collectively called the Kitchen Buffet: it was a line of demarcation between the domain of the Kitchen Office, that of Chiquart and the Kitchen Clerk, Vernetello, and the domain of the Hall for which the Marshal and ultimately the Grand Master of the Household were responsible. The Marshal, the Hall Pantler and the Hall Butler entered the kitchen up as far as that line, and no further. It was at that line that all the initial proving for poisons usually took place.

Albert brought dishware, mostly pewter, silver and gold platters and bowls. He set out most of the gold and silver plate upon the Buffet tables; all of the pewter was spread across the central kitchen table. The Serving Valets in their clean livery were already lining up in the passageway. Chiquart checked the sandglass again. He called to Old Jean.

"Roasts and sauces!"

All four of Old Jean's helpers lugged the rear spit with its beef and mutton to a table where all of Oliver's helpers had rushed to lay into the hot meat with knives and cleavers. One uncut leg of mutton and one uncut shoulder of beef, both for Duke Amadeus's table, were set on enormous gold platters and placed on the buffet; a selection of the better cut pieces was heaped on silver platters. Sauces were ladled into twenty gold and silver bowls. In the same way pieces of hot sausage were cut and distributed over plates. Bernard's help passed a stout pole through the handle of the cauldron of Hare Civet and bore it to the centre of the room by the table; most of the pieces of hare were set out onto plates and the broth again ladled into a score of bowls. The same was done with the two cauldrons of the Savoy Broth, and finally the green stewed vegetables. On average roughly half of each preparation—except for the sauces—remained in the pots and cauldrons, and in the wicker trays the more sinewy of the pieces of meat.

As each preparation was dished out Chiquart stood with the Marshal and Sir Simon, the Grand Master of the Household, to prove its wholesomeness, slicing bits from each meat, dipping thin fingers of bread into each of the sauces. To the Hall Pantler, Sir Reginauld, Albert delivered the assay horn from its ornamental receptacle in the Pantry. As always, the Grand Master muttered a few words of approval about the savory dishes he proved, and as usual Chiquart simply nodded his acknowledgement of this compliment.

Albert also passed a variety of other items to his Hall counterpart and this latter's liveried assistants: pillows, towels, silver and gold vessels for the Hall Buffet, silver spoons and carving knives, the salt boat and cellars. Robert brought up the wines for the first course and emptied his jugs into the silver cruets and pewter pitchers of the Hall Butler and his assistants. The Marshall organized the procession. The Chapel bell chimed distantly. The door at the far end of the passageway opened wide. The procession for the first serving moved off.

When the door to the Hall had closed behind the servers, Chiquart's kitchen help continued to dish up but this time onto very large plain wooden platters and into deep wooden bowls. A small parade of the castle retainers, members of the guard, the stablers and carters, the chamber attendants, and so on, came in by the courtyard door, picked up what Bernard directed each of them to take and, without the slightest trace of ceremony, retired quickly and wordlessly with it. For the Accounts Office, enough for thirteen; for the trades, eighteen; for the Chancellery and scriptorium, seven; for the Laundry, twelve; for the Guardroom, thirty-five; and so forth. Throughout the castle, in the guardroom or stable or attic storage areas, everyone would be eating at least something that had come from the kitchen and that had been made initially for the Duke's table. All of the commons in the Duke's castle knew that in other households, right across Europe and maybe beyond, their counterparts would be receiving a plain, inferior sort of food that had been made expressly for them and with as cheap ingredients as possible. In the matter of food, though the meat might get skimpy toward the bottom of the pot, the exceptionally generous treatment they benefitted from here in the Duke's service made them value their positions all the more.

Chiquart went to see Schroeder in front of his oven. The firedoor below was open and Chiquart could see that Fernand had shovelled out all of the coals and ash. Schroeder swung back the oven door, inserted a palette and withdrew a pie for his Master to examine. The pastry was taking on a rich golden glow and the upper crust was beginning to heave with succulent vapors.

"They will be just right," Schroeder assured him, and Chiquart agreed.

"Tell Bernard to hold back six for the Kitchen," he asked Schroeder. Schroeder grinned.

Chiquart went off to the latrine.

2. Afternoon and Supper

By midafternoon the Kitchen had settled into the work of preparing for supper. The sun had travelled around to the west side of the castle, and because the breeze had followed the sun and Bernard had opened the window boards on that side of the kitchen in order to let in the fresh flow of air, a stream of the sun's rays was entering along with the breeze.

All of the dishes of the dinner's second course had eventually been served up, the roast fowl and their sauces, the Furmenty-and-Venison and Chiquart's Parma Fish Pies. Wafers, some fruits, cheeses, nuts, candies and hypocras had followed this second course in due time as well. As soon as the procession of hall servants had returned with the remnants of the first serving, the scullions began their principal job in earnest: they scrubbed. Armed with rags and brushes at the two large stone sinks along a wall in the Well Tower, they scoured and rubbed and swabbed and rinsed. In theory Albert should have supervised them in order to keep an eye on all the silver plate and gold vessels he was responsible for, but, as it usually happened, he had been far too busy setting out more of the same dishware from his well-guarded stores for the next course. Experience reassured him.

Several bulging basketfuls of scraps had been accumulated for the Duke's hounds and for the poor. By now the Almoner with his acolyte would have carted them and an iron pot of surplus broths and sauces, mixed, across the castle's drawbridge and distributed their contents to the indigent. The large metal spoon the Almoner used had virtually become his symbol; the poor blessed the Duke's name because his Almoner's spoon slopped into their wooden bowls a much better fare than they got at the town's hospice.

So now the Kitchen worked on supper. As with dinner the menu was fairly straighforward, containing nothing that Chiquart's lieutenants couldn't manage quite satisfactorily on their own: roast meats and wildfowl, their sauces, jellied meats, a Trimollette of Partridge, cream flans, a Chivrolee of Stag (made with beef since this was after all still only mid-April) and Calaminee with Cold Sage, as well as the assortment of wafers (baked by Schroeder and stored in the Larder) and spiced candies (confected by Chiquart and stored in the Pantry) that would constitute the meal's normal conclusion. He foresaw no exceptional problems. Schroeder needed the oven for a large batch of trencher bread that would do for the next half week, but the flans could bake briefly in the residual heat from that batch. Afternoons normally afforded a conference time for Chiquart, so he confirmed with Bernard and Hugh the quantities that he had estimated the previous day and left them to the practical work of supper. In his own mind he prepared the proposals he would make for the next day's two lean menus, dinner and supper. Then he went off to find Vernetello.

Together the two men crossed the courtyard, now a little more animated with men and women taking a post-prandial stroll in the afternoon sun, grooms leading horses to and from the stables, minor officers of the court and messengers hurrying importantly on some insignificant errand, a chamber porter bearing a huge sack of dirty straw he had swept up from a floor somewhere. They made their way to the small, low-ceilinged chamber above the guard-room in the Alexander Tower. It was there in the Accounts Office that the Duke's three financial officers worked. It was stuffy, horribly cramped for space, and it was called, with grandiose irony, the Treasury. It looked more or less like what it was, an incommodious attic garret. Chiquart supposed that the amounts handled by the Master of the Treasury and his clerks of behalf of the Duke, the income and outgo not only of the castle and ducal household but of the entire duchy, must be considerable. Certainly he knew that the moneys that were spent for food and drink, daily and monthly, in contracts and individual purchases, were huge. But all Chiquart had ever seen in the Treasury were sheafs of paper, rolls of parchment, bound quires on the dusty shelves and bundled rolls standing compactly in bins. The sole responsibility of the Master of the Treasury seemed to be to keep track of figures.

Vernetello had brought the Kitchen accounts. He passed the page of coarse paper solemnly to the Master, a taciturn, self-confident Italian whose name was Luccio. Seated before a large-format ledger, quill in hand, the Master checked yesterday's actual expenses—in terms of processed foodstuffs and other materials used—against the recorded (and approved) estimates, reviewed each of the entry details that Vernetello had carefully enscribed there, rapidly verified his arithmetic, and apparently found nothing egregiously improper. He passed the sheet to one of his clerks at the sloping writing desks behind him.

"Remember that the monthly inventories of the Larder and Pantry are due next Wednesday," he said to Vernetello. He always said it at about this time in the month, and it was always unnecessary.

Sir Simon came into the room at that moment. Without a word the three men grouped themselves around a wall-mounted pupitre on which Vernetello spread out another sheet. Though the scant free space of the Treasury did not invite meetings, the schedule of the Grand Master of the Household brought him there regularly at this time and a meeting of the three persons most concerned about the castle's food had become part of their daily routine.

Chiquart's memory did not need Vernetello's list: he had already drawn up those tentative menus for tomorrow and talked it over with the Kitchen Clerk. He recited it. "Lean day. Dinner: Roast pickerel and carp, salt herrings, Red Eel Soringue, fish pies, Sops of Stewed White Leeks, Almond Milk Flans, Camelin fish broth. Wines: Romania and Spanish Bastard. Supper: salted trout and salted dolphin and rice, Larded-Boiled Tench, Gravy of Fish Tripe, Parmesan Fish Pies. Wines: Greek Moscatello."

"His Grace particularly liked the Saupiquet Fried Fish the last time you did it, Master Chiquart," Sir Simon said. "Could you work it in tomorrow? Maybe in place of the Larded-Boiled Tench?"

"Did Gregory say anything about it last time?" Master Gregory was the plump Ducal physician who lived in town but who seemed to manage to be in the Castle at most mealtimes. He was, after all, entitled to eat at the Duke's board.

"About the Saupiquet? No, only that if you boiled the fish before frying it, the dish could do no harm to anybody. He certainly didn't think it would harm *him*," Sir Simon added with a sarcasm that was not lost on the two Kitchen officers.

"How would it be, then, if we put a Russet Broth of Fish in place of the tench dish in the second course? Much the same cost, because there are fewer pike fillets. I'd use pike. We have plenty on hand to be roasted tomorrow."

Sir Simon nodded. Vernetello dipped a pen and scratched a correction in his list.

"Any need to show this to Gregory?" Chiquart and Vernetello remained silent. "Well, it won't hurt if I do, as always. Anything else?" Sir Simon looked the question first at Chiquart and then at the Kitchen Clerk.

Chiquart volunteered: "Sometime next week, say next Thursday, I'd like to do some water-fowl, storks, herons, bittern, moorhens, and the like. They should be ordered from the little man in Montrosso by tomorrow." Sir Simon nodded. Vernetello again scratched.

"Hugh in the Larder is still complaining about Nardoccio," the Kitchen Clerk stated, a little tentatively. "He says that Nardoccio sent an order of filberts that had become mouldy. But that hardly seems ... "

"He has been slow shipping pinenuts, too. Two weeks overdue. We're very low now. And he promised pomegranates back in March. He's taking on more than he can handle."

"You're suggesting a change in supplier?" Sir Simon asked.

"If the contract isn't fulfilled .... " Chiquart shrugged his shoulders to indicate the inevitable consequences. "Pomegranate seeds make a nice garnish on fish dishes, but there are alternatives. Pinenuts, though, ... if we run out of pinenuts ... "

Sir Simon turned to Vernetello. "Go see him. Let him know we're upset. Give him a warning. We can't tolerate shoddiness or missed deadlines. There are other suppliers. It won't be the first contract we've reassigned. Anything else?"

Chiquart thought that he could speak privately to Vernetello about Oliver's concern over the quantity of hares and other small game that the Kitchen was receiving. Vernetello, however, was clearing his throat about something else. "Well ... Albert has complained about Robert again, and wants me to lodge a formal grievance with you. It seems that some of his linen boulting cloth ... "

"It's a small matter," Chiquart interrupted. "I'm trying to do something about it. It will blow over." He tried to sound confident. At the back of his mind he added a prayerful reservation. Sir Simon seemed content to leave the problem with the Chief Cook.

Their conference broke up and Sir Simon went to speak with Master Luccio about other household accounts. As the two from the Kitchen went out the door and started down the spiral stone stair, Sir Simon turned and called: "Chiquart! His Grace wants to see you about the banquet. He'll probably be free in about an hour."

The banquet! Chiquart hurried back to the kitchen, but only to check rapidly on the progress of supper. As he cast his eyes around the kitchen from the doorway, he noted that the large roasting fire was back to blazing the full length of the veal and kid that were mounted along two twelve-foot spits. Old Jean and his helpers had had them on their spits and ready to be hoisted into position just as soon as the spits with with the beef and mutton had come down for dinner. Across from the great fireplace Fernand was compacting more intense blazes for the cauldrons of Chivrolee and Trimollette. Squatted on his little haunches beside the hearth and raptly following every action of the older boy was the four-year-old noble prince who clearly had yet once again evaded the lackadaisical jurisdiction of his nursemaid. Chiquart could see himself assuming another function, that of a sort of court fetch-um dog: "Go fetch Phillip! Bring him back! That's a good dog!"

He was pleased to see that Andrew and Jeannet, the simple-minded apprentices and notoriously the two worst jokesters and laggards of the kitchen, were busy at a central table chopping herbs for the Cold Sage. And they looked as if they were concentrating silently on their work; it was clear that Bernard himself must have been busy brow-beating them! Hervé was swabbing out his three large mortars; Chiquart remembered the days when he had had to watch Hervé closely and shout at him that he didn't empty a mortar and then simply reload it with next batch of things to be ground up, moistened and sieved. Everything had to be continually scrubbed and scoured; no ingredient residues, no dirt or smoke contaminations, no foul tainting due to shoddy or lazy procedures. Cleanliness and godliness, Chiquart thought; but even God would have to run a close second to a persistent pursuit of spotlessness in any kitchen for which he, Chiquart, was responsible. God, he also thought, would probably approve.

Over in Oliver's corner—the butchers were always the first to be working hard—Young Jean and Martin were bringing baskets of pheasants and partridge that had hung in the lower Larder, and Oliver's other help were hacking and hewing, as always with such expansive, energetic movements, it seemed to Chiquart, as if they were a crew of misplaced woodsmen.

There was something enormously satisfying about all this single-minded activity. Despite the problems and bickering and blunders and petty animosities, when things were running more or less as they should in the kitchen, and when the clock had just the right number of minutes in an hour for everything that had to be done, then he enjoyed a brief glimpse of contentment. Not that he ever let himself get so far as complacency, of course, because as a Chief Cook, despite everything and despite the most carefully thought-out menus, you never knew . . . .

The jellied meats had been at the back of Chiquart's mind all morning but he had not had the time to check on them. Strained last evening out of a kettle into silver and pewter bowls of meat, the boiling mixture of vinegar, spices, capons, pork and sheep's hooves had been left to set in one of Hugh's lower storerooms. The gelling of such preparations was rarely a sure thing; he had been badly embarrassed before to discover a dozen large bowls of opaque mush just half an hour before he expected to be able to serve a Galentine of Lamprey. He caught Bernard as he was calling after Hugh to change some of the cheese for the cream flans. They needed a combination of old and new cheese that was richer with the Parmesan; Valerian had brought too much old.

"Have you been able to look at the gelatin? I should have thought of it earlier."

"Yes," Bernard answered. "It's fine. And I told Hugh to bring it up with the fruit." The bowls of gelled capon and pork chunks would stay cool as long as possible before being served. The Cold Sage, for which Andrew and Jeannet were working on the first ingredients, might just get down to their temperature in time. "I'll have our two jokers here separate the eggs when they're done with the greens. Eight score?"

"No, make it twelve. The commons will get Calaminee tonight. You'd best do the checking that they are boiled through hard. And watch that they start with cold water. Tell them. In fact tell them everything clearly twice, and then keep an eye on them. I should be back in time to do the Cold Sage."

He crossed the kitchen to where young Phillip was still entranced with Fernand's ministrations to the second pottage fire. Fernand himself seemed a little disappointed when Chiquart came to take his attentive audience by the hand again. But Phillip wasn't hauled, once more, directly across the courtyard to the remarkably inattentive Anne de Beaumont. The big fetch-um dog got only as far as the kitchen doorway with his quarry when, Cook and Prince, they ran into the Prince's mother, nursemaid and siblings.

The group stood in the kitchen doorway, at least the Duchess did with little the two-month-old baby—Yolande it had been named—in her arms. Occasionally when Chiquart saw her, Marie of Burgundy seemed surprisingly young to be both a duchess in her own right, like her mother and her father's two sisters-in-law, but also to be a mother of three living children. She was certainly younger than the incompetent Anne de Beaumont. She wore the robe of pale peach samit that he had seen earlier; its light sheen was slit in the upper arm where an inner cotte of rich burgundy protruded, and at the neck where the same fabric set off the dark blonde swirls of her braided hair. Unlike Lady Anne she wore no cap.

Even though she was reluctant to step beyond the doorway where she stood, the Duchess seemed just as interested as her eldest child in the operations of the kitchen. She folded the wanderer under her free arm and made the polite sounds of reassuring herself. "I hope he hasn't been a nuisance here. We know you don't like children getting among your pots and pans, and that's sensible. But there *is* such a lot to see, such a lot going on, isn't there?"

She let her eyes wander around the room, as Chiquart had done fifteen minutes before, but with more curiosity than scrutiny. Chiquart backed up a step or two and the women accepted that as an invitation to penetrate at least a little into his realm. The turn-spit stared at them as if exotic African zebras or giraffes had turned up out of the blue. Stealthily Phillip slipped back to Fernand.

"How . . . ," the Duchess Marie began tentatively, " . . . I've often wondered, Master Chiquart, how you get the color you do in your Rosé Broth." Glimpsing their extraordinary visitors, all of the butcher's help set to smiting the carcasses in front of them with extraordinary vigor and bustle. Even the goof-off artists, Andrew and Jeannet, in a flurry of unwonted activity treated their bundles of parsley, sage and marjoram to as ferocious a hacking as any such bundles had ever received. And simple Hervé looked as if he might drive his pestle through the bottom of the mortar.

"A root, my lady. A root of a plant called alkanet." Chiquart went to a shelf and withdrew a stubby, twisted dark object from a leather bag. He showed it to the Duchess, and in spite of its earthy filth she took it in her hand and examined it closely. With the knife at his belt he peeled some of the outer skin away, but what was revealed was only slightly less dark. "We peel it and slice it and boil it in good olive oil, and the oil leeches a very red dye from the wood. Then we strain the oil. We clean the root first, of course," he apologized as the Duchess rubbed the dirt from her hands.

Lady Anne de Beaumont was having difficulty restraining the year-old Catherine, who, if there was nothing to hang onto upright, could make extremely good time on her hands and knees, even on the flagstones of the kitchen. The nursemaid still asked the question that was burning her.

"And what makes the pig breathe fire through its mouth like a dragon?" Chiquart smiled, though not because that particular trick belonged to some culinary branch of the occult cabalistic art, like a freemasonic secret.

"Aqua vita, my lady. It possesses the virtue of being inflammable. With camphor soaked in it, too. The camphor prolongs the burning of the aqua vita and lends a pleasant scent to the air—rather unlike the breath of real dragons, I imagine. You use a finely shredded rag or a ball of wool dense enough to hold a supply of the aqua vita, and you put that into the boar's mouth. And light it. It's like a continuous wick, my lady." Chiquart thought for a moment of offering a demonstration but then dismissed the idea. Robert wouldn't appreciate such a waste of his precious distillates.

"And the camphor?" the Duchess pursued. "Where do you get that from? It's not obtainable within the Duchy, is it?"

"Not naturally, my lady. It's brought by merchants from far eastern lands, from China, I believe I heard, and is sold by them to any who wish to buy it. They supply two varieties, natural lumps that are harvested directly from a certain tree, and a distillate that is made by boiling the sap out of the wood of that tree or some other—in the same way as an alembic distills wines to make the aqua vita." Chiquart thought he was probably straining the Duchess's interest, but concluded, a little lamely: "Doctors of physic value it too to purify the air against the pest."

The sunlight, beginning to stream through the western windows, played on the visiting group. The brilliance put the rest of the kitchen into relative obscurity and made it difficult for the Duchess to make out the details of all she seemed curious to see. Except around the blazing fireplaces opposite, which is where she did see her Phillip, and called out to him that it was time to go. Chiquart unstrapped the sheath of his knife, dropped it inconspicuously on the seat of his "throne" and accompanied the ladies and children as they withdrew again across the courtyard.

Taking leave of the Duchess and Lady Anne, who were going out for an afternoon stroll around the moat with the children and with several other ladies of the court and *their* young children, Chiquart recalled that earlier in the day he had promised himself to do just that himself. He might still manage a brief minute or two for a spring walk before nightfall.

The Duke's apartment was on the second floor of the southern wing of the castle's square, the wing that adjoined the block in which the Hall and the kitchen were located. At its entrance near the corner of the two wings Chiquart felt the glance of a guard, unobtrusively inspecting for weapons. Within the doorway he turned and started up a spiral stair. The first opening brought him directly into the ante-room of the ducal chamber. There seven or eight individuals stood around, including several chamber valets wearing the liveried tunic of the Duke's quartered yellow and blue. There were ten of these valets in all on the Duke's household rolls, and seemingly arrogant to a man. What Chiquart had seen of them when they came to the kitchen to demand and fetch sickdishes for some invalid in the Duke's family had not endeared them to him or to any of his crew in the kitchen. Besides the valets another guard, armed with a gleaming-headed pike and a long knife in a scabbard, minded the inner door, the door to the Duke's chamber.

In the ante-room as well, a little off by themselves, Chiquart recognized the First Master of the Household and the Chamber Butler, gentlemen whose duties brought both frequently to the kitchen. The first, Sir Guthried of Bourgetto, of very short physique and quick wit, was entrusted with much of the difficult formal ceremonial arrangements of the court. When dignitaries came to visit, his dwarfish body was invariably seen flitting in the background, preparing, organizing, checking, above all sorting out foul-ups of one sort or another where others had bungled. *His* master, the Grand Master, Sir Simon, gave the orders that the Duke wanted given; Sir Guthried made sure that, whatever the obstacles, they were carried out. The anomaly of his bearing the title of First Master of the Household and there being no Second (or subsequent) Master was felt to speak to Sir Guthried's efficiency.

Chiquart rarely had much to do with Sir Guthried, perhaps because the Kitchen ran relatively smoothly, or at least had its own routines for solving its own problems.

"Master Chiquart!" The little man came over to him, his short legs moving as always in a way that in someone else would have looked as if they were sore. Chiquart greeted him politely. "Sir Simon may not have told you. A baron and his wife and family have just come in for the night. The Duke received them. They're returning to Lausanne from a pilgrimage and it seems that all of them have been touched by some sort of contagion during their travels. The Duke sent word to Master Gregory to go pay a visit to them."

Chiquart understood from much past experience what the First Master was getting at. "Will Master Gregory tell me what regimen they need for their distemper, Sir?"

"He may or he may not. Wringing an explicit diagnosis from him is often difficult. He may play it safe and say nothing to you. If so ... well something bland and of moderate virtue. You know. Safe." Indeed, Chiquart did know. And he knew, too, how often Master Gregory had heaped blame on him with Sir Simon and Sir Guthried for having prepared a sickdish that he, the physician, protested vociferously (and, invariably, *post facto*) was inappropriate for some current invalid, whether too warm for a bilious disturbance or too cool for a melancholic or phlegmatic one. Chiquart was relieved to realize that Sir Guthried at least recognized some of the games that chubby, complacent Master Gregory, for all his esoteric learning, resorted occasionally to playing.

When the heavy, studded door to the Duke's chamber opened, Sir Thomas à Seaton, the Chamberlain, emerged, nodded to Sir Guthried and disappeared down the staircase. From the doorway the rather disdainful tones of a valet summoned them: "Sir Guthried and Master Chiquart!"

Amadeus of Savoy sat at a short board on trestles in the embrasure of the chamber's window. Chiquart knew him to be just under thirty years of age; his beard was closely trimmed, his thick chestnut hair cut short of his shoulders. He wore a loose-fitting doublet of very fine white wool. The way it hung from his shoulders reminded Chiquart of an ecclesiastical alb. Before him were spread a number of sheets of paper and of parchment. In the corner of the chamber to his left his secretary sat at a similar table, but with a heap of crinkly paper in folio format to one side and to the other several rolls of parchment with other rolls about him on the floor. Furniture in the room was sparse: two unoccupied folding chairs, a stool or two, two very large chests, another chest standing on end, its lid open like a door, and the Duke's blue-and-yellow baldequined bed. Two ceiling-to-floor tapestries, strong with blue hues, adorned the long wall opposite the window. The chamber valet resumed his position beside the door. A floor candelabrum stood by the bed with last-night's half-burnt tapers still in it.

"Our banquet, gentlemen," said the Duke without preamble. "Sir Thomas and I have settled on Comb Abbey for the 18th of July. Two days." He looked up at Chiquart and added, "They'll both be meat days. The Abbot is being told." He nodded over to his secretary. The secretary scratched a reminder to himself.

Chiquart began immediately to try to visualize the kitchen at Comb Abbey such as he remembered it from ten years before. He found the vague picture rather disquieting. He was certain that no comparable event had ever visited itself upon the quiet precincts of the Abbey during the entirety of its long and holy history. It was a cloistered backwater if ever he had seen one. "The Abbot is also being told to expect you two and our Purveyor. You'll want to see what you have to deal with there and what you'll need. Clear all expenses through Sir Simon."

"For how many people, my Lord?" Chiquart asked.

The question made the Duke pause. He was not in the habit of counting his guests like some agent of his own poll tax. "That depends, I suppose. It's for Burgundy as you probably know, so there'll be ... fifty of them, fifty of us? A hundred? It depends on who comes with my father-in-law, whom he brings along with him. I shouldn't think much more than fifty. One hundred, then, for the banquet. And another whatever, three hundred? four hundred? in his suite. His military people will look after themselves as always, but we should likely count on at least three hundred along with our own people. What does that make? Between seven and eight hundred mouths might be safe. Over four days, of course, because we'll arrive on the 17th and leave on the 20th or 21st. And Burgundy, too, doubtlessly."

The enormity of these figures that dropped so nonchalantly from his master's mouth, their immense significance for his responsibilities, did not even begin to make an impression on the cook's imagination. The scratching of the secretary's quill on paper certainly meant that he would be able to ponder their meaning at greater length when he left the Duke's presence.

But it was to be a banquet and therefore what was important was quality. Amadeus was going on. "I want it to be noble. You'll need to plan an *entremets* at each dinner, and I want something really impressive. You'll give us substantial fare throughout, I'm sure, Chiquart. I know I can count on you. The Duke and Duchess of Burgundy won't have ridden three hundred leagues just to insult their bellies and have a good laugh at the rustic vulgarity of a bumpkin's court. The banquet has to be honorable, and I'm confident you'll know how to do it."

The Duke let the injunction sink in and then asked, generally, "What problems do you foresee?" And then of the stocky, reliable Lord of Bourgetto: "Guthried?"

"Lodging, my lord. We can coerce the Abbot into offering space for perhaps fifty people only. Their guest dormitory is fairly new but I don't think it is very large."

"For the Burgundians, then. Tents for most of our people and all of the commons. I'll be in a tent myself if necessary. If my brother-in-law comes along, it might even be preferable for me to be off in a tent."

"Particularly with the Abbey, my lord, the Abbot and the Chapter," Guthried went on. "There's always a lot of resentment ...."

"That won't be the case at Comb. There are obligations, and ... well, I'd be surprised if there isn't a fair amount of cooperation. They've been promised .... Anyway, if there isn't, speak to Sir Simon about it. Chiquart?" He turned to his Master Cook with his eyebrows raised.

"Provisions, space, utensils and workers, my lord. In that order. Most of the utensils will have to go with us five days before. Twelve wagons probably, another five for plate and linen. For the space and the workers I'd have to see what is there now. As you know we can set up an adequate lean-to or a series of tents for the four or five days—as we did when you arranged the tournament at Chillon, for instance. For provisions ... "

"The Purveyor should look after all that. Just tell him what you need. Domestic and game. He has my full authority to requisition whatever you need, against fair payment, of course. Just give him a list." He looked back and forth between the two of them. "That's all then? Robertet here will give you each a copy of the numbers and dates. Let Sir Simon know if any serious problem comes up."

It was a dismissal so Sir Guthried and Chiquart made a decorous exit from the Duke's presence. They separated at the foot of the stair, Chiquart deciding to return to the kitchen by way of the Great Hall.

Normally he enjoyed a walk through the Great Hall, to feel himself within its airy space, even to hear the brushing echoes of his soft suede footsteps on its paving stones. The Hall had exactly the same height as his own kitchen further along under the same roof ridge, but was twice the length and was roofed with a series of wonderfully carved rafter beams. In the ornate stone seats of the roof beams skilled sculpters had also brought forth heads, some human, some animal, some, like many people, indistinctly one or the other, along with intertwined vines, branches, trees. But above all the room was bright from the western sun that flooded into it at this time of day through the three tall recessed windows that overlooked the moat. But bright too because all the stone walls of the Hall were whitewashed and some were hung with the colorful banners, shields and motifs of Savoy.

Entering the Great Hall as he did from the Duke's wing he stood beside the Hall Buffet and was on the dais of the Duke's board, raised some three feet above the rest of the room. The view from this corner encompassed the whole Hall, but Chiquart was not as moved as he normally was. Rather what he had in his head were the logistics of collecting and transporting pots and cauldrons of all sizes, large frying pans, a dozen—no, a score of them—a dozen tubs, fifty buckets, a hundred pails, six heavy mortars, a dozen of the largest grills, a dozen rasps of various sizes, a hundred wooden spoons, twenty-five long-handled stirring spoons of the holed type that he liked, and knives, knives, knives, six strong meat hooks though the Abbey was bound not to have any at all, twenty flat oven shovels—what sort of oven did the Abbey have, anyway? entirely inadequate, doubtlessly: he would have to have masons build one for fifty loaves—twenty spit-trees, one hundred—no, one hundred and twenty—strong iron spits thirteen feet in length, and maybe another three dozen lighter spits of the same length for fowl and piglets, and skewers, four dozen of them to hold meat whose glaze is being set, and .... The list that kept surging up into his mind went on, and on. Not just of the kitchen hardware he would have to have, but of things like various weaves of fabric for his filters—sixty yards of fine cloth just for jellies, and much more for the mulled wines and for a dozen other uses; five or six hundred yards of coarse cloth to spread on the dressing tables and to cover baskets and keep dirt off semi-prepared food. Baskets: at least a hundred large ones, for all sorts of purposes, before, during and after the meals.

The sooner he got a scrap of Robert's paper and began his lists, Chiquart thought, the better. Normally he disdained notes; his memory had never failed him yet in the kitchen. But this was different: too much depended upon everything being available that he would need. He couldn't take any chance of forgetting *any* vital element. He must begin to write it all down.

He would have to remind the Purveyor to be certain to make arrangements for all of the game at least six weeks before the banquet. His hunters and suppliers must deliver everything four days before so that we can hang it properly and work on it. And the water there, Chiquart thought with horror. What if the Abbey well yielded only a brackish water; or, immeasurably worse, what if there were not enough of it for all the necessary scrubbing? He must see whether there was a stream nearby, or whether he would have to commission tank-carts to bring in a daily supply.

He stood overlooking the Great Hall of the castle, its two rows of trestle tables still set up from dinner and stretching down its length, its minstrel gallery at the other end perched over the panelled screen and the double two serving door—and he saw nothing. His brain was awash in quantities and schedules and arrangements. Provisions, space, utensils and workers, he had told the Duke. That was simplifying it very neatly. And he hadn't even mentioned fuel! Each of those so simple categories of his concerns contained an infinite number of worries. For instance, the question of personnel. As a minimum, with enough lead-time on the site, and all the other arrangements working out as they should, the kitchen could manage such a banquet with seventy strong and tireless workers, in all of the offices including butchery and buttery. But that figure depended on another question: how efficient, how experienced would these workers be? How many of regular crew, from kitchen, pantry, bakery, butchery, saucery, buttery, scullery and larder could he afford to take there? Afford in the sense that he was naturally obliged to leave enough good and responsible workers in all of the offices—under Bernard or Old Jean?—to continue to provide a week of meals for the commons of the castle and the guard that remained. How rapidly and effectively could he train the necessary local recruits on the site? Could he even get the workers locally that he would need? That question must go on his list for the visit he would make to the Abbey. And what about carpenters and painters for the two *entremets*, whatever they would turn out to be? How much of those *entremets* could be prepared and pre-assembled here and carted to Comb without damage?

The chapel bell rang, a little louder here in the Hall since the chapel was in the same wing as the Duke's apartment, and recalled Chiquart to the present and *its* problems. Should he go see the Duke's sick visitors, to ask whether they had been put on any particular regimen? No, that was Master Gregory's job. Let him earn the exorbitant fee he would undoubtedly charge, and let him send explicit word to the Kitchen about the diet he prescribed for his patients. A cook should know better than to meddle in a physician's business. Even if he might in fact know that business almost as well as certain physicians.

The bell was of nones. In an hour most work in the kitchen would have to pause while everyone there, except for the turn-spit and pot-stirrers, shuffled like a subdued and disreputable mob to the courtyard outside the open chapel windows and heard Vespers chanted. Chiquart left the Great Hall by the well-trod passage that ran between the Pantry and Buttery and directly into the kitchen itself. Were it not for the moat tightly girdling the castle, making of it a compact little island, Richard the mason would undoubtedly have sited the kitchen off by itself at some distance from the Hall and the ducal living quarters. As it was, the length of this paneled passage, down which was borne a hundred loads of Chiquart's prepared dishes every day, served as a makeshift filter for the noise and any offensive smells of the kitchen.

Back in his kitchen the Chief Cook discovered that all of the extraordinary energy that had been expended for the benefit of the Duchess's visit had exhausted itself very quickly: at the various tables and fireplaces the pace of work had returned to normal. Perhaps the pace was even a little more leisurely than usual, because of the warm spring sun that cast a soporific glow over the whole room. With a twinge of worry Chiquart checked the progress of each of the dishes and sauces and satisfied himself that nothing was unduly behind schedule. Then he strapped on his knife in its sheath again, tied his canvas apron about his waist and took up his working position at the end of the larger centre table.

In point of fact there was no need for him to prepare anything himself, particularly for the smaller meal of supper. Whenever possible, though, he liked to be involved somehow with one of the dishes. He felt that in a sense the physical activity validated his function. He may have been Chief Cook but he was still, and primarily, a Cook. And he could prove that only by seeing a dish through from its raw ingredients to the moment when the garnished platter or bowl was borne down the passageway to the Great Hall. The excess number of workers in the kitchen, between eighteen and twenty-four, those who had been kept so busy for the dinner but who were not needed for the smaller supper menu, were regularly reassigned to other labors in the afternoon. Almost without exception these other labors consisted of cleaning and of the initial preparation of foodstuffs for the next day's meals.

To himself this afternoon Chiquart had assigned work on the sauce known as Cold Sage.

As everyday sauces went, the Cold Sage was relatively simple. He called Schroeder's boy for sixteen mounded loaves of bread. Andrew and Jeannet had left eight large wicker baskets of parsley and sage stacked on the table, each basket holding roughly a bushel in quantity. Perhaps because of the Duchess's visit earlier the herbs had been particularly well washed of their sand, drained and chopped. He began by toting a basket of each over to Hervé to be ground, and while the other was pounding he sliced and chopped two of the pillow-like loaves and fed the cubes into the mortar. When satisfactorily reduced to a green paste, that first batch was removed into a five-gallon two-handled bowl and replaced with another until all of the herbs were done. He then turned to the spices. From the leather pouches on their shelves he measured out four handfuls of ground pepper and another four of ground grains of paradise. Then from another leather sack he dumped maybe a score of ginger roots onto his table, chopped them and dumped them into one of Hervé's smaller mortars to be ground. All three spices he stirred together with his hand in the bowl. The aroma of the mixture asked for another handful of ground grains of paradise, which he gave it. Together the spices amounted to something like three quarts. From a box under the table he added half a handful of ground salt.

To steep these spices Chiquart drained vinegar into a three-quart jug from a cask which lay by Robert's door. Still with his hands he worked the mixture until the granular mush became a more or less consistent slush. Borne on the vinegar fumes the spices clouded his head with their powerful scent. When he was satisfied that the vinegar had leeched as much as possible from the ginger and from the coarser grains of the other two spices, he set up a filter frame over another bowl. Into the frame he fixed two yards of medium-mesh boulting cloth which he doubled over.

Then, slowly, he poured his suspension of spices into the strainer.

When the dripping stopped, about half of the liquid had drained through. He examined it closely, passing his hand through it and trying to see just how fine were the particles still in the vinegar. He tasted it off a finger, added more ground grains of paradise to that second bowl, stirred and strained everthing again. Then he combined the spicey vinegar with the green herb paste in the five-gallon bowl and mixed it all thoroughly by hand until his arms began to feel the strain. He had two scullions carry the bowl to one of Hugh's cellars. The Cold Sage was ready.

He had only the garnish to do. He washed his hands and arms at the stone sink in the corner and called to Valerian for eggs. He would just have time to boil six dozen before Vespers. While the cauldron in which he set them came to a boil over one of the pottage fires, he made the rounds of the kitchen, watching, approving, suggesting, correcting, helping a hapless apprentice correct some bungled procedure, insisting that a lazy scullion rasp and scrub a chopping block again, sending a witless porter back for the right variety of cheese. At the roasting fireplace he noticed that Old Jean's lads had just mounted some veal shanks on wooden spits and had them turning over the hot flames. He knew that the Roaster would never have sanctioned that, and in his absence told them to remove the meat immediately and to remount it on proper iron spits. He thought he had had all of the kitchen's wooden spits put away into reserve in Hugh's cellar long ago, and explained patiently to the lads that, even though meat might mount more easily along wood, it simply wasn't worth the risk of losing that meat *not* to use the iron spits.

Chiquart took his six dozen eggs off the fire and scooped them out of the vat to cool on his table. Then the Vespers bell rang and, with desultory chatter, most of the Kitchen personnel filed languidly out to the far end of the castle courtyard.

At the end of the service a push cart of Montfort & Fleury, the fish merchants, rumbled under the portcullis and into the courtyard. Chiquart waited until the two men at its shafts came up to him. They were cheerily insouciant of the blast that awaited them.

"Fish," they announced vacuously, recognizing the cook.

"What the hell do you mean bringing them along now when I've got to use them tomorrow? Tomorrow! The hake has to soak for twelve hours! The order was due two days ago. Why wasn't it here?"

"Well," the speaker wasn't sure whether he should even attempt an excuse or just stick with a short formal apology on behalf of the company. "I heard that the month's shipment was slow coming up the Rhone valley. A lot of rain this spring, bad roads. Your order got loaded as soon as it came in."

Chiquart recruited several of his men to help take the bales of dry hake directly into the kitchen, to pass the forty bundles of salted fish in through the Larder window, and to stow the two vats of live sea-fish in a shady corner of the courtyard. He didn't know whether the man from Montfort & Fleury had really exonerated his company or not. He knew that he simply could not tolerate the uncertainty of never knowing whether he would have the fish he was counting on. He could imagine old Fleury behind his desk in town muttering that the Castle wouldn't really need their Friday's fish before Vespers Thursday, and therefore other, more demanding customers such as the Collegium could be served first.

He would still speak with Vernetello, even though Hugh swore that it did little good. Fitz-Thomas, despite his noble Norman name, was a local merchant who handled all the castle's needs for fresh-water fish that weren't answered by the castle's fishponds. And he did it punctiliously, which is what Chiquart was most concerned about. His was a much smaller operation than Montfort & Fleury, but he might be interested in expanding into the procuring and merchandising of sea-fish. Vernetello could at least look into it.

The kitchen resumed its preparations for supper. When he had finished chopping the hard eggwhites that were to garnish the Cold Sage, Chiquart put them in a dish and covered it with a cloth. Then he gave orders to Andrew and Jeannet to prepare a Chicken Cullis and a Chicken Whitedish for four. The Duke's invalided guests would have something substantial even if Master Gregory didn't deign to drop by the kitchen and prescribe for whatever turned out to be wrong with them.

In due time the Hall Marshal appeared with his liveried Serving Valets. The Kitchen Buffet was covered and laid with precious dishware. The meats were carved smaller and set out and, after them, each of the preparations was dished up in quantities more than sufficient for the Hall: Chivrolee of Stag, Trimollete of Partridge, jellied meats (which had indeed jelled properly), stewed vegetable greens, Cream Flans (sugared), and finally the Calaminee and Cold Sage on poultry. Chiquart himself saw to the garnishing of this last bi-partite dish when the two sauces had been poured, separately, over the chunks of meat, with diced eggwhite on the Cold Sage and colorful spiced candies on the Calaminee. Everything was properly proved, then the Valets hoisted the platters and, at the distant sound of the chapel bell, the procession moved off down the corridor.

With much less ceremonial the commons were then served. The wafers, hypocras and *dragees* were laid out on the Kitchen Buffet. And, as far as the Kitchen was concerned, supper was done.

3. Evening

But already the eternal washing up had resumed, and already Chiquart began to think out the initial preparations for tomorrow. Friday: a lean day. No eggs. Eels and nuts. The smell of fish roasting on all of the grills, or frying in a dozen pans, a smell that would waft pungently out the kitchen windows and pervade the whole of the castle. Mustard Sauce. And the ever-pressing need to look ahead, far ahead: small game animals and fowl to be procured from local hunters and fowlers, to be skinned and plucked and hung; bags of flour to be resifted because a fragment of millstone had broken a count's tooth; firewood in the courtyard to be restacked because the green wood had ended up on top, and the coal bunkers in the big shed on the other side of the moat to be restocked; stocks of ground spices in leather bags to be topped up; several twenty-pound cones of sugar received from a merchant in so hard a state that they had proven almost impossible to break up and should be returned; and Ricardo, the suspected pilferer, who finally had been caught yesterday by the drawbridge guard with a small plucked pheasant under his tunic. Ricardo had a constant shifty expression to his face but apparently he did as honest a job for Oliver as any of the Butcher's Boys, as they called themselves. He would probably lose a finger or two if not the whole hand. And unfortunately never hold a butcher's knife again.

And Chiquart had the grand banquet to think about, with its various *entremets* to plan. Someday, maybe when the banquet had been done and castle life had returned to normal, he would be able to devote himself more seriously to the book the Duke had graciously suggested that he write. It should be a record of the best of his work, the Duke had said, for the Savoy archives. The request, or rather command, had been flattering in the extreme, and repeated on three occasions now, so that Chiquart could not think it was any mere passing whim of the Duke. He would have to start a tentative outline of that, too, but he had never in his life seen anything like a cookery manual to give him any guidance in the matter. He would have to think about the most sensible outline to use. But first, the Duke's banquet.

From the bottom of the kettle of Trimolette he scooped a last wooden bowlful for himself and went into the Pantry to sit at Albert's table by the barred window. The sun was very low on the horizon and glinted off gleaming ripples across the moat. At this time of day Albert was always away to the Laundry to deliver and count his precious, dirty linens. All the flames in the kitchen were dying except for a low pottage fire under a vat of boiling rice for tomorrow. Even the men's voices, muted a little by fatigue, were less dominant than the clatter as pots were lifted roughly into and out of the stone wash basins. The smokey air of the kitchen had almost cleared, but was not yet comparable with the perlucid calm of the dimming scene to the west of the castle.

To Chiquart it was always a time of great peace, this moment before Compline. He often thought back to the days when he, too, as a lad of fourteen struggled with the huge cast iron

369

cauldrons, tipping them from their three legs in order to scrape and scrub out the burnt layers of meat or peas encrusted on their bottoms. He thought with a little wonder of his bewilderment in those first days, his awe at the hugeness of all that went on in the kitchen, his terrors of the Master, Old Antonio, certainly a gruff bear if ever there was one, but also his timid respect for the lesser gods, the assistant cooks and the section heads, all of whom seemed to incarnate authority and limitless competence. But the job was a coveted one in town and it did bring a little needed money to his family.

And despite the sheer drudgery of so much of what he had had to do, there had always been a lot of home-made fun, nonsensical horseplay he remembered vaguely, with the other lads of his age in the kitchen. Then when Antonio accepted him as an apprentice, all that seemed to matter was his pride, his profound sense of the worth of his work. With each procedure learned under the sour tutelage of Antonio, with each recipe that the master watched the apprentice work through and then in turn accomplish by himself, there had grown a conviction that he would eventually be a good cook. Antonio had endlessly insisted on filling his memory accurately with absolutely everything that had to do with cooking; even at the end of a day when he was dropping with exhaustion, he got no comfort from his master who would drill him and test him over and over on ingredients, mixtures, colors, consistencies, cooking times. But even so, as the consciousness of his craft grew so did the awareness of his mastery of it. When Antonio at last became too sick to carry on and, wonder of wonders, recommended him, the humble journeyman Chiquart, to Sir Simon, and when Sir Simon in turn suggested him to the present Duke's father, who named him Chief Cook for the person and house of Savoy, the sun beamed with supremely glorious rays that day. Never had he been so overwhelmed by both the grandeur and the responsibility of his position. When one was elevated to an exalted place, exalted things were expected of him.

The stark awe he had once felt for Master Antonio came fleetingly back to him, as an elusive pungent tang in a long-forgotten sauce. Was it the man's knowledge? Chiquart had that now, and perhaps more. Was it his power? Again, Chiquart's kitchen was busier, employed more, produced more now. Just his personality? Any supervisor had to make his superior knowledge and power be felt and respected. What had evoked that awe in the young apprentice, then? It couldn't have been just the man. It must also have been the job, too.

To cook, and to cook well, that was the essence of what Antonio *was* as well as what he did. If anything stirred awe in Chiquart in his younger years it was surely the sight of a man who understood—who *knew* in all his being—that cooking was in its essence a quasi-divine calling, and who devoted himself to it as a priest would to his vocation. As Master Cook he enjoyed the trusting faith of a large number of his fellow human beings, and in return for that faith he provided sustenance, health and pleasure.

Chiquart stood up. The sun had set, leaving in the sky only a bright warm glow which still reflected across the moat. He took his bowl to the sinks by the well tower where hundreds of similar bowls in gold and silver, pewter and wood, were stacked waiting for their turn under the scullions' rags. But he washed it himself quietly and replaced it where all the wooden bowls belonged, under the central worktables. The kitchen was getting dark; it was a nice question whether he would have to have torches lit tonight before all of the work was done. In company with Vernetello he visited in turn the Buttery, the Larder, the Bakery and the Pantry to inspect the detailed inventories which each officer had drawn up, and then to go over the specific needs of tomorrow's menus and to advise each person of any exceptional demands on their respective Offices foreseen for the coming week. Albert seemed at least to have forgotten his grievance against Robert.

Then in the very dim light that still descended from the western windows and glowed from the one low pottage fire, he directed his two apprentices, Andrew and Jeannet, on how to set salted fish to soak overnight. He had them fill a kettle with Robert's worst wine and carry squirming eels from the courtyard vats to it. He had them shell and skin and wash a batch of almonds, an exercise they had done scores of times before, but he showed them how to pass quickly through them and sort out the bitter ones or those that were past their prime. With one of Hervé's smaller mortars he had them grind the batch into milk and showed them just how much the fish broth (reserved from Dinner) to add to the almond paste to prevent it from becoming oil. He had them bite a stick of stale cinnamon, and then distinguish on their tongue between old and newly ground cinnamon. He had them demonstrate when the peas were properly cooked for pureeing.

And always he would ask them to name the ingredients for Saupiquet, for Almond Milk Flans, for German Capon Broth, and the relative quantities of each. Although it was getting late, they remained a cheerful pair through all this drill. Jeannet in particular looked more sober, tried a little harder to remember exactly what went into a Cony Buchat or a Spanish Gratunee, and in just what variety of ways one could drop the batter for rishews. His answers seemed to be couched with respect for the Master, his glance to show an earnestness to win his Master's respect.

At last Chiquart let them go. Bernard had seen that all of the dishware went back to where it belonged, and that the clean pots and pans, kettles, vats, spoons and knives were in place and ready for the next day's work. Most of the kitchen help had homes in town and went off there with full bellies; some lodged for a fee in the dormitory over the Buttery, but even they went off with the others to see what fun the town offered after Compline. Apart from the hapless lad who had been left to lift down the rice, the kitchen was now empty. Hugh and Robert had bolted the shutters over their respective courtyard windows; Albert had locked up the Pantry with meticulous care and shuffled off to his meticulous house and meticulous life in town. Fernand had set fine dry kindling in front of the oven for Schroeder's early batch of table bread.

Chiquart sent the pot-stirrer on his happy way and took over his long, holed spoon. When the night guard on his rounds looked into the kitchen a moment later all he could make out was the silhouette of a man standing with a spoon by a large pot which hung over the glowing embers of a dying fire.

Index

Please note. Of the numbers below, those in **bold** type indicate the page at which a recipe begins. Numbers in plain (non-bold) type refer to pages where it is suggested that the recipe might also be considered as appropriate among the other dishes or preparations in that chapter; the recipe itself is located elsewhere.

No accents were written in Old French. Conventionally, modern editors write an acute accent on a final *e* in order to distinguish between this final vowel with and without a tonic accent: for example, *georgé* and *George*.

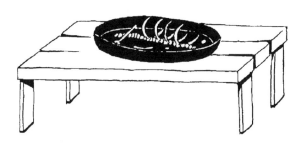